the
Magic
of
Opera

DA CAPO PRESS

the
Magic
of
Opera

J. MERRILL KNAPP

New introduction by the author

Library of Congress Cataloging in Publication Data

Knapp, J. Merrill.
  The magic of opera.

  (A Da Capo paperback)
  Reprint. Originally published: New York: Harper &
Row, 1972.
  Bibliography: p.
  Includes index.
  1. Opera. I. Title.
ML1700.K6 1985   782.1   85-10442
ISBN 0-306-80251-1

Published by Da Capo Press
A Member of the Perseus Books Group
http://www.dacapopress.com

Introduction to the Da Capo Edition

The original purpose of this book still seems a valid one. It was meant as an introduction to opera for college students and the interested adult. The first half, dealing with the elements of opera, attempts to explain some of the common features of the genre, even though most later twentieth-century specimens have modified traditional components such as recitative and aria. Since the best way to explain an art is to get right into the middle of it, the second half of the book concentrates on certain works and even just parts of these works as examples of the high moments in operatic history. It does not attempt to be a comprehensive survey with many names and titles. The examples chosen can stand for others not mentioned and should lead the reader on to further exploration.

What has happened to the operatic world since 1972? Not much on the surface. The big houses still concentrate on the familiar repertory with an occasional venture into a new or unfamiliar work. Those interested in statistics for this statement can do no better than to consult George Martin's *The Opera Companion to Twentieth Century Opera*, which gives a fascinating picture of the repertory in the world's leading opera houses during most of the nineteenth and twentieth centuries. The data also indicate which operas have had the most performances and show quite clearly why the operatic stage has often been called "a museum."

What *has* undergone change is the physical side of opera production. For better or for worse, the stage director and his associate, the designer, have become more important figures in the opera house. Press criticisms of a performance often start with a description of the staging and then get to the voices and the musical rendition later. If anything can stir the operatic public out of its familiar routine and possible doldrums, it is a new production which has been "reinterpreted" by some famous director. Stage scenes and direction have ranged from the "gimmicky" to something enlightening and enhancing. When Wotan in *The Ring* is depicted as a nineteenth century industrialist with striped pants and a top hat and Rosina in *The Barber of Seville* makes her entrance from one of the breasts in a huge, enlarged female torso, there are growls and mutterings which exceed the usual opera-lover's complaint about distortion of the librettist's and composer's directions. Germans and Scandinavians have come to see the Seattle production of Wagner's *Ring* because they know they will actually witness the representation of an ash tree in *Die Walküre* and some form of the *Siegfried* dragon in more or less traditional staging.

The most exciting operatic events in the United States and, to a certain extent, in the rest of the English-speaking world, still take place in smaller cities, university centers, and summer festivals. Many new operas are being produced there as well as worthwhile revivals of older works not generally found in the standard repertory. It would be nice to report that there has been a resurgence of American opera, or more rightly, opera composed by Americans; but this is hardly the case. Familiar figures such as Gian Carlo Menotti, Virgil Thomson, and for lack of a better designation, the "folk group," still dominate the American operatic stage when so-called native operas are given.

The most interesting operas on English texts seem to originate from Britain. Benjamin Britten is still the outstanding figure of the century with his *Peter Grimes, Albert Herring, Billy Budd, Turn of the Screw, Midsummer Night's Dream,* and *Death in Venice* achieving something like international status. Others, including Michael Tippett (*The Midsummer Marriage, King Priam, The Knot Garden*), the Scottish Thea Musgrave (*The Decision, The Voice of Ariadne, Mary, Queen of Scots*) and several younger British men and women are experimenting with the idiom and writing operas that deserve attention and possible transportation across the Atlantic.

Another figure who has risen enormously in international esteem during the last ten years is Leoš Janáček. Although his operas will always suffer in translation from their native Czech, works like *Jenufa, The Cunning Little Vixen,* and *The Makropulos Affair* have attained considerable acclaim and more frequent productions in both Europe and America.

The important and seminal twentieth-century composer, Béla Bartók, wrote only one opera, *Duke Bluebeard's Castle* (1911), seldom seen on the stage but available in nine or ten commercial recordings. The operas of such familiar Russian figures as Serge Prokofiev (ten operas) and Dimitri Shostakovich (two operas and several ballets) are rarely performed in the West any more, although at one time *The Love of the Three Oranges* by Prokofiev was heard regularly.

Because Alban Berg's *Wozzeck* has such an important place in the modern repertory, the recent production (both in New York and abroad) of a full-length *Lulu*, his other opera, has generated much excitement in the operatic world. Many musicians feel it rises to even greater heights than *Wozzeck*, and look for further performances so it will become better known. Another German opera that has been brought to the attention of the public, largely because of its literary and musical collaboration, is Berthold Brecht's and Kurt Weill's *The Rise and Fall of the City of Mahagonny* (1930), a satire on American life, which, along with their *Three Penny Opera*, had a renaissance in this country.

So-called avant garde opera, involving the use of electronic media, still remains at the edge of operatic interest and attention. Experimental works by Krysztof Penderecki, Luigi Nono, Luciano Berio, and others of many nationalities are occasionally heard, but they have not entered the main stream and it is a question whether they ever will, in such a conservative medium as opera.

The extraordinary rise in popularity of ballet in this country in the last ten years has inevitably cast a certain shadow over opera. In the areas of advanced musical theater, drama and music have been pushed somewhat into the background in favor of action and gesture. Ideally, ballet and opera should exist side by side as both independent arts and related ones. Too often ballet, when it appears in opera, has been just a diversion from the main course of the plot and not an integral part of the production.

Television opera (either a live performance or one that is pre-filmed from the stage or studio) still offers the best opportunity for opera to reach a wider public. Although the sonic quality of the average television set is minimal, classical radio stations have begun to broadcast these operas simultaneously. If listeners can adjust their stereo and television equipment so that the aural and the visual are heard and seen together, the effect is quite good and perhaps second-best to being in the opera house. Other elements in televised opera that have improved are the English sub-titles and dialogue at the bottom of the screen, in foreign language productions. An even more promising technical achievement that may eventually attain the ideal coordination of sight and good sound are the various video systems and laser disks which are gradually coming on the market to transform home-viewing.

And so opera survives in spite of the prophets of doom, and it continues to fascinate those who find in it the ideal amalgam of the arts. Its magic still exerts a strong pull in spite of deficits, voices that come and go, and fashions of the moment. When the various energies of opera all ignite, the conflagration of drama, music, and spectacle can be a very exciting and rewarding one.

—J. MERRILL KNAPP
Princeton University
June 1983

Note: For this new edition, the Suggested Readings at the end of the chapters have been slightly revised, and on pp. 354–356 more recent books on opera have been listed.

Contents

TWO   HISTORY

Preface

Opera should have a wide appeal. As a unique combination of several arts, it deserves to reach a larger audience than it does. In the past too many sensible people have associated it with diamond tiaras, exclusive theater boxes, opening night social snobbery, and haughty prima donnas. Fortunately most of these associations have faded or disappeared. Opera in this country is coming into its own as a vital theatrical experience, and it is growing more popular in spite of economic strain. There is no longer one opera company but many But more understanding and knowledge are needed to get rid of past impressions and to prove that opera is both within the comprehension of the ordinary person and worthy of high aspiration and serious study.

This book attempts to supply some of that knowledge and to convince the reader that opera can be readily understandable, very dramatic, and highly enjoyable. The text is designed primarily for the college student but also for the general reader who wishes to know more about this "exotick" art. There are two general sections. the first treats the forms of opera, the second gives a brief historical survey with particular attention to certain selected works. Rather than attempt to be comprehensive, the book concentrates on a few great masterpieces, to get to the essence of the drama and the music and give some notion of why the individual work has retained its luster.

Some technical terms have been used where necessary to explain the music. Most of them are relatively familiar, but a glossary has been provided for those readers who may wish more explanation. Musical examples are often a stumbling block to anyone who does not read musical notation. Opera at least has the advantage of words, and much of the music can be followed through them. The musical examples have been simplified and adapted for illustrative purposes. It is hoped that they will illumine the text and even send some readers who know the signs back to the piano for direct confirmation.

The suggested readings at the end of each chapter could have included many more books, particularly those in foreign languages. But the aim was to restrict suggestions to books in English and primarily to those recently published or readily available in paperback form. For those who wish to delve more deeply, the bibliographies in many of the books mentioned are a good starting point. Opera titles are first given in their original form with translations into English and the year of their first performance. In the case of Wagner's *Ring* and Berlioz' *The Trojans*, the dates include both composition and performance, since the works were not performed for many years after they were composed.

The author is particularly indebted to Mr. Winton Dean for reading the manuscript and offering suggestions for improvement, to Mr. Walter Lippincott, Jr., whose enthusiasm and passion for opera gave the impetus to this project, and to Mrs. Sally Cerny, whose editorial patience and skill helped immeasurably in bringing the work to a conclusion.

J. MERRILL KNAPP

the Magic
of Opera

ONE STRUCTURE

1 The Nature of Opera

Opera, for those who love it, has an endless fascination. The singers, the spectacle, the music, even the maligned drama, are all topics for debate and subjects of delight. For some, opera is the *ne plus ultra* of art because it blends music and drama. When these two arts complement each other in perfect proportion, each strong in its own right, the result can be thrilling. But because each component generally pursues an independent existence outside of opera, the balance is delicate. Should the music push the drama aside or the drama overwhelm the music, the structure suffers, and the result is "a concert in costume" rather than a genuine opera as we understand it.

If it is to be successful, opera must be regarded with "a living imagination." As George Marek put it:

It [opera] does not call so much for an imaginative ear as for an imaginative eye, an eye which can see beyond little absurdities toward great truths. Opera demands, as does poetic tragedy, a cooperation of mood. Robust, powerful, and sufficient though it is, opera needs a sympathetic audience.[1]

Two arts can make uneasy bedfellows. Each must *accommodate* the other and out of this accommodation should arise a new union in

[1]George R. Marek, *A Front Seat at the Opera*, Crown, New York, 1948, pp. 4–5.

which each enhances the other. Pietro Metastasio (1698–1782), himself a great librettist and literary figure, spoke elegantly of this union.

. music is an ingenious, marvelous, delectable, and enchanting art which, by itself, is capable of working miracles. But when it applies itself with poetry, and makes good use of its enormous wealth, it is able not only to confirm and express all the changes of the human art but also to illumine and increase them.[2]

The key words here are "makes good use of" and "illumine." Even Boito could not take Shakespeare's *Othello* as it was (with necessary cuts) and have Verdi set it to music. He had to construct a libretto based on the original play and its Shakespearian language. Then Verdi composed the music. The result was illumination: not an improvement on the original, but a different achievement in a different sphere.

Opera obviously has not always found this illumination. Whether because of an imbalance among its parts, a poor performance, or a badly staged work, opera may fail. When it does, it often falls harder than a single art because it is carrying so much baggage. For this reason, it has been a favorite target for criticism since its birth at the beginning of the seventeenth century.

Some of the most famous criticisms of opera often give the wrong impression because they are quoted out of context. Saint-Évremond (1613–1703) once said:

If you want to know what an opera is, I tell you it is a bizarre mixture of poetry and music where the writer and composer, equally embarrassed by each other, go to a lot of trouble to create an execrable work.[3]

Saint-Évremond, an intelligent, witty Frenchman living in England in the 1670s, was merely trying to be amusing for the sake of the Duke of Buckingham, to whom he included the above remark in a letter. The rest of the letter (on opera in general and the differences between French and Italian opera) is more thoughtful and serious. He states some of the natural objections a classically trained Frenchman, brought up on Corneille and Racine, would have to this relatively new art. Since some of his objections have been heard throughout operatic history, they are worth repeating.

First, he mentions the difficulty of setting flat prose to music.

the whole piece is sung from beginning to end, as if the characters on

[2]Ulrich Weisstein, ed., *The Essence of Opera*, Free Press, (Norton Library paperback), New York, 1964, pp. 100–101.
[3]*The Essence of Opera*, pp. 33–34.

stage had conspired to present musically the most trivial as well as the most important aspects of their lives. Can one imagine that a master sings when calling his servant or when giving him an order? That a friend confides a secret to another musically? That deliberations in a council of state are sung?

He is even impatient of the device music has created to get over these everyday situations—the recitative (see Chapter 5). "And who can endure the boredom of a recitative, which possesses neither the charm of the song nor the forcefulness of the spoken word?" Although he recognizes the beauty and passion of music which can be set to poetry for singing (he was a lover of music and an amateur composer himself), he wants to confine it to choruses which comment on the action like Greek tragedy or have it used as accompaniment in intermittent songs. But if this role for music is accepted, the result is not opera as generally understood. It is drama with music or plays with songs and choruses—a quite different sort of entertainment, where the two arts are contiguous but hardly joined together. Finally, Saint-Évremond speaks of the necessity for the librettist to subordinate himself to the musician, a long-standing complaint in the history of opera. "The best poet is obliged to degrade himself in favour of the musician, since his lines must be arranged, less for the meaning he would have them represent, than for the convenience of the musician and the smoothness of his songs."[4]

The second oft-quoted criticism, that Italian opera was "an exotick and irrational entertainment," was made by Dr. Samuel Johnson (1709–1784). Dr. Johnson was notoriously unmusical, and he was speaking about the Italian opera of his day, which, with its male sopranos and altos, its glorification of the singer and the spectacle over the drama, its performance in London in the original language, might be termed "exotick and irrational" for the average Englishman.

Then there have been the sheer music-haters like Charles Lamb (1775–1834) whose words in a "Chapter on Ears" were merely a reflection of his exasperation with music in general.

I have sat through an Italian opera till, for sheer pain and inexplicable anguish, I have rushed out into the noisiest place of the crowded streets, to solace myself with sounds which I was not obliged to follow, and get rid of the distracting torment of endless, fruitless, barren attention.

Yet opera, in spite of these and other barbs, has successfully survived and continues to flourish for a devoted clientele. It may be a museum piece in the contemporary world, but the true opera lover is not daunted. He is always seeking an amalgam in perfor-

[4]*The Essence of Opera*, pp. 32–33.

"Opera, in spite of   barbs, has successfully survived and continues to flourish for a devoted clientele." Central City Opera House after restoration. (Courtesy of Denver Public Library Western Collection)

mance which will produce a miraculous result—that moment when drama, orchestra, singing, and spectacle unite to achieve what is promised by a composer and librettist of genius. Mozart, Verdi, Wagner and others believed in opera as a genuine art form. They devoted their best efforts to it. If the artistic world is any judge, many of these efforts are supreme, and they deserve to rank with the greatest of man's aesthetic achievements. An investigation of their worth is an important task.

The Literary Source   Opera starts not with music but with its literary source (story or plot), whether it be history, biography, fiction, or mythology in the form of poem, play, drama, novel, or original libretto. Not every subject is fit for musical representation, and transformation of literary material into a workable libretto demands great skill (see Chapter 2).

Many critics of opera firmly believe that unless the dramatic structure of an opera possesses strength, validity, excitement, and pace, not even the best music will save it. However, others contend that drama in opera can never be an equal partner with music because music is too powerful an element in the combination. Acrimony on this subject results from confusion between drama for music and the spoken drama—the two differ greatly in length, language, and emphasis. Scathing remarks about the quality of the average opera libretto generally stem from a person's not reading the text *with music in mind*. The libretto can be a work of art but it has to be judged in terms of the music which makes special demands on it.

MYTHOLOGY   The earliest seventeenth century librettists and composers sought to revive Greek tragedy in a new form, and therefore mythology was regarded as the best subject for opera. Myths had the advantage of being remote in time yet humanly believable; they observed eternal truths, portrayed dramatic action, and provided an opportunity for spectacular display—all important ingredients in the operatic mixture. The earliest operas (*Dafne, Euridice, Arianna,* and *Orfeo*) took their plots from mythology. Francesco Algarotti, an eighteenth century writer (*Essay on Opera,* 1754), writes eloquently on the value of myth for opera.

At the poet's behest, mythology brought to the theater all the pagan gods, taking the audience now to Olympus and the Elysian Fields and then to Tartarus as well as Thebes and Argos. With the appearance of these gods, the strangest and most marvelous happenings become lifelike. And by raising, to a certain extent, everything above the human level, mythology made the singing in opera seem to be the natural language of the characters.[5]

The tradition of using mythological subjects as a basis for opera librettos has been a long one. Among others, Monteverdi's *La favola d'Orfeo* (The Fable of Orpheus, 1607), Handel's *Semele* (1744), Gluck's *Orfeo ed Euridice* (Orpheus and Euridice, 1762), Berlioz' *Les Troyens* (The Trojans, 1863–1890), Wagner's *Der Ring des Nibelungen* (The Ring of the Nibelungs, 1869–1876), Strauss' *Elektra* (1909) and *Ariadne auf Naxos* (Ariadne on Naxos, 1912) are based on mythology

HISTORY
AND CON-
TEMPORARY
DRAMA   The earliest operas were presented at court or in an Italian palace. After the first public opera house was opened in Venice in 1637 and opera became a public spectacle, economics and the taste of the

[5]*The Essence of Opera,* p. 70.

audience forced a change to historical plots. Mythology was too remote and demanded an educated taste. Although the history drawn upon (mostly late Roman Empire and the Middle Ages) was equally remote, the characters seemed nearer to reality. The company of gods and goddesses was exchanged for that of human beings. Plots could be touched up and embroidered to create more excitement and thrill for the audience since the stories were obscure and little known. Historical validity was a relative matter.

But before long, something more contemporary was demanded. By the time of Mozart in the second half of the eighteenth century, opera librettos were based on recent plays. These plays dealt with up-to-date problems and circumstances, and they took place in the present. *Le nozze di Figaro* (The Marriage of Figaro, 1786) is a case in point. Beaumarchais' play, *La Folle Journée* (The Crazy Day), which Lorenzo da Ponte used as his source for Mozart's libretto, appeared in Paris in 1784; Mozart and da Ponte's opera was heard in Vienna in 1786.

NATIONALISM In the nineteenth century when political nationalism was ascendant, operatic subjects reflected the current mood. The audience wished a reminder of their own immediate or remote past, or they wished to feel the local color of a setting that could be underscored by the drama and the music. Thus Weber's *Der Freischütz* (The Marksman, 1821) is very German, Bizet's *Carmen* (1875), Spanish, even though written and composed by Frenchmen, Smetana's *Prodaná Nevěsta* (The Bartered Bride, 1866), Czech, and Mussorgsky's *Boris Godunov* (1874), Russian.

Operatic subject matter has also come from Shakespearian plays, epic poems, novels, and contemporary plays—in fact, from the spectrum of drama and literature. The play has been the chief source because it most nearly resembles the opera libretto. Yet, by drawing its net widely, opera has been able to touch upon most of human experience.

The Music Without music opera is not opera. Music lifts the words to a new dimension and creates the magic of an opera. It is the essential element. However clever, powerful, and beautifully constructed a libretto may be, it must have music of similar quality to sustain it or else it fails as opera. Historians estimate that about 40,000 operas have been written since 1600. The vast majority have disappeared, and it is safe to assume that the chief cause of oblivion has been the second-rate music. This is why the composer is always mentioned before the librettist, even though the librettist should rightfully share the credit and the title page.

Throughout the history of opera, two basic components of music have been essential: the *human singing voice* and the *orchestra*. Without singing, there is no opera. The human voice in all its manifestations—not just soprano, alto, tenor, and bass, but the range and timbre of voice as well—gives each role its unique quality. The singing voice, like the human being, has infinite variety. Often an opera lover will recognize a certain singer as quickly as he recognizes a familiar voice speaking over the telephone. The art of singing, even though it has had much nonsense written about it, is at the center of opera. People who disdain the voice will lose most of opera's flavor. It is like the occasional spectator of baseball versus the true *aficionado* who knows not only the players by the way they stand at the plate but also their batting and fielding averages and their extracurricular love affairs. In order to capture the magic of singing, one must get as fully involved in its tribulations as in its triumphs, and be ready to accept the consequences of each on any given evening.

The orchestra is equally essential. Because an opera orchestra remains largely out of sight (except for the conductor), the notion has grown that it is less important than the symphony orchestra which performs on a platform in full view of the audience. On the contrary, the opera orchestra is a full-fledged orchestra of major proportions. Often it has led the way in innovation and change, and in all cases it has developed along with orchestral music generally. Composers do not shift gears when they write an orchestral score for an opera; they only use these resources differently because of the added dimension of voices. In most operas, the orchestra does not "accompany" the voice in the secondary sense of that term; it joins with the voice or voices as a partner. Often the orchestra will tell what is going to happen before the words are sung on the stage. Music with its unique ability to instill a mood, predict a passion, or anticipate an event, is often more specific and meaningful than verbal language; and opera draws on its orchestra to give depth to its presentation. Some moments in an opera will be purely orchestral: for example, overtures and interludes. Indeed, a common complaint throughout operatic history has been the "noisiness" of the orchestra, its drowning out of the voices. (If some singers had their way, there would be hardly any orchestra.) As orchestras have grown (more brass, more winds, more special instruments), the "noise complaint" has become more valid. With Wagner and Strauss the limit of sheer bulk seems to have been reached, for in the later twentieth century, relative numbers have declined somewhat. More important than size, however, is how the orchestra is used. Is it merely an "oom-pah-pah" for the voice as it can be in some Italian operas (including Verdi), or is it a valuable and exciting musical element which lifts high both singers and stage production? The second is its true function.

The Spectacle

Another operatic resource, often neglected, is *dancing*. French opera of the seventeenth and eighteenth centuries (Lully and Rameau) gave ballet as much emphasis as the voice and the orchestra, but Italian and German tradition generally placed it on a lower level. Unfortunately, operatic ballet has often received a bad name—and rightly so. The "Dance of the Seven Veils" in *Salome* by a less-than-sensuous 170 lb. diva, or the Egyptian belly dance of a portly *corps de ballet* in *Aida* has led more to giggles than aesthetic enjoyment. Fortunately, the post-World War II years have seen a resurgence of the ballet. Since the dance can be part of the action as well as something "atmospheric," it must be rehearsed and staged as carefully as the singing. Practically every opera calls for some kind of formalized dancing or at least movements of the body that approximate dancing. These movements must sustain the energy and level of the rest of the production and not become tiresome interruptions rather than a delight. Some of the finest "operatic" music has been music written for ballet. Pantomime, dancing, and music, when combined well, can make ballet a unique artistic achievement.

Yet ballet is only one element in the entire *spectacle*, in which acting, scenery, costumes, and lighting can be grouped for convenience. The *mise-en-scène* (putting into production on the stage) of an opera is one of its most important elements. Because an opera by definition is bound by certain conventions and because it often involves large groups of people (crowds, choruses), it has certain limitations which may be overcome or counteracted by a fine stage production. Also, many operas may be handicapped by historical and esoteric material that is notoriously difficult to represent convincingly. An Oriental potentate, a Chinese princess, a Mantuan sixteenth century adventurer, a Norwegian sea captain are a few of the characters whom opera singers are called upon to impersonate. It goes without saying that a beautiful voice is not always lodged in a body that either looks the part or can act it. In a telegenic age when visual appearance has become almost as important as the brain or message behind it, the contradiction between image and reality on the operatic stage is often painful. Performers must be disguised with make-up and clever costumes. Stage designers have to decide whether their scenery is to be realistic or representational and how it will reach the back row of the gallery (scenery problems are compounded because opera houses generally are much larger than theaters). King Henry's followers in Act I of Wagner's *Lohengrin* must be dressed somewhat like men of the tenth century and not extras in nondescript clothes with old hats on their heads. Even if the less realistic and more timeless illusion is sought on the order of Wieland and Wolfgang Wagner's Bayreuth productions of their grandfather's *The Ring*, it too must carry conviction. One encouraging recent development is the imaginative use of lighting. With modern technology almost any kind of shading and color is possible.

All these resources offer great potential for an art if they can be managed well and placed in proper relation to each other. Human frailty (the vagaries of the vocal cords), opera economics (the enormous cost of good production), and too many ingredients in the boiling pot make the struggle for perfection a hard one. But struggle is a way of life in the operatic world, as it is in the theatrical world in general; and the color, variety, and excitement engendered by each attempt keep the humble chorus singer, the *Heldentenor*, the regisseur, and the listener devoted to his or her task, hoping next time the ideal will be attained. Opera shows no signs of dying yet.

SUGGESTED READING

Brockway, Wallace, and Herbert Weinstock, *The World of Opera*, Pantheon, New York, 1962. Operatic history with full "Annals of Performance" at end.

Dent, Edward J., *Opera*, Penguin Books, London, 1959; Reprint, Kennikat Press, 1972.

Grout, Donald J., *Short History of Opera*, 2nd ed., Columbia University Press, New York, 1965. Best book in English for operatic history although somewhat dry reading. Most thorough opera bibliography in any language.

Martin, George, *The Opera Companion: Guide for the Casual Opera-Goer*, 2 vols., Dodd, Mead, Apollo Books paperback, New York, 1961. Popular in approach and style but interesting. Contains valuable statistical information.

2 The Conventions
of Opera

If any art is to be understood, its conventions and limitations must be considered. Painting is on a flat surface; sculpture is multidimensional; architecture is immovable; music proceeds in time. Conventions we take for granted exist all around us. If examined occasionally, they help to broaden our understanding and increase our perception. To complain of them is to "complain of Shakespeare that people don't in fact talk in poetry; or of an ordinary play that a room shown on the stage has only three walls .. ; or of a film that characters couldn't get from one place to another as quickly as they appear to do."[1] Then there is the modern convention of drama, music, and spectacle (and commercials) coming out of various-size boxes called television. The idea of a screen projecting sound and a picture, whether it is cinema or television, is today hardly given a second thought. But it is still artificial in that what is seen and heard is on a flat surface and comes over air waves, wires, and other equipment and is not directly in front of the viewer. Even spoken drama has its conventions which are just as far removed from reality as are operatic conventions. An example is the "aside" when a character says something to the audience he does not want another person on the stage to hear,

---

ionel Salter, *Going to the Opera*, Penguin Books, London, 1955, pp. 11–12.

yet the words are perfectly audible. Or an actor in a soliloquy thinks aloud when realistically he should be quiet. What are the specific conventions of opera?

Musical Convention

First, the drama is set to music, *generally* all the way through. This is the supreme convention, and the listener must accept it easily and naturally. The distinction between opera and subbranches of the musical stage like operetta, light opera, and musical comedy generally hinges on whether parts of the text (mostly conversation) are spoken or sung. Even with this broad definition, however, exceptions come immediately to mind. Two of the greatest operas, both by major composers, are operas with spoken dialogue. One is Mozart's *Die Zauberflöte* (The Magic Flute, 1791), and the other, Beethoven's *Fidelio* (1805), the only opera Beethoven ever wrote. Both are technically *Singspiele* (German for "sung plays"). All of Mozart's operas with German texts (his most famous operas, *Don Giovanni* and *The Marriage of Figaro*, are in Italian) are Singspiele: that is, they have spoken dialogue. Almost as well-known as *The Magic Flute* is *Die Entführung aus dem Serail* (The Abduction from the Seraglio, 1782), the first important German opera. Both of these are so-called "comic operas" but are great works of art because of Mozart's genius. Beethoven's *Fidelio* is hardly comic, though it has light features in the first act. Beethoven kept the structure of a Singspiel because in his time (1770–1827) operas with German texts were written in this form. After the death of Carl Maria von Weber (1786–1826), the so-called founder of German Romantic opera who wrote Singspiele, except for *Euryanthe*, German operas with spoken dialogue were generally regarded as light or comic opera while serious opera had continuous music. Of the three great European traditions in opera (German, French, and Italian), the Germans at first stressed opera with spoken dialogue; the French generally used it in light opera (opéra comique); but every kind of Italian opera was sung all the way through.

Types

The Italians long ago recognized that dramatic verse and speech had its lyrical, dramatic, and conversational moments, to which music had to adapt itself. Early in the seventeenth century, they began to divide operas in a loose sense into *recitative* (conversation, dialogue), and *arias* (lyricism) (see Chapter 5). Shortly thereafter, John Dryden in England spoke of these divisions from the poet-playwright's point of view in his Preface to *Albion and Albanius* (1685), which became an opera of sorts:

> the recitative part of the opera requires a more masculine beauty of expression and sound, the other, which for want of a proper English word, I must call the *songish part*, must abound in the softness and variety of numbers; its principal intention being to please hearing more than to gratify the understanding.   The chief secret is the choice of words; and by this choice, I do not here mean elegancy of expression, but propriety of sound, to be varied according to the nature of the subject.[2]

Music accommodating itself to the words; text accommodating itself to the music: here is the ideal juncture of the two arts.

Opera of the nineteenth and twentieth centuries, which tries to get away from formally set divisions of music such as the aria and recitative still demonstrates the rise and fall, action and repose, of music set to words. Even Wagner, who prided himself on the continuity with which his music (after *Lohengrin*) flowed from one scene into the next without a break, still shows moments in his later operas when either song-like or recitative-like passages are predominant. The labels are gone, but the music still acts out this natural division of the text. Even when opera is sung all the way through, there is enough variety with the music to prevent it from becoming monotonous. Sung speech or verse has its limitations, but these limitations can be surmounted and even made into assets through the power of music.

Quality of Music Since most operatic conventions deal with music, several of its qualities must be considered. First, music takes *time to unfold*. A single chord or a brief series of notes are striking in the context of what has preceded them. Because of music's rhapsodic nature, it usually has to be organized formally to create an impact. Its discursiveness is given form and balance by repetition (rhythmically, harmonically, melodically), by a return to previously stated material after something different has intervened, by anticipation of what is to come, by endings or breaks that signify a small or a large section, and by phrases, sentences, paragraphs (in a figurative sense) which organize large entities. Dramatic verse moves much more quickly than

[2]Ulrich Weisstein, ed., *The Essence of Opera*, Free Press, (Norton Library paperback), New York, 1964, p. 37

music. A line or a few words are sufficient for the playwright to make his point. Seldom, except for a special kind of effect, can the composer do this in a few measures. He needs time to reach his climax.

It is for this reason that the dramatic action often stops while the music unfolds. A familiar example in the opera house is the dying hero or heroine who has been stabbed, shot, or otherwise mortally wounded, yet manages to sing an aria or duet of some five minutes duration (which takes breath) before expiring. Gilda at the end of *Rigoletto* has supposedly been stabbed to death by an efficient assassin, Sparafucile, who, in the dark, mistaking her for the Duke, does his deadly work, and puts the body in a sack to be delivered to Rigoletto. In the haunting moment (one of the most moving in opera) when Rigoletto, exulting over the supposed body of his daughter's seducer, hears the Duke within the tavern singing "La donna è mobile," tears open the sack to discover his beloved daughter, there is time for Gilda to sing a farewell of some duration and ask her father's forgiveness for substituting herself for the Duke. Verdi and his librettist, Piave, felt that Gilda had to survive that long in order to let the music give the tragic situation its full weight. Realistically, she should have been dead when Rigoletto opened the sack.

Another convention which the nature of music forces upon opera is the *repetition of words*, in itself undramatic. Edward Dent in his splendid little book, *Opera*,[3] speaks trenchantly on this point:

> one of the most ludicrous conventions is that by which a character who ought to be in the greatest hurry to leave the stage remains in front of the footlights for several minutes informing us melodiously and with many reiterations that he "must away" or "can no longer stay"

Listeners are often astounded to discover on reading a libretto that an operatic aria, which may last five to ten minutes in performance, consists of four lines of verse. Although the following famous cavatina at the beginning of Act II of Mozart's *Figaro*, where the Countess asks the goddess of love to restore her husband to her, is hardly a long aria, the music in its effect gives great breadth and dignity (implying length) to a mere four lines.

Porgi amor, qualche ristoro
Al mio duolo, a miei sospir!
O mi rendi il mio tesoro
O mi lascia almen morir

---

[3]Penguin Books, London, 1949, p. 17

Render, O love, some solace
to my grief, to my sighs.
Return my beloved to me
or else let me die.

If lines have been varied skillfully enough by the composer, repetition is not distracting. In fact, the avid listener *wants* the words repeated in order to hear once again a melody or motive that has enraptured him by its beauty. Whether this repetition is contrary to sense or not is no longer important because the music has captivated the ear and swept everything else before it.

Other Forms of Music

Some other conventions that stem from music can be mentioned briefly. One is the *overture*. Originally it was designed to quiet a noisy and boisterous audience so the singers could be heard. In Jean-Baptiste Lully's time (1632–1687), overtures became tripartite: a slow first part, a fast, imitative, middle part, and a final, slower section. The dignified section probably accompanied the entrance of Louis XIV and his court who patronized these operas, the lively Allegro drew attention to the stage and what would take place there (ballet, colorful action); the return presumed everyone was seated and the opera ready to begin. Overtures have taken various forms over the years. Many have been bustle and notes, signifying nothing, apparently designed to fulfill only their original function. Others have attempted to foreshadow the action by reference to themes which will be heard in the opera. A few overtures, notably those by Gluck, Mozart, Beethoven, and Wagner, have been great works of art, either summing up the action or setting the mood for what is to follow. Some recent composers (Puccini and Strauss) have dispensed with the overture, jumping right into the opera and avoiding the problem entirely

Then there is the *chorus* (if called for), which is notoriously difficult to handle. A play or a drama may call for a crowd scene which has a direct part in the action. But many operas use the chorus primarily for musical and not dramatic reasons. The problem then becomes what to do with the chorus singers while they are on stage but not participating in the movement of the opera. Their function as commentary on the action is a valuable musical asset, but somehow their presence must be separated from what is taking place. Too often this distinction is not made clear. Some particularly violent action may be transpiring downstage (a duel, a fight, a strangling), and upstage eight or ten strapping soldiers or townspeople look on with vacant expressions, to the amusement of the audience. A good stage director will anticipate this problem and make the scene visually realistic.

Similar to the chorus are the various *ensembles* which the music of opera demands. These may be duos, trios, sextets, or finales where the chief characters sing together. The presence of the people involved is as often dictated by musical considerations as by the action. Mortal enemies ready to leap at each other's throats conclude an act by singing a tuneful duet together. Two sets of characters who cannot abide each other's presence spend some time standing next to each other singing words (mostly asides) which are meant for the audience (if they can be understood) but not for each other. These conventions have become such a part of opera they are seldom even noticed. But in a great finale, like the conclusion of Act II of Mozart's *Figaro*, where action and music combine to produce a miraculous result, there is no creaking of the machinery and no awkward stage business; rather, a wonderful musical and dramatic flow from one episode to the next. The clever librettist and supreme composer have demonstrated beyond any doubt that drama and music are both compatible and unifiable, and in this opera they have gloriously transcended the limitations either art may have placed on the other.

Dramatic Convention

Acting in opera makes special demands upon singers. Because music moves much more slowly than speech, the singing actor or actress must often prolong an action, mood, or idea to lengths a speaking actor would find intolerable. The singer must concentrate not only on the melodic line and his vocal production but on the meaning of what he is singing, so that a total projection of music and drama is conveyed to the audience. Unless the person knows precisely what he or she will do with gestures, facial expressions, and movements of the body while singing, the result can be disastrous. Meaningless gestures, exaggerated motions, grimaces which convey pain when joy is meant are merely a few of the faults that can be common in the opera house. Good singing does not always imply good acting, and many an opera star must train and practice continually to play a role convincingly. In days gone by, operatic acting was often given scant consideration, the theory was that the public came to hear the voice and paid little attention to acting or production. Today, while it is hardly possible to say that every Violetta, Gilda, and Mimi is sylph-like, beautiful to behold, has a glorious voice, and can act,

singers are more conscious of their figures and their acting ability than they have been before.

Even Verdi in 1848 was concerned about the appearance and voice of a certain singer in *Macbeth*. In writing to one of his librettists, Cammarano, he said.

> The part of Lady Macbeth has been assigned to Tadolini, and I am much surprised that she should lend herself to it. You know how much I esteem Tadolini and she knows it herself, but in our common interest I would consider it necessary to think this over a bit. Tadolini has too great qualities for the part. Perhaps this will seem absurd to you. Tadolini's appearance is good and beautiful and I would like to have Lady Macbeth deformed and ugly Tadolini is a perfectionist in her singing, and I would like to have her not sing at all. Tadolini has a marvelously bright, clear voice, and I should like to have for Lady Macbeth a stifled, hollow, harsh voice. The voice of Tadolini has the quality of an angel, the voice of the Lady needs something of the devil.[4]

Verdi did not literally mean "not sing at all"; he wanted the person who took Lady Macbeth's part to have a harsh singing voice, not an angelic one.

The listener often wonders why some opera singers tend to be heavy, with less than youthful figures. Singing demands great physical exertion of the whole body and after three hours of it (with little to eat beforehand), a singer is famished and likely to stow away astonishing quantities of food and drink. Another difficulty, often forgotten, which makes it hard to find a Rodolfo of 19 or a Juliet of 17, is the physiological fact that the human vocal cords and larynx are among the last organs in the body to mature. Also the diaphragm and chest cavities must be developed and used to their utmost. A voice seldom gains the tone and staying power demanded of a major operatic role before a singer is in his middle or late twenties.

Extraneous Conventions Finally, there are those extraneous conventions in the opera house, such as the *prompter*, the *claque*, and the *encore* which always intrigue a newcomer. The prompter's box, a recessed and hooded opening on

[4]Gaetano Cesare and Alessandro Luzio, *I Copialettere di Giuseppe Verdi*, Verdi Commissione, Milan 1913, pp. 61–62.

the stage just in back of the footlights, houses the prompter who has the musical score and either mouths or speaks the text to aid the singer. (Occasionally he gives a pitch.) If the same opera were given night after night (as is done now with a new play in the theater and was the rule in the seventeenth and eighteenth centuries with opera), a prompter would hardly be necessary. But most of the world's large opera houses (and many smaller ones) are committed today to the repertory system, in which a number of "old" works are alternated during a given series of weeks. Each singer may play 20 to 25 roles, if not more; he may sing *Tosca* in Buenos Aires one week and jet to London for a performance of *Il trovatore* the next or even the same week. In such cases a prompter may be of crucial importance. Some people never need prompting, but others are always grateful for such a crutch and bless the aid that comes when loss of memory threatens.

A *claque* is a paid group of listeners (mostly standees) who are hired by individual singers or the management to applaud lustily or firmly at the proper moment (generally after an aria or at the end of an act when curtain calls are taken) so that a particular singer is kept before the public and gains the popularity that will mean larger fees and greater *réclame* in the future. The stories about claques, their leaders, their loyalties, and their discipline (the right moment to clap or withhold applause) are legion in the opera house, but today few claques remain (except in some of the smaller Italian opera houses). In a sense, the phonograph recording has replaced them. Recording gives a singer not only additional income but also an entrée to the public, often in more favorable circumstances (the sound engineer manipulates the voice) than in the opera house with its limited and fickle audience. Opera recordings have almost become a substitute for performance because the sound as sound (with the visual element lacking) is made superior, by tape splices and retakes, to anything that can possibly be heard in an opera house under performing conditions. Thus singers are known even before they arrive in a strange city or a different country for an appearance.

Encores also are largely a thing of the past. Naturally, to repeat an aria or an ensemble violates any dramatic sense of continuity, and most major opera houses today will not tolerate it. But the revival of Bellini, Donizetti, and Rossini, proponents of "the singers opera," where the coloratura soprano, ornamentation, and the cadenza are featured, sometimes leads to moments when the demand for an encore becomes overwhelming. A particularly brilliant cadenza or *fioritura* lets loose all the exhibitionist tendencies in singer and audience and what should be a musical triumph becomes an acrobatic one where the crowd wants to have the stunt performed again.

Conventions may be acceptable (an encore is not) within the framework of a fine operatic performance. The danger comes with the second-rate. Opera, an intensely professional art, must call forth the best from all its individual parts. If any one part sags, then each convention, which normally can be taken in stride, becomes too prominent and the audience finds difficulty in accepting it. But when the impact of the work as a whole is so satisfying and complete, so exciting and overwhelming that all the rough edges become rounded and smooth, everything falls into place and conventions are forgotten. Opera then fulfills itself as a noble art.

SUGGESTED READING

Kerman, Joseph, *Opera as Drama*, Knopf, Vintage Books paperback, New York, 1956. Sharp, critical, but highly penetrating series of essays on opera aesthetics. Some famous operas discussed in detail.

Rosenthal, Harold, and John Warrack, eds., *Concise Oxford Dictionary of Opera*, Oxford University Press, 2nd ed., London, 1979. Excellent for operatic material: musical terms, names of singers, operas, brief resumé of plots, and other general information.

Weisstein, Ulrich, ed., *The Essence of Opera*, Free Press, 1964, Norton Library paperback, New York, 1969 A fine collection of writings on opera over the centuries.

3 The Libretto

The libretto has had a difficult role in the history of opera. It has seldom been treated as a form of literature, even a special one, and critics have been loath to call it drama because it must always be read with the music in mind. A spoken libretto is an anomaly unless parts of the text have been specifically conceived for spoken dialogue. As Christopher Hassall, a contemporary English librettist and translator says: "There's no such thing as a good libretto in the abstract, though a particular text or a particular theme devised for a particular musician may prove itself in the event to have been a good one."[1] The poet W H. Auden is even stronger: "The verses which the librettist writes are not addressed to the public but are really a private letter to the composer. They have their moments of glory, the moment in which they suggest to him a certain melody; once it is over, they are as expendable as infantry to a Chinese general: they must efface themselves and cease to care what happens to them."[2]

Many librettos can be read with pleasure, provided the imagination is always at work and the reader realizes that, with the help of music, a few words or a few lines can say what a paragraph or a long passage of verse may say in a drama. There are really two dramatists in an opera, the librettist and the composer. As already discussed (see

[1]"Words, Words   " (An Open Letter) in *Fanfare for Ernest Newman*, Arthur Barker, London, 1955, p. 109
[2]"Reflections on Opera as a Medium," *Opera News* (February 9, 1953).

p. 14) the composer controls "stage time," the amount of time it will take for any set of words to be sung. But the librettist must fashion the scenario, see to it that the relationship of the characters is properly balanced, the language is fit for music, and the meaning is clear. The libretto must often be more straightforward than an ordinary drama need be with the opportunity of many more words to explain itself. Words, action, gesture, and voice inflection accomplish for the drama what music in itself often does for opera. Ernest Newman, one of the best writers on opera, has the following wry comment to make about librettists:

The musical world pullulates with schools and instruction books for pianists, fiddlers, singers, conductors, composers, and what not. It still lacks, however, a school for librettists. To recast a novel or a play as an opera text calls for a special technique; yet after three hundred years there is still nothing resembling a code for the guidance of a librettist in his fumbling hand-to-mouth practice. What generally happens is that the poet . . (to employ what in this connection is generally no more than a technical term) and the composer, after an infinity of discussion, correspondence, and from time to time heated recrimination, eventually settle down to a rough-and-ready compromise between the claims of the drama and those of music: despite the struggles of the poor librettist the composer always has the last word, and we know from history, that it is not always the most rational word.[3]

Ideally, the librettist should know a good deal about music, so that he will instinctively realize what sort of language is best for singing, where climaxes come naturally, and where the text must race forward or slow down. Arrigo Boito (1842–1918), Verdi's librettist for *Otello* (1887) and *Falstaff* (1893)—his last two magnificent creations, was an ideal collaborator in this respect because he was a musician himself, a composer with two operas of his own. Boito was able to construct from Shakespeare two of the finest librettos ever written, not only because of his literary ability but also because he understood the problems of musical setting. Presumably an even more desirable goal is to have the librettist and composer be one person, as in the case of Richard Wagner (1813–1883). But this poses problems. A perfect equilibrium between two sides of a creative personality is rarely attained, although the possibilities for opera are greatly enhanced when one person is responsible for both words and music. Today Wagner's poetry is hardly regarded as the literary equivalent of his music. At their worst, his texts are turgid and obscure; at their best, good serviceable poetry for music. As the architect of a plot, however, Wagner was a first-rate dramatist.

[3]Ernest Newman, *Great Operas*, Vintage Books paperback, New York, 1958, vol. 2, p. 218.

Throughout operatic history, the names of librettists have hardly been known. We speak of Mozart's, Verdi's, and Puccini's operas but not often of the people who wrote the librettos for them. This is hardly fair. A good or bad libretto does not necessarily seal the fate of an opera, but it can have a decisive effect upon it. Librettos have been constantly compared to the plays or novels on which they were based, to the detriment of the libretto. Unless a critic knows how a libretto works and hears the music to it, the comparison is useless. There have been enough first-rate librettists in the past to prove that the drama can attain a level comparable to the music: Busenello with Monteverdi, Quinault with Lully, Calzabigi with Gluck, da Ponte with Mozart, Boito with Verdi, Hofmannsthal with Strauss are all artists worthy of serious consideration in a special medium. Their accomplishment deserves to be analyzed and praised for what it is and not for what it might be under different circumstances.

If one really wants to understand an opera, then, the libretto must be a primary consideration. One reads it thoroughly and if possible, examines its model, if there is one, to see what material has been omitted, contrasted, or heightened to help the music. Unless this reading of the libretto is done, a great deal will be lost. Half the people who are exposed to opera and then lose interest do so because they have failed to read the libretto. They do not really know what is going on and why, and they rely almost entirely on the music to carry them through the spectacle.

It is particularly important for the American and English opera public to know the libretto because they usually will not understand the sung text. Most operas in the regular repertory have been written in Italian, German, or French, and major opera houses in America and England generally perform them in the original language. Proponents of opera in English rightly maintain that this is one of the chief reasons opera has never become an important popular entertainment in the two English-speaking countries. Unless they are devotees, people will not go to hear something they cannot understand. Germans and Italians expect respectively to have Verdi sung in German and Wagner in Italian (though this is changing). Why not the Americans and English? In the early eighteenth century when Italian opera in Italian became the rage in London, Joseph Addison in *The Spectator* said, "For there is no question but our great Grand-children will be very curious to know the Reason why their Forefathers used to sit together like an Audience of Foreigners in their own Country, and to hear whole Plays acted before them in a Tongue which they did not understand."[4]

[4]*The Spectator*, No. 18 (March 21, 1711).

Yet, *translated opera* has both advantages and disadvantages. It has the obvious very great advantage of letting the native audience know, at least partially (words get swallowed up by the music or poor enunciation), what is transpiring on the stage. Plot synopses help, but they are only a substitute. On the other hand it is desirable to hear an opera as the librettist and composer wrote it. Translation at best is a compromise. Vowel and consonantal sounds are never exactly the same in another language. A further problem is the criteria for translation. If the translation is to be *sung*, literary and musical abilities of no mean order are demanded of the translator. Vowel sounds of the original must be approximated, and the length of lines and accentuation of words must correspond closely to the original, or else the music and text are distorted. If the libretto is primarily meant to be *read* as rhymed English verse (the original being in this form), the translator must be something of a poet and a musician, as well as thoroughly conversant in two languages. Yet he can be freer in his choice of words with this kind of verse. If the translation is to be a *literal* one, in which the English is as close to the original as possible with little regard for literary style or rhymed verse, then plain, understandable prose is in order. Too many translations are a disoriented hodgepodge of these three approaches. Consequently, the reader is confused and disillusioned at the outset when he ought to be eager for a new experience. Fortunately, many of the record companies have commissioned new translations of favorite operas with their recordings, and the situation is much improved over what it once was.

Writing a Libretto

What are some of the problems inherent in writing a libretto? First, there is obviously *meaning and content*. If the text is action prose ("Where are you going?" "I must help her."), then there is little difficulty. But if dramatic poetry is demanded in moments of emotional stress (love, hate, jealousy, fear), then the poetry must be clear and not too abstruse or idiosyncratic. Contemporary poetry with its love of elliptical and complicated imagery is very difficult to set for opera because its meaning is often ambiguous or hidden. The following stanza is an example.

At the first turning of the second stair
I turned and saw below
The same shape twisted on the banister
Under the vapour in the fetid air

Struggling with the devil of the stairs who wears
The deceitful face of hope and of despair

T. S. Eliot, *Ash Wednesday*[5]

If the poetry is isolated and independent (composed as a separate lyric which might be set to music), then the situation calls forth a different response. But in opera, irony and ambiguity are apt to get lost because the gesture has to be large and plain, unless the work is chamber opera on an intimate scale. To quote Hassall again. "A libretto requires the unfashionable and peculiar virtue of the eighteenth century era—the virtue of being at once direct and concise without flatness.... Poetry in a libretto exists only by virtue of its serving a purpose not its own."[6]

Then there comes the matter of language, *the selection of words to be sung*. It is indisputable, for instance, that it is easier in English to sing the word "soon" than the word "stuck." Two factors are at work here: first, the short vowel sound of "uh" has not nearly the vocal carrying power "oo" has; second, hard consonantal sounds like "k" are harder to articulate than the softer ones like "n." The composer can overcome textual difficulty by the construction of his musical line, but the librettist's choice of words will be very important. Where it is necessary for the intent of the plot that the words be clearly understood, the librettist must make his meaning doubly clear because the music will inevitably submerge some of the diction. The composer, on the other hand, has an obligation to see his music does not overpower the words. The meat of a libretto is generally expressed through "action" words: verbs and nouns. Adverbs and figures of speech have to be treated warily. When the plot calls for a moment of lyrical reflection (an aria) and the librettist puts it in the form of a rhymed stanza of four to eight lines, his words and phrases must bear repetition since the music will probably demand it. If the words are awkward when sung the first time, they will be doubly and triply so when repeated.

Librettists have always complained about the pressure they are under to reduce their lines to the barest minimum in order to accommodate the composer. Mozart's and Verdi's letters to their librettists are filled with suggestions for cuts of existing verse. Occasionally they want something added, but for the most part pruning and excision are requested. The poet within the librettist naturally rebels against this elimination of his creative children. E. T. A. Hoffman

---

[5]*Collected Poems 1909–1962*, Harcourt Brace Jovanovich, New York, 1963, p. 89.
[6]"Words, Words. ," p. 114.

(1776–1822), poet, painter, composer, and one of the first Romantics, wrote an essay in 1813 called "The Poet and the Composer" (in *Die Serapionsbrüder*), in which, speaking as the poet in the dialogue between the two, he said.

> It is the incredible brevity you demand of us. All our attempts to conceive or portray this or that passion in weighty language are in vain, for everything has to be settled in a few lines which, in addition, have to lend themselves to the ruthless treatment which you inflict upon them.
>
> When we have striven ever so hard to give the proper poetic expression to every portion of our work, and paint each situation in glowing words and charming, smoothly running verses, it is frightful to see how mercilessly you obliterate our finest lines and mangle our best verses by twisting, inverting, or drowning them in music.[7]

In spite of all his creative instincts, then, an important part of the librettist's craft is *the art of omission*. What can be left out without harming the plot or doing less than justice to the characterization or dramatic situation? The decision is never easy, and the poet will naturally complain when the contraction becomes so terse it sounds abrupt. His medium is words, but the words sometimes get in the way of the music. One of the best ways to demonstrate this art at its best is to put a page of Shakespeare next to that of Boito and see what the latter had to omit in order to write an effective libretto.

Another delicate situation for the librettist arises in an ensemble where three or four characters are singing together but each is saying something different. Because the music functions as a unit and is apt to overpower any differentiation in the text between one person and another, the librettist tends to despair of his words ever coming through and merely hopes that somebody will read them in order to understand what is really going on. Yet this need not be the case, as is demonstrated in that over-familiar but telling example of the famous quartet from the last act of *Rigoletto*. Here Verdi comes to the rescue of his librettist, Francesco Piave, and by musical means enhances the differing sentiments of the four characters in the text while simultaneously creating a perfect musical whole. Verdi gives to each person a distinctive theme which not only expresses the mood of the character but at the same time is combined contrapuntally and chordally to make a fine musical entity. The crafts of librettist and composer here become one.

Perhaps the most frustrating moment for librettists occurs when important lines of text are lost through the inept pronunciation of singers. Richard Strauss (1864–1949) once said he expected about a

[7]Ulrich Weisstein, ed., *The Essence of Opera*, Free Press (Norton Library paperback), New York, 1964, p. 169

third of the words to be swallowed up in any one operatic performance. It goes without saying that good singing *is* good enunciation. The finest artists have always been proud of their ability to "project" a role. Such projection demands not only beautiful tone but also articulation of it through diction to reach every member of the audience. Nevertheless, the librettist must see to it that the words are the sort that carry and have distinct meaning.

If it is inevitable that some of the text will be swept aside— whether by the singers, by the music, by poor staging, or by the acting—then the librettist must be certain that *the dramatic action on the stage* is quite clear. Information can be shown as well as sung or spoken. It can be demonstrated by decisive gestures, by exits and entrances, and by other stage actions. Physical movement is even more important for the librettist than for the ordinary dramatist. He cannot leave it to the whims of the stage director. His text must indicate exactly what has happened or is about to happen. Since music will often hold up the action, even the meaning of the static moment must be made clear. Hoffman has the composer say some words to the poet on this subject:

> he must be doubly careful to arrange the scenes in such a way that the action unfolds clearly and distinctly before the eyes of the audience. For even while barely able to comprehend the text, the spectator must be in a position to reconstruct the action from what happens on stage. No other dramatic poem is so much in need of lucidity, since apart from the fact that even with the clearest enunciation the words are difficult to understand, the music itself tends to distract the listener's attention, so that it must be constantly directed toward the points of the greatest dramatic effect and concentration.[8]

None of these desired ends come easily and automatically [9] The best librettos are the result of a constant dialogue between composer and librettist, each adapting himself to the other to achieve the finest result. The composer does not necessarily have to have the last word. The most able composers are keenly aware of what a well-constructed libretto will do for their music, and they are as anxious as the poet to have a fusion of efforts. They realize that cooperation and com-

---

[8]*The Essence of Opera*, p. 177
[9]When Benjamin Britten collaborated with Eric Crozier and E. M. Forster on the opera *Billy Budd*, drawn from the story by Herman Melville, the libretto went through a series of five drafts before it was acceptable. The first draft was merely a jotting down of episodes in the story, a rough list of characters, suggested stage setting; the second, a synopsis of the plot, dividing the action into scenes; the third, a draft of the entire text; the fourth, a thoroughgoing revision with the composer present and each line rigorously tested; the fifth and last, Britten's own word alterations and changes as he composed.

promise are needed on both sides and that a true union of music and words is the ultimate goal.

| **Historical Background** | In the seventeenth century, the word "libretto" (Italian for "little book") came into general use because the text of an opera was printed separately for the audience who wished to follow the words during a performance. Before opera became open to the public around the middle of the century, the "little book" was not small but of good size with engravings and other elaborate programmatic features which would appeal to the cultivated taste of aristocratic Italians in a private palace or at court. As opera grew in popularity and numbers (by the end of the century the city of Venice alone could claim seven theaters devoted exclusively to opera), the "book" became smaller, to be handled more conveniently. It literally reached pocket size and evidently was carried in the pocket. Theaters were never entirely darkened, so reading during a performance was possible. Even so, illumination left a good deal to be desired, and little candles were sold to the audience to be attached to the top of the librettos. These candles left wax stains on the paper, and extant library copies of librettos bear these marks of usage. Most of the early librettos had a florid dedication to a patron (from whom monetary support was expected), and they were signed by the librettist, the impresario, and sometimes even the printer. Generally the composer was not even mentioned. If anybody was singled out, it was the scene designer, who in a baroque age of extravagant stage sets and machinery was a key figure in operatic production. |

For the opera historian, the libretto is often just as valuable a source as the music. It may contain stage directions not found in the musical score. (Even with Mozart this is true.) The libretto frequently had portions of explanatory text which the composer did not see fit to put to music, but which were important for an overall understanding of the opera. It generally gave a cast of characters and sometimes actual names of singers, and included the date when an opera was first performed. Most seventeenth and eighteenth century librettos also included an *Argomento* (argument), which could be both a plot synopsis and a summary of the action that had taken place before the opera began. They also had a sentence to the effect that fates and gods who determined action should not be construed in any religious sense.

Today's libretto has changed very little from the early days of opera. The dedication to a patron and the argument have disappeared, but the text and stage directions for the work are included as

SOSARME,

Re di MEDIA.

DRAMA.

Da Rappresentarsi

Nel REGIO TEATRO
DI
HAY-MARKET.

Done into *English* by Mr. HUMPHREYS.

LONDON:

Printed for T. WOOD in *Little-Britain*, and are to
be sold at the King's Theatre in the *Hay-Market.*

M DCC XXXII.

[Price One Shilling.]

"The text of an opera was printed separately for the audience who wished to follow the words during a performance." Title page of an eighteenth-century libretto printed in London for Handel's *Sosarme* in 1732. The original Italian and its English translation were printed on facing pages. The Italian on the title page reads, "*Sosarme, King of Media,* Drama. Presented at the Royal Theater in the Haymarket." (Courtesy of Princeton University Library) completely as possible. If the opera needs a translation, it appears on the opposite page from the original so the reader can see both languages. The libretto also generally includes a plot synopsis.

The Libretto Versus the Music

Throughout the history of opera one thing has remained constant: the eternal battle as to whether the words should serve the music, or the music the words. As discussed, this argument is largely futile if both librettist and composer determine that neither is going "to conquer"—that their collaboration will serve both arts and not either one singly. Nevertheless, the polemic has raged from the beginning, almost to the point of obsession. In 1677, Saint-Évremond could declare, "The music must be made for the words, rather than the words for the music." Early in the eighteenth century, the Italian critic Lodovico Muratori wrote, "At one time, music was the servant and waited on the poetry; now the poetry is the servant of the music." This comment pertained to the *opera seria*, a type of Italian opera which swept Europe in the second half of the seventeenth and the first half of the eighteenth century and was exemplified in the works of Handel. It was rather rigidly (though not so much as commentators declare) divided into scenes of recitative and *da capo* arias, which were constructed largely for the solo singer and not for the dramatic progress of the plot. Ensembles and choruses were few, and the opera revolved around the individual singer and his music. In the process the poetry suffered, although Pietro Metastasio was able to make an art of this kind of libretto. Even before his time, the aria had become the center of musical interest, and librettists turned out quantities of doggerel to enable the composer to have free play. Smooth quatrains with numerous end-rhymes (what we would call the Tin Pan Alley complex, where "tune" always rhymes with "moon,") were the order of the day. The seventeenth century equivalent of this was:

Bellezza sdegnosa	*Mi piace, e m'alletta*
Gradirmi non può	*Sol rigido amor*
Sembianza vezzosa	*M'invita, e diletta*
Io sempre amerò	*Superbo rigor*
	(Nicolo Minato, *Scipione Africano*, 1678)

Disdainful beauty	*Stern love*
I cannot accept,	*pleases and entices me*
a pretty face	*proud severity*
I shall always love.	*invites me and delights me.*

The plots of these librettos had some historical basis with familiar names of characters and their relations to each other, but love, intrigue, and honor became somehow the ruling factors in their lives. Examples from Roman history were Julius Caesar conquering Egypt but falling in love with Cleopatra, or Nero wanting Poppea and getting rid of his lawful wife, Octavia. Librettists were also forced to contrive a happy ending, which often made the final untying and tying of knots a ludicrous and improbable denouement. It is important to remember, however, that opera seria was popular entertainment and not solemn grand opera. The audience in Venice (the gondoliers in the pit and the aristocracy in their boxes) went to be seen and to converse with friends as well as to hear the music; even business and diplomacy were transacted.

In the middle of the eighteenth century, the pendulum had swung so far in the direction of music that it had to reverse direction. This "reform" was a gradual process but it can best be seen in the work of Christoph Willibald Gluck (1714–1787). Gluck and his librettist, Calzabigi, turned back to mythology and the classics. They attempted to rid the plot of subsidiary, complicating action (a feature of opera seria) and concentrate on one noble subject with language to fit. In the process, the set musical forms were partially, but not entirely, replaced by a more free-flowing musical line. Poetry once more assumed its rightful place in the spectrum. Gluck's oft-quoted remarks are rather a justification of what he had already done than a call for future action. Of course, he speaks for the composer rather than the librettist.

My intention was to purify music from all the abuses which have crept into Italian opera through the vanity of the singers and the excessive compliance of the composers and have made the most splendid and beautiful of all arts the most ridiculous and boring. I tried therefore to bring musicians back to their real task of serving the poetry, by intensifying the expression of emotion and the appeal of every situation, without interrupting the plot or weakening it by excessive ornamention.[10]

A few years later, Mozart, who was primarily a musical dramatist, in that he made the plot and words live through his music, said in a letter to his father (October 13, 1781):

I should say that in an opera the poetry must be altogether the obedient daughter of the music. Why do Italian comic operas please everywhere — in spite of their miserable libretti . . . Just because there the music reigns supreme and when one listens to it all else is forgotten.[11]

[10] Preface to his opera, *Alceste* (1766).
[11] Emily Anderson, ed., *The Letters of Mozart and His Family*, Macmillan, London, 1938, vol. 3, pp. 1150–1151.

What Mozart meant was that a good libretto was so hard to find, it was better for him to impose upon the drama his music, which had the power to shape it more convincingly than the words themselves. When eventually he found an ideal collaborator in Lorenzo da Ponte, the librettos came up to the level of the music composed for them. Wagner (1813–1883) reopened the whole question when, as his own librettist, he felt the necessity in his polemical *Opera and Drama* to reemphasize the literary part of opera and what it stood for in relation to the music.[12] In modern times (1942), Richard Strauss wrote an opera, *Capriccio*, on a text by Clemens Krauss, in which the characters occupy much of their time discussing whether the music or the words should have pre-eminence in opera.

If any conclusion can be drawn from this survey, it is that the libretto is always in danger of being subdued by the music. Each time, in a so-called reform period, poetry has had to be reemphasized after being overpowered by its ally. And surprisingly, the composers have been the first to recognize the necessity for this. The more clear-sighted composers, Monteverdi, Gluck, Mozart, Verdi, and Wagner, instinctively realizing that opera is an amalgam and not exclusively musical, have urged the balancing of the scale.

To follow the course of the libretto in operatic history is a fascinating undertaking, although there are many arid stretches. But the "little book" has persistently been the key to what comes later in the act of creation. We must always start with it and treat it with the respect it deserves. Without it, the music would merely be an outpouring of sound and not a dramatic realization of verse and plot. Opera is drama and music.

SUGGESTED READING

General   Smith, Patrick, J., *The Tenth Muse, A Historical Study of the Opera Libretto*, Knopf, New York, 1970; Reprint Schirmer Books, New York, 1975. One of the first books in English to discuss the libretto intelligently.

Plot Summaries   Cross, Milton, and Karl Kohrs, *The New Milton Cross Complete Stories of the Great Operas*, rev and enlarged ed., Doubleday, Garden City, N.Y., n.d. Strictly plot synopsis with some musical titles. Familiar repertory
Cross, Milton, and Karl Kohrs, *Milton Cross' More Stories of the Great Operas*, Doubleday, Garden City, N.Y., 1971. 45 of the lesser known works.

[12]"The error in the art-genre of opera consists herein: that a Means of Expression (Music) has been made the object, while the object of expression (the Drama) has been made a means."

Kobbe's Complete Opera Book, rev. ed., Putnam, New York, 1963 The oldest and most complete of all the plot synopsis books.

Simon, Henry, *100 Great Operas and Their Stories*, rev. ed., Doubleday, Dolphin paperback, Garden City, N.Y., 1960. Useful coverage of most operas in the repertory

4 The Music

What is the alchemy that makes one opera a perennial favorite and another, even by the same composer, a forgotten work? Is it the music, the characters, the dances, the plot, the stage settings, the total effect? Eight times out of ten it is the music that makes the difference. Few operas can win lasting fame without music of high quality. Some "old chestnuts" may remain whose longevity can be attributed to other factors: a special part for an unusual kind of voice, spectacular stage display, appeal to patriotism, a few familiar arias with catchy melodies. But these are exceptions. Certainly every work does not pretend to possess the weight of Verdi's *Aida* (1871) or Wagner's *Götterdämmerung* (The Twilight of the Gods, 1876). Equally great in their sphere are comedies which touch the lighter side of life: Mozart's *Così fan tutte* (So Do They All, 1790), Rossini's *Il Barbiere di Siviglia* (The Barber of Seville, 1816), Strauss's *Der Rosenkavalier* (The Knight of the Rose, 1911). In every one of these works, the music is superb in its own right and is combined with a fine libretto, a masterwork has been created.

The music of an opera means many different things to different people. To some, it will be the melodies of two or three striking arias which they will wait impatiently to hear. To others it will be a particular ensemble (a duet, a trio, a finale) which brings a special thrill. Or, for the less vocally minded, it will be the orchestra—its interludes, its accompaniments, its motives—which is important.

The professional listener may pay more attention to the harmonic and rhythmic structure of the music, how the voice fits with the orchestra, the transitions from one moment to another, the instrumental scoring of the work, and the contour of a melodic line.

These attitudes, in concentrating on the physical sound of music, neglect what is perhaps music's most significant contribution to opera: its function as a dramatic force. Gerald Abraham has written eloquently on this point:

What matters above all in the opera house is not the ability to write beautiful music, but the much rarer ability to create characters and dramatic situations in music, just as an ordinary dramatist creates them in words. Observe that they must be created *in* music, not taken ready-made from the librettist and set to music; the librettist can and must provide dramatic possibilities, or at least sketches for the characters, but he cannot create them in opera. Only the musician can do that. No composer can succeed as a musical dramatist simply by supplying a good libretto with appropriate music; he must himself have the gift of visualizing dramatic situations, of living in them, above all of thinking himself into the skins and skulls of his characters, no matter how diverse or how different from himself. Verdi, Wagner, Moussorgsky possessed this gift, Puccini had it in a more limited range. Mozart was most richly endowed with it.[1]

This vital function is one of the most difficult to analyze and describe in operatic music because it is often so subtle and elusive. Many little musical elements which are tremendously important may pass unnoticed: a turn of a phrase, a sudden dynamic mark, an interrupted cadence, a rhythmic diversion, a key change, instrumental coloring, a harmonic shift. Yet these are the musical means that delineate the dramatic force of the action. Without their detail and intricate delineation the strokes get either clumsy or too broad, and the composer is merely setting words to music, not creating characters and situations. A good ear unconsciously takes in these subtleties without necessarily identifying or labeling them. Technical knowledge is not a prerequisite for artistic enjoyment. But the ear must hear the differences, understand what the composer is attempting to do, and grasp the intent of word, action, and setting, so that the opera claims the attention of all the senses and brings them into coordination and balance with one another.

Operatic music has provided us with considerable stylistic innovation. Monteverdi's use of orchestral color in *Orfeo* was far in advance of his time, as was his treatment of harmony (freely introduced seventh chords, modulating sequences), dissonance,

---

[1] H. C. Robbins-Landon and Donald Mitchell, eds., *The Mozart Companion*, Oxford University Press, New York, 1956, p. 283.

syncopation, and ensemble. Although these innovations had appeared in his madrigals, they were brought together with cumulative impact in the two great operas that survive, *Orfeo* (1607) and *L'Incoronazione di Poppea* (The Coronation of Poppea, 1642). When another Orfeo (*Orfeo ed Euridice*) by Gluck burst upon the musical world in 1762, it also pointed the way to the future through the power of its music. Gluck's superb handling of chorus, orchestra, aria, and recitative demonstrated that music had a cumulative dramatic power all its own. Each part of the opera blends into the other without interruption: the chorus as furies, as shades of Elysium, or as commentator on the action; in powerful recitative and melody of heart-rending beauty; the instruments singing above the voices or standing out in solo. Then a hundred years later, Wagner's new style in *The Ring, Tristan und Isolde* (1865), *Die Meistersinger von Nürnberg* (The Mastersingers of Nuremberg, 1868), and *Parsifal* (1882) became the guiding force for music of the late nineteenth and early twentieth centuries. Wagner's harmonic style, particularly in *Tristan*, which leads to the breakup of the tonal system as it was known for two centuries; his elevation of the orchestra to an importance it seldom had before; his *leit motiv* (leading motive) system, not new but carried to great complexity and ingenuity—these innovations are among opera's most significant contributions to music.

National Traditions

Before launching into a discussion of music's contributions to opera, it is important to know a little about opera's national traditions, since they have helped to mould the art. Every composer is different, be he Italian, Polish, or English, and therefore it is often difficult to generalize about traditions. Yet certain musical attributes, commonly recognized, can be assigned to different cultures with some degree of safety.

Native opera in countries other than Italy, France, and Germany generally has been neglected by opera historians. Yet Russians, Czechs, Slovaks, and other Slavs have contributed much to opera. *Boris Godunov* (1874) by Modest Mussorgsky, for instance, is generally acclaimed one of the world's great operas. The use of folk melodies, harmonies, and rhythms by composers like Mussorgsky (Russian) and Janáček (Czech) is familiar enough, but their total work and that of other Slavs should be better known. (Unfamiliarity with the language and simple ignorance keep us from studying these works.) Scandinavia has never developed a native operatic tradition comparable to that of its other art forms, the same is true of Spain and Portugal. In England there are few names to point to between Henry Purcell (c. 1659—1695) and Benjamin Britten (1913—1976). Opera in America is largely European. English and American opera may yet come into its own, but at the moment it has only a weak hold on the operatic public. A view from the mountaintop does not always include all the valleys below, and though there is much to be studied in various national traditions, the great majority of operas *which have held the stage* have been Italian, French, and German. Consequently, these traditions demand most attention.

ITALY The main bulk of opera is Italian. Opera (the name itself is Italian for "work") began in Italy around 1600 and has flourished there and elsewhere ever since. During the seventeenth century Italian opera was the dominant operatic medium, although the French tradition was an important and flourishing one. In the eighteenth century, most of Europe, including Russia, Austria, Spain, Scandinavia, and England, was an Italian province operatically speaking, whether it was opera seria or *opera buffa* (comic opera) that occupied the stage. France kept to its native tradition and German opera was just emerging.

What comes immediately to mind when Italian opera is mentioned is *melody* The word must not be construed in its narrow sense of a tune or theme with a fixed beginning and ending. Rather, one should think of song in the larger sense: of the surge, thrust, and fall of a long curve, of a sequence of notes in succession that capture the ear and the imagination. Melody can be long or short, but something in it raises the spirit and stirs the emotions. In opera, splendid melodies can be played by the orchestra, but generally the voice is the medium.

Secondly, the best Italian operatic music has been highly *dramatic* —elementally so. Life, at least in the less sophisticated parts of Italy, has always been lived close to the surface, and human passions are not bottled up for very long. Most Italian dramatists and musicians have understood this and created in their works uninhibited realization of love, hate, jealousy, pride, greed, and compassion, generally in a simple and clear manner. This desire to penetrate to the essence of life has meant that Italian opera appeals to the emotions directly and boldly, not obliquely or intellectually This has been particularly true of the "verismo" (realism) school of composers where a Ruggiero Leoncavallo (1858—1919), a Pietro Mascagni (1863—1945), and a Giacomo Puccini (1858—1924) have sought to represent life on its brutal and sordid side, as Emile Zola and other French naturalistic writers of the time did in the novel.

The third characteristic of Italian opera is that its harmonic structure tends to be *simple* and uncomplicated. Moments of climax come as a result of plain but strong progressions. The accompaniment to an aria may be simple to the point of banality, but it is clearly understood by the ear. That is not to say that Italian musicians have lacked the technical equipment and ability to write a complicated score; rather, simplicity seems to be a natural part of their musical language and heritage. For opera in Italy is as common as eating pasta. It is not treated with grudging respect, as it is apt to be in Anglo-Saxon countries, but with an enthusiastic and loving embrace.

To illustrate these three qualities, one can dip into Italian opera almost anywhere. On the grounds that the public is sometimes right in its estimation and esteem, and the favors it bestows are not meretricious but essentially valid, one of the most popular operas ever written is Puccini's *La Bohème* (The Bohemian, 1896). *La Bohème* is perhaps "a warhorse," but no opera house today can do without it. Everything that makes for excitement is in it. a moving love story, a colorful background (bohemian Paris of about 1830), memorable melodies, superb orchestration, telling characterization, and a clear, straightforward plot (really a series of scenes or tableaux). It is easy to smile at its sentimentality, and its charm may fade with time, but there is no sign of such weakening in the late twentieth century Since its first performance under Arturo Toscanini in Turin, Puccini's opera has penetrated to practically every country on the globe, and it has even been given in such languages as Urdu and Swahili.

A balanced judgment on Puccini is difficult to find. The operatic public has always adored him, while many critics have been hostile. Whatever his faults (and they are apparent), there is no avoiding the fact that he was one of the most effective opera composers who ever lived. Few people have had his ability to evoke an atmosphere or setting. In the Latin Quarter scene of *La Bohème* where the four artist friends, Rodolfo (poet), Schaunard (musician), Marcello (painter), and Colline (philosopher) sit in the Café Momus with Mimi, and Musetta makes an appearance with her "sugar-daddy" Alcindoro, very little happens, but the color and vivacity of the crowd scenes are unexcelled.

Our primary interest, however, is in Puccini the melodist and dramatist. Few scenes have ever touched the imagination more than the meeting of Mimi and Rodolfo in Act I. Mimi, who lives upstairs, has lost her light (a candle) and timidly knocks on the friends' door. Everybody has left for the café but Rodolfo, who is trying to finish some work. He is enchanted by Mimi's prettiness and delicacy (she coughs violently). When she drops her key, the two search for it on the floor in the darkness and their hands meet. Sudden love for each other overcomes them, and glorious themes well up out of the orchestra and in the voice. They are mostly short melodies which are built up in sequences with changes in key and orchestration. Once heard, they impress themselves indelibly on the memory and are always associated with the opera and its atmosphere.

Above all, they show Puccini's melodic gift in a simple, direct way and demonstrate how his music makes more poignant a dramatic situation. In Example 4-1a, Rodolfo and Mimi have just said goodnight to one another. As Mimi goes out the door, she remembers she has no key. Turning back to the threshold of the open door, she sings a phrase asking about her key Since this missing article is going to be the reason for the two to search the floor and to fall in love, Puccini incorporates the musical idea later into love

Example 4-1   ⓐ   Puccini, *La Bohème* (1896)

(Oh! thoughtless me! The key to my room, where have I left it?)

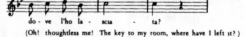

ⓑ   Andante lento (♩ = 52)

(At times, from my coffer, two thieves steal all the jewels: they are your beautiful eyes.)

ⓒ   Andante lento (♩ = 40)

(They call me Mimi, but my real name is Lucia.)

ⓓ   Allegretto moderato (♩ = 144)

(Alone, I make dinner for myself.)

music, where its contour assumes prominence and implies that the accident led to the passion of the two for each another. Example *b* is another moving melodic phrase, this time Rodolfo's impassioned climax to his declaration of love which is reiterated in the love duet that follows. Examples *c* and *d* are always associated with Mimi— in the first, she tells her name; in the second, she is describing the narrow pattern of her life. Both become particularly important in the last act when she is about to die. All four of these melodies are woven into the fabric of the music so skillfully they become a personification of the two lovers.

FRANCE   In the first half of the nineteenth century, the center of interest and excitement in opera swung from Italy to France. French prominence in politics—the Revolution, the rise of Napoleon and the Empire, the Revolutions of 1830 and 1848, the pomp and magnificence of the Second Empire—were reflected in the artistic life of the nation. The embodiment of this new spirit was *grand opera*: a huge, five-act, heroic, and historical spectacle of music and drama, two of whose great exponents were foreigners (Gasparo Spontini, 1774–1851, Italian, Giacomo Meyerbeer, 1791–1864, German). The emphasis on stage effect meant that *incidental music* (marches, lyrical interludes, ballet music) played a very important role, as it has in all French opera before and since. Although "incidental" implies something subordinate and of minor importance, this was not the case. The marches and dances were integral parts of the action, and many large ensembles and crowd scenes were absolutely dependent on them for total impact. Some of the finest ballets come from French opera, and some of the best ones, extracted for public performance, have remained great favorites long after the opera has been forgotten. (The ballets from Delibes' *Lakme* (1883) are an example.)

Although stage spectacle and the music for it has been a constant French preoccupation, the visual for the sake of the visual has never gained the upper hand. The French, with their passion for *raison* (reason), want loose ends tidied up and everything to fit in its proper place. Consequently, French music has an *order and logic* to it which befits the tautness and clarity of the French mind. Whether for the dance, the voice, or the orchestra, the music tries not to overstep the boundaries of "good taste." Emotions are important to show, but they must not become excessive or overbalanced. It is better to understate than to overstate. A French composer would hardly indicate "pppp" (quadruple pianissimo) in his music, as Verdi and Puccini often did (but rarely got from their singers, conductors, and orchestras) because a "pp" if properly performed would give the necessary effect.

Yet restraint and order should not be construed as pallid or bland. Most French opera music has *a spirited quality* which is very appealing. Above all, it can supply *élan* and verve. The emotions may not delve as deeply as they do in some Italian music, but there is generally a *delicacy* in French opera which compensates. These attributes are particularly evident in *opéra comique*. The French term is misleading because operas in this category were not always comic. Rather, like the German Singspiel, they were operas with spoken dialogue. Grand opera, in contrast, was sung all the way through. Bizet's *Carmen*, one of the greatest of French operas, was originally composed with spoken dialogue, but had recitatives added later.

Likewise, the most popular French opera of the last hundred years, Charles Gounod's *Faust* (1859) was originally written as opéra comique. Gounod (1818–1893) is generally described as a minor composer, but his dramatic and musical ability should not be taken lightly. His *Faust*, based primarily on Goethe's play but using only the part of Faust's love for Marguerite (and for this reason called *Margarethe* in Germany to avoid confusion with the complete work), is the only one of his operas to find a lasting place in the general repertory. It is not an oddity that has somehow managed to hold the public's affection. The quantity of tuneful music in *Faust* is quite extraordinary, and Gounod, handicapped by a rather sentimental libretto, managed to create a fine work by combining the best qualities of French opera with a strong dramatic sense. The number of popular "hits" in this opera is legion—waltzes, arias, march music, and ballet.

Example 4-2 gives a number of the most famous tunes. They all exhibit that spirited or delicate quality which characterizes French opera. Example 4-2a occurs in the opening scene when Faust, a scholarly old man, is approached by Mephistopheles. Faust has called down a curse upon the world because it has refused to reveal its secrets to him. Now he is old and about to die. Perhaps Satan can help. Mephistopheles offers gold and glory, but Faust wants his youth back. He invokes the joys of youth—love, passion, rapture—in the gay melody of "A moi les plaisirs," which gallops along in a torrent of feeling. Example *b* is sung by students at the fair (second scene) as they hail the power of wine and beer. Gounod captures their youthful spirit superbly in this lively duple time chorus. Example *c* is the beginning of Mephistopheles' famous Song of the Golden Calf, an invocation to the graven image of Mammon, which celebrates only the most carnal joys. Example *d* is the endearing waltz the maidens dance and sing as Siebel, Faust (now transformed into a young man), and Mephistopheles wait for Marguerite, the lovely girl Faust has seen and desired in a dream.

Example 4-2   Gounod, *Faust* (1859)

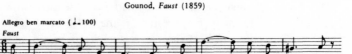

ⓐ Allegro ben marcato (♩.=100)
Faust

A moi   les   plai - sirs,_____ les   jeu - nes maî - tres - ses!
(To me the pleasures, the young sweethearts!)

ⓑ Allegretto (♩ = 84)
Chorus (men)

Vin ou_____ biè - re,   Bière ou_____ vin,
(Wine or beer, beer or wine,)

ⓒ Allegro maestoso (♩=92)
Mephistopheles

Le veau d'or_____ est tou - jours de - bout!
(The calf of gold is always standing!)

ⓓ Tempo di Valzer (♩.=72)
Waltz

ⓔ Allegretto agitato (♩=88)
Siebel

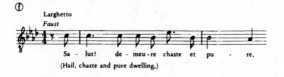

Fai - tes lui mes a - veux,_____ Por - tez_____ mes voeux!
(Make my avowal to her, bring my wishes!)

ⓕ Larghetto
Faust

Sa - lut! de - meu - re chaste et pu - re,
(Hail, chaste and pure dwelling,)

ⓖ Allegretto leggiero (♩=50)
Marguerite

Ah! Je ris_____ de me voir, Si belle en ce mi - roir!
(I laugh to see myself so beautiful in this mirror!)

ⓗ Tempo marziale
Chorus (men)

Gloire im - mor - tel - le de nos a - ieux_____
(Immortal glory to our ancestors)

Siebel is also in love with her. The music, in rapid triple meter with syncopated accents on the last beat of the measure, is gaiety personified. Example *e*, Siebel's song to Marguerite, captures the spirit of the young lover. Like *a*, it is in fast 6/8 meter with a rush of eighth notes in many measures. Example *f* is Faust's cavatina to Marguerite, sung outside her dwelling as he waits for her to appear. Tender and restrained in feeling with emphasis upon the melody itself, the air shows Faust as a man deeply in love. In *g* Siebel has left a simple bouquet of flowers for Marguerite but Faust's gift (conjured up by Mephistopheles) is a rich casket of jewels. As Marguerite opens it to find sparkling gems, her naive delight comes trilling forth in the well-known Jewel Song. A tripping cascade of notes spills out as she looks at herself in the mirror. Finally, there is the stirring Soldier's Chorus, *h*, sung by Valentin, Marguerite's brother, and his fellow soldiers as they return from the wars. This tune has become so famous that it has written itself unforgettably into operatic music. *Faust* may seem somewhat faded, but for sheer tunefulness, it has seldom been duplicated.[2]

GERMANY In spite of Mozart's German works and Beethoven's *Fidelio*, not until the first half of the nineteenth century did a national tradition of German opera assert itself. It is mostly associated with the rise of *romanticism*, which was a reaction against the eighteenth century and the Age of Reason. Romanticism in literature turned to the fairy tale, to legend and myth, to the mysterious Middle Ages, and often to the Orient as source and setting for its stories. German composers, in turn, drew on *folk melodies* for inspiration. At the same time their music reflected German *love of nature*. Often they depicted naturalistic scenes: a storm, a moonlit night, the oncoming of spring, the depths of the forest. They used *orchestral color*—horns, combinations of woodwinds, the entire palette—to create the desired feeling. German music, even in opera, drew upon the orchestra for a *solidity* in the texture, which the Italians often found heavy and ponderous. The German tendency toward *seriousness* found its outlet in counterpoint, complicated harmony, rhythms that march instead of dance.

Romanticism runs through most nineteenth century German opera. Wagner's first three significant works, *Der fliegende Holländer* (The Flying Dutchman, 1843), *Tannhäuser* (1845), and *Lohengrin*

[2] By the 1880s in New York, the work had become so popular it was chosen as the first opera to be performed in the Metropolitan Opera House when it opened in October, 1883.

(1850), not only draw on legend for their plots but also embody folk and religious elements in their music (Senta's ballad in *The Flying Dutchman*; pilgrims' chorus in *Tannhäuser*; the bridal scene in *Lohengrin*). In his later works, the orchestra becomes a dominant feature, and Wagner lays out specifications for new brass instruments to bear the weight of his inspiration for the gods in Valhalla and the race of the Gibichung in *Götterdämmerung*. Even Richard Strauss, who wrote at a later date and under different circumstances, cannot escape the mantle of late romanticism in his early operas, *Guntram* (1894) and *Feuersnot* (Need of Fire, 1901).

The earliest true exponent of German tradition is Carl Maria von Weber's *Der Freischütz*. The story is drawn from an old folk legend. Samiel, a wild huntsman, who is the Devil in disguise, must ever find new victims. Max, a young huntsman in love with Agathe, daughter of the hereditary forester, has to win a shooting trial to gain her hand. His luck and skill have gone bad and in desperation, he turns to Kaspar, a friend, who has already sold his soul to Samiel. Kaspar promises magic bullets if Max comes to the haunted Wolf's Glen with him to get them. In this famous scene, the cradle of musical romanticism, Kaspar casts the bullets by secret incantations under the most eerie circumstances (ghosts, devilish uproar, apparitions). Samiel finally appears. Six bullets will find their mark, but the seventh has evil powers. At the trial, Max shoots six successfully but the seventh nearly kills Agathe and lodges in Kaspar, who dies horribly. Max confesses his sin and is nearly banished. Finally pardoned, he may marry Agathe if he acquits himself well for a year.

The opera has not only an irresistible series of melodies which have become part of German folklore but a magnificent overture, several fine choruses, an embryonic motive system, and orchestral coloring that points the way to Wagner and the rest of the century. The music is typically German and yet international in its appeal. The amount of spoken dialogue in the opera has prevented it from finding a wide audience outside Germany, unless it is given in translation.

Example 4-3 illustrates some of the more striking passages in *Freischütz*. As indicated, the overture is a classic. Weber includes in it Max's and Agathe's main themes, and also in the beginning Adagio, an evocation through pure orchestral color of the forest and the mysterious Wolf's Glen, where the magic bullets are to be fashioned. The instruments chosen to represent the dark German forest are the horns; two of them in 4-3*a* sound their call and summon us to the sylvan setting. Max, in *b*, sings of his former joy in roaming the forests, hunting for game, and returning to find his love,

Example 4-3 ⓐ   Weber, *Der Freischütz* (1821)

Agathe. His happiness has been shattered recently by his inability to have his bullets find their mark. His aria, recalling past delight, breathes the freshness and vigor of a young man at the height of his romantic ardor; *c*, which is the concluding part of the air, however, indicates the fear of evil powers that surround him (this section has a prominent position in the overture). Examples *d* and *e* display two sides of Agathe as she awaits her lover at dusk. The beginning (*d*) is a prayer to the heavens (a beautiful starlit night) and the Lord to watch over her. There is a simplicity and tenderness in the melody that reminds one of folksong. The second half is eager anticipation of Max's arrival; it is the triumphant final theme of the overture in which Weber tells us that the love of the two will have a happy ending. Example *f* is the chilling diminished chord (low woodwinds, pizzicato string basses) which accompanies Kaspar's call to Samiel in the Wolf's Glen. The directions read. "Kaspar, in shirt-sleeves, is making a circle of black stones; a skull is in the center; nearby a ladle, a bullet-mould, and an eagle's wing. A thunderstorm is coming on. He raises his hanger aloft, with the skull upon it, and turns around three times."

The music, then, of the three great national operatic traditions generally possesses a special character which gives flavor and color to the total work. It is not always clearly distinguishable for the good reason that composers of genius transcend boundaries of race, language, and culture, and bring to their art a quality which is true, recognizable, and lasting for all peoples and all places. Music has always been an international language that speaks to any audience no matter what their tongue may be. When it is combined with drama of distinction, powerful music raises opera to that high level of artistic achievement which is good for all time.

SUGGESTED READING

Jacobs, Arthur, and Stanley Sadie, *Great Operas in Synopsis*, Crowell, New York, 1966. Good overall guide with some musical illustrations; 61 operas.

Music in Opera, A Historical Anthology, Elaine Brody, ed., Prentice-Hall, Englewood Cliffs, N.J., 1970. A very handsome selection of musical examples (mostly complete) from all periods of opera. Good accompanying commentary

Newman, Ernest, *Great Operas*, 2 vols., Vintage Books paperback, New York, 1958. Perhaps the best "guide" to 30 of the operas. Treats both plot and music.

von Westermann, Gerhard, *Opera Guide*, Harold Rosenthal, ed., Anne Ross, trans., Dutton paperback, New York, 1968. More operas with briefer summaries but still excellent. Originally for a German audience.

5 The Components of Music

Music, even in a pure state, is an art that reveals itself in successive stages. Because it exists in time, the simple elements of repetition, sequence, phrase, and period are essential to its organization (see Chapter 2). Just as paragraphs, sentences, and grammar are the essence of prose, so music has been arranged to give coherence and structure to the passage of sound. These units are instinctively recognized by the listener even though he may not be able to give them a name. They are common to every art but naturally take different form according to the nature of the medium—painting, sculpture, architecture, poetry, or music.

In opera the organizational powers of music have been adapted to a dramatic text, and in the course of its history, certain musical components have become characteristic. These forms arose because they were peculiarly fitted to the combination of stage action, music, and drama, and gave to the whole enterprise a working musical mode of operation.

Recitative The English word recitative has been adapted literally from the Italian *recitativo* and corresponds to the French *récitatif* and German *recitativ* The root is the Latin word *recitare*, meaning to read, recite, or declaim. When an opera is sung throughout, recitative is the musical name given to the narrative, as opposed to the lyrical portions of the text. From the late seventeenth century to the mid-nineteenth century, there is a sharp distinction between recitative and the lyrical sections of the opera such as aria and ensemble. Either the recitative comes to a halt in a cadence or the character of the music changes quite markedly when it ends. Early seventeenth century Italian operas do not observe this division, although there are differences between narrative and lyrical passages in the music. The same is true of late Wagner, late Verdi, and most opera composers of the twentieth century. Although their style is naturally quite removed from early opera, there are both narrative and lyrical portions amid Wagner's "unending melody" and Verdi's ripe texture.

Recitative attempts to imitate and emphasize the natural inflections of speech. The speech may be prose or verse or a mixture of both. If the text is a narrative or dialogue between two characters which concentrates on pushing the action forward rapidly with a considerable number of words, the passage is known in English as plain recitative. In musical terms, this probably means a syllabic treatment of the words (a note for each syllable), rapid reiteration of the same note, a narrow range of inflection (the pitch intervals of the notes are relatively close to one another), and an irregular rhythmic structure (measures are not strictly metrical but conform to speech rhythm).

The Italians called this style *recitativo secco* or dry recitative. It flourished at the end of the seventeenth and through the eighteenth century in both opera seria and opera buffa. Composers like Rossini continued it in the nineteenth century. Although primarily suited to the Italian language, recitativo secco was taken over into other languages as a general procedure. The adjective "secco" refers to the somewhat inexpressive character of the vocal line rather than to the type of accompaniment. The accompaniment itself was mostly isolated and broken chords which came just enough to support the singer, direct the harmonic progression, and give substance to the structure. The accompanying instruments were generally the harpsichord (sometimes a lute or a similar instrument) with a cello and/or double bass to reinforce the bass line.

Example 5-1 is an example of secco recitative from Mozart's *Figaro* and occurs just after the opening of the opera when Figaro has been measuring the room he and Susanna will have after their marriage, and Susanna has been trying on a hat. Almost every syllable has a note. The vocal line also resembles the up-and-down inflection of the voice if the words were spoken. Susanna's question emphasizes "mio" (my), which is given a quarter note compared to the other eighth and sixteenth notes. Figaro's answer is straight

Example 5-1

Mozart, *Le nozze di Figaro* (1786)
Act I (recitative)

(Susanna: What are you measuring, my darling Figaro? Figaro: I am looking to see if the bed which the Count has given us will fit well into this space.)

narration, but he stops momentarily to catch his breath after "Conte." (Only the vocal line and bass were written originally, the small notes being "the realization" of the chords implied by the bass line and played by the harpsichordist.)

This "realization" typifies the *basso continuo* principle which dominated seventeenth and eighteenth century music. Alternate designations for it are *figured bass* or *through* (old spelling was *thorough*) *bass*. *Through* or *thorough* is a translation of the Italian word *continuo*, meaning a bass running through the music. *Continuo* was a technique used in performance by the supporting instruments. It was indicated by bass notes only. Attached to these notes, above or below, could be figures indicating to the harpsichordist the chords he was to play. These figures were a kind of shorthand that described intervals, chromatic alterations, even the voice-leading in the vocal line if desired. They enabled the harpsichordist to follow the singer with a minimum of confusion. Many times they were absent because the chord was understood in the context of the bass line (*Figaro* example). In the meantime, the string player merely played the bass. The system was an effective way of accompanying rapid musical speech, and it disappeared only when composers felt this style was no longer applicable.

Plain or secco recitative was not the only type used during the baroque and classical periods of music. When the text was of a much more dramatic and expressive nature, the opera composer turned to *recitativo accompagnato* (that is, recitative which was accompanied by the orchestra). A fully written accompaniment took the place of the single bass line. From the second quarter of the nineteenth century onward, recitativo accompagnato was almost always the type used. The music could indicate a full body of strings or more instruments. With it the singer lost the rhythmic freedom he had with the secco because more metrical regularity was needed to hold the orchestra and singer together.

Recitative—a device peculiar to opera, oratorio, and cantata—has had its share of criticism and ridicule (see Chapter 1). It is seemingly unnatural, particularly in a language the audience does not understand. The classic comment on it was made by Joseph Addison in 1711 when Italian opera first began to invade the English stage:

There is nothing that has more startled our *English* Audience, than the *Italian Recitativo* at its first Entrance upon the Stage. People were wonderfully surprized to hear Generals singing the Word of Command, and Ladies delivering Messages in Musick. Our Countrymen could not forbear laughing when they heard a Lover chanting out a Billet-doux, and even Superscription of a Letter set to a Tune.[1]

Recitative is the part of the opera people are bored with most easily Singers often take less trouble, enunciating and singing it badly, while waiting to do the aria or ensemble that shows off their vocal powers. In the heyday of opera seria when many works were written in a hurry, little time and effort was spent on recitative. In several instances, Italian composers even delegated the writing of recitative to their pupils, the way Rubens' assistants filled in a large painting. Yet behind the conventions and routine formulas there could be striking variety Recitative can be dramatic, exciting, and moving. A single chord beneath a key word, a sudden leap in the vocal line, an abrupt stop—each can produce a powerful effect, well worth waiting for.

In late nineteenth and twentieth century opera, the problem of writing recitative per se disappears, for, in a sense, the recitative *is* the opera. The modern composer does not regard his task as one which divides the opera into separate compartments: recitative, aria, ensemble, and chorus. Rather he seeks a unified approach, combining features of several forms that are suitable vehicles for the words. Debussy's *Pelléas et Mélisande* (1902), for instance, is technically neither recitative nor aria but delicate musical speech, utilizing a restrained, beautiful, haunting musical language. More recently, a musician like Gian Carlo Menotti (1911–   ) wrote in his *Note on the Lyric Theatre*: "For the contemporary composer the exciting challenge is the recitative. It is the logical instrument of action, and he must find the way to make it work for him musically and dramatically."

[1]*The Spectator,* April 3, 1711.

In order to avoid the monotony recitative can sometimes engender, Arnold Schönberg (1874–1951) and his followers, particularly Alban Berg (1885–1935), turned to a form of it which may have been heard in Greek drama: a cross between speech and recitative which uses every musical element except exact pitch. This *Sprechstimme* (speaking tone) is particularly effective in Berg's *Wozzeck* (1925), one modern opera that seems to have established itself in the repertory The composer indicates the rhythmic pattern, the tempo, and the dynamics of a musical passage—even the rise and fall of the voice inflection—but the notes themselves on the staff are merely a series of crosses or asterisks, showing that exact pitch is not to be observed (see Chapter 16, Example 16-4). The desired effect is nearer to speech although it still has musical qualities. Whether this practice will be taken up by future opera composers remains to be seen.

COMPOSITION
OF
RECITATIVE

Although by definition recitative imitates the inflections of speech, it is controlled by the laws of music. Musical elements determine the structure; the writing of a recitative is not haphazard or piecemeal but conforms to a musical logic of its own.

First to be considered in writing recitative are the *rhythmic values*: accentuation, quantity, and stress. Verbal and musical rhythms are not always similar and they often contradict each other. When the two conflict, the composer does not bow to verbal values; otherwise he would cease to be a musician. Yet he must make the music fit the words and not sound awkward. Second, he must indicate *note pitch*. A high note cannot always coincide with a climactic word, nor a low one come at the end of a line. Contemporary music often employs wide leaps in a vocal line, but normal progression in pitch generally gives the singer confidence and makes the recitative flow.

Third, a composer must consider *harmonic support*. Most musicians feel that if the harmony does not specifically reinforce or emphasize a word or series of words, it should remain in the background. Nevertheless, logical progression is necessary to prevent aimlessness, and beginnings and endings need definition. Finally, there is *melodic contour*—and good recitative must have it. Contour here does not mean a theme or a tune but rather phrases that rise and fall to avoid monotony.

An English composer and teacher, Arthur Hutchings, once demonstrated how he would set lines of Shakespeare to music as recitative.[2] He chose at random the opening lines of *King Henry*

[2] Arthur Hutchings, *The Invention and Composition of Music*, Novello, London, 1958, pp. 125–126. Reprinted by permission.

IV, Part 1, which are primarily narrative. The object was not to create something original but merely to show how a composer would write recitative, drawing on all the factors mentioned above except harmonic support. The lines are·

So shaken as we are, so wan with care,
Find we a time for frighted peace to pant,
And breathe short-winded accents of new broils
To be commenced in strands afar remote.

The verse does not particularly lend itself to music, but Hutchings' example demonstrates a possible solution. He divides his exercise into two parts. The first is purely rhythmic with no pitch beyond one note. The natural iambic scansion of the first lines is reproduced rhythmically. Exact accentuation, however, would bring monotony, so the notes do not correspond precisely to the poetic rhythm. Moreover, Hutchings organizes his beats metrically and does not give the recitative that freedom which comes from a nonmetrical unit (Example 5-2a). But when he came to put this music into final form with pitch and melody, his ideas changed slightly (b). Among his revisions were the sliding dissonance on "wan", the diminuendo (a means of accentuation) for "care"; the raised note for "shaken", the triplets for words running together; the emphasis of "new broils", and the top climax melodically on "afar." The music not only supports the words but heightens their meaning.

OPERATIC EXAMPLES Great composers of every age have naturally faced these problems differently because style and taste have varied with time and place. But their aims have been essentially the same. Each has sought the best possible marriage of music and text. As early as *Orfeo* (1607), Monteverdi demonstrated how recitative could be skillfully written through melodic progression, rhythmic variation, and harmonic changes (mostly dissonance and chromaticism). In Act IV, Orfeo has finally persuaded Pluto, through the intervention of Proserpine, to allow Euridice to return with him from Hades on the condition that he not look back at his beloved. Euridice misunderstands Orfeo's presumed coldness and entreats him to look at her. Orfeo disobeys Pluto's command, and Euridice dies a second time.

Orfeo's dilemma and anguish are beautifully portrayed by Alessandro Striggio, the librettist, and Monteverdi, the composer (Example 5-3). In the recitative the two *"Ohimè's"* stand out most poignantly with their dissonant intervals. The rise and fall of the vocal line in measures 4 and 5 underline Orfeo's uneasiness almost like the question itself. The same is true of measures 7, 8,·and 9, where Monteverdi uses a similar pattern for the second question,

Example 5-2   Hutchings, *Recitative Exercise*

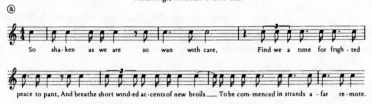

So sha-ken as we are so wan with care, Find we a time for frigh-ted

peace to pant, And breathe short wind-ed ac-cents of new broils___ To be com-menced in strands a-far re-mote.

Bass recit.

So sha-ken as we are so wan___ with care, Find we a time for frigh-ted

peace to pant, And breathe short wind-ed ac-cents of new broils__ To be commenced in strands a-far re-mote.

Example 5-3   Monteverdi, *Orfeo* (1607)

Orfeo

Ma men - tre jo can - to, Ohi - mè!___

Chi m'as-si - cu - ra ch'el - la mi seg - na? Ohi - mè!

Chi mi na-scon-de del - le ja - ma - te pu-pil-le jl dol-ce lu - me?

(But while I sing, alas, who can assure me that she is following me? Alas, who is hiding from me
the sweet light of her beloved eyes?)

Example 5-4   Lully, *Amadis de Gaule* (1684)

Florestan

Je re-viens dans ces lieux pour y voir ce que j'ai-me. Cha-que mo-ment est cher pour

moi. Mais au sang qui nous joint, je sais ce que je dois. Je ne puis vous quit-

-ter sans un - e peine ex - trè-me, Dans la dou-leur où je vous vois..

(I return to this place to find here that which I love. Each moment is dear to me. But in the name
of the blood which joins us, I do not know what I should do. I cannot leave you without great pain.
In the unhappy position I see you...)

54   The Magic of Opera

and yet Orfeo's voice droops as if he were not quite sure whether Euridice was there. Monteverdi's ability to underline faithfully and vividly the feeling and meaning of the text is extraordinary

French opera of the seventeenth century usually had a more measured and formal structure. Since French is the only romance language without a tonic accent (without a heavy fall on one syllable of a word of two or more syllables), the natural rise and fall of the spoken tongue presents even more strongly the need for metrical organization. Jean Baptiste Lully (1632–1687) was the first great master of this art, and the opening recitative of his opera, *Amadis de Gaule* (1684), libretto by Philippe Quinault, demonstrates his skill in setting French text to music. In the opera, Florestan and his half-brother, Amadis, meet at the court of Lisart, King of Great Britain. Amadis is deeply in love with Oriane, the king's daughter. In Example 5-4 Florestan addresses Amadis.

Looking at the example we can see that the change in metrics fits the rise and fall of the voice. In a prosodic sense, anything goes, but phrases are grouped together and organized in units. The descending passage in measure 6 leading to the low C sharp of "extrème" with the turn to four-beat time (from three) is a good example of word painting.

Henry Purcell, whose great work, *Dido and Aeneas* (1689) is one of the landmarks of English opera in spite of its chamber quality, was outstanding in his delineation of English recitative. His setting of Dido's words on Aeneas' departure as she prepares to take her life demonstrates beyond any doubt that the English language is richly capable of being adapted to music if handled properly (Example 5-5). The lengthening of the second syllable of Belinda's name and the pause on "shade" show the natural accentuation of the words and the phrases. The melodic line, revealing in itself, starts from an almost stationary position with the opening notes. Then it quietly but sadly (melisma on "darkness") sinks downward by slow degrees to the final note. Along the way Purcell delays the inevitable ending by having the voice fall hesitantly, dwelling almost agonizingly on "bosom," "would," "death," and "now" by the use of appoggiaturas. The phrases are short and breathless, separated by rests, as if Dido could hardly say them. Only death as a welcome release points the line temporarily upward in the next-to-last measure. "Rest" and "guest" are goals of motion and serve to anchor the restless movement. This recitative is a simple but extraordinary achievement.

Jumping ahead more than a hundred years to an outstanding example of recitative accompanied by orchestra, there is Beethoven's *Fidelio* and Leonora's magnificent outburst when she learns

Example 5-5   Purcell, *Dido and Aeneas* (1689)

Example 5-6   Beethoven, *Fidelio* (1805)

(Coward! Where are you hurrying to? What are you up to? What are you planning in such wild fury? Can the call of pity and the voice of mankind no longer move your tigrish mind? Rage and fury still storm in your soul like the ocean billows. But for me a rainbow, resting brightly on the dark clouds, lights the way. It shines so quietly, so happily, recalling memories of days gone by, and my heart is newly refreshed.)

Example 5-7   Verdi, *Otello* (1887)

(And you, how pale you are, and weary, and silent, and beautiful,)

that Don Pizarro, evil governor of the prison where her husband is being held, is intent on murdering him (Example 5-6).

In the opening measures before the voice enters, the strings each play an agitated motivic figure rising up the scale to a held diminished chord. Leonora cries out in anger and distress, each of the first three phrases being separated by sharp, exclamatory chords. The initial figure storms in again but trails off suddenly and quietly with a change in tempo (Poco adagio) and a modulation to suit "Des Mitleid's Ruf" (pity's call). But anger returns with mention of Pizarro's tigerish impulses (rushing strings). At the word, "Farbenbogen" (rainbow), the mood changes again and the winds (flute, oboe, clarinet, and bassoon) sustain a high, clear chord, followed by an angelic phrase signifying Leonora's happy thought. As the words describe stillness and happiness, the winds barely breathe in short, repeated notes, and the recitative slides into the aria. Here the orchestra, with infinite resource, echoes and points up the drama of the text.

Lastly, there is the recitative which relies on the voice alone, as if the moment is too painful to tolerate anything else. One of the most moving places of this kind comes at the end of Verdi's *Otello* (1887), when Otello realizes he has been tricked by Iago and by his own jealousy. He looks at Desdemona's strangled body and is ready to take his own life, singing heart-rending words of description and farewell (Example 5-7). Not until "bella" does the orchestra finally return to underline the fact that the Moor has lost not only a faithful wife but a beautiful one. Verdi's perception of what is musically right at this unbearable moment is extraordinarily penetrating.

These examples show that recitative can be flexible and effective in the hands of great musicians. Recitative is musical speech, capable of enhancing the word and raising it to a different level from the spoken variety. As a device it need not be boring or mechanical but can be alive and vibrant. Examination of its resource must not be neglected.

Aria An aria, an elaborate song, is generally accompanied by instruments, and is found in operas, oratorios, and cantatas of the last three centuries. Aria is the Italian word for "air," but the word loses its international flavor in translation. An operatic aria may be complicated, simple, long, or short, but its text primarily fulfills a lyrical function. It can be dramatic, but its general purpose is not to create an action so much as to reflect upon or express an emotion generated by that action.

Why has the aria become such an important element in musical drama? The key to the answer can be found in music itself. Early Italian composers soon realized that a continuous diet of narrative rarely created a healthy opera. There had to be moments of repose and lyrical reflection; times when music could exert its unique power of expression without interruption; times when the sentiment of the words was more generalized. This "songish" part of the opera, as Dryden called it, then began to alternate with the recitative. At first, it was only a brief interlude, a slowing of the action. As the singer gained importance and music tended to

"Each principal character was developed through a series of these arias, the total of which was the complete representation." Beverly Sills in Donizetti's *Lucia di Lammermoor* (Photo by Beth Bergman)

overshadow the drama, the aria become more formalized—almost the center of the opera. Its musical design was as important as the text. Recitative existed only to explain the plot and lead up to the aria. Some arias became so stereotyped they were put into categories: a rage, hate, love, jealousy, or pity aria. Ordinarily, each principal character was developed through a series of these arias, the total of which was the complete representation. There was naturally a reaction to this formalism when drama reasserted itself (see Chapter 3). Elegant though it may have been, the da capo aria was essentially undramatic since, by definition, it repeated what had already been sung, largely for the benefit of the singer. It was the singer's task to ornament the repeated part while the orchestra or accompaniment remained substantially the same. Composers like Gluck and Mozart retained the best of this style but refused to be hobbled by it. When the situation demanded it, their arias were much freer, being incorporated into ensembles and choruses or consisting of one or two parts rather than the ubiquitous da capo. On occasion, Mozart moved the action forward during solo singing.

A demonstration of how recitative and aria were linked together in the old opera seria can be shown through the text alone. Emotionally the recitative "loaded the gun" and the aria "fired" it. A Handel Italian opera presented on the London stage in the early eighteenth century can serve as an example. The opera is *Giulio Cesare in Egitto* (Julius Caesar in Egypt, 1725). Cleopatra is in love with Caesar, and her brother Ptolemy is plotting against her. He has killed Pompey, whose widow Cornelia, and her son, Sestus, have come to Egypt to revenge his death. Cleopatra is alone.

RECITATIVE   Cleopatra. *In vain my Brother thinks himself secure. Already I have fomented Caesar's wrath. And stirr'd the just Complaints of Sestus and Cornelia. If he [i.e., Ptolemy] attempts to occupy the Egyptian throne by himself, certain Ruin will attend him.*

ARIA   *A pleasing Hope shall urge me on*
And crown my Wishes with Success.
My constant Heart undaunted shall remain
And mighty love with its Power make known.[3] *D.C.*

(The first two lines are repeated for the da capo. They read in Italian: "Tu la mia stella sei, amabile speranza/ E porgi ai desir miei un grato bel piacer." The English is a free translation.)

A very different kind of example comes from an opera buffa by Mozart. Dorabella, one of the ladies in *Così fan tutte*, sings of her love

[3]From the English translation of the original Italian libretto: *Giulio Cesare in Egitto*, London, 1725.

for Ferrando, even though half seriously she has just threatened to take poison. She is addressing Despina, her servant.

RECITATIVE Dorabella. *Oh, go away! Beware the sad result of a desperate love. Close those windows. I hate the light—I hate the air I breathe—I even hate myself. Who derides my grief? Who consoles me? Alas, leave. For pity's sake! go away and leave me alone.*

ARIA *Implacable frenzy that stirs me, enter into this heart and do not let up until anguish makes me die. I'll give this miserable example of a dismal love to the Furies. If I stay alive, it will be with the horrible sound of my own sighs.*

The aria in both instances comes as a result of what has been said in the recitative, the Handel aria more directly than the Mozart. They both, however, stop the action. Cleopatra tells what she has done to accomplish her ends (recitative) and hopes it will happen (aria). The music of this aria heightens this emotion and brings out not only her ambition and drive but also her love for Caesar. Dorabella flutters in her recitative in a series of pretended little actions that do nothing to conceal her love for Ferrando, which is commented and reflected on humorously in her aria. Mozart keeps a running string figure through the music to signify her single obsession. He sets the whole stanza twice but varies it harmonically the second time to bring the music back to the home key. In the coda Dorabella's sighs become literal and end the piece with a comic and ironic twist.

TYPES OF
ARIA

Throughout operatic history, composers have let their imaginations roam with the aria because it has been music's moment to come to the fore. Although some arias were show-pieces for the singer with little musical content (rapid series of notes, extraneous decoration, big jumps in the vocal line, held high notes), the majority have tried to capture the inner meaning of the text and enhance it through musical setting.

A favorite early style of aria was the *strophic aria* which repeated the same music for several stanzas of verse. Instrumental interludes could appear between the lines of a verse, or the singer could decorate the vocal line in repeating it, but essentially the music remained the same for each strophe. One of the most famous operas of the seventeenth century which employed the strophic aria was a court opera written for the wedding of Emperor Leopold I of Austria to the Infanta Margherita of Spain and performed in Vienna with extraordinary display and richness of setting. This opera, *Il pomo d'oro* (The Golden Apple, 1666—1667) by Pietro Antonio Cesti (1623—1669), had 66 scenes in five acts with 24 different stage sets and a ballet as the feature of each act. It told the story of Paris

Example 5-8   Cesti, *Il pomo d'oro* (1667)

(Stanza 1: And wherever you roam among the mourning souls, you hear nothing here but plaints and sighs. Pains and torments encumber everything with horror, with shrieks, with lamentation, and with grief. Stanza 2: La Tantalo geme/ Per l'esca fallace,/ Qui Sisifo preme/ Il sasso fugace,/ La rostro vorace/ Di crudo avoltare/ Sbrana di Tizio/ Il rinascente core.
(There Tantalus groans for the false bait; here Sisyphus rolls the escaping stone; there the voracious beak of the cruel vulture tears to pieces the reborn heart of Tityus.)

and Helen (Paris carrying off Helen and precipitating the Trojan War) but also brought in every other classical allusion the authors could think of. One scene takes place in Hades where Pluto and Proserpina are seated on their thrones. Proserpina, who, according to mythology, had to spend part of her time in Hades, is troubled by what she sees, and describes her painful surroundings. Cesti had a great gift for writing tunes, and it is remarkable how effective his strophic aria is with its varied orchestral accompaniment (Example 5-8).

The music represents a complete strophe. It consists of two main sections according to the division of the text, but every line except the first two is repeated to give emphasis to the melodic structure. Notice the similarities and differences between measures 6–12 and measures 13–18 with the same text; also measures 23–36 and measures 39–53 When the second strophe is sung, it retains the same pattern with slight variations in the vocal line and accompaniment. The regularity demonstrates how music, with its demand for form and repetition, began to dominate the operatic medium.

The da capo aria has already been mentioned. Musically it consisted of three parts (ABA), only two of which were written out. The third part, a repeat of the first part, was indicated by the sign D.C., which appeared at the end of the second part (B). At the conclusion of the first part (A), the word "fine" marked the end of the third part. In time, da capo arias became very elaborate the A section itself was divided into two parts (repeated text) with a cadence on the dominant or relative key in the first half and a return to the original key in the second half. This A section often opened and closed with a purely instrumental passage called "ritornello" (Italian for "refrain"), which also appeared in the middle before the intermediate cadence. The musical material of the initial ritornello was usually an anticipation of what was to come in the vocal line. The B part generally had melodic material related to the A part, but presented in a different key with reduced scoring. Occasionally, because of the text, it was a complete contrast to the A part. There was a great deal more variety in the da capo aria than historians have been willing to grant. Any departure from the formal structure, such as beginning without a ritornello, was immediately noticeable and had greater musical impact.

One of Handel's oratorios, *Semele* (1744), is really an English opera. It is based on a William Congreve text derived from a classical legend. Jupiter has fallen in love with the mortal Semele and has transported her to heavenly regions. She expresses a desire to see her beloved sister, Ino. Jupiter promises to bring Ino to her, and they will both dwell in an Arcadian paradise. This takes place before the tragedy, when Semele, consumed by human curiosity, asks Jupiter to make love to her in his divine form, and she is destroyed by a thunderbolt. The recitative and da capo aria are sung by Jupiter as he describes the paradise which awaits the two sisters.

RECITATIVE   Jupiter. *Now all this scene shall to Arcadia turn,*
              The seat of happy nymphs and swains,
              There without the rage of jealousy they burn
              And taste the sweets of love without its pains.

ARIA   *Where'er you walk, cool gales shall fan the glade;*
        Trees, where you sit, shall crowd into a shade.
        Where'er you tread, the blushing flowr's shall rise,
        And all things flourish where'er you turn your eyes. D.C.

Example 5-9   Handel, *Semele* (1744)

The aria (Example 5-9), one of Handel's greatest and an example of pure, unexcelled melody, has two distinct parts. Part B is similar to A, although in a different key; introductory, intermediate, and concluding ritornellos (not shown) give body to the aria and separate the various sections from one another. Tonally, part A proceeds from the home key (B flat) to F (its dominant) at measure 6. Then it goes back to the B flat, utilizing the same text (measures 7–14). Part B ("Where'er you tread"—measures 15–21) falls into the related minor key (G minor) at first and then ends in C minor, from which it returns to the beginning. The melody of the first part is so familiar it might seem bizarre to decorate it on the repeat. But the eighteenth century only tolerated the da capo because it was ornamented and varied when heard the second time. Admittedly this practice demanded great artistry, but when the singer was capable, it created an excitement and delight which captivated the audience.

When composers broke away from the prevalent da capo pattern, their arias took a number of different forms. Some of them are hardly classifiable; others can be recognized as variants of what had gone before. One was the *arietta*, a small aria of two parts, the sections of which were brief and light enough to be repeated (AABB). The arietta appeared often in comic opera because it was short and unpretentious and could be undertaken by singers of moderate ability. Many are found in opera buffa and opéra comique. When part of an aria lost its formal structure and began to resemble recitative, it was called *arioso*. This cross between aria and recitative was more prevalent in oratorio and cantata than in opera. In the eighteenth century, the composer often wanted at the beginning of an act to create a quiet mood which would not demand a full-blown aria. He then wrote half a da capo aria, (the first part). This was called a *cavatina*, and many of them are particularly beautiful. One, whose text has already been mentioned (see p. 15), comes at the beginning of Act II of Mozart's *Figaro*. "Porgi amor" has always been a favorite of connoisseurs. It is over so quickly that the audience hardly has a chance to assimilate its rare beauty; and it must be sung by a good actress as well as a fine singer. The Countess is sitting in front of a mirror (in some productions) contemplating her face and figure. She is young (in her twenties but married in her teens), feels she has lost the days of her first youth, and that her charm has faded because her husband, the Count, has been philandering. She implores the goddess of love to restore her beloved to her. Mozart, by the most artful use of instrumental accompaniment, sighing phrases, and a melting melodic line, manages to convey this nostalgic mood in a remarkably brief space. There are 17 measures of introduction (longer than usual), but Mozart portrays the Countess through a lovely clarinet melody, violins that anticipate the sighing accompaniment which follows, and syncopation to show her inner agitation. The cavatina divides generally as the first part of the da capo aria did, but its second section (measures 28–51) lengthens with word repetition to give a sense of climax (Example 5-10).

In the nineteenth century, another type of aria appeared, first in opera buffa and then in all opera. It was called a *cabaletta*. Originally it was a simple song with a uniform accompaniment and vocal line to match; then the term came to be used for the second section of a two-part aria, the first section of which was fairly plain and deliberate, and the second, longer and in a faster tempo. Rossini was particularly fond of this type, and his operas are filled with cabalettas that begin slowly and simply, then end in a great burst of excitement. Verdi complained about the prevalence of this pattern in opera of his time and said that the animated section made everything sound like an engine that started slowly, gathered speed, and ended at a breakneck pace.

One of Rossini's famous cabalettas is "Una voce poco fa" from *The Barber of Seville*, a favorite for coloratura sopranos (originally mezzo coloratura). The opera was derived from the play by Beaumarchais which Mozart used for *Figaro*. In this

Example 5-10

Mozart, *Le nozze di Figaro* (1786)

(Bring, o love, some comfort to my grief and to my sighs. Return my dearest one to me or let me die!)

aria, Rosina, the heroine, who has been kept in hiding by her guardian, Dr. Bartolo, sings of her love for the "unknown" soldier, Lindoro, to whom she has just been writing a letter and who later turns out to be Count Almaviva in disguise (Example 5-11).

The orchestral introduction (Andante) begins in a formal, serious fashion (*a*), as if Rosina wants to impress upon her listeners the weight of her intention to capture this handsome soldier. The strings, however, soon convey the vivacious, lively nature of a young girl, excited at the idea of a lover (*b*). Her opening vocal line recalls the serenade he sang to her, an echo of its melody coming on "mi risuonò" (*c*). At first, she says that Lindoro will be hers, even if her guardian refuses the match. She will sharpen her wits and get the best of the doctor (example not shown). The second part (Moderato) also has an orchestral introduction (not shown). It anticipates Rosina's slightly guileful remark that she is inherently a docile, respectful girl (*d*); but when she is crossed in love, she can play a hundred tricks (*e*). The rest of the aria develops this theme with numerous rapid scale passages and coloration which create rising excitement, aided at the end by an even faster tempo (Più Allegro) and a rise of the vocal line to a high B natural (b^2)*,

*See Glossary· Abbreviations.

Example 5-11 ⓐ　　　　　　　　　Rossini, *Il barbiere di Siviglia* (1816)

Andante

Tutti

etc.

ⓑ

Strings

Clar., Horns

etc.

ⓒ Andante

Rosina

Un - a vo - - ce po - co fa　　qui nel cor　　mi ri - suo - nò;
(A voice I heard just now has thrilled my very heart;)

ⓓ Moderato

Io　so - no___ do - ci - le,　　son ri - spet - to - - sa,
(I am docile; I am respectful,)

ⓔ Moderato

(ᵈ)　*E cen - to trap - po - le pri - ma di ce - de - re fa - rò gio - car,*
(And I shall play a hundred tricks before giving way,)

Example 5-12　　　　　　　　　　　Verdi, *Aida* (1871)

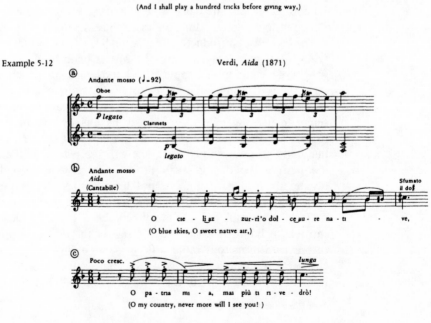

ⓐ Andante mosso (♩=92)

Oboe

P legato

Clarinets

legato

ⓑ Andante mosso

Aida

(Cantabile)

Sfumato il do♯

O cie - li az - zur - ri'o dol - ce au - re na - ti - ve,
(O blue skies, O sweet native air,)

ⓒ Poco cresc.

lunga

O pa - tria mi - a, mai più ti ri - ve - drò!
(O my country, never more will I see you!)

which can bring the audience to its feet. An aria of this sort has a built-in appeal and verve which is difficult to resist.

Finally there is the kind of aria that cannot be categorized. In more modern times, composers have increasingly favored freer treatment. Their arias are still musically logical and coherent, but follow none of the particular patterns mentioned so far. In Act III of Verdi's *Aïda* (1871), the slave girl, Aïda (who is really the daughter of Amonasro, Ethiopian king, but now a servant to Amneris, daughter of the Egyptian pharaoh), sings a touching lament for her native land ("O cieli azzurri"), while waiting for her lover, Radames, general of the Egyptian armies, to appear. Verdi added this aria (he called it a *Romanza*) for the performance at La Scala in Milan after the opera had first been given in Cairo. Eventually the aria became famous.

Beginning with a haunting little orchestral phrase, scored only for oboe and two clarinets (Example 5-12a), Verdi then (b) has Aïda longing for the blue skies, green hills, and scented shores of her country she may never see again (no matter that the description hardly fits the geography of Ethiopia: the important thing is the mood). The accompaniment (not shown) to her first words is not only striking but original—three flutes, clarinet, bassoon, and pizzicato cellos and basses, with upper strings added later. Verdi wants this beginning to sound like a verse to which there is a simple refrain (c). To be noted is the interesting musical direction *sfumato* (evaporate like smoke) at the end of the initial phrase (b). The same procedure is repeated. instrumental introduction (shortened), the verse with a new kind of triplet string accompaniment, and the refrain which is an apostrophe to "O patria mia" (my country) with a heightened ending (high C) (c^3). However, it trails off in an echo of despair with the plaintive introductory winds (a) in the background. The scene is evocative, mournful, beautiful, and musically taut. Its simplicity is art that conceals art.

The aria, then, is a flower that changes its hue according to its season, soil, and musical climate. Often, too much has been made of it because, as the musical climax of the solo voice, it can easily overshadow the more pedestrian recitative beside it. Nevertheless, it invokes feelings and emotions as only music can, and, in doing so, is an integral part of the operatic scheme.

Ensemble An ensemble (the French word for "together") is a vocal group of two or more singers who perform together. The designation "together" is misleading: it does not necessarily mean the artists sing *simultaneously*; they can also sing separately but their voices must have some relation to each other. Duets, trios, and quartets are all ensembles. An ensemble can be one of the most effective operatic devices in that it enables the composer and librettist to portray two, three, or more different emotions, moods, or feelings at the same time. It also can emphasize a particular situation by having two or more people sing the same words at differing musical pitches and with different timbres. If two lovers speak the same words at the same time in a play, they either will seem ridiculous or they are creating a special effect. Music, however, makes this simultaneity a genuine artistic experience. Two voices are joined and yet distinct in timbre, quality, range, and musical expression.

Admittedly, when two or more people sing together there is danger that the words will be lost (see pp. 27–28) and the larger the ensemble the greater is this problem. Librettists often compensate by writing more general texts for the ensemble, and the composer ideally constructs the music so that the words *can* be heard if properly delivered. There is no easy answer to this problem. It has been solved satisfactorily in the past and will continue to be solved by dramatists of distinction but there have been failures too. The secret, if any, is variety and musical and dramatic realization of the particular situation. Too often a duet or trio is believed to be two or three people warbling together in sixths or thirds with repeated words that go on interminably to the final cadence. This parody of an operatic ensemble occurs just enough in second-rate music to create an impression that it happens regularly.

In fact, most good operatic emsembles are a combination of solo and concerted singing. Very rarely do two or three singers start and continue together through an entire section of music unless the occasion is a very formal one involving a stop of all action and a set "concert number" aimed at the audience. More often, there is a dialogue between characters in which each sings *separately* at first and then joins with the others in moments of climax. Technically, a duet or trio may be two or three people singing primarily *at* each other and not simultaneously. The advantages of this scheme are self-evident. There is more flexibility, and the composer is not bound to have the entire ensemble sing at all times. Words and action can be more pronounced, and there is less danger of musical stagnation.

A duet, trio, or other combination of singers can be static or dynamic. When the ensemble sums up a tender expression of love, parting, or grief, the static quality is a legitimate halting of the plot in order to have the lyrical episode run its course. On the other hand, if the composer can both write memorable music and keep the action going, he creates an ensemble that combines the best of two worlds. A miracle of this sort is the finale to Act II of *Figaro* where da Ponte and Mozart show us the enraged Count trying to get the key to a dressing room where he believes Cherubino is hidden. When he does get the key from his wife and opens the door, out walks Susanna, mystifying both the Count and Countess. The Count realizes he has been tricked but reconciliation seems imminent. Then Figaro bursts in; wedding preparations for his marriage to Susanna are complete, and he wants the ceremony to proceed. But the Count wishes the mystery cleared up: who wrote the anonymous letter? Susanna and the Countess have already told the Count it was Figaro, but Figaro is unaware of this. As the situation gets warm again, the usually drunken gardener, Antonio, fairly sober at this point, says somebody has ruined his flower beds by leaping out the window. Figaro tries to say it was he; but Antonio hands him Cherubino's army comission which he picked up outside the window. The women get Figaro out of this difficulty; but Bartolo, Basilio, and Marcellina enter to press Marcellina's claim on Figaro. The Count, realizing that allies are at hand, joins this delegation so that Figaro's and Susanna's marriage can be delayed. The act ends with Susanna, the Countess, and Figaro arrayed against the Count, Marcellina, Basilio, and Bartolo. And how does Mozart treat this? In a brilliant mixture of solo singing, duet, trio, quartet, and at the end, septet—all linked by key structure, parallel tempo changes, dialogue alternation, and contrasts. It is a masterpiece of ensemble writing.

Opera composers can also treat an ensemble in the familiar recitative and aria form, the difference being that two or three characters are involved instead of one. In Verdi's *La forza del destino* (The Force of Destiny, 1862), there is a very powerful scene between Don Alvaro (tenor) and Don Carlos (baritone). Alvaro, who has been wounded in battle, entrusts to Carlos a casket of private letters, they swear eternal friendship. But unknown to Alvaro, Carlos is the brother of Leonora, whom Alvaro loves and tried to elope with, in the process accidentally killing her father, the Marchese di Calatrava. Don Carlos has sworn to avenge his father's death, but only finds out later who Alvaro is.

RECITATIVE Alvaro. *Where am I?*
Carlos. *Close to your friend.*
Alvaro. *Let me die.*
Carlos (with surgeon). *Our treatment will save you. Your reward will be the order of Calatrava.*

Alvaro (startled). *Of Calatrava. No, never!*

Carlos (aside). *What! Does the name of Calatrava shock him?*

Alvaro. *My friend, a word alone.*

Carlos (to the surgeon). *Please leave us briefly.* (The surgeon withdraws to the background. Alvaro motions Carlos to come close to him.)

DUET

Alvaro. *At this grave time, you must swear to do my wish.*

Carlos. *I swear it.*

Alvaro. *Look for something near my heart.*

Carlos (does so). *A key!*

Alvaro. *With it open and pull out a packet of letters which I confide to your honor There is a mystery in them which must die with me. Please burn them.*

Carlos. *I swear I shall do it.*

Alvaro. *Now dying I am at peace. I press you to my heart* (embraces Carlos with deep emotion).

Carlos. *Be faithful, my dear friend. Trust in heaven.*

(These last lines from "Now dying" are sung together.)

Verdi continues the action in the duet by having Alvaro entrust his precious letters to Carlos. The two men still sing separately here because the words must be clearly understood to carry the story forward. Only when Carlos has agreed and made a promise can the lyrical moment take place; the voices join together, mostly at cadences, and bring the ensemble to a climax. Technically, the encounter is a duet but in reality it is a carefully worked-out scene in which Verdi portrays vividly the characters of the two men: Alvaro, with a triadic, soaring C major melody; Carlos, by a darker, baritone, more monotonous line.

VARIOUS TYPES There are two or three famous ensembles in opera which have often been extracted from their settings, sung independently, satirized, and praised. While they are well-known as music, the average person has no idea what they were meant to express in the operas from which they came.

One such ensemble is the famous quartet from the last act of *Rigoletto.* After he had seen the opera Victor Hugo said that Verdi with the quartet had actually improved the scene from his play, *Le Roi s'amuse,* on which the opera was based. The ensemble is a supreme example of how that great musical dramatist, Verdi, was able to picture four different characters with four different emotions and have them sing together in such a striking way that we often remember the music and forget the action. Some knowledge of the background is necessary. The act takes place on the banks of the Mincio in sixteenth century Mantua at a lonely, dilapidated inn. Rigoletto, hunchback and court jester, is trying to prove to his only child, Gilda, that the Duke, whom she loves, is a libertine who will toss her aside as easily as he has done others. Through a crack in the wall, he shows her the Duke, disguised as a cavalry officer, making an arrangement with Sparafucile for wine and a woman. Sparafucile has been hired by Rigoletto to lure the Duke to this desolate spot and to kill him. When the Duke is left alone momentarily, he sings the famous "La donna è mobile" (Woman is fickle), perfectly expressing his philosophy that women are to be loved and abandoned. Meanwhile, Sparafucile steps outside and asks Rigoletto whether his victim should be dispatched now or later; Rigoletto says to wait. (This is not heard by Gilda.) Sparafucile goes off, and the musical interest shifts to the Duke and Maddalena, Sparafucile's sister, inside the inn (she has come down stairs at a signal from her brother). The Duke showers attention upon the coquettish Maddalena. Gilda sees what is happening and gives short, bitter cries of anguish and pain as the Duke professes ardent love and tries to embrace Maddalena. Rigoletto joins in at the end of this E major section, asking his daughter if the scene is not enough to persuade her. There is a significant pause. Then Verdi, through a wonderful enharmonic change in the music, begins the familiar quartet, with the Duke (tenor) pleading for the fulfillment of his love with the charming girl (Example 5-13a). (The melody is almost a little aria in itself with the opening phrase varied on its repetition; a middle part; then the opening part varied at the end—AA'BA'.) Maddalena's reply (contralto) is a rapid, sixteenth note patter, saying the Duke is a practiced flatterer but she rather likes it (b). Just after that phrase, Gilda (soprano) sings a broken, chromatic little melody to the effect that to see love treated so lightly is torture to her (c). After the two women sing their phrases again to different words (Maddalena: "I laugh to think of how many girls have fallen for these lines"; Gilda. "He said the same things to me"), Rigoletto (baritone) joins in on a stern, largely one note, reiterated phrase, saying it is useless for Gilda to weep now (d). The four join together for the first time, expressing the sentiments already sung individually and bringing this section to a close. The Duke then resumes his initial melody after a lingering cadence on a dominant chord, going up to a B flat (b^1). This time all four sing together, Gilda and Rigoletto supplying the outer voices of the harmony, their vocal lines fitting together, while the Duke and Maddalena continue their inner patter. As the music grows in excitement, Gilda's cries become more broken and breathless in the soprano and Rigoletto's judicial comment in the bass becomes more agitated (e), while the Duke and Maddalena continue their musical courtship. The pair inside the inn are unaware of Gilda

Example 5-13 Verdi, *Rigoletto* (1851)

Bel - la fi - glia del - l'a - mo - - re,
(Lovely daughter of love,)

Ah! Ah! ri - do ben di co - re, che tal ba - ie co - stan po - co,
(Ah! I laugh heartily because such flattery costs very little,)

Ah! co - si par-lar d'a - mo-re
(Ah! to speak that way of love)

Ta-ci, il pian-ge - re non va - le;
(Hush, Weeping has no value)

In - fe - li - ce   Ch'ei men - ti - va,
(Unhappy)   (He was lying,)

and Rigoletto outside; yet the musical identification of each character is so exact there is never any doubt about the differing sentiments. The quartet is a magnificent musical and dramatic achievement.

Another equally famous ensemble is the sextet from Donizetti's *Lucia di Lammermoor* (Lucy of Lammermoor, 1835). In spite of its musical quality, however, the sextet has much less dramatic power than the *Rigoletto* quartet. Donizetti, an able but facile composer, was often carried away by his musically creative moments and his characters lost their individuality, becoming little more than a group of people singing in ensemble on the stage.

The sextet comes at a very striking moment in the opera. Lucy Ashton (her name and those of the other characters are Anglicized here according to Scott's novel, *The Bride of Lammermoor*, on which the work was based) is in love with Edgar Ravenswood, her brother Henry's mortal and hereditary enemy. The lovers have met secretly; but Edgar has gone off to France (it is the sixteenth century when the Scots were conniving with the French for power and constantly

Example 5-14  Donizetti, *Lucia di Lammermoor* (1835)

(Edgar: Who restrains me in such a moment? Who cuts off the course of my anger?
Henry: Who holds back my fury and the hand that wants to turn to the sword?)

quarreling among themselves at home). Henry Ashton intercepts Edgar's letters to Lucy, and he forges a letter from Edgar to Lucy indicating Edgar has married another woman. Lucy, in despair, is pushed into a marriage with Arthur Bucklaw, who will help to retrieve Ashton's sagging fortunes. Just after a marriage contract has been signed by the frantic Lucy and the ceremony is about to take place, Edgar bursts in and accuses Lucy of violating her word to him. Edgar (tenor) and Henry (baritone) begin the ensemble, their words supposed to be an aside (Example 5-14*a*): Edgar is accusing Lucy of faithlessness; Henry, fearing that Edgar's dramatic entrance will prevent the wedding, is longing to use his sword. Donizetti takes an attractive tune sung by Edgar and has Henry provide the lower harmony to it. Lucy (soprano) and Bidebent (bass), her trusted advisor, join in by singing the same tune with the two men filling in middle harmony. Finally, Alice, Lucy's companion, and Arthur, Lucy's intended bridegroom, are added to the ensemble. Their reason to join is to add two more voices to the group. Henry and the orchestra, however, add another memorable phrase to the ensemble, which carries it along further (*b*). Meanwhile, below the six, the chorus fills in chords to give further body to the singing. Musically, there are some lovely moments but dramatic surge is lacking.

Two ensembles of quite different character can be drawn from Mozart's *Magic Flute*. In the first act, Tamino, an Egyptian prince, learning that the Queen of the Night's daughter, Pamina, is being held by the magician Sarastro, falls in love with her picture and, accompanied by Papageno, the bird-catcher, resolves to rescue her. Tamino and Papageno are given a magic flute and bells, respectively, to protect them from perils on the way. In the first ensemble (a trio sung by three ladies-in-waiting to the Queen), they are told that three spirits will watch over them (Example 5-15a). Mozart does not distinguish between the three ladies very much except in the range of their voices; most of the time they sing together and act as an entity. He is careful to see that their high register is balanced by delicate orchestral accompaniment, which gives a unique quality to their singing.

In the last act, Tamino must penetrate the temple before he can be reunited with Pamina. Two men in armor show him the gates he must enter to pass through fire and water. In this second ensemble, the two men (a tenor and a bass) sing a German Protestant chorale (*Ach Gott, vom Himmel sieh darein*) an octave apart, under which Mozart writes a Bachian counterpoint, perhaps to indicate the presence of death or at least a very strenuous and difficult trial (*b*). The combination of the two men sternly outlining the chorale melody above active orchestral polyphony is musical imagination of the most vivid sort.

Example 5-15

(Three spirits, young, beautiful, gracious, and wise will guide you on your journey;)

(Whoever wanders this burdensome pathway [must be purified by fire, water, air, and earth])

74   The Magic of Opera

Chorus The chorus has always been important to opera. There was a time in the late seventeenth and early eighteenth centuries when it almost ceased to exist in Italian opera because solo singing (see p. 31), ruled supreme; but in France and Germany it has had a long and honorable history. Choruses have varied in size and importance. Most common is the four-part chorus of women's and men's voices, but there also have been men's choruses, women's choruses, and even double choruses where eight or more parts are realized in the musical texture. Some operas have featured the chorus; others have practically ignored it; others have used it mainly for color and background.

Opera demands the same qualities of its chorus as it does of individual singers: the chorus has to be able to *sing*, or it remains just a crowd. A group of slim, beautiful girls, such as one might find in the chorus line of a musical comedy, will rarely be seen in an opera; the ability to act and dance tends to be of secondary importance. The primary qualification is the voice, not lovely legs, a beautiful face, or graceful gestures. Consequently, opera choruses have not always looked so attractive or convincing as they have sounded.

Nowadays when the stage director and producer have become more important (sometimes to the point where an opera is overstaged and overproduced), the chorus is more artfully grouped on stage. Making a group of villagers or soldiers look natural without distracting from the principal actors takes skill and planning—too much movement is fatal, too little is stultifying; there has to be a happy mean. The chorus should be able to *see* the conductor (or an off-stage assistant) when singing. After a chorus singer has sung the same music many times, he may feel an inescapable desire to spread wings. But in independence lies anarchy and, unfortunately, a chorus out of step with the conductor is all too common. Directing a chorus is like the balancing act on the high trapeze at the circus: the body or the pole leans too far, and the audience holds its breath, fervently hoping the next step will put matters to right. A chorus of 80 or 100 people is hard enough to control when stationary; when these gypsies, soldiers, brigands, or courtiers are moving around the difficulties are compounded unless everybody is sure what is expected.

The opera chorus plays one of three roles: (1) a participant in, (2) commentator on, or (3) background to the action. In operas like Mussorgsky's *Boris Godunov* and Rossini's *Guillaume Tell* (William Tell, 1829), the people of Russia and Switzerland are chief participants in the opera. Yet in other operas the chorus can stand outside the mainstream of the plot, like the chorus in ancient Greek drama representing the audience's fears and joys. Because of the nature of a chorus—its bulk, its inability to portray anything but a collective emotion—this role is its most common and useful one. As a commentator, it is more effective in making a point or reaching a climax and it is easier to control.

A chorus can provide *background* to the action: it lends local color or sets a mood. This third category spills over into the extra or supernumerary sphere (spearholders, guards of the king, village onlookers); but it is still important for the total effect. Sometimes all three roles for chorus can be combined; for example, at the end of an act when a big climax is desired.

The musical make-up of a chorus can vary greatly according to the composer's wishes. Although soprano, alto, tenor, and bass are the most common combination whenever both sexes are singing, numerous groupings are possible. Five parts (first and second soprano, alto, tenor, and bass) are quite common, as is three parts: one female voice and two male ones. There is also the special color of men's (two tenors, two basses) or women's (two sopranos, two altos) voices alone—a favorite device in grand opera of the nineteenth century when numerous choral effects had to be distinguished from each other. Finally, there is the excitement of having a chorus sing in octaves or in unison; when a melody is to be emphasized or is particularly beautiful by itself, the impact of such a sound at the right moment is very great.

Choristers in most good opera companies now are professionally trained and recognized in their own right. In European houses, they have tenure or nontenure just as the orchestra and some of the major singers have. As choristers become older, though, tenure can create difficulties. Fortunately, opera like life seldom demands that everybody be under 25. There is plenty of call for the middle-aged and even the elderly. A good chorus voice can last longer than a solo one because less is demanded of it; voices retain quality if not volume and vigor.

A good chorus can create variety and excitement, even though composers have sometimes ignored it. In early Italian court opera, choruses were of modest size; in seventeenth century Italian opera when the singer became the focus of attention, the chorus was an expensive luxury which almost disappeared. In such operas there was a "coro" at the end, but it was merely an ensemble of the six or seven members of the cast. In France during the same period, however, the chorus and ballet were featured. Most of Lully's operas employed large numbers of singers and dancers in a lengthy prologue dedicated to Louis XIV, in order to give the massed effect so pleasing to the court at Versailles. Opera buffa gradually brought groups of people back into the main operatic stream, but it was not until the nineteenth century that the chorus achieved its full glory.

Part of this popularity was attributable to the rise in the 1830s and 1840s of nationalistic sentiment which glorified the "folk" — the people who could join in the action or provide background or local color. German opera after Weber seldom lacked a chorus (witness its importance in Wagner's early operas); and in Italy, fretting under the Austrian yoke, the opera chorus became almost a political force, expressing the longing of a people for independence. The twentieth century with its diversity of styles in neo-classicism, chamber opera, Wagnerian neo-romanticism, and other influences, has utilized the chorus in opera when it fitted the context.

FAMOUS CHORUSES In the writing of choruses for opera (or any other medium), the composer is concerned not only with the text (how it serves one of the three purposes outlined above), but also with the sonority desired. A series of regularly spaced chords in the middle register of the voice serves one purpose. Voices can sing in a chordal or polyphonic fashion and entries can be staggered, the sopranos first, altos second, etc. The choral voices can be spread out far from each other or they

Example 5-16   Verdi, *Il trovatore* (1853)

(See! the great arch of heaven removes its dark, nocturnal remains:)

(Who brightens the gypsy's days?)

77   The Components of Music

can be bunched. There is the special sound of men's voices which can be rich and full; or the ethereal quality of women's in their high register (a favorite representation of angel choirs). The possibilities are numerous and varied.

Verdi's *Il trovatore* (The Troubadour, 1853) has two choruses which have become famous. One is the Anvil Chorus at the beginning of Act II. The stage directions read:

A ruined habitation at the foot of a mountain in Biscay; within, through a wide opening, a fire is seen. Day is dawning. Azucena is seated by the fire. Manrico is lying on a low couch at her side, wrapped in his mantle, his helmet at his feet, a sword in his hand, on which he is gazing intently. The Gipsy band is scattered about the stage.

The chorus here plays role three: it provides background and color for the setting and for Azucena's roving life. The men do most of the singing while beating time with their hammers on the anvils. The words tell merely of the rise of dawn, of wandering existence, of the faithful gypsy women who give the men sustenance and some occasional wine. Verdi's vocal line is inspired simplicity—a rising series of chord outlines starting from the key note goes up and then down again. The tenors and basses sing in unison (Example 5-16*a*); the women join (*b*) at the octave, and harmony is reserved for the final cadence. This chorus is seldom forgotten, because of the tune and its orchestral background.

Another unusual chorus of octave singing appears in Verdi's *Nabucco* (Nebuchadnezzar, 1842), his first operatic success and one

Example 5-17   Verdi, *Nabucco* (1842)

(Go, thought, on gilded wings; go, put yourself on hills and mountains,)

Example 5-18

Chorus of Sirens (grouped in the background, sound like an echo)
Wagner, *Tannhäuser* (1845)

(Approach these shores; approach these lands where in the arms of burning love)

Chorus of elder Pilgrims (at a great distance, slowly approaching)

(Blessings be upon thee, O native land, which I see once more, and happy greetings to thy lovely meadows;)

which spread his name throughout Italy. The opera deals with the fortunes of the Jews during the Babylonian captivity. The chorus, "Va, pensiero, sull'ali dorate," sung by Hebrew slaves longing for freedom, became a revolutionary manifesto. It was taken up by patriotic Italians who heard in it a similar cry for freedom and independence from the Austrian monarchy. Each time it was sung, many in the audience broke into tears. Interestingly enough, its effect comes not through power and a large orchestra but through a quiet, intense melody (almost an operatic psalm) that engraves itself upon the memory. Not until the middle does the chorus break into a forte and full harmony, and in the end it sinks back into the original melody, and trails away softly (Example 5-17).

Wagner's *Tannhäuser* (1845) has several well-known choruses. In the opening scene (the interior of the Venusberg) naiads are bathing, sirens reclining, and Venus is on a couch with Tannhäuser at her knees. In a rosy light, nymphs dance, and the sirens sing a haunting phrase that tapers off in languid beauty as if it could go on forever— an effect Wagner creates by an altered chord that refuses to resolve fully. The timbre of the women's voices gives an angelic and caressing impression in the music; it is background of the most subtle and penetrating kind (Example 5-18*a*).

Also there is the Pilgrims' Chorus. In the last act, Wolfram, Tannhäuser's faithful friend, and Elisabeth, Tannhäuser's beloved, wait at a shrine in the valley below the Wartburg Castle for the pilgrims to return from Rome. They hope that Tannhäuser will be among them. He had gone to ask the Pope forgiveness for his sin. he betrayed Elisabeth by consorting with Venus and her maidens and has been eternally damned unless he is shriven. The pilgrims are heard approaching from afar, singing their famous hymn—one of Wagner's fine creative touches with its rich grouping of men's voices and mixture of harmonic simplicity and complexity (*b*). As they come nearer, Elisabeth and Wolfram anxiously scan the faces, singing a few short phrases above the pilgrims' voices. As the hymn reaches its climax and fades away, Elisabeth has one sad comment, "Er kehret nicht zurück" (He has not come back), and the choral sound evaporates in an inconclusive cadence. The pilgrims are active participants in the drama, and their music also conveys the religious atmosphere of medieval Germany—the fanatic belief that their way must be followed by all righteous souls.

Summary   Recitative, aria, ensemble, and chorus are the basic musical components of opera. Although they tend to melt into one another in modern times, there is enough distinction from Monteverdi to Verdi to single them out so that the opera lover can recognize differences. Because individual functions help to give variety and excitement to operatic texture, they are treated as free forms and not fixed, inviolate mechanisms that cannot be altered. Opera composers have found enough leeway within these structures to develop remarkably different idioms and still abide by essential patterns established previously. The distinctions will probably remain, in some form, for years to come.

SUGGESTED READING

A Dictionary of Opera and Song Themes, compiled by Sam Morgenstern and Harold Barlow, Crown, New York, 1950. For those who wish to find their favorite aria or chorus by first line of text, composer, or musical beginning.

Hamm, Charles, *Opera*, Allyn and Bacon, Boston, 1966; Reprint Da Capo, New York, 1979.

Hope-Wallace, Philip, in collaboration with Raymond Mander and Joe Mitchenson, *A Picture History of Opera*, Hulton, London, 1959 A fine collection of singers in costume, stage sets, and theater interiors (full captions and introductory text) from every period in operatic history.

Pauly, Reinhard G., *Music and the Theater· An Introduction to Opera*, Prentice-Hall, Englewood Cliffs, N. J., 1970. A book similar to this one in purpose.

6 The Singers

Singing is the lifeblood of opera. Other elements—orchestra, acting, stage setting—are important but supplementary It is the human voice with all its idiosyncracies, charm, and magnetic power that captures the audience. No mechanical instrument can express the full range of color, timbre, and emotion of which the voice is capable. But along with its extraordinary capacity for delicacy, pathos, and mood comes fragility; the voice is subject to the ills of the body and can be hurt or destroyed overnight. Just as an athlete keeps in good physical shape, so must the singer protect and coddle his voice. It can easily be injured by strain, overwork, peculiar voice production, or a poorly functioning respiratory system. No wonder that singers become professional hypochondriacs! Even if their voices are preserved properly, age takes its toll sooner than in other parts of the body An operatic career of 25 to 30 years is the most one can hope for; the average is more likely 20 years, so that the age of 45 or 50 is usually considered the dividing line, particularly for women.

The human larynx (the voice box, containing the vocal cords, in the lower throat—the "Adam's apple" prominent in men) is partially hidden from view (If it were not, there might be much temptation to manipulate it as a means of fame and fortune.) As important as the larynx in producing sound are the resonators (mouth, nose, head, and upper part of the throat), the articulators (tongue, palate, teeth, and lips), and the wind supply (the lungs as well as the diaphragm which control the emission and force of air). The actual sound-producing agents are the two vibrating strips of cartilage called the vocal cords, which are separated by an expanding and contracting opening, the glottis. The epiglottis, the cartilage at the root of the tongue, during swallowing covers and protects the vocal cords.

Because voice production is a slightly mysterious process, it has been the subject of some of the most abundant nonsense ever written or spoken. Books have been written on the subject, but most of them use a language and a terminology that rivals medieval astrology in its obscurity. There are certain scientific principles involved in producing a fine vocal sound, but most of them stem from what comes naturally in singing and not through any forced or mechanistic "method." Generally, the greatest singers have been those who could produce tone in an easy, natural way. Of course, discipline and control have to enter in, but the stamina necessary for three hours of strenuous exercise derives from the security of knowing the sound is forthcoming without forcing. And then, with any other human endowment, one must be graced at the beginning with the *potential* for a good voice. Without the potential, all the production methods in the world will do little good.

Once a voice has been technically developed so that steadiness of tone, accuracy of intonation, clearness of sound, and articulation are good, only half the battle has been won. Particularly in opera, the singer must be a good musician, an actor or actress, and a performer who has enough personal magnetism to make contact with an audience. There have been singers who did not read music and learned everything by rote, but good singing generally means a thorough knowledge of music, intelligent shaping of a phrase, emotional intensity behind the words, and the articulation and understanding of several foreign languages. Moreover, in repertory, singers must assume an astonishing variety of roles which test both their musical and histrionic abilities. Years of difficult and arduous study are involved, but when a singer is able to combine a fine, trained voice with innate musical and dramatic ability, he stands at the center of opera, making opera exciting and vital.

Categories of Voice

The singing voice is generally assigned to one of four categories: for women, *soprano* and *contralto*; for men, *tenor* and *bass*. These four divisions signify the high and low registers respectively in each sex. In reality, there should be *six* divisions of voices (true for all singing); many people find their best range is in between the usual four categories. This central range is called *mezzo-soprano* for women and *baritone* for men. Such middle voices may not have the brilliance of very high or low notes, and often are not given equal billing with the top or low voices, but they are just as important.

The natural span of an untrained voice is about an octave and a half. An operatic voice should have a range of at least two octaves. (Extraordinary voices have had ranges up to three octaves.) Many of the great singers of the past have been able to sing in almost any register, even though technically they were in one of the usual categories, increase in vocal range usually comes from training and discipline.

Perhaps even more important than range is the *quality* of a voice. A tenor inherently has a lighter color to his voice than a bass, a soprano than a contralto. (It is better to use the word contralto for a woman's low voice rather than *alto*, which should mean a boy's low voice, even though the two words are generally used interchangeably.) No matter in what register a voice falls, it can usually be characterized as a heavy or light voice according to its weight, volume, and sonority. This distinction is particularly important in opera where voices are commonly labeled *dramatic* or *lyric* according to their quality. A dramatic voice is a heavier, bigger one, capable of carrying over the orchestra by itself or in an ensemble; a lyric voice is lighter, sweeter, more gentle—it cannot be forced or pushed too far or it loses its quality and becomes shrill and ugly. This characterization holds true for both women's and men's voices, but it is largely applied to the upper voices (sopranos and tenors) rather than to contraltos and basses.

The public often does not realize that most opera composers in the past have written their music with *specific* singers in mind. Since an individual voice has strengths and weaknesses (less volume in a certain register, shrillness above a certain note, a velvety quality in the middle, a trumpet-like sound at the top), the composer has naturally written his vocal lines to emphasize the strengths and play down the weaknesses of a particular performer. Fortunately, patterns of assets and liabilities in singers have tended to repeat themselves over the years, and most people with a certain quality of voice fit into a role without great difficulty. Music created for a dramatic soprano by Verdi will generally be comfortable for most dramatic sopranos today.

SOPRANO What further classifications of operatic voices can be made? The highest voice of all is the *coloratura soprano* (inaccurately named, in that coloratura literally means rapid passages, trills, and ornamentation). A genuine coloratura has an unmistakable light, bird-like quality to her voice. She often sounds much like a flute or piccolo, and these instruments often are given music to accompany her. Two of Mozart's most famous operatic roles were written because his sister-in-law, Josefa Weber Hofer, was a coloratura, and she sang the parts of the Queen of the Night in *The Magic Flute* and Constanze in *The Abduction*. A number of operatic roles call for high sopranos with voices of great flexibility which can trill, sing scales with the utmost rapidity, and make wide jumps, but do not go to the astronomical heights (F or F sharp, two and a half octaves above middle C) of Mozart's coloratura or Zerbinetta in Richard Strauss' *Ariadne*. Some of these roles, with top notes of an E flat or an E natural, are Lucia in Donizetti's *Lucia*, Gilda in Verdi's *Rigoletto*, and Norma in Bellini's *Norma* (1831). The flutter of the vocal cords in high registers demands constant practice (presumably a soprano high C gives off about 1,025 vibrations per second). A coloratura must be a slave to vocal exercises that keep her voice in tip-top condition to prevent the vocal cords from thickening.

The *lyric soprano* is the embodiment of the high, bright, clear female voice. Susanna in *Figaro* and Mimi in *Bohème* are examples. This is the voice of young womanhood or of the youthful heroine. When the role is quasi-comic, the description *soubrette* (French for "cunning," "shrewd") is often applied. Another term used is *spinto* (Italian for "pushed" or "urged"), which signifies a soprano whose tones have greater brilliance and carrying power than the usual lyric soprano. Many Verdi heroines are in this group· Leonora in *Il trovatore*, Elisabetta in *Don Carlos* (1867; 1884), Leonora in *La forza del destino*.

Last in the soprano group is the *dramatic soprano*. This voice is rarer because it often takes on the heavier and darker hue of a mezzo or a contralto but is still a genuine soprano with a high range and ringing sound. It is generally a big voice with very full medium and low tones. The voice may not develop fully until the late 20s or early 30s although it is embryonically present earlier. Two of the most famous dramatic soprano roles in opera are Brunnhilde in Wagner's *Ring* and Isolde in *Tristan und Isolde*. Leonora in Beethoven's *Fidelio* also is a dramatic soprano.

MEZZO-SOPRANO Below the regular soprano is the *mezzo-soprano* (Italian for "half," "middle"), really the most common among untrained female voices because it is in the middle. The range might be that of a dramatic soprano, but the voice is generally lower and has a darker, thicker quality than that of a true soprano. Opera composers have not been generous with roles for the mezzo-soprano; the poor mezzo has often had to settle for the less sympathetic (but still important) roles of Amneris in *Aida*, Azucena in *Il trovatore*, or Ortrud in Wagner's *Lohengrin*. There is one role, however, that every ambitious mezzo covets: Carmen. When she succeeds as Carmen, her career is assured. There are lighter mezzo roles, often ones that portray a male adolescent (a "trouser" role), such as Cherubino in *Figaro*, Siebel in *Faust*, and Octavian in *Der Rosenkavalier*. There is even a *coloratura mezzo*, a low soprano who can negotiate the trills, ornaments, and notes of a high soprano, although her voice may not reach the very top of a true coloratura. (Rossini was fond of this voice, using it with great success for Rosina in *The Barber of Seville*.)

CONTRALTO   The true *contralto* is the lowest of the female voices. There are not so many of them as one would expect. Popular singers who sound like contraltos are largely forced mezzos who push their voices into the low register to get the throaty, dark effect presumed to be the essence of passion and sex. Operatic contraltos are generally assigned matronly roles—mothers, elderly women, middle-aged queens. Although they seldom take a leading part, contraltos do have opportunities to shine: Orfeo in the Gluck *Orfeo* is a contralto;[1] Ulrica in *Un ballo in maschera* (A Masked Ball, 1859), and Mistress Quickly (technically a mezzo but generally sung by a contralto) in *Falstaff* (1893) are examples in Verdi. Mamma Lucia in *Cavalleria Rusticana* (Rustic Chivalry, 1890) and Annina in *Rosenkavalier* are important supporting roles.

TENOR   The first thing to recognize with men's voices is that they are less flexible than women's. When a boy reaches puberty and his voice changes from treble or alto to tenor or bass, either gradually or overnight, the vocal cords thicken. The same process does not take place with a girl. (Male vocal cords are about seven-twelfths of an inch thick; the female ones about five-twelfths of an inch.)

The operatic *tenor*, the highest of the male voices, has always been a somewhat serio-comic figure. Perhaps it is because many have been small in stature and inclined to put on weight. Also, since they are in great demand, many tenors have developed considerable egos (Frances Alda once wrote a book entitled *Men, Women, and Tenors*). The representation on stage of a short tenor hero and his two-or-three-inch taller soprano heroine has been a favorite operatic caricature for generations. It is refreshing to know that there have been (and are today) tall, slim tenors who can hold their own with shorter gentlemen in elevator shoes.

[1] It was originally written for a castrate male voice. See Glossary under *Castrato*.

Tenors, like sopranos, are generally classified as lyric or dramatic, depending upon the quality of their voices. The demand for flexibility and ornamentation in the male higher register is less than it would be for a woman, but tenors often have to develop greater stamina, because as heroes and men they are expected to be stronger and louder than their female counterparts. Dramatic tenor roles like the Count in *Rigoletto,* Alfredo in *La traviata* (The Woman Led Astray, 1853), and Rodolfo in *Bohème* are well-known in nineteenth century opera. There are also character tenor roles, some of which are comic, like Pedrillo in Mozart's *Abduction* and Don Basilio in *Figaro.* Lyric tenor parts like Don Ottavio in Mozart's *Don Giovanni* demand elegance and finesse more than power since they have a different function in the opera.[2] A *tenore robusto* or *Heldentenor,* usually assigned roles in the Wagnerian repertoire (Siegfried in *The Ring,* Tristan in *Tristan und Isolde*) or Otello in Verdi's *Otello,* must have a very strong, trumpet-like voice to carry over powerful orchestral forces. Interestingly enough, many of the great Heldentenors have started as baritones and then moved up in register so that the darker part of the voice sustains the volume called for in the big, ringing tenor roles.

Before leaving the tenors, a word should be said about a virulent disease that often strikes them, as well as other singers, particularly sopranos; it might be called "high-note-itis." At endings or after a long cadenza, there is a strong temptation to take a note an octave or a fifth higher than written, hold on to it, then descend to the last note to the accompaniment of "bravos." It is a form of acrobatics which is a sure source of applause but has little to do with music. Composers have been plagued with this practice but the audience is delighted with it. Some composers have succumbed by writing a high note into the part; others have tried rewriting the part so that there is no high note possible. Done tastefully and not too often, taking a high note other than the one written can be a legitimate operatic practice (particularly in Italian opera), but when extra notes become too numerous and the singer is more conscious of exhibiting his vocal ability than of relating to the part to be portrayed, then the disease needs radical treatment to effect a cure.

BARITONE   After the tenor there is the *baritone,* the middle range of the male voice. Some of the finest dramatic roles in opera have been written

[2] Up until almost the end of the eighteenth century, the leading male heroic roles in Italian opera seria were taken by *castrati.* They were gradually supplanted by tenors. The French tenor voice often differs from the Italian. It is apt to be less robust, more nasal and reedy.

for him: Rigoletto, Scarpia (*Tosca*), Escamillo (*Carmen*), to name a few. Attempts have been made to divide baritones into high and low categories, but a good baritone can sing up to f^1 and g^{1*} with no trouble and still maintain a fine middle and low range. If a baritone has strong low notes, he is generally called a *bass-baritone* (Wotan in *The Ring* calls for this kind of voice). There is little distinction between this and what the Italians call a *basso cantante*, a bass with a highly developed upper register.

BASS Lastly, there is the real *bass*, much commoner than the true contralto. Like the contralto, he is generally called upon for the older roles—a father, a dignified king, an elderly priest, a general of the army. Some familiar bass parts are Sarastro in *The Magic Flute*, Sparafucile in *Rigoletto*, the Grand Inquisitor in *Don Carlos*, and Baron Ochs in *Rosenkavalier*. Among vivid *basso buffo* parts for the bass are Leporello in *Don Giovanni* and Basilio in *The Barber of Seville*. A special kind of bass is the *basso profundo* who can sink to the lowest notes (E flat and D) and hold them as if they were sixteen-foot organ stops.

Before proceeding further, it should be emphasized that these divisions really only became definite after the mid-nineteenth century as a result of the demands (mostly volume and endurance) that Verdi and Wagner put on their singers. Before that time, the best sopranos were expected to sing dramatically and lyrically and to be something of a coloratura in the bargain. The eighteenth and the early nineteenth centuries were the ages of *bel canto* (a term nearly impossible to translate correctly because of its many associations; literally, however, it means "beautiful singing"). It was a style of legato phrasing, rounded tone, and immaculate articulation in which every singer was expected to be proficient. Rossini, Bellini, and Donizetti were its primary exponents as operatic composers. Tastes have changed, and although this style lingers, singers have been placed in special categories where voice is more important than the style of singing.

Another caveat must be said as an epilogue: every voice is an individual one. Each voice has its own character and timbre which can easily be recognized—on stage, in a recording, over the telephone. The unusual voice transcends the usual categorizing; some great singers have sung both high and low roles over a long operatic career. Most voices tend to lose their top notes as age comes on, but there are many exceptions; the fascination of singing is that

*See Glossary· Abbreviations.

boundaries can be crossed and occasionally even age can be defied. What is needed is a scientific assessment of the human voice: its capabilities, its strengths, its weaknesses. Was there ever a Golden Age of singing? Is singing less good today than it was yesterday? There are many chit-chat biographies of great singers (who saw whom on what occasion; "How I felt when I first stepped out on the stage") and too few solid, informative ones. With modern sound reproduction a good deal of conjecture has been removed and our descendants will be able to assess their singers against ours and come to some fairly definite conclusions.

Another point to be stressed about opera singers is that not all of them can take the leading roles. The secondary parts—brother, servant, follower, friend—carry the opera. Singers who may not have the voice for a lead specialize in these lesser roles. Through acting and vocal characterization, a good *comprimario* (Italian for "junior lead," "second part") is a very valuable asset to the opera company. And comprimario parts have a habit of "stealing the show" if done well.

Few opera composers have written for children's voices, except for special effects. The lung power of a young boy or girl (treble and alto) is too limited to fill an opera house. A boy's unchanged voice also has a curious, white, sexless quality about it that is very different from that of a woman's. A child's voice is unable to express passion with any force. Benjamin Britten has employed boys' voices with considerable success by using stories that call for boys in central roles (Miles in *The Turn of the Screw* (1956) or the three boys in *Noye's Fludde* (1958). Then there is the child's role in Menotti's *Amahl and the Night Visitors* (1951), where the problem of carrying power is eliminated because the work was designed expressly for television.

The *countertenor* voice, essentially falsetto (forced tone production above the normal register), is rarely used except for early operas (Gluck, Handel, and before). In these operas it has taken the place of the soprano or alto *castrato*, which for obvious reasons no longer exists. Since falsetto or head tone cannot produce much volume, it is still not very satisfactory in operatic parts. Today, women are often used for these castrato roles, even though there may be a loss in dramatic verity; the women can sing the music at the pitch it was written and still give weight and power to the musical line. Moreover, in the seventeenth and eighteenth centuries, many male parts were originally written for female voices.

Another curious fact about the human voice is that some countries seem to have produced more of one kind than of others. Very low basses have been a special Russian contribution, dramatic tenors have flourished in Italy, England has been fruitful in giving opera some outstanding mezzo-sopranos and contraltos, and some of the finest lyric tenors have been French. As yet, America has made no special contribution. When it comes to specific cases, however, individuality and not the country is the determining factor: opera companies are a United Nations of nationalities. The singer will be recognized for his quality, not by his native language: opera is a *lingua franca*.

SUGGESTED READING

Pleasants, Henry, *The Great Singers, from the Dawn of Opera to Our Own Time*, Simon and Schuster, New York, 1966. Mostly biographical. Slightly disappointing in content, but good general survey of famous singers of the past.

Rushmore, Robert, *The Singing Voice*, Dodd, Mead, New York, 1971. Popular and somewhat superficial, but readable and entertaining. Treats categories of voice and assigns roles to them.

7 The Orchestra

History To trace the history of the opera orchestra is to trace the history of the orchestra itself. Many of the orchestral innovations have originated in the opera pit. Indeed, the opera orchestra differs from the concert or symphony orchestra only in the location of the players. One performs in a theater pit, mostly out of sight; the other, on a platform in full view of the audience. In size and composition they are the same. A composer does not shift gears in writing first for a symphony orchestra and then for an opera orchestra; he draws on the same forces but makes different calculations about the sound—how it will be in relation to voices and the stage performance.

The early opera orchestra (seventeenth century) was small, although the size depended upon the nature of the production. The "first operas"—Peri's and Caccini's *Euridice* of 1600 and 1602 respectively and Monteverdi's *Orfeo* of 1607—were all performed in Mantua, but there could be no greater contrast than the extent of their orchestral forces. The two *Euridice* settings were frankly experimental within the Florentine Camerata (a group of singers, poets, playwrights, and composers who were attempting to revive the spirit of Greek drama in a contemporary musical idiom). Because, above all, the text had to be articulated as clearly and correctly as possible, the instruments were few (four) and of the accompanying variety (harpsichord, bass lute, lyre, and another higher lute). They created a varied tonal color, but were restricted to "realizing" the basso continuo which was the only musical line aside from the solo part with text.

Monteverdi's *Orfeo* was a large-scale affair presented at court. The instrumentation rivaled eighteenth and nineteenth century orchestras in size—12 winds and brass of various kinds (recorder, trumpets, trombones, etc.), 14 strings, and 13 accompanying instruments (harpsichord, harp, small organs, lutes, etc.).

After the opening of the first public opera house in Venice in 1637, the opera orchestra assumed a size which remained for the rest of the century, with the notable exception of court operas such as those in Vienna and Paris which always had larger forces. The core of the orchestra, beside the strings, was the accompanying instruments: harpsichord, small organ, and possibly lutes. In the eighteenth century, winds and brass (flutes, oboes, trumpets, etc.) became solo instruments which wove strands of melody around the vocal part and acted as other voices, either while the soloist was singing or in instrumental interludes.

In general, the orchestra was careful not to overshadow the voice, which, as the aria became more prominent, was increasingly the ruling element. Orchestral interludes often echoed the melodic material of the vocal part or introduced it before the voice began (ritornellos). In a continuo aria (orchestra silent except for accompanying instruments), the full orchestra was sometimes saved for the concluding measures where it came in with marked effect. If in an aria there were *obbligato* instruments, they did not dominate the voice but acted as a counterpoint or additional melody. By the late seventeenth and early eighteenth century, however, there was emphasis on the alternation of the full body of strings with a selected few playing against them (the *tutti* and *soli* effect of much baroque music, particularly the concerto). Although these dynamic effects were not always marked in the music, they were understood as a means of creating contrast between *forte* and *piano* and giving added color to the music. These principles were typical of opera seria as demonstrated in the works of Alessandro Scarlatti and Handel.

The conductor of an orchestra was generally the harpsichordist, who held his forces together with the help of a concertmaster at the first violin. By nodding his head or moving his body, the harpsichordist managed to create an ensemble which could respond sensitively to his wishes. Often the harpsichordist was the composer himself. The other continuo instruments (cello, double bass, lute, or harp) were grouped near him, often reading from the score at the harpsichord. Only at Paris and Versailles did the practice of maintaining a time-beater prevail (a conductor who used a piece of parchment or a stick to direct the orchestra). The older system worked well so long as the group was small and the basis of the music was the continuo, the harpsichord and accompanying instruments filling in the harmony and giving rhythmic bite and direction to the music. The average opera orchestra in the early eighteenth century was probably 25 to 30 players. In Dresden, then a court residence for the King of Poland, the orchestra for opera and concerts in 1731 consisted of 6 violins, 3 violas, 4 cellos, 2 bass, 3 flutes, 4 oboes, 3 bassoons, 2 horns (total: 27) and possibly trumpets and timpani when needed.

Toward the end of the eighteenth century (in Mozart's and Haydn's lifetimes), the orchestra began to change: the continuo function gradually faded as did the pre-eminence of the harpsichord and accompanying instruments. Horns and winds lost their predominantly solo or tutti function: oboes no longer played merely solo parts or doubled the violins when all the strings were playing, but joined with the flutes and bassoons to create a woodwind ensemble. This ensemble, with the horns (and other brass, to some extent), began to fill in the inner harmonies and take the place of the harpsichord and associated instruments. The orchestra became the classic orchestra of Mozart, Haydn, Beethoven, and Schubert. It had four groups: woodwinds, brass, percussion, and strings, each of which had a specific function. The strings were in four or five parts (violin I, violin II, viola, cello, and double bass), and there were pairs of flutes, oboes, bassoons, and horns, sometimes trumpets, later clarinets, plus percussion. The strings were the center of the orchestra and the other sections revolved around them. When the full orchestra played, more tone and volume were demanded from the singer to carry over it.

Yet composers like Mozart, who knew Italian opera and singers, were careful to calculate their effects so that the singer was not overpowered. In spite of the increase in numbers, strings would simply accompany many arias, while the body of winds provided color and background. Mozart scored *Figaro* for pairs of flutes, oboes, clarinets, bassoons, horns, and trumpets, plus timpani and strings. But the total force seldom played except at climaxes or in ensembles at the ends of acts.

During the nineteenth century, the trend was toward larger orchestras, and the singers had to develop greater vocal stamina. By 1816 La Scala in Milan had a string section of 50 musicians, and in Paris there were 48. Instead of two winds or brass, there were now three or four in each section. A double process was at work;

mechanical improvements in winds and brass increased their volume so there had to be more strings and special instruments like the English horn (alto oboe), bass clarinet, contrabassoon, and modern harp were introduced.

The size of the opera orchestra reached its peak in the nineteenth century with composers like Wagner and Strauss. Since then, the orchestra has tended to become smaller and more specialized. Wagner, in his early operas, did not differ much from his predecessors, except that he asked for three winds (for example, two oboes and an English horn; two clarinets and a bass clarinet). In *The Ring*, however, he expanded his orchestra considerably. Its roster is worth quoting in detail: 16 first violins and 16 second violins, 12 violas, 12 cellos, 8 double basses, 3 flutes and 1 piccolo (third flute sometimes playing a second piccolo), 3 oboes and 1 English horn (sometimes a fourth oboe), 3 clarinets and 1 bass clarinet, 3 bassoons, 8 horns, 2 tenor and 2 bass tubas (played when required by four of the horn players), 1 contrabass tuba, 3 trumpets, 1 bass trumpet, 3 trombones, 1 contrabass trombone (sometimes instead, a fourth trombone), 2 pairs of kettledrums, 1 triangle, 1 pair of cymbals, 1 side drum, 1 glockenspiel, and 6 harps. The big increase here is in the brass section, where some of the tubas were called "Wagner tubas" (really a hybrid of horn and trombone) since he devised them. The horns and "Wagner tubas" used valves which allowed much greater flexibility and ease of playing than had been possible previously.

Many instruments were added permanently to the orchestra through the opera. In the eighteenth century, trombones were commonly considered sepulchral instruments and confined to church music; but when Gluck began using them for his operas and Mozart made a special point of including them in his *Idomeneo* and *Don Giovanni*, they became a regular part of the brass section. Trumpets and kettledrums were originally used for military bands. When warlike or triumphal scenes were demanded in opera, however, they joined the orchestra. Horns also gradually became a solid element in the instrumental ensemble.

Overtures and Preludes   One of the most interesting duties of the orchestra in opera has been as the opener of festivities—the performer of the overture or prelude. The two words have acquired different meanings: in general, the overture is a larger piece of music, more formal than a prelude, which is apt to be shorter and more compact. In early operas, the overture was a brass fanfare to capture audience attention and let them know the performance was about to begin. Monteverdi's *Orfeo* (1607) begins with approximately eight measures of fanfare for brass, largely on one chord; the opening of his *Poppea* (1642) is longer with more variety, but has predominantly the same purpose: to quiet the audience. In the course of the seventeenth century, the simple beginning was expanded and given more weight. In France, Lully's operas ("tragédies lyriques," written in the 1670s and 1680s) were introduced by a two- or three-sectional work (slow, fast, slow) that came to be known as a French overture because it was a trademark of court opera at Versailles (see p. 16). This French overture, as used by Handel for his operas, generally omitted the third part and often added a stylized dance (minuet, gavotte). With both Lully and Handel, the music generally had no direct connection with the opera but merely gave a formal beginning to the entertainment.

In Italy during the early eighteenth century, another type of overture (often called a sinfonia) evolved. It had three parts of fast-slow-fast, with the middle section hardly more than a few measures of Adagio between the two Allegros or Prestos. It was lighter in style and often served as an introduction to an opera buffa, which needed something gay and quick to set the stage.

One of Gluck's contributions was to have the overture bear a direct relation to the opera itself, setting the mood for the drama. In his famous preface to *Alceste* (1769) (see p. 32), he said, "I have felt that the overture ought to apprise the spectators of the nature of the action that is to be represented and to form, so to speak, its argument." While all his reform operatic overtures do not conform to this dictum (the overture to *Orfeo* is merely a one movement Allegro in the prevailing Italian style), the overtures to *Alceste*, *Iphigénie en Aulide* (Iphigenia in Aulis, 1774), and *Iphigénie en Tauride* (Iphigenia in Tauris, 1779) do, and the second of these three is perhaps Gluck's finest instrumental composition.

The story of *Iphigenia in Aulis* was taken from Euripides by way of Racine and concerns the Greeks gathered at Aulis under the generalship of Agamemnon, ready to sail to Troy to avenge the rape of Helen. The gods are angry (there are contrary winds) and demand a sacrifice of a daughter of Helen's race. Clytemnestra, wife of Agamemnon, is Helen's sister. Calchas, the priest, after consulting the oracle of Diana, says that Iphigenia, Agamemnon's and Clytemnestra's daughter, is to be the one sacrificed. The plot concerns Agamemnon's agony, torn between his duty (an oath) and paternal love. After various complications, Iphigenia is saved at the last minute by Diana and is reunited with Achilles, who loves her.

Gluck in his overture wished to show the various conflicts in the drama. Although he took his initial theme (Example 7-1a) from

Example 7-1

Gluck, *Iphigénie en Aulide* (1774)

an earlier opera, *Telemacco*, its clashing dissonances most effectively portray Agamemnon's state of mind and his dreadful choice. Later (*b*), there is a series of peremptory unisons by the full orchestra to represent inexorable fate in the form of Greek soldiers, ready to sail, demanding the gods be appeased. A lighter, more lyrical theme is the feminine element, striving to placate the men (*c*). A plaintive oboe lament forms another strong dissonance against the first violins as a portrait of the desolate Iphigenia, torn between duty to her elders, the laws of her race, and loss of life (*d*). Gluck combines these elements into a magnificent orchestral picture which leads directly into the opera. Mozart and Wagner were so impressed with this music that one tried to make it into an independent piece (Mozart) and the other reorchestrated it for his own purpose (Wagner). While this practice of linking the overture to events in the opera did not mean that every future opera adopted the same procedure, it at least demonstrated an ideal for unity which was to have a lasting effect.

Mozart's overtures to his well-known operas carried forward Gluck's pattern. There is nothing quite so gay and sparkling as the

Figaro overture which sets the mood for the comedy to follow. The opening threatening D minor chords of the *Don Giovanni* overture tell listeners of the Commendatore's death at the hand of Don Giovanni; the stone statue and its appearance at the final banquet; and the Don's descent to the flames of hell. But the Allegro (D major) following this introduction puts us back into the world of opera buffa where a good part of the work belongs. The overture to *Così fan tutte* is all merriment and mischievous spirits, and it even includes the three-note descending figure which Alfonso sings toward the end of the opera in describing to Ferrando and Guglielmo how the ladies "change their loves a thousand times a day . . ." and "so do they all" (*così fan tutte*), which the young men repeat. In the overture to *The Magic Flute*, Mozart introduces us to the mysterious realm of Sarastro with the opening three trombone chords— Tamino's knocks on the door of the temple. The Allegro theme is comedy (as Papageno and Papagena are in the opera), but a theme given fugal treatment which deepens and makes serious the comedy. There is great variety in Mozart's inventiveness, even under stress: the overture to Don Giovanni was written the night before the first performance!

For most of the nineteenth century, composers felt that a long and complex overture was an intrusion and distraction, that it delayed the central business of the evening, and that it was best not to expend too much effort on it. (Weber and Wagner were exceptions.) The Italians, particularly, often reverted to the idea that the overture was a pleasant diversion used to get the audience settled; consequently, overtures were a potpourri of tunes in the opera, much like the overtures to today's musical comedies. An example is the overture of Donizetti's *Don Pasquale* (1843). Rossini often has some of his finest music in overtures, many of them played today while the operas themselves are forgotten. In *Semiramide* (1823) he actually incorporated themes from the opera into a symphonic structure. Although the *William Tell* overture has been overexposed as background music for films, television, and radio, it is still a stirring and effective piece of music if one can block from his mind the Lone Ranger and his faithful Indian, Tonto.

Verdi rarely wrote large-scale introductions to his operas. His two last works, *Otello* (1887) and *Falstaff* (1893), have no introductions at all but go right into the first scene. Most of his other introductions are entitled "preludes" and simply foreshadow the atmosphere of the opera—sometimes by direct quotation of themes. Two of the best are the Preludes to *La traviata* (1853) and *Aida* (1871). In *La traviata*, Verdi emphasizes two themes in an Adagio of only 49 measures. The first (Example 7-2a) is the plaintive, mournful phrase

Example 7-2

Verdi, *La traviata* (1853)
Prelude

(a)

(b)

Example 7-3

Verdi, *Aida* (1871)
Prelude

(a)

(b)

that comes at the beginning of the last act when Violetta realizes she is in the last stages of consumption (tuberculosis) and has not long to live. Verdi makes this theme a premonition of death to tell us at the beginning that the work ends in tragedy. After a series of temporary modulations with this phrase, he comes to a long-held seventh chord on B, which leads to the passionate love theme sung by Violetta in Act II as she is about to leave Alfredo, her lover, at the instigation of his father, who says that Alfredo's liaison with a kept woman will lead to a family disgrace and prevent his daughter from marrying. This brief and striking melody (*b*), played here by the cellos, is only used once (24 measures) by Verdi in the opera, but it is a memorable summation of Violetta's and Afredo's love and, as such, is the central force of the work.

In the Prelude to *Aida*, there are two themes which spell out the essence of the drama and sum up the conflict which ends in tragedy. The first is the melody associated with Aida (Example 7-3a), the beautiful slave girl in Egypt (in reality, the daughter of Amonasro, the Ethiopian king) who falls in love with Radames, general of the Egyptian armies. Impelled by her father, who has been taken prisoner, Aida makes Radames reveal the secret route the Egyptian armies will follow to surprise the Ethiopians. Radames is condemned by the Egyptian priests to being entombed alive for treachery to his country, and he dies with Aida who has managed to join him. The priests' theme, played softly and unobtrusively in the prelude (b), is later transformed by Verdi into a thundering, accented melody in Act II, as the priests demonstrate their implacable desire to have all the captured Ethiopian prisoners slaughtered. These two musical ideas are played together in the prelude to show the struggle which will dominate the participants throughout the opera.

Richard Wagner spent a great deal of time and effort trying to come to grips with the overture. In his essay "On the Overture" (1840), he examined several of the well-known ones by Gluck, Mozart, and Beethoven and described how these works, in his opinion, did or did not accomplish their purpose. He saw clearly that Beethoven's *Leonore* overtures were dramas in themselves and almost supplanted the need for the opera, *Fidelio*; that Gluck's *Iphigenia in Aulis* and Mozart's *Don Giovanni* overtures did not sum up the drama but pointed out the chief conflicts without resolving or answering them.

Wagner's own operas show every conceivable type of opening, from the portrayal of a storm in *Die Walküre* (The Valkyries, 1870) as Siegmund seeks shelter from his enemies, to the full-fledged representation in symphonic form of the Mastersingers, Eva, and Walther in the Overture to *Die Meistersinger* (1868). One of his most interesting introductions is the Prelude to *Lohengrin* (note it is a prelude, not an overture), where the entire piece is a depiction of the Holy Grail. Lohengrin, as a Knight of the Grail, must return to its holy service because Elsa, his beloved, has asked the forbidden question of who he is and where he came from. The Grail has no direct part in the drama, but it personifies the mysterious force which impels Lohengrin to leave Elsa, and restores Gottfried, her brother, to her and to the throne of his country. The prelude has become a classic of orchestration: Wagner scored it for divided strings in their highest position, dwelling on an A major chord pianissimo to give the music the ethereal, angelic quality representative of the Grail (Example 7-4). The strings gradually descend, and winds are added as well as the lower instruments in the orchestra. The climax comes in a tremendous fortissimo two-thirds of the way through; the music fades away again, ending on the same tranquil note with which it began. The prelude is a tour-de-force of pure music and of the orchestra as the purveyor of operatic meaning without the help of the voice.

Incidental Music

Pure orchestral music in opera encompasses far more than the overture or prelude: ballet, off-stage music, marches, ceremonial pieces, and interludes. Some of the music is trivial; some is quite important, depending upon its weight and its place in the opera.

Dancing on the stage generally has been of two kinds: *social dancing,* enacted by chorus or cast members; and *professional dancing,* executed by the corps-de-ballet, either as a group or individually. Social dancing, which may be background to an action, has music incorporated in the body of the score. For instance, a cast member may be called upon to perform a few steps which will not tax his capacity to sing; obviously, a dance requiring much physical movement is generally impossible for a singer because breath and tone will be affected. One of the few roles, however, in which the singer must also be a dancer of almost professional skill is Strauss' *Salome* (1905), where the dance over John the Baptist's head has to be convincing. Dancing of various kinds (ball scenes, parties, fêtes) is fairly common and generally part of the function of the ballet. Sometimes, principal singers will join in; sometimes all other action will stop; sometimes, the main action will continue in the foreground. Composers have often lavished considerable effort on this part of the score because they knew that the music had to be constructed rhythmically with the dance in mind.

A good example of dancing as part of the plot is the final scene of Act I of Mozart's *Don Giovanni.* Three stage bands, the principals, and the chorus take part. Don Giovanni has invited Zerlina, Masetto,

Example 7-4

Wagner, *Lohengrin* (1850)
Prelude

and the villagers to his villa for refreshments and dancing. In the midst of their enjoyment, three masked people appear: Donna Anna, who suspects Don Giovanni of being the killer of her father; Don Ottavio, who supports her theory; and Donna Elvira, who seeks to expose Don Giovanni for making love and then abandoning her. They are asked to dance: Donna Anna and Don Ottavio do the minuet, proper for the aristocracy; Don Giovanni and Zerlina do a contradanza; Leporello gets Masetto to do a rustic country German dance. Mozart cleverly writes these three dances so they can be put together, if only for about 25 measures (Example 7-5). While the music is playing, Don Giovanni manages to get Zerlina offstage, where he intends to make violent love to her. She screams, the dance stops, and the stage bands are superseded by the orchestra. This combination of orchestral music on stage, singing, and dancing is a clever synthesis of differing elements, which is over so quickly the audience scarcely has an opportunity to realize its deftness and skill.

Professional dancing plays a different role in opera. It is usually part of a crowd scene or big triumphal celebration. Perhaps a king and queen are entertained by dancers, and the principals stop to watch the spectacle. Some of this dance music has become almost as famous as the opera itself; consider the "Dance of the Hours" from Ponchielli's *La Gioconda* (The Gambler, 1876) or the dances in Delibes' *Lakmé* (1883). Ballet has always been a French speciality, even in the early days of opera. Lully's operas are filled with ballets and dances, as are those of Rameau later and Berlioz later still.

Dancing and the music for it can be an important part of the

Example 7-5

Mozart, *Don Giovanni* (1787)
Dances

Example 7-6

Verdi, *Aida* (1871)

spectacle of opera; though primarily outside the action, it must not be entirely extraneous to what is taking place on stage. This is a matter of choreography and the skill of the composer. If the dancing is merely a tiresome distraction, then it might well be discarded; if it fits, then it is an integral part of the opera.

One of the most famous scenes in opera, where march music, ballet, and plot all come together, is the triumphal Act II finale in *Aida* with victorious Egyptian soldiers, headed by Radames, returning with Ethiopian prisoners from war. They parade in front of the Pharaoh, his daughter Amneris, and members of the population (officials, priests, slaves, citizens), who have opened the scene by singing a paean to Isis, the monarchy, and Egypt. As the troops file by, special trumpets and a stage band blare out a march tune that has left its imprint on generations of opera-goers and almost every high school marching band in the country. (Example 7-6a). Dancing girls appear, bringing the spoils of the conquered, and Verdi writes for them a considerable dance sequence with several attractive and memorable motives (*b, c, d, e*). The ballet fits into the scene in an appropriate fashion and is not distracting because the cumulative effect of the procession can be built through movement of the march and the dance.

Orchestral interludes in opera take several forms. They may be purely orchestral introduction to an aria or ensemble where the setting or mood of the characters about to sing is represented in musical terms before words are heard. The same function holds true for postludes: the summary after the event. Interludes may be strictly inter-scene or inter-act music when a curtain has been drawn to indicate change of time (or for the practical purpose of moving scenery). With the visual element withdrawn, the orchestra becomes the central part of the drama with music assuming the role of protagonist. In *Carmen*, Bizet wrote three "entr'acte" pieces for orchestra, really preludes in the conventional sense to the act following. The first one anticipates the melody Don José will sing to Carmen when he is released from prison in Act II; the second is incidental music taken from Bizet's previous *L'Arlésienne*; and the third is music of the bullring, anticipating the tragic scene of the last act. They all serve as musical supplement to the drama and give the orchestra opportunity to demonstrate its importance in the general scheme.

Aside from overtures and preludes, dance and incidental music, the orchestra has a dramatic function which is very important. occasions in opera when there is no singing, and the actors must indicate by gesture and motion the events taking place. These moments are critical because the composer must time his music to the action on stage; if it does not fit perfectly, the audience will mistake a meaning, laugh in the wrong place, or otherwise lose the flow of the plot.

What are examples of such "speechless moments" when panto- mime rules the action? One is the end of Act II of Puccini's *Tosca*, where Tosca stabs Scarpia, the police chief. She then has to get the passport out of his dead hand, extinguish the lights, and put candles on either side of his head and a crucifix on his chest, before the curtain falls. While Puccini does not specifically indicate that certain actions must take place during certain music, there is only so much time for Tosca to accomplish these actions.

Another famous orchestral interlude tied to gesture is the end of Strauss' *Rosenkavalier* where, after the young lovers, Sophie and Octavian, have embraced (Sophie dropping her handkerchief), and run off the stage hand in hand, the directions read: "Then the center door is opened again. Through it comes the little black boy [one of the servants], with a candle in his hand. He looks for the hand- kerchief; manages to find it; picks it up; then trots out. The curtain falls rapidly." The boy's movements are synchronized with 21 mea- sures of Strauss' music that lightly and deftly follow the boy as he accomplishes his errand.

Changing Role of the Orchestra Throughout operatic history, the role of the orchestra has fluctuated greatly. For some composers, it has been primarily accompaniment to the voice where the musical content has been centered. With some of the greatest opera composers, however, the orchestra has reinforced characterization and drama by being independent of the voice, not subordinate to it. It is especially effective in the use of dramatic irony: for example, to tell what a character is thinking when he may be speaking or acting differently. Such an accomplishment has not been confined to any particular age or time: Monteverdi, Handel, Gluck, Mozart, Verdi, and Wagner have all demonstrated it in their works.

This function of the orchestra is much more easily recognized in more recent music than in that of earlier periods. Verdi and Wagner are good examples. In early Verdi, the orchestra serves mostly as accompaniment by playing simple chordal blocks, by reinforcing harmonies outlined in the voice, and by not straying rhythmically too far from a pattern established at the beginning of a piece. Beginning with his great "threesome" (*Rigoletto, Il trovatore,* and *La traviata*), Verdi began to conceive of the orchestra as not only accompaniment but also as an independent unit that, by means of counterpoint, harmonic subtleties, and rhythmic differences, made the orchestra equal to the voice.

Wagner carried this evolution even further by giving virtual primacy to the orchestra over the voice in some of his operas, particularly *Tristan.* He did it not only by the accumulation of mere size (see p. 94) but through his well-known "leading motive" system, where a theme representing a character, object, or situation was heard in the orchestra and repeated in variation and transformation throughout the opera. In these circumstances, the voice became another strand in the fabric—vitally important, but by no means predominant as it had been previously.

This "development" has not been consistently adopted in the twentieth century. Composers like Richard Strauss have tended to give the orchestra the same weight Wagner did; others have felt differently and tried to restore more of a balance, even returning to an eighteenth century conception, as Stravinsky did in *The Rake's Progress* (1951).

The orchestra is no fixed musical element in opera, but one changing in function and size according to the style of the age and the composer's wishes. It can be musical accompaniment or musical protagonist—subordinate or speaking in accents of its own. Its tonal palette the composer draws on for color is almost as varied and responsive as the human voice. While the voice in opera is what most audiences come to hear, the seasoned listener will devote more and more of his attention to what is happening in the orchestra to gain richness and fullness in aural satisfaction.

SUGGESTED READING

Bekker, Paul, *The Story of the Orchestra,* Norton, 1936, published as *The Orchestra,* Norton Library paperback, New York, 1963. Not strictly on the opera orchestra as such, but contains many insights on the orchestra in general.

Carse, Adam, *The History of Orchestration,* 1925, Dover Publications paperback, New York, 1964. More technical, but a fine survey.

Lawrence, Robert, "The Orchestra in Opera." Five successive issues of *Opera News* (December 9, 16, 23, 30, 1967; January 6, 1968) entitled respectively· Ensemble, Play of the Winds, The Brasses, Kingdom of Strings, Beat of the Percussion. Brief but interesting summaries of the different orchestral sections as they pertain to opera.

8 Production of Opera

Producing an opera is far more complex and difficult than producing spoken drama. In opera all the normal theatrical components (scenery, costumes, lights, make-up) are present, but the pre-eminence of music brings a new dimension to each of these. The movements of singers, the coordination of orchestra to stage action, the shifting of scenery—all are determined by the flow of the music. Music is the drama's clock; no component within the play can move faster or slower than it dictates.

In a stage play the director coaches and rehearses his cast, but for the actual play he steps behind the scenes and lets the actors perform together at their own (albeit preplanned) pace. In opera there is always a conductor in the pit who directs both the orchestra and the singers on stage. He and the stage director have decided how the drama will be presented. Should their interests conflict, the demands of music generally win out, since the singers are singers first and actors second. Ideally, the conductor, the stage director, the scene designer, the technical director, and the singing actors will agree on artistic aims and coordinate their efforts. The result should be a genuine fusion of music and drama. Yet there is inevitably compromise—compromise with high intent so that the different elements create something greater than their individual parts.

Because opera has so many conventions and most opera productions are old, established ones, the greatest problem is to keep the production alive and see that it does not settle into routine. The danger of stagnancy is particularly great in the world's large opera houses where productions are costly and changes come slowly. Since most of these houses are committed to the repertory system where a season is announced, subscriptions are sold, and schedules are announced in advance, adherence to a routine is mandatory. There is little opportunity for experimentation. Most "name" singers today (and even the stage directors and scene designers) are travelers who stay at an opera house a few days or weeks. Singers playing the key roles change from performance to performance; even where there is opportunity for plenty of rehearsal, some of the principal parts must be assumed temporarily by understudies because the chief singers are not present. Gestures, movement, location onstage, and tempos of the music have to become standardized so that the production does not fall apart. A singer with time for only one rehearsal cannot suddenly be faced with "new business" for a performance. Productions become stereotyped so that everything can be put together in a minimum of time.

In many ways the Italian "stagione" system, where a production is given repeatedly for a limited period of time, is superior to the repertory plan. At least the cast must be in residence for the weeks the opera is being presented, and there is greater opportunity for teamwork. Stage personnel and technical directors are not under pressure to change their sets and stage business every night and they can concentrate on one thing at a time. The system may give the audience less variety from night to night, but it does create a more unified ensemble.

Both the repertory and "stagione" have disadvantages if they operate under the star system: famous singers who join the opera company for several performances may be good for the box-office but are not necessarily beneficial to the teamwork of the group. The impresario is in a dilemma. He knows that voices (well-known ones) are the big attraction of opera for the general public. The dedicated who are more interested in the production as a whole are in the minority. There is no easy solution.

Once a decision has been made to produce a certain opera, the singers have been hired, and rehearsals start, who are the people who make the production possible in the opera house and carry through the project from its initial stages to the finished product?

Musical Direction   Since the music is of primary importance, the natural start is with the conductor who supervises the musical details. His first task is to determine what will be sung and played in the work to be performed. Few operas have emerged unscathed over the years; there have been cuts in the music, transpositions of arias from one key to another, and other forms of rearrangement brought about by different productions, singers, and local conditions. Tampering with the music may seem scandalous, but it has been fairly common practice in the opera house. Illness, human vagaries, and technical difficulties make improvisation a way of life because no two performances are exactly alike. The composer's actual notes are generally respected, but traditions of various kinds have crept in and become a settled part of the routine—an omitted scene, cuts in a long solo, a pitch taken an octave higher or lower, changes in dynamics, a slowing or speeding up not indicated in the score. A few of these alterations may have been sanctioned by the composer himself when he heard a passage that might be improved; most, however, have been added after the composer's death. The conductor must decide how many of these interpolations he will abide by. Often he has no choice. The orchestral parts have been copied out to agree with an established production of the company. To change them or revert to the original conception would be too large a task in the time available unless the conductor has the kind of reputation which enables him to dictate his own terms.

Back of the conductor are several assistants who rehearse singers with piano, supervise interpretive details determined in advance by the *maestro* (the master or head conductor), and help pull the musical elements together. If the opera calls for a chorus, there is a chorus master who trains his group for their part of the performance. Once the production goes into orchestral and stage rehearsal, details must be agreed upon so there can be no confusion.

Conducting from an opera pit demands more professional skill and flexibility than does the direction of an orchestra in concert. The orchestra is more spread out because of the nature of the space, lighting is dim, and cues can be missed. The conductor has not only a full orchestra to supervise but all the singing on stage. Tempo changes with different stage situations, constant starting and stopping, transition from recitative to aria (and vice versa in older operas)—all demand secure baton technique. The conductor must be aware of singers' problems; yet he cannot allow too much gazing in his direction or the dramatic illusion is spoiled. Singers must obey his beat at all times and be aware of what he wishes. The conductor must achieve the proper balance of dynamics between the singers and the orchestra because being on top of the orchestra

"Once the production goes into   rehearsal, details must be agreed upon."
Josef Krips rehearses singers for Mozart's *The Magic Flute*. (Photo by Louis
Mélançon)

he has little opportunity to judge acoustics in the back of the auditorium. With knowledge and experience these problems are carefully worked out and solved.

Finally, the conductor must be fully aware of what is happening
on stage and why. He cannot concentrate solely on the music and let
the dramatic elements be slighted. Some conductors have become
so involved in stagecraft that they have insisted on being both stage
and musical director. (Rarely has this dual function been successfully
combined in one person.) When Wagner produced his later operas
in the Bayreuth Festival Hall, built to his specifications, he insisted
on letting one of his protegés conduct, so that he, the composer and
renowned European conductor, could assume full stage direction of
the work and be sure his ideas of acting and staging were conveyed
to the audience.

Stage Direction Equally important in opera are the stage director and the people who help to make the visual and dramatic production a success. This includes scene, lighting, and costume designers, and technical crew. The stage director is generally in charge of the purely theatrical elements in the opera: acting, movement on stage, and the entire mise-en-scène (settings, lights, costumes, and properties). Obviously, he and the conductor must work together to get the best results. The stage director generally has a vocal score of the music prepared with blank pages inserted opposite each page of music (the production book). On these pages, the stage action is written or diagrammed, so that there is no doubt about what is to occur on stage at any time with the music.[1]

The stage director has the problem of making actors out of singers, yet not allowing their vocal performance to suffer. Gestures and movements of the body have to be adapted accordingly. He has to determine how musical introductions and interludes are to be filled onstage and how much freedom can be allowed without detracting from the music. The wise director knows it is better to have singers motionless than to indulge them in excess movement. Pantomime plays a greater part in opera than it does in the theater, and the stage director must know how to use it effectively. He must also train a chorus or ensemble to look natural onstage, a problem not often encountered in the spoken theater. He must have a clear concept of style in scenery, lighting, and design so that these elements cohere. For this reason, his bond with the various designers has to be a close one.

In the early days of opera, the stage director as such never existed. The singers' positions on stage, their gestures, their relationships to each other were rigidly prescribed, and there was little departure from these norms. The more important characters were placed at stage right (left side looking from the audience) and the less important, stage left, in a tableau of two or more people. If the occasion demanded it, one actor could step a little in front of the others for emphasis. Stylization and symmetry were all-important. Arias were sung from the middle of a group; entrances and exits occurred on the ritornellos of the arias. Movements of the arms, legs, and head were stereotyped according to the emotion being portrayed; when

---

[1] Nathaniel Merrill, one of the Metropolitan Opera stage directors, writes, "I believe that all opera stage direction should spring from the music.   . Singers are not meant to be actors in the same sense as in the legitimate theater. My main function as stage director is to place singers in the position onstage where they can be most comfortable for singing." "The Making of a Director," *Opera News*, February 17, 1968, p. 8.

the singing started, the action froze so that there could be concentration on the music.

While it would be erroneous to declare that this picture was completely reversed in the nineteenth and twentieth centuries, the trend was certainly toward naturalism and lifelike action and away from formal representation. The hero or heroine had to die naturally; lovers turned to each other and not to the audience while singing— acting was no longer simply statuesque posing. Yet singing has always imposed certain limitations upon movement—limitations as binding today as 200 years ago. Breathing, phrasing, and enunciating cannot be effective if the body is in too awkward a position (for example, lying down or bent over). The nature of opera creates some formalities which will always remain.

In the twentieth century, the stage director has become an increasingly important figure in opera. This change has had both good and bad results. So many factors are involved in opera production there is generally a need for a dictator to coordinate individual elements on the stage. This is particularly true in an age where the ensemble is a frail reed. A strong personality can unify and blend the components if he is given the proper authority and uses it with tact and discretion. Yet what is probably most necessary is that the stage director be something of a musician. He must not only understand music and how it works but also be able to read an orchestral score, study it carefully, and see what the composer had in mind when he and the librettist wrote the opera. Then he and the conductor can speak the same language and discuss stage business together, so that the fusion of their efforts is a genuine collaboration.

The difficulty is compounded in an intensely visual age of television. Appearance has become the catchword, and music has suffered accordingly. Often well-known directors from the spoken stage have been brought to opera and have imposed their personal vision upon the spectacle without knowing much about music. In many instances, this new approach has helped to let fresh air into the stultifying atmosphere of opera. Although the experiments of Wagner's grandsons at Bayreuth may have included extremes (one wit said the characters in several productions needed seeing-eye dogs to find their way around an almost completely darkened stage), the positive attributes of their performances have outweighed the negative ones. On the other hand, some stage directors have gained such an exaggerated idea of their own importance in opera that they have refused to undertake a production unless their ideas are rigidly followed (even to changing the music). Too often these ideas have been "stage mechanisms" or "tricks" to catch attention, not ones to further the spectacle as a whole. In an art form that is

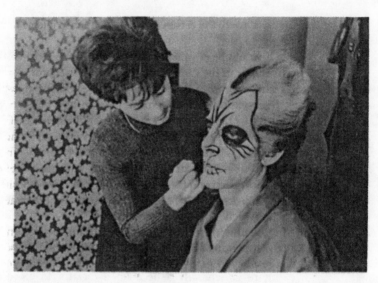

"Appearance has become the catchword." Making up Norman Treigle for Boito's *Mefistofele* is an art unto itself. (Photo by Beth Bergman)

a combination of arts, collaboration and cooperation are vital. To relegate the stage director to a minor position because of occasional excesses would be as foolish as to give the musical director sole authority over acting (if he knew little about it). The ideal situation is mutual respect for both the music and the drama so that one heightens the effect of the other.

Stage Setting

Stage setting depends upon the nature of the opera, the size and capability of the theater (space and acoustics), and the resources available. The problems are those which face any theatrical production, except that opera is often performed on a large stage, and the scenery must be adapted to a grander scale. Moreover, the majority of operas performed today are nineteenth and twentieth century works demanding choruses, rather large casts, and sufficient space for considerable movement. (Chamber opera with five or six characters is rather rare, but fortunately growing more common.)

Operatic stage setting began rather magnificently in the seventeenth century Some of the greatest architects and painters of the baroque era, including the Torelli and Galli-Bibiena families in Italy and Inigo Jones in England, devoted their energies to the problems of scenery for opera, masques, and plays. They helped create stage perspective by using a series of flat wings which could be pushed back and forth on runners from either side of the stage to create new scenes in a hurry. They also designed sophisticated cloud machines which could bring down the deus ex machina who reconciled the warring elements in a happy ending. Previously, perspective was largely a matter of a painted backdrop which remained stationary. Movable seventeenth century "wings," borders, and shutters were two-dimensional but very flexible (at first, they were controlled by hand, but later, winches were used to get better coordination). A clearer division between audience and stage was created by an actual proscenium, not just a painted one. Usually there was no curtain; any change in scenery was merely a quick movement of the flats. The numerous scenes in seventeenth and eighteenth century opera librettos did not necessarily mean a new setting but rather the arrival or exit of a character. Because there was not much space in the sides of the early theaters, a good deal of the action took place far forward, sometimes on an apron going out into the orchestra space. Candle and oil lamps illuminated the sets.

In the eighteenth and much of the nineteenth centuries, the existing apparatus was only refined. As sets became more complicated, they became three-dimensional; there was much greater demand for realism. Consequently, curtains had to be constructed and pulled, so the sets could be moved about unseen by the audience (not in full view—the delight of the baroque theater). Singers and actors moved away from the front of the stage and became part of the scenery. Costumes were adapted to the historical period portrayed, and great care was taken to create a representational and realistic effect. With three-dimensional scenery came larger flats, and then electric lights which supplanted gaslight. More space was needed backstage to handle the equipment. In the early theater, the proportion of space in front of the proscenium to that in back was about 1.1; in the twentieth century, the formula has become something like 1.3, with three-quarters of the necessary area being backstage.

The basic concept of a stage setting independent of what transpired on the stage changed toward the end of the nineteenth century. Instead of creating a picture and having the singing actors wander about it as best as they could, attempts were made to interpret the opera through the dramatic impact of the stage picture. Scenic effects were related more directly to the human figures within them, and a setting was not complete until the singers had taken their places on the stage. This theory of stage design became prominent just after Wagner's time through the writings of Adolphe Appia (a Swiss), Gordon Craig (an Englishman), and others. Adolphe Appia, himself a devoted Wagnerian, wrote two books on the aesthetic principles of modern stage design. *La Mise-*

en-Scène du Drame Wagnérien (The Staging of Wagner's Music Dramas, 1895) and *La Musique et la Mise-en-Scène* (Music and Stage Setting, 1899). Most of what Wagner's two grandsons, Wieland and Wolfgang, presented on the German stage in the 1950s and 1960s came directly from Appia, with the refinement of more sophisticated and complicated lighting. In general, Appia wished to unify a stage setting by suggesting mood and atmosphere to enhance the dramatic values of a performance. To him, a three-dimensional painting on stage was false, particularly when the scenery needed full light to get its maximum effect. Rather, the stage was to be a flexible unit shaped around the characters. This meant the stage floor was broken into slopes and planes, hummocks and hills; objects were cast in shadow and not in full light. If the moment was heightened, light was focused and directed on the persons or objects creating this moment. The stage became a microcosm of the world and not a toy, cardboard theater with light spread equally over everything. Light gained a fluidity and an ability to represent light and shade which was almost the counterpart to the music.

Unfortunately, many of Appia's concepts for opera have been adopted only in part, though they are now commonplace in the theater. Since opera is so traditional and loath to experiment, new ideas in stage development have come slowly. Many new opera houses are constructed following the same pattern as the ones evolved centuries ago and the stage setting is apt to be equally old-fashioned. There are hopeful signs among the some of the less well-established companies abroad. This spirit will have growing influence.

The Opera Theater

Physical surroundings may not determine the success or failure of any given art, but they can enhance or detract from a performance. From the beginning opera has been an intensely social art, and the opera theater has had a powerful effect upon the nature of the spectacle.

The history of this kind of theater mirrors opera development itself. By the early seventeenth century the operatic audience and singers were already separated by a fixed proscenium; and two-dimensional scenery, set up on runners, could provide perspective and recede into the background as necessary Private boxes or loges mounted in rows one above the other evolved because of social distinctions engendered by an aristocracy who demanded not only privacy but decoration and splendor. This architecture continued into the eighteenth century, as can be seen by the eighteenth century theaters (La Fenice, Venice—1755; San Carlo, Naples—1737; La Scala, Milan—1779) which survive today. These tiers of private boxes are far from the democratic Greek amphitheatre, where the sight-lines and acoustics were excellent from every seat and as many as 15,000 people could be accommodated at one sitting. The opera house made no pretense of serving the general public; it fulfilled its own select purpose.

Only in the late nineteenth century did the European opera house begin to change. In 1876, with the financial help of King Ludwig of Bavaria, Wagner designed and built his "ideal" opera theater for his own music in Bayreuth, Germany. This new opera house did away with boxes and had an amphitheatre auditorium with bench-like rows of seats rising steeply from the stage. The decor was simple and each seat had an unobstructed view of the stage. The orchestra pit was lowered out of sight. The curtain parted from the center; and

"The opera house made no pretense of serving the general public." George Cruikshank's cartoon, drawn in 1818, depicts both the interior of a private box and the "dandies" who can swoon in it with ample privacy, space, and personal attention. (Courtesy of the Raymond Mander and Joe Mitchenson Theatre Collection, London)

A Dandy fainting or — An Exquisite in Fits.

the auditorium, which had always been partially illuminated, was darkened during a performance. These innovations, commonplace today, were revolutionary in Wagner's time.

After World War II, many European opera houses had to be rebuilt after they were destroyed by bombing. Some architects experimented, drawing on the Bayreuth model for their new theaters. Yet Vienna, Milan, and East Berlin rebuilt their old grand opera houses (with enlarged backstage space), demonstrating how the old baroque model could extend its influence into the twentieth century. Even the new Metropolitan Opera house at Lincoln Center in New York is a compromise between the old and the new; it retains the private boxes on the lower levels.

Many of the new opera theaters in Germany (Cologne, Frankfurt, Hamburg, and Mannheim, among others) have adopted more democratic seating arrangements, using mainly orchestra floors and balconies. Some have included a compromise box arrangement: a mixture of balcony and old-fashioned private boxes that satisfies the older patrons and gives a slight air of tradition to the theater.

Naturally the greatest changes in the opera theater have come backstage, where technical advancements have brought revolving stages, elevator stages, turntables of all kinds, plastic scenery, and much more. Lighting has become an art unto itself: floodlights, spotlights, and overhead projectors, at the side, front, back, on the floor, can brighten, fade out, and suddenly reappear, controlled from a central console. Lighting rehearsals, as a consequence, have become as essential as dress rehearsals. Extra space for side stages, scenery storage, elevator bridges, etc., have become mandatory. New German opera theaters have wisely restricted their seating capacity (Hamburg—1650; Cologne—1360; Berlin Staatsoper—1800), which they can do because of the large number of performances they give and careful calculations about their attendance. The main Italian, French, and English opera houses are larger (Paris—2150; Covent Garden, London—2000; Rome—2500; La Scala, Milan—2800). In the larger theaters, chamber opera or experimental opera is a rarity because the public is conservative and prefers its old favorites.

The theater, then, has a major influence upon the nature of opera produced. Large traditional houses help to perpetuate the grand spectacle which has become a synonym for opera itself. Yet the future of such sumptuous production is uncertain. It would be much healthier if opera were put on a less lofty pedestal, if it drew its support from a larger segment of the public; if it were accepted as a community undertaking to which one went as regularly and unceremoniously as to the neighborhood movie house; if it were housed in a building less grandiose and more practical to run. Then musical drama might attain the recognition and the backing it deserves.

Economics
The costs of production (orchestra, singers, costumes, maintenance of house, etc.) have been so great that there has generally been some form of *subsidy*. In the early days of opera, subsidy came mostly from princes, kings, or the aristocracy. The audience was a narrow segment of society, the entertainment not designed to have a broad appeal. The number of opera houses (from seven to twelve at different periods) in seventeenth century Venice has always been cited as a marvel of musical culture at an early date. Yet these opera houses held about 300 people at most. There was no chorus or ballet and generally only 10 to 15 singers. The theaters were supported by various Venetian noble families who either owned the theater or owned the boxes in them and rented them for substantial fees. The boxes were handsomely equipped with anterooms as well as forward seats, and were more often meeting places for diplomacy, gossip, and intrigue than places to view the opera. The general public was allowed in the pit (mostly standees) but was treated as an appendage to the whole operation.

Early eighteenth century opera in London was a shareholding enterprise in which certain of the nobility guaranteed fixed sums for the production of opera; for this they received stock which made them part-owners. Even with a presumably secure financial base (and an added subsidy from the king), the Royal Academy of Music (1720–1728) had to cease operations because expenses were so much greater than income; there was bickering among the singers, and the public got tired of hearing opera in a language (Italian) they could not understand.

Subsidy, then, is essential if opera is to survive. In Europe and South America today, governments support productions. They contribute enough money for the opera house to break even; thus they assume responsibility for the inevitable deficit. In Germany and central Europe, where there is an opera house in almost every large city and in many medium-sized ones, national, state, and city funds are available. Yet in the United States, there is no regular federal or state subsidy for opera except from some state Arts Councils which provide funds. Local governments may aid community operas; but this support is, at best, intermittent. The Metropolitan Opera in New York is able to survive only through large private donations, some minor tax relief, and the contributions of the public at large. During the 1969–1970 season almost 1000 people were employed by the company in various capacities. This number included singers, chorus, orchestra, ballet, conductors, stage directors, managerial officials, stagehands, office personnel, wardrobe department, box-office men, ushers, ticket-takers, and porters. The budgeted deficit for the following season before contributions was $4,600,000. Under these conditions, it is a miracle the opera company can survive. The same is true on a lesser scale for Chicago, San Francisco, Los Angeles, and other large opera undertakings in the United States.

Further factors make commercial opera in the United States a hazardous undertaking. Union wages are among the highest in the world, and more unions are involved in opera (orchestral musician's union, chorus union, ballet union, stage unions) than in the ordinary theatrical production. A strike from one union can paralyze the whole operation. The budget is tight, and rehearsal time is at a premium. Moreover, there are very few small companies which can train and prepare personnel for larger companies the way farm teams can train players in professional sports. Most native American singers must get their training and experience abroad. Also, since opera is largely regarded as an exotic and esoteric art in the United States, there is little sense of public participation. Opera-going is a rare event rather than the habit it is in many European countries. Each production must make a greater initial impact to hold its audience.

While the picture in Europe is by no means completely rosy, the difference is striking. National, state, and local subsidy is taken for granted in Germany, Austria, Switzerland, Italy, and most of the countries in eastern Europe. There is subsidy in Spain, Portugal, France, and England, though not on quite such a handsome scale. West Germany has about 130 subsidized theaters of which some 60 are devoted to opera alone. Austria has a population of approximately 7 million people (less than New York City); yet it supports two full-time opera theaters in Vienna, not to mention other Austrian cities. Because these state subsidies are guaranteed on a regular basis (annually or for longer periods of time), long-term planning is possible, and an air of stability permeates the operatic scene. More time is allowed for rehearsal, and more than one or two new productions a year are possible. As a rule, the operas are performed in the native language of the country, so that they have greater popular appeal. (This policy is changing in cities like Vienna, Munich, Hamburg, and Milan where the original language of the opera is often heard; but the average German opera house still sings Verdi in German, just as Wagner is heard in French in Paris and Italian in Italy.) If this policy of translation had been adopted in America, the history of opera in this country might have been different.

While it is unlikely that American opera houses will be granted any substantial subsidy in the near future, there is hope. Distinctions must be made between different kinds of opera. When opera is mentioned, most people think of "grand opera" as heard at the Metropolitan Opera in New York: a lavish production with famous singers, of a familiar work in the original language. This type of opera has slim chance of survival without government subsidy because expenses mount too rapidly, and the capacity of the private purse to finance such a venture is increasingly limited. Of more promise is what might be called "community opera." A city decides it will help the local symphony orchestra (which is also the local opera orchestra) by giving a tax-free theater and sufficient funds for several modest opera productions. Stage and house expenses are deliberately kept low, the singers are young and do not demand huge fees, ensemble is stressed, and the majority of the performances are in English; thus the operas tend to be artistically and financially more feasible. Today there is a devoted and growing audience for this kind of opera. To them, opera-going is a natural part of their cultural life and the work itself is more important than the glamor of a magnificent stage setting or the fame of a highly touted voice. The success of the New York City Opera Company is an indication that community opera of this sort is practical, and perhaps the best solution for opera in the United States.

There is a third type of American opera: operas given by groups in colleges and universities. Although consisting largely of amateurs, these groups often give performances of professional quality and scope. Because they are subsidized by their educational institution, they can experiment in ways hardly feasible for commercial opera. For many contemporary opera composers, the college group is almost the only outlet he has for performance of his work. If opera is to be a growing, living art, new works must be produced and heard, otherwise the form becomes a fossil preserved in a museum.

The operatic situation, then, is not the same everywhere; many different factors determine the quality of a production. Seldom is it possible to reconcile each factor to everybody's satisfaction. Yet if opera is to survive under modern conditions, it must seek a solution that will weld these contradictory elements together. This can be done if the work of art (not an individual voice, a striking bit of scenery, a virtuoso conductor) is kept in mind. Whatever enhances the total effect of the opera will find its proper place within the production. Then the production becomes a successful one and a vital experience in the musical theater.

SUGGESTED READING

Eaton, Quaintance, *Opera Production, A Handbook,* University of Minnesota Press, Minneapolis, 1961; Reprint Da Capo, New York, 1974. A compilation of about 500 operas, giving plot synopses, necessary performing forces, and how musical material can be rented.

Goldovsky, Boris, *Bringing Opera to Life,* Appleton-Century-Crofts, New York, 1968. An excellent, practical book on operatic acting and staging with detailed outlines of scenes from familiar operas. Musical examples and diagrams.

Graf, Herbert, *Producing Opera for America,* Atlantis Books, Zurich, New York, 1961. Survey of various problems.

Mitchell, Ronald E., *Opera, Dead or Alive,* University of Wisconsin Press, Madison, 1970. Discusses the production and performance with chapters devoted to selected operas.

Volbach, Walther, *Problems of Opera Production,* 2nd ed., Texas Christian University Press, Fort Worth, Texas, 1967 A good general survey of opera production, aimed primarily at college opera workshops.

TWO HISTORY

9 Opera Before Mozart

Relatively little of our current repertory of opera was written before the late eighteenth century. If opera is primarily a revival of older works and not contemporary scores, then it seems unduly restrictive to limit the choice to those written in the last 180 years. Operatic history covers a period of some 370 years and only half of it is represented. Why are great opera composers like Monteverdi, Lully, Alessandro Scarlatti, and Handel so seldom performed on the modern stage? The superficial answer is that these composers speak in a language that is no longer relevant to modern audiences. But this reasoning is hardly convincing when baroque music is enormously popular and practically every Corelli, Vivaldi, or Geminiani concerto has been preserved for posterity in recordings. The musical language, then, does not seem to be the chief culprit. It may be the nature of the operas themselves: difficult, complicated, and often absurd plots, a formality in structure that another age finds puzzling, and great emphasis on a kind of bel canto singing which has largely disappeared. Whatever the reasons, the operatic stage is poorer because these composers are scarcely represented. Complaints about narrow choice (too much Verdi and Puccini, for instance) might well be mitigated by the inclusion of some of these early works. Proper care would have to be taken to insure a performance of both stylistic accuracy and of living musical theater. If the same loving artistic preparation lavished on a new production of *Tosca* or *Rigoletto* were directed to this end, the public might be surprised at the effectiveness of the result.

Monteverdi   One early composer contemporary opinion is regarding more and more highly is Claudio Monteverdi (1567–1643). He is certainly the first great master of opera; some musicians even label him "the creator of modern music." Yet his operatic reputation is based on only three works—the only ones to survive of twelve he wrote. Monteverdi spent most of his life in two Italian cities, Mantua and Venice. His early career in Mantua, from 1590 to 1612, was in the service of a Gonzaga at a ducal court. Most of his activity involved music for the chamber and the church—madrigals and other secular and sacred vocal works. But also during this period came *Orfeo* (1607) and *Arianna* (1608), both produced at court. They were operas in the new recitative form pioneered by the Florentine Camerata. Unfortunately, only a recitative and a lament survive from *Arianna*, but *Orfeo* has come down to us relatively complete, and in it there is a cornucopia of vocal and instrumental effects: sinfonias, ariosos, instrumental interludes, and quasi-arias (see p. 60).

After 1612, when Vincenzo Gonzaga died, Monteverdi sought other employment. In 1613 he was appointed *maestro di cappella* (choir director) at San Marco in Venice—one of the leading church posts in Italy. But Venice, a cosmopolitan city, was also a center of secular theatrical and musical entertainment, and Monteverdi took part in it. In 1637, the first Venetian public opera house, Teatro S. Cassiano, was opened; by 1641 there were four opera houses. These theaters provided a milieu for operatic production unsurpassed in its day; because of them, Venice became a center for Italian opera.

Of the stage works that Monteverdi wrote while in Venice little is known but the titles and the librettos. However, his last two operas, *Il ritorno d'Ulisse* (The Return of Ulysses, 1641) and *Poppea* (1642) survive and establish him as a great musical dramatist. *Poppea*, which Monteverdi wrote when he was 75 (a very advanced age for that day), is regarded as the supreme operatic work of the first half of the seventeenth century. It corresponds in musical imagination and power with *Otello* and *Falstaff*, which Verdi wrote in his old age. It is also one of the first historical operas, most of the previous ones being drawn from mythology. Roman history and the unbridled passions of Nero's world give the composer a unique opportunity to portray human character and emotion.

The subject of *Poppea* is the triumph of love without regard for morality, virtue, honor, or fidelity. The action is set in Rome of 65 A.D. and takes place within a 24-hour period. Nerone (Nero) loves Poppea and is determined to make her his Empress, in spite of the fact he already has a wife. Ottavia (Octavia), Nerone's wife, learns of his infidelity and vows revenge. She plans Poppea's death, with the help of the disillusioned Ottone who has returned unexpectedly. Ottone (Otho), one of Nerone's generals, also loves Poppea, but had been sent on a military expedition to get him out of the way. Seneca the philosopher (and Nerone's teacher) tries in the name of virtue and law to prevent the Emperor from carrying out his plan. Because of his opposition, Seneca dies. Various plots are exposed in the last act: Ottone's attempted assassination of Poppea is thwarted and he is sent to exile with Drusilla, a lady-in-waiting, who loves him; Ottavia is banished from Rome and put to sea in an open boat; Nerone publically crowns Poppea his Empress.

The virtue of the libretto is its concentration on human passions. There are sub-plots, but they are subordinated to the main issue of Nerone's love for Poppea and her ambition to be Empress. The subject is scandalous but historically true, as told by Tacitus. Betrayal, hatred, and all-consuming love lead to suicide, wrecking of lives, and self-abasement. Busenello, the librettist, has no moral to portray; he merely shows the characters as they are. Fortunately, he had Monteverdi to translate the story into music.

Dramatic characterization in the score is superb. Through the voice and its accompaniment, Monteverdi accomplishes his purpose in a singularly free and flexible way. There is almost no pure recitative, pure aria, or pure instrumental music; rather it is a mixture of all three—a kind of dramatic recitation which unites these elements and foreshadows late Wagner and Verdi. There are monologues, duets, and other kinds of ensemble but very little chorus. The orchestra is much reduced from that which Monteverdi used in his earlier *Orfeo*, where he had the resources of a wealthy court. The continuo instruments (two harpsichords, two archlutes, and a chitarrone) and the strings provide the chief support. Some winds are used, and a trumpet when martial music is desired. Yet emphasis is not on the orchestra but on the vocal line and the text. A great variety of voices is demanded: boy trebles, castrati sopranos and altos, as well as the usual men's and women's voices. A performance or a recording inevitably has to be a compromise because of the voices to be used and the orchestration, fragmentary in some spots, which has to be filled out. When done properly, however, the quality of this fine work is evident.

Toward the end of the opera, after Ottone and Drusilla have been sent into exile, Nerone swears to Poppea that she will be his bride

Example 9-1   Monteverdi, *L'incoronazione di Poppea* (1642)

(My heart's idol, at last the time has come when I shall enjoy my love)

(No longer have I a heart in my breast: you stole it from me, yes)

(Farewell Rome, farewell country, farewell my friends. Though innocent, I must leave you.)

that very day. Poppea, about to see both her ambition and her desire fulfilled, turns to Nerone and throws herself into his arms. She takes the lead vocally, and her passion is vividly portrayed in a line that feels the embrace of the two in its breathless pauses; Poppea can hardly get the words out in the emotion of the moment (Example

9-1*a*). But she catches her breath and goes on in a rush of rapid feeling that vocally starts high and gradually descends as if she were spent with the fullness of her happiness (measures 9—14). The music here is a flexible recitative, ideally adapted to Busenello's words. When Nerone joins in (*b*), the bass line and voice grow rhythmically more regular, as the two lovers sing to each other. Monteverdi joins the lines with a quasi-ostinato bass which acts as a unifying force in the musical structure.

Another striking moment in the opera comes when Ottavia takes leave of Rome and her friends. The vocal line again demonstrates the powerful emotion of the moment (*c*). Ottavia can hardly get off the main note; she sings it repeatedly. Even the word "Addio" cannot be sung consecutively because of her pain and torment. For seven measures the harmony is unchanging A minor. After bidding farewell to Rome and country, the parting from friends is made more poignant by a leap from d^2 to g^1 sharp*. Then she continues more conventionally, claiming her innocence. Monteverdi's musical perception, always at work, is a tribute to his ability as a musical dramatist.

Handel It is a long journey from Monteverdi to George Frideric Handel (1685—1759). When Handel's name is mentioned, the immediate association is *Messiah* and oratorios, not opera. Yet Handel spent most of his life as an Italian opera composer and only turned to oratorios in middle age.

He was cosmopolitan. Born in Germany and initially receiving the same kind of Lutheran church training that Bach had, Handel soon caught the operatic fever and went to Hamburg, one of the few German cities where opera already had become established. After writing three operas in the prevailing half-German, half-Italian manner, he went to Italy and spent his formative musical years there. The Italian operatic style was to influence him throughout his life. Eventually, Handel settled in London and, aside from several trips to Germany and Italy, remained there the rest of his life; in 1727 he became a British citizen. From 1710, the year of his arrival, until 1741, he wrote 36 operas for the London stage; before his death they disappeared from the stage almost entirely, and were not revived again until the early twentieth century.

In order to understand Handel's operas, some knowledge of the changes which had taken place since Monteverdi's death is neces-

*See Glossary· Abbreviations.

sary. During the second half of the seventeenth century, Italian opera became more formal in its structure—particularly, aria and recitative became distinct from one another. The singer also assumed great importance. It was the beginning of the bel canto era when the dramatic substance of the libretto was subservient to vocal and scenic display. In Venice and other Italian cities there were virtually no choruses and only a small cast of expert singers (see p. 76). In France, the local tradition of court opera with its lavish ballet and choral effects remained, but throughout the rest of Europe, the Italian opera seria was triumphant. It was the heyday of the *castrato* voice and fortunes were made by these men who were the idols of an adoring public. Librettos contained many subplots and comic scenes which depended for their effect upon mistaken identities, "truthful" accidents, coincidences, and an invariably happy ending—everything hurriedly straightened out in the last act. The public wanted to be entertained, not enlightened. They were captivated by the clever stage designs, the spectacular displays of the baroque stage, and the pyrotechnics of the human voice.

Under the influence of French classical tragedy, opera librettos took a more serious turn in the first quarter of the eighteenth century. Italian poets such as Apostolo Zeno (1668–1750) and Pietro Metastasio attempted to make the libretto a literary form. They used more elegant language, adhered to "the unities" (action within a set time and place), and omitted unnecessary complications and irrelevant comic characters in order to give logic and coherence to the plot. Since most of Zeno's and Metastasio's librettos were performed as operas at the Viennese court where both men were the king's official poet at different periods, there was much emphasis on honor, duty, virtue, and the magnanimity of princes and kings.

Handel's opera librettos were a mixture of the two currents: attempts to adapt an older seventeenth century libretto to the new Metastasian style. Sometimes the adaption was successful, sometimes not. One of the most popular of Handel's operas, *Giulio Cesare in Egitto* (1725), (see p. 59) is a work of this kind; it is derived almost entirely from a 1677 libretto of the same title. Some of the earlier spectacular battle scenes are omitted, much dialogue is compressed, minor characters are eliminated, and new arias have been added. The story has nothing to do with the Julius Caesar in Rome or the soldier on his campaigns every schoolboy knows. Rather it deals with the same episode in his life that George Bernard Shaw used as the source for his play, *Caesar and Cleopatra*.

In the opera, Caesar has pursued Pompey, his traditional enemy, to Egypt. Pompey is murdered there by King Ptolemy, who is warring with his sister, Cleopatra, for the throne. Ptolemy tries to win

Caesar's favor by presenting him with Pompey's head. Appalled, Caesar joins forces against the tyrant with Cornelia, Pompey's widow, and her son, Sextus, who are intent on revenge. Cleopatra uses her own obvious attractions to allure Caesar. Sextus finally kills Ptolemy, and Caesar is acclaimed as conqueror and as lover of Cleopatra.

The opera is largely a succession of arias and recitatives, but Handel does not hesitate to vary the pattern at great dramatic moments. Like Monteverdi, he incorporates a mixture of forms into a large and powerful scene, increasing dramatic impact because of departure from the norm. He also writes strikingly beautiful da capo arias which sum up a mood or emotion with stunning effect. Vocal ornamentation done with taste and skill on the repeat lifts the music to a higher plane.

In the third act of *Giulio Cesare*, Caesar, by throwing himself into the sea after Egyptian conspirators have tried to murder him, has narrowly escaped death. He has managed to reach the shore and now believes himself abandoned with no hope of support or rescue. The scene opens with an orchestral introduction, the ritornello of the chief aria which Caesar sings. It also represents the calm after the storm of his flight. It is based on the instrumental figure of measures 15 and 16 in Example 9-2a, and for 22 measures Handel manages to convey both the peace of the setting and the lapping of the waves on the sand. When Caesar sings, he first tells in calm accompanied recitative what has happened, and how glad he is to be alive (not shown). Then as his desperate plight grows more apparent, his accents become more jagged and breathless (a) as he asks a series of rhetorical questions, punctuated vehemently by the orchestra. The contrast of piano and forte measures toward the end of the recitative (measures 12 and 13) show his increasing distress. But the breezes will perhaps bear him to his beloved Cleopatra and assuage his turmoil.

The first part of the aria that follows (measures 17 and 18) is a lovely lyrical moment in the midst of difficulty. Then Caesar's troubles crowd back on him and what would normally be the second part of the aria becomes accompanied recitative again with reminiscence in the orchestra of the motivic "wave" figure between outbursts of the voice. Yet the power of love is deep, and he returns to his memory of Cleopatra in a repeat of the first part of the aria. Handel's imaginative musical conception transcends the ordinary seria conventions and molds the scene into living drama.

Another magical moment occurs at the beginning of Act II when Cleopatra is trying to bewitch Caesar. The orchestral introduction calls for alternating orchestras, one in the pit and one on the stage.

Example 9-2

Handel, *Giulio Cesare in Egitto* (1725)
Act III, scene 4

(But where shall I go, and who will give me help? Where are my troops and my legions? How shall I find my way through to eventual victory? Must the monarch of the world wander alone on these deserted sands? Sweet breezes, oh, take pity)

(I adore you, pupils and arrows of love; your sparks are lodged in my breast;)

The first has the usual string complement, but the second contains oboe, viola da gamba, harp, and theorbo plus other strings and bass. Cleopatra's aria (b) is an outpouring of love, assisted by lovely strains from the two orchestras. There is a second part to the aria, but before Cleopatra can return to the ornamented da capo, Caesar, deeply enthralled by the spectacle of the beautiful Queen, interrupts the course of her song by a recitative. It lasts only a moment but serves to show his emotional reaction to both sight and sound.

There are equally striking places in other Handel operas. Hard things said about baroque opera ("concert in costume," etc.) are by no means always justified, but the conventions of it have to be understood, and these conventions have held back popular acceptance. Baroque opera was primarily aristocratic; it was geared to an aristocratic audience and at its best in a sumptuous setting with emphasis on noble actions and rarefied singing. Expert performance was needed to achieve full effect; anything less showed the seams. By the middle of the century opera seria was regarded as old-fashioned, and the time had come for a change.

The "Reform" of Opera in the Eighteenth Century

In the course of its history, opera has gone through a series of reforms. These reforms have been considered necessary because music has always tended to overbalance the drama. Music, by capturing attention, can bring the plot to a standstill and even make the drama seem superfluous; yet the overpowering force of music in opera has been exaggerated. Composers and librettists have been the first to see that their work did not flourish in an atmosphere where either music or drama was strictly subordinate to the other (see Chapter 1). When change came, the creators of opera were ready for it.

Changes of styles in art come gradually. A new or different technique may originate with one man but only be taken up slowly by others. But the ripple in the pond does spread, and the style of the new work becomes common parlance. Gluck's reform operas, first given in Vienna in the middle of the eighteenth century, are an example: audiences knew they were hearing something new, but the form took time to be absorbed. Later in Paris, when some of these works were presented with new music and scoring and in French rather than Italian, their innovative force was felt.

The Italian opera seria as written by Scarlatti, Handel, and a host of others, was dominant in Europe in the first half of the eighteenth century. These operas were as popular in St. Petersburg and London as they were in Florence or Naples. The nationality of

"Baroque opera was primarily aristocratic; it was   at its best in a sumptuous setting." Pietro Domenico Olivero's painting portrays the interior, in 1740, of the Royal Theater in Turin during a production of Francesco Feo's *Arsace*. (Courtesy of the Civic Museum of Turin, Italy)

the composer had little to do with what he wrote; musical language and style followed an international pattern. Emphasis was on polished Metastasian Italian verse sung exquisitely in arias by a virtuoso singer (see p. 31). Metastasio developed extraordinary skill in making these conventions rounded and complete. But his language, beautiful as it was, had a bloodless quality. His dramatic situations, carefully suited to the singer, lacked passion and variety; action was largely limited to the recitative delivered dramatically with only continuo accompaniment. There was very little ensemble because the audience wanted to hear the singer alone. Characterization was built in a series of "pure" moods (rage, love, hate, jealousy, compassion) expressed musically in the arias—the sum of a person's arias was the sum of his character. Great artistry was displayed in polishing these arias into jewels of musical and artistic expression but their formality was too removed from life. Composers wanted to break away from the inevitable aria-recitative-aria succession, as Handel did, and to overthrow the inevitable da capo aria designed primarily for the singer, not the drama. They also wished to use the chorus to comment and to take part in the action.

Italy itself influenced operatic reform through the rise of opera buffa—not strictly comic opera in the English sense, but a more earthy, popular entertainment that dealt with everyday situations, not just affairs of royalty. Its progenitor was the *commedia dell'arte* (the Italian native comedy). Much of the impetus came from comic *intermezzi*, interludes given between the acts of opera seria in Naples and other Italian cities. Often in local dialect, these bright little entertainments (*La serva padrona*, "The Maid as Mistress," 1733, by Giovanni Battista Pergolesi (1710–1736) is always cited as typical of its kind), drew on popular songs and dance tunes to parody the older opera and make the buffa characters more distinguishable in a moment, not over the period of the whole opera. Fast, comic repetition of words developed a different kind of recitative—the rapid, secco variety—as near to speech in music as the Italian language could get. In these intermezzi, joy, wit, and humor were more desirable than elegance, and above all there had to be fast pacing to make the action move and come alive. Arias, ensembles, and popular songs were thrown together at the end of an act to create an uproarious conclusion. From this came that artistic achievement of Mozart, the finale of continuous music, which was so powerful an influence on later opera.

GLUCK There was nothing in Christoph Willibald Gluck's (1714–1787) early career to show he was cut out to be a reformer or innovator. Born in

Bohemia (one of those shifting areas in central Europe which has been German or Czech at various times in history), he may have been of Czeck stock; his father was a forester in the service of various German princes. Gluck himself was given a good education, particularly in music. After secondary school at a Jesuit college, he matriculated at Prague University and then decided to pursue music seriously. He first served as a chamber musician to Count Lobkowitz (an ancestor of the man who befriended Beethoven 70 years later). In the 1730s and 1740s, Gluck's travels took him to Italy where he wrote operas that were performed in Milan, Bologna, and elsewhere. On one trip (1745–1746), he went to London, where two of his works were heard. During these years, Gluck was no different from any other conductor and composer of the time; his operas (all Italian) were in the contemporary seria style, competent but not striking or original.

Around 1750 he married a well-to-do Viennese lady. This gave him leisure for composition and a respite from the arduous existence of a traveling performer. He settled in Vienna and in 1754 was appointed musical director to the court. The Austrian royal family were eclectic in their tastes. Aside from Italian opera, which was performed regularly, they were partial to French ballet and opéra comique. Gluck was asked to arrange and compose many of these entertainments for his aristocratic audiences, and he acquired considerable proficiency in the French style, both serious and light. He also absorbed the Rousseauian doctrines of the Enlightenment: a desire to get away from the artificiality and formality of the past age and return to natural sentiment and simple feelings. The new classicism turned back once more to Greece and mythology as a source and inspiration.

Just at this time, a skillful Italian man-of-letters, Ranieri da Calzabigi (1714–1795) began to exert artistic influence at the court. Calzabigi, a jack-of-all-trades with literary ability, was excited by the new cultural forces of the day, and had spent some time in France. His own words in the third person describe how Gluck's first reform opera, *Orfeo ed Euridice* (1762) came to be written.

The then intendant of the spectacles of the imperial court, Count Durazzo, believed that Calzabigi (who had shortly before come to Vienna with some reputation as a poet) might have some opera books in his desk, and invited him to dispose of them to him. Calzabigi was obliged to accede to the request of a man of such weight. He wrote *Orfeo* . and chose Gluck to set it to music. Everyone in Vienna knows that the imperial poet, Metastasio, belittled Gluck, and that the feeling was mutual, for Gluck thought little of Metastasio's meticulous dramas. He was of the opinion that this high-flown poetry and those neatly manufactured characters had nothing that was great and elevated to offer to music   Gluck liked emotions captured from simple nature, mighty passions at boiling point. . . "[1]

The three men—Durazzo with political power at court, Calzabigi who shaped the libretto, and Gluck who wrote the music—were the begetters of reform. (Gluck later gave Calzabigi the major share of the credit for directing the venture successfully.) Yet what was this *Orfeo* that created such a furor? It was hardly unique in plot construction, the story is too simple. Orfeo, the great singer, whose music has power over animate and inanimate objects, appeals to the gods to restore his dead wife. They take pity on his suffering and are overcome by the beauty of his song. He may go to Hades to fetch her but cannot look at her until they are clear of the gates of the dreaded underworld. As he leads her out, striding ahead, Euridice doubts his love because he will not face her, and she implores the gods to send her back to Hades. Her lament is too much for Orfeo; he turns; she drops lifeless at his feet. In the Greek legend, Orfeo is torn to pieces by the Corybantes when he returns to earth, but in the opera Calzabigi had to have a happy ending. When Orfeo in despair tries to kill himself, Eros, the God of Love, stays his hand, recalls Euridice to life, and unites the lovers again.

The opera is a series of tableaux; it moves majestically from picture to picture. There is none of the dramatic action—wedding festivity, explanation, messenger with news of Euridice's death— that Monteverdi had in his *Orfeo*. But Gluck's music makes it a moving experience. Orfeo's role in the original Viennese production was taken by Guadagni, an alto castrato. When this version is given today the part is generally sung by a female contralto. When Gluck revised the work for Paris in 1774, the lead became a tenor. The work lost and gained something in its French version. The orchestration was richer and more varied but the key relationships were disturbed by the change to tenor. Eros was given a new (superfluous) aria to satisfy the Paris singer; some of the added transitional music was richer than the original. An ideal version of the opera might combine the best features of both the Italian original and the French revision.

The three most original features of Gluck's *Orfeo*, compared to opera seria, were that the recitative was only accompagnato with no secco; the arias were fitted more closely to the words with no da capos; and the chorus and ballet both had significant roles. Gluck concentrated on the main action (no side issues and complications), and he had only three characters. His music was deliberately statuesque and noble. The typically ornamented vocal line gave way to

[1] As quoted by Alfred Einstein, *Gluck*, Dent, London, 1936, pp. 66–67

melodies of inspired simplicity. The great danger in producing the opera today is that the grandeur becomes frozen and vividness is lacking, but this need not be.

Act II, for instance, is perhaps the strongest part of the work. It shows Orfeo at the gates of Hades. The spirits of the underworld, in answer to his questions, refuse to admit him, and in a series of terrifying "no's" bar his entrance. But the beauty of his song melts even the Furies, and the doors swing open to admit him to the beautiful light and splendor of the Elysian Fields where Euridice awaits him. This simple action is hardly enough to occupy a whole act, but Gluck through his music transforms it into a magnificent scene, famous in the history of opera. By repetition of phrases, changes in scoring, interplay of chorus and solo voice, the act builds to a powerful climax that makes the timing of the single action wonderfully right in its context.

The setting for the opening of Act II is the entrance to Tartarus beside the River Styx. An orchestral prelude (a series of thundering orchestral unisons) depicts Orfeo's knocking at the gates of Hell. His courage falters after he knocks, and the violins taper off in a hesitant diminished chord (Example 9-3a). Nevertheless, he tries again, his grief at the loss of Euridice pushing him on (a series of descending, dissonant suspensions). The chorus of dread Furies answers his knock in a massive outburst of pounding rhythm in octaves, ending on the dominant. They ask who the foolish mortal may be who dares to cross the barrier (b). The spirits surround him in a fiendish dance. The chorus repeats its question but adds another phrase of warning (ending on a diminished chord) about the terrible fate which awaits him unless he is a god (c). After more ballet, there is a modulation to E flat major from the incessant choral C minor. With harp accompaniment in triplets, Orfeo pleads his cause, to be answered each time by the terrifying "no's" from the chorus (d). He perseveres, and the charm of his appeal gradually gains an effect.

As Orfeo sings entreatingly, the Furies find themselves relenting. The gates gradually open as the chorus slinks away, muttering that they have been vanquished. The doors reveal the blessed realm of Elysium; and as the scene unfolds, the orchestra plays the famous ballet of the happy spirits who usher Orfeo into their

Example 9-3   Gluck, *Orfeo ed Euridice* (1762)

(a) Maestoso

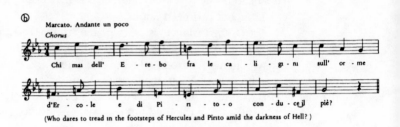

(b) Marcato. Andante un poco
Chorus

Chi mai dell' E - re - bo   fra le ca - li - gi - ni   sull' or - me

d'Er - co - le   e di Pi - ri - to - o   con - du - ce il piè?

(Who dares to tread in the footsteps of Hercules and Pirito amid the darkness of Hell?)

(c) Andante
Chorus

D'or - ror l'in - gom - bri - no   le fie - re Eu - me - ni - di   e lo spa -

ven - ti - no   gli ur - li di Cer - be - ro   se un dio non è!

(The dread Furies block his way with horror and the howls of Cerberus terrify him if he is not a god!)

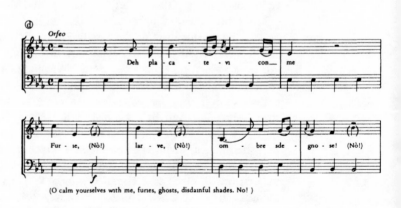

(d) Orfeo

Deh pla - ca - te - vi   con____ me

Fur - ie, (Nò!)   lar - ve, (Nò!)   om - bre sde - gno - se! (Nò!)

(O calm yourselves with me, furies, ghosts, disdainful shades. No!)

(e) Andante
Ballo
Fl. I + II

Vln. I
Vln. II

Vla.

Bass

140 The Magic of Opera

verdant fields (*e*). It is a magical moment, and Gluck makes the most of it.

Gluck's and Calzabigi's achievement made a great impression in France when *Orfeo* was revised there in 1774 as *Orphée et Eurydice*. His other operas performed on the Parisian stage were *Iphigénie en Aulide* (1774), *Armide* (1777), and *Iphigénie en Tauride* (1779). Their influence was felt much less in central Europe and Italy where the older opera seria and opera buffa held sway. Nevertheless, Gluck's works pointed to the future. They still represent a significant landmark in the chronicle of opera.

SUGGESTED READING

General   Palisca, Claude V., *Baroque Music*, Prentice-Hall, Englewood Cliffs, N.J., 1968. Has four good chapters on opera of the period.

Robinson, Michael F., *Opera Before Mozart*, Hutchinson University Library, London, 1966. A clear, intelligent survey with some musical examples not found elsewhere.

Worsthorne, Simon Towneley, *Venetian Opera in the Seventeenth Century*, Clarendon Press, Oxford, 1954. Emphasizes the spectacle as well as the music.

Monteverdi   Arnold, Denis, *Monteverdi*, Farrar, Straus & Giroux, New York, 1963. Good chapter on the dramatic music.

Arnold, Denis, and Nigel Fortune, *The Monteverdi Companion*, eds., Faber & Faber, London, 1968. Two chapers on the operatic composer by Robert Donington and Janet E. Beat.

Handel   Dean, Winton, *Handel and the Opera Seria*, University of California Press, Berkeley, 1969 Series of lectures that embrace all of Handel's art.

Dent, Edward J., "The Operas" in Gerald Abraham, ed., *Handel: A Symposium*, Oxford University Press, London, 1954. The best brief survey

Lang, Paul Henry, *George Frideric Handel*, Norton, New York, 1966. Biography, but most of the operas are discussed.

Gluck   Einstein, Alfred, *Gluck*, Dent, London, 1936. Biography with considerable discussion of opera.

Howard, Patricia, *Gluck and the Birth of Modern Opera*, St. Martin's Press, New York, 1963 Gluck's techniques of composition.

Newman, Ernest, *Gluck and the Opera* (Reissue of original 1895 edition), Gollancz, London, 1967 Still a fine book on the subject.

10 Mozart

Wolfgang Amadeus Mozart (1756—1791) is one of the few composers to whom the title "universal genius in music" is applicable. Whether it be concertos, symphonies, chamber music, church music, or opera, his creative efforts are among the greatest in all music, and he crowded them into a brief lifetime of 35 years. But if any part of the field of music could be said to be his favorite, it was opera. His letters to his father bear this out. One dated Mannheim, February 1778, reads: "I beg of you to do your best to get us to Italy. You know my greatest desire is—to write operas. . . . I envy anyone who is composing one; I could really weep for vexation, when I hear or see an aria. But Italian, not German. . . ."[1]

Two factors in Mozart's crowded life help to explain much about him as a composer. The first was his incredible ability at an early age. A child prodigy, a good deal of his musical training came at a time in his life when his contemporaries were playing with toys. This training was absorbed quickly and thoroughly, so that by the age of ten or twelve he had the musical sophistication and perception of an adult. The second grows out of the first: by reason of his precocity in performance he traveled all over Europe while still a child. Shepherded by his father on these travels (Leopold

[1]Emily Anderson, ed., *Letters of Mozart and His Family*, Macmillan, London, 1938, vol. 2, pp. 682—683.

Mozart was himself an accomplished musician—a violinist and the author of a treatise on the instrument), he heard and absorbed the best music of the day in Austria, Germany, Italy, England, and France. Consequently, he was in a unique position to draw on all the musical currents around him when he started to compose. People who worship Mozart profess to see a work of genius in everything he wrote, but a good deal of his very early music is superficial—the kind of music a very talented child might write. What is amazing is its technical proficiency. From the beginning Mozart's music always sounded well, even if the maturity was lacking.

Opera was the gateway to musical success in the second half of the eighteenth century. The musician's Mecca was still Italy. Although Mozart was performing before the crowned heads of Europe at the age of six, and by ten had been all through Germany, Switzerland, and Holland as well as to Paris and London, it was not until 1769, his thirteenth year, that he visited Italy. But this was not too great a deprivation because he undoubtedly heard all kinds of Italian opera on his travels. Also Salzburg, Austria (his home), was practically an Italian outpost. The court of the Archbishop in Salzburg, one of the old Holy Roman episcopates, used Italian as the official language. Leopold, and eventually Wolfgang, were both attached to the court in a musical capacity, and presumably had to have knowledge of the prevailing tongue. Stylistically, the musical language in Austria was Italian, particularly in Vienna, the capital, where the Hapsburgs' musical establishment had been Italian since the seventeenth century.

Because of opera's powerful appeal, it was natural that Leopold Mozart should encourage his talented son to write one. *La finta semplice* (The Pretended Simpleton, 1768), an opera buffa with stock comic characters, was meant for Vienna, but the Imperial Opera impresario was doubtful about an opera by a 12-year-old boy and the work never reached the stage there. It was heard the following year in Salzburg, but not performed because Salzburg had no theater. The music is lively and spirited but hardly notable. In 1768, he also wrote a little German operetta, *Bastien und Bastienne*, for Vienna. German music was still considered somewhat uncouth by the aristocracy, but was known by Mozart and others. This little work was put on in the garden of Dr. Anton Mesmer, the Viennese physician whose experiments with hypnotism gave us our word "mesmerism."

As a result of a tour to Italy in 1769, the young composer was commissioned to do an opera seria for Milan in 1770. The work, *Mitridate, rè di Ponto* (Mitridatus, King of Pontus), has some lovely music in it, but fails to hold together under the weight of an old-fashioned libretto. Other commissions on later trips were for serenatas, another opera seria, *Lucio Silla*, 1772, a further attempt at buffa, *La finta giardiniera* (The Pretended Gardener's Wife, 1775) for Munich, and even some incidental music to German plays. In all these works Mozart was feeling his way dramatically. The music has some beautiful moments, but it lacks that dramatic quality for which Mozart was to be known in his later operas.

The great works of his maturity can be grouped under the three categories that characterize opera in the late eighteenth century· opera seria, opera buffa, and Singspiel. In the first group are *Idomeneo, rè di Creta* (Idomeneus, King of Crete, 1780) and *La clemenza di Tito* (The Clemency of Titus, 1791); the second consists of *Le nozze di Figaro*, 1786, *Don Giovanni*, 1787 (not strictly an opera buffa but a "dramma giocoso"), and *Così fan tutte*, 1790; the third, *Die Entführung aus dem Serail*, 1782 and *Die Zauberflöte*, 1791.

The two opere serie have not been produced regularly until recently, having been overshadowed by Mozart's better known operas. *Idomeneo*, particularly, is a remarkable work. It was written with Gluck's French reform operas in mind, attempting to blend their simplicity and statuesque quality with the older Metastasian tradition of aria and recitative in succession and a work based on the supremacy of the voice. There are a number of choruses, ballets, and marches in the opera, and the chorus has an important dramatic role. The story concerns a period after the Trojan war when Idomeneo, King of Crete, is returning home with his fleet and is beset by a terrible storm. To appease Neptune, he promises to sacrifice the first person he sees on reaching shore. This person is none other than his son, Idamante, who is in love with Ilia, King Priam's daughter. After many misadventures in which Idamante is nearly killed by a sea monster and Idomeneo and Ilia threaten to sacrifice themselves, the gods take pity on the sufferings of the principals and let them live in peace. There are few ensembles and little secco recitative but a good deal of accompanied recitative. The orchestration, being Mozartean, is magnificent in its use of woodwinds and brass. The opera has been criticized because it contains heterogeneous stylistic elements, but it is a splendid achievement. *La clemenza di Tito* was written in a great hurry in the last year of Mozart's life when he had great financial worries and was already ill. Mozart had to compose it in eighteen days for the coronation of Leopold II, Emperor of Austria, as King of Bohemia, in Prague. It is a much more old-fashioned opera seria than *Idomeneo*, but it is by no means negligible; it is decidedly worth hearing.

Mozart's most telling operatic achievements were with buffa and

Singspiel, and there is no doubt that *Figaro, Don Giovanni,* and *Magic Flute* are among the greatest operas ever written, although their quality has only been fully grasped in the twentieth century. *Così fan tutte* has seldom been properly appreciated for what it is—the essence of high-spirited and artificial comedy. There are only six characters, and the work should be performed as a chamber opera and with the utmost delicacy. It loses its charm in a large opera house; the three men and three women seem like a group of puppets being manipulated at a distance. It is literally an opera of ensembles in every combination and for some Mozarteans the quintessence of his art. *The Abduction* came about because of the interest Joseph II, at that time Emperor in Vienna, had in developing a national drama and opera. It was adapted from a previous libretto and changed a great deal before production. Most of the singers had been trained in the Italian style, and Mozart wrote for them in that manner, interspersing the score with simple German songs. This jumble of styles means that the work does not hold together very well, but a good performance reveals a work of considerable charm and power.

One of the ironies about Mozart's great Italian operas is that they have never found the same acceptance in Italy that they have in German-speaking countries in inferior German translations. The subject of Mozart's relation to Italian audiences is a complicated one. Edward Dent[2] said Italians have always been puzzled by Mozart operas because they have never known when to applaud. There are very few bravura arias that end with cadenzas or a burst of excitement, and the listener may feel let down. Dent's remark may be considered a witticism which is too hard on the tastes of the opera-going public in Italy, but there is much truth in it. Mozart wrote operas which do not immediately appeal to the galleries. There are too many subtle touches, too intricate a combination of intellect and emotion to satisfy on one hearing. Like so many of life's deepest pleasures, Mozart's music must be savored and heard again and again. Even though Mozart loved the human voice, he could not subordinate everything to it. He was too much a complete musician, skilled in the ways of counterpoint and the orchestra, to place these important elements in an inferior position. His pride in his craft never let him descend below a certain level even in his lightest moments. There is a solidity of structure and content that rarely weakens its grip.

But his great operas, remarkable as they are musically, also provide that fusion of music and drama which is the ultimate goal

[2]Edward Dent, *Mozart's Operas,* 2nd ed., Oxford University Press, London 1947

of opera. For his significant Italian works, Mozart had the services of Lorenzo da Ponte (1749–1838), whose name should be honored with other great librettists in opera like Busenello, Calzabigi, and Boito. He knew the theater and how to get the best out of a libretto; he had the knack of creating language for music; he knew what to omit and what to include. He respected Mozart's wish to pare down, compress, and make everything move rapidly. Although a rascal (his memoirs make spicy reading), he was a thorough professional in the musical theater, and much of the magic in *Figaro, Don Giovanni,* and *Così fan tutte* can be attributed to him.

As stated earlier (see p. 36), Mozart had an uncanny ability to make his characters come alive through music. He made their dramatic situations seem real. He always collaborated with his librettists to help strengthen the drama; in comedy, he wanted the subjects to be gay and lively, but he could bring on tears as well as laughter. He was a very practical man of the theater, as his letters attest; he knew what would be effective on the stage and what would not. He knew the assets and liabilities of his singers and adapted his music for them. His timing was a marvel of conciseness and directness. With all his attention to detail, however, Mozart always had the unity of his work in mind whether it was a matter of key or the rounding-out of a character.

He used the standard forms of opera—recitative, aria, ensemble, chorus—but molded them to his purpose. In the Italian opere buffe, his secco recitative is light, rapid, quasi-musical speech. Almost headlong in its dash, less measured and deliberate than opera seria, the recitative races along with only a few broken chords for accompaniment. Yet it is not superficial—the shape and thrust of the line still bring out character. Accompanied recitative is reserved for more emotional and dramatic moments; for the more serious characters (Donna Anna in *Don Giovanni*, the Countess in *Figaro*); or to make a transition between secco and a longer, more highly developed aria. Here the orchestral comment to the vocal line is the ingredient that paints the situation or delineates the character.

Although his arias, of necessity, are more static than the recitative, they are never stereotyped. Mozart can push the action forward by writing a quick second part which spells out a decision after a first-part contemplation. These two sections are generally contrasted by tempo—the first, moderate or slow speed; the second, an Allegro. The effect is that of a nineteenth century cabaletta without the contrivance of that form. Mozart's arias are captivating in their variety: cavatinas, ariettas, two parts, modified three parts, serenades, and, at formal moments, even the old da capo. They range from the quick, tuneful, and comic such as Example 10-1 (Figaro's farewell to

Example 10-1

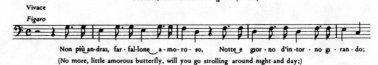

Vivace

Mozart, *Le nozze di Figaro* (1786)

Figaro

Non più an-drai, far - fal-lone__a - mo - ro - so,   Notte_e gior - no d'in -tor - no gi - ran - do;
(No more, little amorous butterfly, will you go strolling around night and day;)

Example 10-2

Allegro vivace

Cherubino

Non so più co-sa son, co-sa fac -cio,   or di fo -co, o-ra so - no di ghiac-cio,
(I don't know any more what I am and what I am doing. At one moment I'm on fire, the next, like ice,)

Example 10-3

Allegretto

Mozart, *Don Giovanni* (1787)

Don Giovanni

Deh vie - ni al -la fi - nes - tra,   o mio_____ te - so - ro,
(O come to your window, my treasure,)

Example 10-4

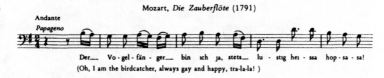

Andante grazioso

Don Ottavio

Il mio te-so - ro in - tan - to   an - da - te, an - da -

- te a con - so - lar
(Go to my love, meanwhile, and console her.)

Example 10-5

Andante

Mozart, *Die Zauberflöte* (1791)

Papageno

Der__ Vo - gel - fän - ger__ bin ich ja, stets lu - stig hei - ssa hop - sa - sa!
(Oh, I am the birdcatcher, always gay and happy, tra-la-la!)

Example 10-6

Larghetto

Sarastro

In die - sen heil' - gen__ Hal - len kennt man die Ra - che__ nicht,__
(In these sacred halls there is no revenge,)

Cherubino as he goes to the army—a tune withheld by Mozart until the last minute for fear it would become too popular if heard beforehand and spoil its effect in the first performance), to the adolescent fancy of what Cherubino feels like to be in love (Example 10-2). Then there is the smooth, accomplished, almost seductive serenade by Don Giovanni in "Deh vieni alla finestra" (Example 10-3) as against the sweetness of Don Ottavio's "Il mio tesoro" (Example 10-4). Mozart has a different style for his German arias than he does for his Italian: Papageno's "Der Vogelfänger bin ich ja" is a simple strophic song in three verses (Example 10-5); while Sarastro's "In diesen heil'gen Hallen" is almost a hymn (Example 10-6).

In both his Italian and German works, however, it is the ensembles (mostly duets and trios) that are Mozart's favorite means of revealing character. The byplay and contrast of male and female, of collaborators in action, the aristocratic and the peasant world, the fool and the schemer, two lovers, the haves and the have-nots—all these are brought into vivid focus by the magic of Mozart's music. The combination or separation of voices, the shape of their melodic lines, the orchestral accompaniment or commentary, the harmonic and rhythmic changes are the musical means at Mozart's disposal.

A striking example comes early in *Figaro*. Figaro, the Count's valet, and Susanna, the Countess's maid, are planning to marry. When the opera opens, they sing a duet in which each is engaged in different actions. Figaro is pacing up and down a partly furnished room in the Count's palace with a yardstick in his hand, making calculations as he walks. Susanna sits before a mirror, trying on a new flowered hat. She attempts to make Figaro see how pretty she looks, and finally gains his attention. In the following recitative, we learn that Figaro has been measuring the room to see where a bed might fit into it, and that the room is next to the Count's quarters (there are evidently two suites in the palace for the Count and the Countess). The Count has promised the couple this room after their marriage because it is commodious and it is convenient to his own—Figaro can get to him quickly. For some reason she will not disclose, Susanna does not favor this plan. Figaro is puzzled because there is no better room for them in the palace.

This is taken directly by da Ponte from Act I of Beaumarchais' *Le Mariage de Figaro ou Une Folle Journée*, 1784, on which the opera was based. In Paris the play was a harbinger of revolution because it made the aristocratic class look ridiculous in the eyes of its servants. Da Ponte greatly toned down the more political speeches by Figaro against his masters and emphasized the purely comic and human elements in the plot; for the most part he kept very close to the original. Beaumarchais' text at the point just described reads as follows.

Figaro. *You are turning down the most convenient room in the castle. It connects with both suites. At night, if my lady is unwell and wants you, she rings—and crack! there you are in two hops. Is it something that my lord requires? A tinkle from his side, and zing! I am at the ready in three strides.*

Suzanne. *Right enough! But when he's tinkled in the morning and given you a good long errand, zing! in three strides he is at my door, and crack! in two hops he—*

Figaro. *What do you mean by those words?*

Suzanne. *You'd better listen to me carefully.*[3]

Da Ponte kept close to the French but rephrased in this way:

Figaro. *If the Countess should call you at night—ding, ding!—just two steps from here and you'd be with her And then, if the Count should want me—dong, dong!—in three jumps I could be at his side.*

Susanna. *And so, if one morning, the dear little Count—ding, ding!—sends you three miles away—ding, ding, dong, dong!—the devil would bring him to my door—and then in three jumps—*

Figaro. *Be calm, Susanna.*

Susanna. *Listen, now!*

Figaro. *Tell me quickly.*

Susanna. *If you want me to go on, discard your nasty suspicions! They only wrong me.*

Figaro. *I want to hear the rest of it, but my doubts and suspicions make my blood blood run cold.*[4]

Mozart made this dialogue into a duet for strings and two each of flutes, oboes, bassoons, and horns. There is a threefold repetition of the initial phrase: first, in an orchestral introduction; then sung by Figaro; then divided between orchestra and Figaro. It is a smooth, gay little tune, at the end of which (the third time), the woodwinds imitate the sound of a high bell for Susanna which Figaro promptly echoes by singing (Example 10-7a). Like the classic sonata form of

[3]*Beaumarchais' Figaro's Marriage*, Jacques Barzun, trans., Farrar, Straus & Giroux, New York, 1961.

[4]Robert Pack and Marjorie Lelash, trans., *Mozart's Librettos*, World Publishing, New York, pp. 100–102. Copyright © 1961 by Meridian Books, Inc. Reprinted by permission.

Example 10-7

(If the Countess should call you at night—din-din; in two steps you would be with her.)

(And then, if the occasion comes that Count wants me—don-don; in three jumps I could go to serve him.)

(And so, if one little morning, the dear little count—din-din—sends you three miles away,)

a symphony or sonata movement, the key of F major (dominant to B flat) has been reached. The second full phrase is in the nature of an answer to the first statement, as Figaro describes the advantages of the room's location for him. The general contour of the melodic line this time is descending (the initial phrase was ascending), and the sound of the bell is characteristically masculine (bassoons and horns before "don-don") (*b*). The modulation is back to the tonic key (B flat major). Suddenly the orchestra slides down to G minor (contrast; also perhaps warning of trouble) as we hear Susanna's phrase three times in the same succession as Figaro's—first, orchestra; then Susanna; then orchestra and Susanna. This phrase (*c*) is rhythmically almost the same as Figaro's but with a different melodic outline. Musically, Mozart not only establishes a connection between the two but also distinguishes them slightly. A masterful touch is the varied pitching of the bell at the end of Susanna's phrase (*c*, measure 6) to indicate suspicion and innuendo. The emphasis is even stronger at the end of her following line ("and sends you three miles away") when both the female and male versions of the bell are heard one after the other. Figaro's phrase from the beginning (in the tonic) is now sung by Susanna only once to the words, "the devil would bring him to my door," followed by "and then in three jumps" on a high f^2*. But before she can continue, Figaro, who has finally understood the point of her remarks, interrupts in comic fright with the words "Susanna, pian, pian" ("Susanna, softly, softly," or as translated, "Be calm"), as the phrase is broken up between them, and the horns have heralded Figaro's realization with a strong sforzando. Susanna's "Listen now" and Figaro's "Tell me quickly" is marked recitative by Mozart and serves to separate the first section from what follows. The final part is based entirely on Susanna's and Figaro's last lines and is more a musical entity than a dramatic one. Susanna keeps saying she will only tell Figaro about the situation when he discards his nasty suspicions; but he, torn, wants desperately both to hear what is really happening and to reserve judgment. Mozart bandies their lines in a buffa repeated fashion until they both sing together, signifying that Figaro has agreed to listen quietly and Susanna has the upper hand. Mozart is at his best here in character delineation: Susanna, pert, knowing; Figaro, at first confident, preoccupied, then quite literally frightened (not angry, because he is a servant) at the implication of what Susanna is saying. After the duet, the audience learns in recitative about the situation: the Count has tired of his wife and seeks amorous adventure elsewhere; his eye has fallen on Susanna and he intends to make love to her. But Mozart already has succinctly and humorously anticipated this part of the plot in the duet and at the same time, given a memorable little vignette of the two characters. The accomplished musical dramatist is at work.

Later in the act there is a trio between the Count, Susanna, and Basilio, the music master, who is not averse to helping the Count in his adventures. An elaborate comedy has just taken place in the previous recitative. Cherubino, youthful page who is smitten with the Countess' charms, has come to Susanna's room to try to get some keepsake of the Countess from Susanna. He is surprised there by the Count but manages to hide behind a chair. The Count openly expresses his love for Susanna and begs her to meet him in the garden that night. After this declaration, Basilio is heard outside, and the Count, fearing compromise, hides behind the very chair where Cherubino has been. Cherubino in turn slips around into the chair itself and Susanna throws a cloak over him. Basilio, coming in, tries to further the Count's suit by implying he saw Cherubino around earlier and Susanna is carrying on with him. He also insinuates that

*See Glossary· Abbreviations.

Cherubino is smitten with the Countess and she returns his affection. This is too much for the Count, who pops up from behind the chair to confront the two.

In the trio, the Count says he will get rid of Cherubino at once; Basilio hypocritically declares he came in at an awkward moment when really he is delighted at the intrigue; Susanna is upset by the possible scandal. Mozart paints each character vividly with an individual phrase (Example 10-8). The Count's is blustering and peremptory, broken chords coming between short exclamations. Basilio's is unctuous and oily, a series of filled-in downward fifths in a rhythmic pattern that personifies Basilio and his activities all through the opera (*b*). And Susanna's is all fluster and agitation with minor coloration and many passing notes (*c*). As the tension increases, Susanna starts to faint (or pretends to) in the dominant key second section, and the two gentlemen, temporarily deterred, show solicitude. As they lead her toward the chair where Cherubino is hiding, she rapidly recovers, stops them, and indignantly accuses the pair of mistreating her. In this classic development section (of a sonata form), the Count gradually gains the upper hand again and declares in quasi-recitative he caught Cherubino the day before in a locked room with Susanna's cousin, Barbarina. As he describes how he went searching for the young man around this room, he illustrates his mission by going to the chair where

Example 10-8

Mozart, *Le nozze di Figaro* (1786)

(What do I hear! That little seducer must go and be thrown out immediately,)

(I am here at an unfortunate time; excuse me, my Lord)

(What trouble, I am wretched, I am overcome with grief;)

Cherubino is hiding and lifting the cloak, to everybody's consternation—Basilio is delighted, the Count enraged, and Susanna quite frightened. They conclude their remarks individually and collectively in an ensemble which is a whirlwind of comedy.

Mozart portrays the scene with superb artistry. During the Count's narration, there are titters in the orchestra (rapid sixteenth note figuration) as if to prepare the audience for the absurd disclosure. As the Count approaches the chair, his vocal line utilizes Basilio's theme (Mozart telling us thereby the Count's actions are hypocritical in themselves?), and goes lower and lower until the orchestra settles on a low F (dominant of the key). This note is held for some time to create suspense (it is reached just as the Count is about to lift the cloak), and also to prepare for the recapitulation. At first, the three lines react differently, but then Mozart puts them together in an ensemble alternating sotto voce and forte that ends with a wonderful buffa coda, gradually fading away into three mocking double pianissimo chords. The result is a marvel of concise comedy

The literature on *Don Giovanni* is enormous, largely because the opera is *sui generis* and a tremendous achievement musically. Unlike *Figaro*, a pure comedy with a slight bittersweet taste, *Don Giovanni* contains both tragic and comic elements. It has elicited powerful comments from people as diverse as Kierkegaard (he saw in it the eternal riddle of mankind) and George Bernard Shaw. The Germans have written tomes on the psychological and symbolic meaning of the opera, using terms like "demonic life force" or "man's essentially evil nature tempered by society." The Don Juan story of a profligate nobleman who kills a man and then is dragged down to Hell by the stone statue of this man is a familiar one in older Spanish and Italian literature. It was never treated with much seriousness and even found its way into the Italian commedia dell'arte. One of its first forms was a drama by a Spanish monk, Tirso de Molina (1571–1641); plays by Molière and Goldoni were two of many that treated the subject. Each time the story was used, variants and additions were made (extra characters; different women Don Giovanni had seduced). By the late eighteenth century, it was well-known on the stage.

The immediate impetus for the opera came from Prague, where *Figaro* had been given with such success. Mozart was asked to write another work and he turned again to da Ponte for a libretto. Da Ponte, occupied with commissions for two other librettos, cast about for something he could do quickly and easily. He seized on a 1775 one-act libretto by Giovanni Bertati called *Don Giovanni Tenorio o sia Il convitato di pietra* (Don Giovanni the Rake or The Stone Guest) as a basis, but wrote his in a more elegant literary style.

The original intention from Prague was to have another *Figaro* with plenty of incidents, and opportunities for arias and ensembles for the singers. Da Ponte was clever in arranging such things and, in this case, had to do so because the opera had a limited number of dramatic actions: Don Giovanni's killing of the Commendatore, father of Donna Anna; Don Giovanni's invitation to dinner to the Commendatore's statue (erected in record time); the statue's arrival and the Don's descent to Hell; and the moral drawn by the surviving characters at the end. Interspersed are scenes with other characters: Leporello, the comic servant; Masetto and Zerlina, the peasants (Don Giovanni tries to seduce Zerlina); Donna Elvira, a former love whom Don Giovanni abandoned in Burgos; and Donna Anna (whose attempted seduction in the first scene led to her father's death) and her faithful fiance, Don Ottavio. Many of the incidents came from Bertati, but da Ponte invented a few himself.

With arias and ensembles (including a quartet and a sestet), Mozart clearly brings out the relationships of all these people. There is the same deft phrase, the unusual harmonic coloring, the concise utterance that characterizes *Figaro*. While the seria parts (Donna Anna, Don Ottavio, and, to a certain extent, Donna Elvira) are more stereotyped, Mozart gives them some glorious music to sing and recompenses for any loss in dramatic realization.

In *Don Giovanni* as in *Figaro*, Mozart makes a lasting contribution to opera through the construction of the continuous finale (already mentioned), a marvelous synthesis of diverse elements—aria, duet, trio, and consistently changing combinations. In the Act I finale at Don Giovanni's palace, there is a party to which the peasants have been invited. At this party many things take place: Don Giovanni's attempt on Zerlina; his pretense that Leporello is the culprit; dancing and entertainment for the assembled group; the arrival of three masked people (Donna Anna, Don Ottavio, and Donna Elvira); and their exposure and accusation of Don Giovanni. These events take place in a continuous musical fabric of great tonal and structural unity. In the final scene of Act II (*Don Giovanni* was compressed into two acts, compared to the four in *Figaro*) Don Giovanni is gaily entertained at dinner by three musical selections—two arias from operas by Mozart's contemporaries and his own "Non più andrai" from *Figaro*. Donna Elvira begs him to give up his dissolute life; he scornfully refuses, and as Elvira goes out the statue appears, summoning the Don to the nether regions. The statue's cold, icy grip from which there is no escape, the flames and disintegration of the set, and Mozart's powerful music combine in a memorable display of operatic drama. Leporello survives to tell the others of his master's disappearance, and they all comment on the wages of sin.

Mozart's music manages to mix tragedy and comedy in equal proportions, and the effect points up his extraordinary ability to make this difficult balance seem effortless.

The Magic Flute, Mozart's last great operatic work, is an experience in art which is difficult to describe because it transports the listener into a mysterious, magical, and supernatural world that loses touch with reality. There is less human characterization so prominently and delightfully portrayed in *Figaro* and *Don Giovanni*; the bizarre and the child-like in the libretto make reason subordinate. But the music dispels all doubts and transcends the everyday world. Gerald Abraham writes:

No one comes away from a performance of *Die Zauberflöte* worried by the muddled dramatic motivation or the violent contrasts of musical style, of buffoonery and solemnity, or by the lack of roundness in the character-drawing of even the most normal human beings in the opera, Tamino and Pamina. One is no more troubled than one is by the incoherence of a dream. When *Die Zauberflöte* has been experienced in the theatre, the final, total impression is of a de Quinceyian dream in which the ultimate secret of the universe has been revealed—only it has unfortunately been forgotten in waking.[5]

The story concerns two realms—that of the Queen of the Night (evil) and of Sarastro (good). Pamina, daughter of the Queen of the Night, is being held captive by Sarastro. Tamino, a prince, who has fallen in love with her picture, determines to free her with the help of a bird-catcher, Papageno. They are given a magic flute and a set of magic bells to help them. Tamino learns that Sarastro's realm is guarded by a Temple of Wisdom and Temple of Proof. He finds Pamina, but they cannot be united until he undergoes certain trials by fire and water. With the help of the magic flute, these dangers are conquered and the couple are joined together. Papageno is also promised a lovely bride if he can show courage and keep silence; with the help of the magic bells, he wins the day, and an ugly old woman who has pursued him becomes lovely Papagena.

Mozart poured some of his most beautiful and serene music into this score. Although the opera is in German with spoken dialogue, it contains German and Italian musical elements. Papageno and Papagena are the German comic figures. Sarastro's music and the

[5]"The Operas" in H. C. Robbins Landon and Donald Mitchell, eds., *The Mozart Companion*, Oxford University Press, New York, 1956, p. 312.

choruses of priests take on a religious significance, some of it clothed in Masonic symbolism, in which Mozart was then immersed. The Queen of the Night is opera seria coloratura. Her three ladies-in-waiting give the ensembles with Tamino (tenor) and Papageno (baritone) a warm, rich quality unique in Mozart's music. Again, the finales to the two acts are masterpieces of drama and music. Mozart not only rises above the inconsistencies and slight absurdities of the plot, but makes his audience take it seriously with an occasional smile. It is not too much to call the opera a masterwork.

Mozart, then, belongs among the elite in the operatic world. As long as the art is recognized for what it should be—the heightening of drama through music, his major works will hold an honored place. Time and change in fashions may bring another such eclipse of his operas as the one that overtook them in the late nineteenth century, but greater knowledge and familiarity will make this eventuality unlikely. Once known, these operas remain close to the hearts of those who cherish them.

SUGGESTED READING

Abraham, Gerald, "The Operas," in H. C. Robbins Landon and Donald Mitchell, eds., *The Mozart Companion*, Oxford University Press, London, 1956. A fine general essay

Dent, Edward, *Mozart's Operas*, 2nd ed., Oxford University Press, London, 1947, paperback, 1967 Scholarly, thorough, and illuminating. A great deal on the sources of the librettos.

Hughes, Patrick C. (Spike), *Famous Mozart Operas*, Hale, London, 1957

Letters of Mozart and His Family, Emily Anderson, ed., 2nd ed., 2 vols., prepared by A. H. King and M. Carolam, St. Martin's Press, New York, 1966. Perhaps the liveliest and most interesting of musical letters.

Moberly, Robert, *Three Mozart Operas*, Dodd, Mead, Apollo Editions paperback, New York, 1968. Detailed analysis of *Figaro, Don Giovanni*, and *The Magic Flute* but meant for the general reader. Should be read with vocal scores on hand.

Mozart's Librettos, Robert Pack and Marjorie Lelash, trans., World Publishing, Meridian Books paperback, New York, 1961. The five chief operas with German and Italian texts opposite the English.

11 Italian Opera in the Nineteenth Century

During the late eighteenth and early nineteenth centuries, opera in Italy became a popular art; in addition to the large cities, there were operatic performances in almost every town of moderate size in the Italian peninsula. Much of this popularity was attributable to the rise of opera buffa, which the common man could laugh at and enjoy without pretension. Intellectually, it made no great demands and was ideally suited to the Italian genius for wit, gaiety, sparkling dialogue, attractive tunes, and comic situations. Sunshine and the sap of life were imbedded in the music and the plot. Composers like Giovanni Paisiello (1740–1816) and Domenico Cimarosa (1740–1801), names largely forgotten by the general public, were masters in musical characterization, deft orchestration, and lilting melodies of this light art. Their operas were known not only in Italy but throughout Europe. Opera seria continued to survive mostly under aristocratic patronage in larger cities. But opera of either kind became a national passion, almost supplanting the theater and other musical entertainment. Audiences, intrinsically musical, took a personal stake in an operatic production, giving vocal vent to their prejudices and likes. This popularity had good and bad effects—good, in that opera became familiar, common, loved, not placed on a pedestal; bad, in that so much popularity inevitably led to dross, second-rate productions, and feeble creative efforts. To achieve its best results, opera has always demanded first-class voices and ample resources, not always available in small Italian towns. But local pride meant that an attempt had to be made. There is an amusing account by the French novelist Stendhal (*The Red and the Black*, *The Charterhouse of Parma*), a devoted adherent of Mozart and Rossini, of the typical Italian opera company of the day (around 1810):

A *contractor*—usually the wealthiest burgher of some petty township .
—undertakes to run the theatre in the town whose leading citizen he has the honour to be; so to start with, he forms a company, which invariably consists of: a *prima-donna*, a *tenore*, a *basso cantante*, a *basso buffo*, a second (female) and a third (male) buffo singer. Next, the *impresario* [i.e., the contractor] engages a *maestro* (composer) to write an original opera for him, having always due regard, in the setting of his arias, to the particular characteristics of the voices of the singers who are to perform them. The impresario then purchases a text (the *libretto*· always in verse), which may cost him anything from sixty to eighty francs, the author being usually some wretched *abbé* parasitically attached to one of the wealthier households in the neighborhood. . Next, the impresario . proceeds to hand over all the business management of the theatre to his agent, who is usually a lawyer, and in fact the same archscoundrel who manages his personal business in private life; while he (the impresario) is more properly occupied in falling in love with the prima donna; at which point, the great question which arises to tickle the curiosity of the entire neighbourhood is whether or not he will offer her his arm in public.

Thus "organized", the company eventually gives its first performance; but not without previously having survived a whole month of utterly burlesque intrigues, thus furnishing an inexhaustible supply of gossip to entertain the entire countryside. This *prima recita* is the greatest public happening in all the long, dull existence of the town concerned—so momentous indeed, that I can think of nothing in Paris which could offer anything like an adequate comparison. For three weeks on end, eight or ten thousand persons will argue the merits and defects of the opera with all the powers of sustained concentration with which heaven has seen fit to endow them, and above all, with the maximum force of which their lungs are capable. This *première*, unless blasted at the very outset by some scandal of positively catastrophic dimensions, would normally be followed by some thirty or forty others, at the conclusion of which, the company disbands. A run of this type is usually called a "season" (*una stagione*); and the best season is that which coincides with the Carnival (i.e., from December 26th onward). Any singers who have not been engaged (*scritturati*), usually hang about in Bologna or in Milan, where they have theatrical agents who make it their business to secure them contracts, and to rob them unashamedly in the process.[1]

The larger cities (Rome, Naples, Milan, Venice, Florence, Bologna) with their established opera houses and larger resources, could aim

[1] Stendhal, *Life of Rossini*, Richard N. Coe, trans., John Calder, London, 1956, pp. 104–105.

much higher, but even they suffered under the pressure of too many performances, the demand for new works, the politics of singers and impresarios, and the taste of the public wanting above all melody and melodrama. It was also an age when the singer still ruled the roost.[2] The composer's notes were hardly sacrosanct: they could be embellished at will; and it was not unusual for singers to substitute arias by another composer, arias they happened to like or thought fitted their voice better. Orchestral standards were not very high and discipline was lacking; the day of the powerful and dictatatorial conductor had not yet dawned—the composer still led from the harpsichord or piano. Audiences were vocal to the point of anarchy: if they liked an aria it had to be immediately encored; if they did not, there were hisses, boos, catcalls, and even refuse thrown at the unlucky composer. Another difficulty was the inclusion of ballets between the acts and at the *end* of the opera, making the performance a very long one. Yet these conditions spawned, if not nourished, the most famous Italian opera composers of the century—men like Rossini, Donizetti, Bellini, and Verdi. In spite of struggles, defeats, and discouragement, they asserted themselves and gave the world some of the finest examples of operatic art, at the same time improving standards and raising the level of performance. More than other composers, they fostered the name of Italy as the continuing cradle of operatic music.

Rossini Gioacchino Rossini (1792—1868), the first of his line in Italy, was remarkably influential because his music was individual and distinctive. His operas were a great success in their time, but until quite recently only one of his works has been heard with any regularity— *The Barber of Seville*. This lack is a great loss to the operatic stage because there is enormous variety and vitality in what he wrote. Although he stopped composing operas at the age of 37 (the reasons for which have been a great challenge to biographers and psychologists), he packed a world of experience into what he did write— some 38 operas.

His music is the embodiment of Italian grace, verve, and musicality. Once heard it is seldom forgotten: there is a spontaneity about it which defies analysis. Most of the attraction is in its melody and rhythm, the harmony being simple and often com-

[2] Stendhal says (obvious exaggeration) that Marchesi, a famous Milanese castrato, refused to perform unless his first entrance was made on horseback or from the top of a hill.

monplace. Above all, Rossini knew the human voice and its capabilities. He himself was a singer from childhood and his writing sets a standard for singability. His music is instinctive rather than intellectual; but Rossini, a first-rate orchestrator, also treated instruments with great skill. Because he was a self-taught musician from a humble background in the small town of Pesaro (east coast of Italy), he never paid much attention to his librettos and his works suffered from a series of bad ones. He was also a pioneer in the writing-out of ornamentation, so that singers (in an age dominated by singers) would not distort his vocal line. Ironically, he was afterwards accused of too florid decoration when what he wanted was the avoidance of excess in a practice which had been extempore.

From the musical standpoint his works are in need of reassessment. Because of *The Barber*, Rossini is thought of as a composer of comic operas. But well over half of what he wrote belongs in the seria or semi-seria category. An earlier age was able to hear *Tancredi, Otello, Mosè in Egitto*, and *Semiramide*—the outstanding seria ones—with some regularity. Most of his buffa operas were written between 1810 and 1816 when he was still a young man, he was one of the first to incorporate buffa conventions (ensembles, rapid moving finales, bass soloists) into opera seria. One of the first Italian romantic operas, *La donna del lago* (Lady of the Lake, 1819, adapted from Walter Scott), came from his pen, as did *Le Comte Ory* (Count Ory, 1828), a French comic opera (really an operetta) that had a strong influence on succeeding light opera in France. His last great operatic work, *William Tell*, (1829), also in French, was a herald of "grand opera," the type which was to dominate the French scene for almost a half a century. Rossini's genius was eclectic; he ought to be more widely recognized.

The public has always preferred his comic operas. Rossini's comedy is of a different order from Mozart's. It is more bumptious, more nearly a farce, with few ironic overtones. It possesses satirical humor but hardly ever verges toward the serious side as Mozart did in *Figaro* (for example, the Countess). The comedy is a game which everybody plays, and the characterization is most deft when the audience laughs—both with and at the principals. The pace never falters or the structure might fall apart. In it are the favorite *commedia dell'arte* characters: the shrewd young girl, the pompous doctor, the rascally servant—all familiar to Italian audiences. But Rossini through his music endows them with life: they are not puppets but people with breath, fire, and blood.

Il barbiere di Siviglia, 1816, was first known as *Almaviva ossia La precauzione inutile* (Almaviva or The Useless Precaution) so as to

"Figaro has entree to the Bartolo household as barber and general handyman."
Figaro (Rossini's *Barber of Seville*) practices his trade on Dr. Bartolo. (Photo by
Beth Bergman)

brook no comparison with an already famous *Barber of Seville* by
Paisiello. The libretto was put together by Cesare Sterbini after
Beaumarchais' *Le Barbier de Seville*, which was the companion
play to *Le Mariage de Figaro* and preceded it. Count Almaviva
(tenor) has seen a beautiful young girl, Rosina, (mezzo-soprano)
in Madrid and fallen in love with her without declaring himself.
He learns that she is the ward of a Dr. Bartolo (baritone) of Seville,
who keeps close watch on her and restricts her freedom. When the
opera opens, the Count is in Seville trying to serenade Rosina and
attract her attention with the help of some musicians. He meets
Figaro (baritone), who has been in Almaviva's employ but is now
in Seville as a jack-of-all-trades—barber, errand boy, quasi-sur-
geon, apothecary, and champion intriguer. (Figaro's famous aria,
"Largo al factotum," describes his many capabilities and is one of
the best patter songs in opera, with many word repetitions, reiterated musical figures, and worked-up crescendos, proceeding at
a breakneck pace.) It turns out that Figaro has entree to the Bartolo
household as barber and general handyman. Almaviva enlists his
aid in gaining access to Rosina without telling her his name and

rank: Figaro suggests he pretend to be Lindoro, a drunken soldier quartered on Dr. Bartolo from a visiting regiment. The opera describes the various adventures and comic event that lead to the Count's final success in wooing and marrying Rosina. Dr. Bartolo, determined to marry Rosina himself, is assisted by Don Basilio (bass), the music master to the household. Bartolo and Basilio are aware of the Count's designs but do not immediately see through his disguise. There are numerous merry contrivances: a letter to signify her interest thrown from the balcony by Rosina to Almaviva; a marriage contract to be signed by Bartolo so he can marry Rosina; the Count seeking entry a second time (the first failed), pretending to be another music master, Don Alonso, a friend of Basilio; a "singing lesson" with Rosina; and a storm that interrupts a forced entry of the house by Almaviva and Figaro after the first and second attempts have failed.

The first performance (February 20, 1816), in Rome where Rossini, on leave from engagements in Naples had gone to write an opera for the Argentina Theater, was nearly a disaster because of musical and political enmity against the composer. The second and subsequent performances, however, were highly successful and soon the opera became a favorite all over Europe. It has been one of the most popular operas in the repertory ever since, translated into many languages and produced everywhere. Its dash and musical wit have rarely been equaled.

Of the two acts, the first is probably superior for sheer pace and musical interest. One of the high spots is the duet when the Count is trying to enlist Figaro's help in his cause. Almaviva knows that Figaro is a rascal and that he cannot rely on him simply because of their previous association. The magic means to inspire cooperation will probably be money. At the mention of this commodity, Figaro immediately warms to the problem and promises to help.

Rossini is less formal than his predecessors in his treatment of ensemble. The division between recitative and songlike portions of the opera, whether aria, duet, trio, or other group, is still marked. But within the ensemble there is greater freedom in setting the words. Some lines can be more declamatory if the situation demands it. The text of the duet is:

Figaro. *You should disguise yourself   for example   as a soldier*
Count. *As a soldier?*
Figaro. *Yes, sir*
Count. *As a soldier? What good will that do?*
Figaro. *Today a regiment is expected here.*
Count. *Yes, and the Colonel is a friend of mine.*
Figaro. *Splendid.*

Count. *And then?*

Figaro. *Then, with a billet for lodging, that door will open. What do you say to that, my lord? Don't you think I've found the answer?*

Both. *What a wonderful idea! Lovely, indeed.*

Figaro. *But softly: here's another thought! (see what gold can do!) You must pretend to be drunk, my lord.*

Count. *Drunk?*

Figaro. *Yes, sir, just that,*

Count. *Drunk? But why?*

Figaro. *Because the guardian would be apt to trust somebody who is not quite in control of himself, one who is stumbling around with wine.*

Both. *What a wonderful idea! Lovely indeed.*

Count. *Well, then?*

Figaro. *To work.*

Count. *Let's go.*

Figaro. *Bravo.* (They start to leave in opposite directions.)

Count. *Oh, I forgot to ask you. Your shop. How do I find it? Where is it?*

Figaro. *My shop? You can't miss it Look There it is No. 15, on the left hand side, with four steps, a white front, five wigs in the window, on a placard, "Fine Pomade," a blue showcase in the latest fashion, and a lantern for a sign you will find me there, without fail.*

Count. *I understand.*

Figaro. *Now you better go quickly.*

Count. *And you be careful.*

Figaro. *I'll remember everything.*

Count. *I have faith in you.*

Figaro. *I'll wait for you over there.*

Count. *My dear Figaro.*

Figaro. *I understand.*

Count. *I'll bring with me*

Figaro. *A well-filled purse.*

Count. *Yes, the amount you want, but you do your part.*

Figaro. *Oh, have no doubt. Everything will go well.*

(Count and Figaro together)

Count. *Oh, what a flame of love I feel, messenger of joy and happiness. My soul burns with uncommon fire and pushes me on to greater things. This glorious moment inspires my heart.*

Figaro. *I already hear the clinking of coins gold is coming. It's already here. Also silver filling my pockets . It's already here, my soul burns with uncommon fire and pushes me on to greater things.*

The "volcano" of Figaro's opening line is anticipated in the comic sliding up and down of the strings, sotto voce, under his wide, delighted skips in the vocal line (Example 11-1a). Then the tempo changes to Vivace, and we are treated to a diverting little dotted and grace-noted tune with its delightful syncopated emphasis at the end of the phrase, followed by a series of cavorting triplets that dance and jiggle with the words (*b*). Figaro cannot let this go, and extends it to a cadence. As the Count is about to reply, the orchestra leads him in with a little bouncing figure (first two measures, *c*) which acts as a motive for the following dialogue. The Count repeats Figaro's phrase (*b*) in D major after his initial line, but his triplets are more formal, more dignified. When Figaro comes up with the suggestion of the Count becoming a soldier, the little bouncing motive leads it in, but the question-answer dialogue partly reverts to accompanied recitative (so the audience

Example 11-1   Rossini, *Il barbiere di Siviglia* (1816)

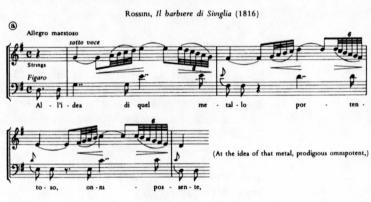

(Number fifteen, on the left side,)

will hear how the soldier plan will work). When they both are captivated by the idea, they sing in duet (mostly jaunty thirds) as the Italian words "che invenzione prelibata" (what excellent invention) are reiterated in buffa fashion. Figaro's second proposal for a drunken appearance finds the music similar to what has occurred during the soldier idea (short figure plus quasi-recitative). Figaro's answer to the Count's "why" is a musical rendition of how he should behave (*d*). The broken, uncertain vocal line with frequent rests and off-beat accents cleverly mimics the ongoing pace of the "well-oiled" soldier. This sends them off again into their gay musical refrain about what a fine idea the second plan is. As they begin a series of march-like chords, the Count speaks in recitative of Figaro's shop and asks him where it is. Figaro's pride as he points it out is nicely underscored by a chromatic scale rising to a held dominant chord. As the orchestra (Allegro, 3/8 time) launches into a typically Rossinian melody, irresistible in its vivacity and catchiness (*e*), Figaro rapidly describes on one note the shop's characteristics. This device of having the orchestra play the tune while the voice speaks a lot of verbal description not only gets through a considerable amount of text but keeps up the excitement. Here it is enhanced by a typical Rossini crescendo on a figure (*f*) ideally constructed for this purpose. The rest of the duet bandies these two musical figures back and forth with increasing intensity. Underneath rapid patter in the voices, a double forte conclusion is finally reached in a blaze of glory. It is Rossini at his best.

Other music in the act is equally attractive. Shortly after the duet, Rosina sings her famous aria, "Una voce poco fa," in which she declares her love for Lindoro (see p. 65). (The music was originally written in E major for a mezzo coloratura—a voice with low notes and a coloratura top. When high sopranos sing it, they generally pitch it upwards.) In spite of its coloratura, it fulfills a good dramatic purpose, describing how Rosina is determined to join her lover and outwit Bartolo. Later, Basilio tells Bartolo that the Count is reputedly in Seville, but he, Basilio, will blacken his reputation so thoroughly he will not dare to show his face. His bass aria, "La calunnia è un venticello, un' auretta assai gentile che insensibile, sottile, legger-mente, dolcemente incomincia a sussurrar" (Calumny is a little breeze, a very gentle zephyr, which imperceptibly, subtly, lightly, sweetly, begins to whisper), has become a bass buffo classic, not only for its text (a comic caricature of the old baroque simile aria) but for the way Rossini treats it. Basilio's deadly whisper becomes a cannon shot in the middle (E flat chord in the key of D) as two striking little themes (Examples 11-2*a* and *b*) work themselves into a whirling crescendo with telling effect.

The finale is a gem. The Count, pretending to be drunk, gets Bartolo's name all wrong on purpose, calling him Dr. Barbaro (barbarous) and even Dr. Somaro (a mule). He embraces him as a fellow doctor, saying that he, Lindoro, is the regimental veterinarian and blacksmith. When Bartolo goes looking for the order exempt-

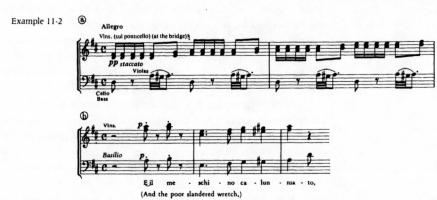

Example 11-2

ⓐ
Allegro
Vlns. (sul ponticello) (at the bridge)
pp staccato
Violas
Cello
Bass

ⓑ
Vlns. *p*
Basilio *p*

E jl me - schi - no ca - lun - nia - to,
(And the poor slandered wretch,)

Example 11-3

Vivace
Principals *sotto voce*
Mi — par — d'es - ser — con — la — te - sta
(My head seems to be [in a dreadful forge])

ing his household from quartering soldiers, Lindoro manages to say a few words to Rosina. When Bartolo finds the order, Lindoro flings it in his face, telling him to go to the devil. Then he tries to get a note to Rosina; Bartolo intercepts it, but Rosina pretends it is a laundry list she happens to have handy and manages to keep the note. Rosina is on the verge of tears, and Lindoro threatens to attack Bartolo for making her so unhappy. Figaro, coming to shave Bartolo, says the hullabaloo has attracted a crowd in the street (Marziale, C major to Allegro, E flat major). Bartolo gets more worked up (the ensemble has been joined by Berta, the maid, and Basilio to fill out the harmony and make a sextet), the noise increases, and finally the town police enter. Bartolo tries to get them to arrest Lindoro as an obnoxious, drunken character (back to C major Andante, then Vivace). The Count shows them his official document, disclosing his rank, and they hurriedly back off (A flat major), which manages to freeze the assembled company in the most delightful fashion, they not knowing what is coming off. Then everybody finds their tongues, and there is hopeless confusion (stretta of finale in C major). Rossini's octave theme for this concluding stage of affairs is unforgettable (Example 11-3).

| **Donizetti and Bellini** | The names of Donizetti and Bellini are bracketed in the history of opera because they represent the period between Rossini's cessation of operatic activity and the rise of Giuseppe Verdi, who was to dominate Italian opera from the middle of the century to its end. In reality, however, their careers and personalities were quite different. Gaetano Donizetti (1797–1848) was an incredibly fecund composer whose 70-odd operas are only a part of his total musical output, but a good deal of it has disappeared from the repertory. Vincenzo Bellini (1801–1834) lived only 34 years and wrote nine operas which were worked over incessantly. (This does not include unpublished works and revisions.) Both men did their best work with romantic opera, although Donizetti's *Don Pasquale* (1843) is one of the finest opera buffas of the nineteenth century, to be ranked near Rossini's *Barber*. Donizetti's *L'elisir d'amore* (The Elixir of Love, 1832), is a splendid Italian romantic comedy, and *La Fille du régiment* (The Daughter of the Regiment, 1840), a French opéra comique for Paris, is one of the best of its kind. Donizetti wrote five operas in French of which *La Fille* and *La Favorite* (The Favorite, also 1840) are the ones which survive. |

Although Donizetti wrote many farces and opera buffas, the

weight of his work was in opera seria and romantic opera. Most of these works had a historical or literary background, either French (for example, Victor Hugo, Scribe) or English (adaptations of Byron and Scott). Some of the familiar ones are *Anna Bolena* (1830) (English Renaissance history), *Lucrezia Borgia* (1833) (Victor Hugo), *Maria Stuarda* (1834) (Schiller and English history), *Lucia di Lammermoor* (1835) (Walter Scott), *Roberto Devereux* (1837) (English history), and *Linda di Chamounix* (1842) (French history). They made great use of choruses and ensembles fully integrated into the action, yet preserving the separate number aspect of earlier opera. There was much greater freedom in interlacing the various elements of recitative, aria, and ensemble into scene complexes, according to the necessities of the plot. Although recitative followed by an aria was still standard procedure, the recitative generally had orchestral accompaniment and was less routine. Arias were often a combination of two parts: cavatina (moderate tempo, lyrical mood), and cabaletta (fast tempo, action) to bring the song to an exciting conclusion. These terms began to be used in a very free way and were applied to almost any solo portion of the opera. There was emphasis on march rhythms in dotted figures (this came from Rossini) which gave the music a jaunty and self-confident air. These figures easily degenerate into a kind of dogtrot which raises a smile and recalls a third-rate band in the village square, but the music is effective. In the orchestra, military effects meant employment for the brass section—a handy aid with processions, temple scenes, acclamation of royalty, and crowd action. Ballet between the acts and afterwards was still popular and occupied much of the evening.

Bellini's operas (tragedies, no comedies) have the same characteristics as Donizetti's but are more delicate and less rough-hewn in their overall effect. Above all, Donizetti and Bellini need sympathetic and skilled interpreters; without them, their operas lose half their appeal. Interpreters, in this sense, means great singers, schooled in bel canto and the art of ornamentation, who can negotiate the treacherous fioritura with ease and conviction. Bellini opera, particularly, is an opera of surpassing and graceful melody—the essence of tuneful contour. Unless the vocal line carries a very special conviction, the structure holds up only with difficulty. On paper, much of the orchestral accompaniment and harmony looks thin and banal—arpeggiated chords, few inner voices, commonplace progression. But when the voice soars, the quasi-emptiness is forgotten, and the music has wings.

In spite of some slighting comments by critics on the weight of his music, Bellini was a very conscientious and careful craftsman who knew the Italian operatic stage well and how it could be used successfully. Born in Catania, Sicily, son and grandson of musicians, he was sent to the Naples conservatory for musical study. His first operas were presented there, but initial success came in Milan at La Scala with *Il pirata* (The Pirate, 1827); most of his operas had their first performances in Milan. Toward the end of his life, Bellini went to Paris to seek added recognition. Shortly after *I Puritani* (The Puritans, 1835) was heard at the *Théâtre Italien*, Bellini was taken suddenly ill and died in three weeks, to the consternation of the musical world.

By common consent, Bellini's masterpiece is *Norma* (1831), his next-to-last opera. He lavished great care on it, trying to get a fusion of words and music that would measure up to his ideal. By good fortune, he had the collaboration of Felice Romani (1788–1865), a good theater craftsman, who wrote most of Bellini's librettos, and some outstanding ones for Donizetti (*L'elisir d'amore, Lucrezia Borgia*). He did not construct his own plots but borrowed them from other sources, mostly French plays. The actions follow one another logically and motivations are generally powerful, although sometimes extravagant according to modern taste. His verses are no better than those of other librettists of the period, but they manage to be serviceable poetry for music. Bellini always said his debt to his librettist was a large one.

The action of *Norma* takes place in Gaul about 50 B.C. during the Roman occupation. The population are Druids, worshippers of nature, and Norma is one of their head priestesses. She has fallen in love with Pollione, Roman pro-consul, broken her vows of chastity, and borne him two children. She has managed to keep this fact hidden from the Archdruid Oroveso (her father) and the other priestesses. She has also prevented her people from waging war on the Roman invaders. Meanwhile Pollione has tired of Norma and taken up with Adalgisa, another priestess of the temple, who returns his love. He proposes to fly away with her to Rome. Adalgisa, tenderly devoted to Norma, tells her of her love for Pollione but learns that he was formerly Norma's lover. Because of this, Adalgisa refuses to go with him. Norma, in despair over Pollione's faithlessness, nearly kills her own children but decides to renounce Pollione in favor of Adalgisa; Adalgisa will not accept, nor will Pollione return to Norma. Warriors and the people gather to declare war against the Romans. Pollione is found in the temple and sentenced to death, but Norma, self-sacrificing to the end, confesses her love and her perjury of the priesthood and says she must be the victim. As she prepares to mount the funeral pyre, Pollione, overcome by her nobility, joins her in death.

Aside from its lyrical beauty, *Norma* has the virtue of sustaining considerable dramatic tension. The title role is a very exacting one: Norma is on the stage constantly; her voice must be that of a dramatic coloratura soprano, capable of singing a bel canto line and of giving it weight as well as feathery lightness in the upper regions. Emotional reserves are needed from beginning to end. Almost equally important is the role of Adalgisa, whose voice must blend with that of Norma in duets and yet be able to ornament on its own; the part requires a mezzo soprano with a large range. Pollione must be a rugged tenor with a good high tessitura. Without the support of these voices, production of the opera can hardly be contemplated.

Act I takes place in the sacred forest of the Druids. Oroveso tells the Gauls they are awaiting the rise of the new moon which will be announced by three strokes upon the sacred gong. Norma will then come to the grove, cut the sacred mistletoe, and, Oroveso hopes, arouse the people against the Romans. After an interlude, in which the audience learns from Pollione and his friend, Flavio, about Pollione's involvement with Norma and Adalgisa, the gong is heard and the people, Druid priestesses, Oroveso, and Norma come to the sacred altar. The group urges war, but Norma says the time is not ripe: the invaders are too strong. Rome will eventually fall, but by decay within; until then, they must keep the peace. The mistletoe is cut, and Norma sings a famous prayer to the goddess who lets the beautiful new moon shine upon them and gives them courage and faith.

Example 11-4   Bellini, *Norma* (1831)

(Chaste goddess, who makes silver these ancient, sacred trees,
turn your lovely face upon us unclouded and unveiled.)

Certain arias in opera have become so famous that a work is remembered when the air is mentioned. Norma's "Casta diva" is such an aria. This extraordinary, limpid melody (Example 11-4), which went through many revisions before attaining final form, is a mixture of lovely calm and mounting tension, reflecting the dichotomy of feelings within Norma herself—torn between her love for Pollione and loyalty to her own people. Its first part consists of two four-measure phrases which are both similar and different. The compound 12/8 meter and Andante sostenuto allow for a gentle stepwise ascent and descent within each phrase which makes the decorative notes between the initial b^{1*} of measure 1 and the second g^1 of measure 2 essential in the progression. Vitality comes through the rhythmic changes in the vocal line which impel it but give repose to the invocation. Particularly skillful is the way Bellini has the second part start a half step higher (measure 5) and reproduce exactly measures 1 and 2 except for the turn ("sacre") of measure 6. This written-out turn which has a tritonal leap and is minor in outline tinges the phrase with melancholy. But the next one-and-a-half measures return the melody to its original tonality (G major), although ending on the third (b^1) of the key. The third part, beginning on the upbeat of measure 8, immediately generates tension through its shorter, broken-up melody, by its E minor outline, and its two dissonant jumps from f sharp^2 to c^2. Before the tension can dissipate, it is gathered suddenly together (repeated "a noi volgi's") and run up to the high, syncopated, and accented b^2s (marked *sempre crescendo al ff*), which in turn reach their climax on the high c^3 and slowly sink in a series of almost agonized resting points that take two full measures to descend to the tonic note. Melodically, the central note of each period has risen upward to give added weight to the thrilling climax (measures $1-4 = b^1$; measures $5-8 = c^2$; measures $9-11 = e^2$). The contrast between these musical sections of the stanza show Bellini's ability both to write a glorious melody and to incorporate it within a dramatic context.

At the beginning of Act II, Norma is in despair. She has learned of Pollione's love for Adalgisa and of her own rejection. Being a woman of great passion and pride who sees nothing but ruin ahead, she has a sudden, terrible impulse to kill her children who lie sleeping before her. The act opens with an orchestral introduction which delineates Norma's mood: two thundering octave Ds at the outset anticipate the final tragedy; the cellos and bass softly outline an ascending D major chord ending in a delicate string—woodwind

*See Glossary· Abbreviations.

Example 11-5

(Both of them are asleep; they will not see the hand that strikes them. O, my heart, do not repent,
they cannot live. Here they would be in torment and in Rome suffer shame, a far worse torment.
Slaves to a stepmother__ no, never! They die, yes. I cannot go near them;)

reply, personifying Norma's natural tenderness and maternal love
for her children (Example 11-5a). After reiteration of this phrase
and some intervening material, the cellos play an extended theme
of grief (D minor), which will be heard later when Norma has
checked her violent impulse but still stands irresolutely over her
two sons (b). Finally, the orchestra dies out on a reiterated A in the
bass, and Norma speaks. Bellini's custom in writing recitative was
to let the voice sing alone as much as possible and have the orchestra
fill in musical comment between phrases with an occasional chord
below the voice to keep the singer on the track.

Norma's opening "Dormono entrambi" is sung entirely without accompaniment (c). The descending line is simple pathos as she describes their slumber, yet there is happiness in the mere possession of her offspring. The orchestra echoes her thought by playing the D major phrase of cello—bass and string—woodwind heard at the beginning of the act (a). But she still is agitated and the next phrase (d) shows this in the rise to the e^2 and its downward dissonant leap. Then comes vivid musical speech by means of short phrases and word emphasis in the vocal line: the single note of "Qui" (here); the breaking up of "supplizio, e in Roma" (torment, and in Rome), and "obbrobrio avran" (suffer shame); the sudden melodic change (E flat) and octave leap on "schiavi" (slaves); the veritable exclamation of "ah! no, giammai" (no, never). If she has raised her dagger to strike her children after "muojani, si" (they die, yes), the orchestra tells us in a series of limp and isolated seconds directly afterward (not shown) that her hand has fallen as she confesses she cannot bring herself to commit such a ghastly act (e).

The remainder of this moving recitative shows Norma again trying to work herself up to carry out her threat. But she fails even more dramatically just when she is about to strike. Overcome, she tells her confidante, Clotilda, to summon Adalgisa.

Although praised for his melodic ability, Bellini was also a skilled operatic dramatist and this passage demonstrates his fine hand in constructing an intensely vivid scene. He and Donizetti were quite capable of writing more than a series of pretty tunes. Their intrinsic operatic abilities were considerable and should be given greater recognition.

Verdi The name of Giuseppe Verdi (1813–1901) has become synonymous with Italian opera. The musical affection this great Italian has inspired in the hearts of his countrymen is as powerful today as it was in his own lifetime. His best known operas have had an extraordinary hold on the operatic stage not only in Italy but throughout the Western world. If *Rigoletto, Il trovatore, La traviata,* and *Aida* were withdrawn from production today, most opera houses would cease to operate. Since they were written these four have retained great popularity with the public. They represent a common ground on which critical opinion and public affection meet and agree.

Yet Verdi's reputation has not always been so high. In the early twentieth century, shortly after his death, he was barely tolerated by the *cognoscenti.* They considered his works crude and lacking in finesse. They admitted he could write a tune but said the orchestration of his early and middle operas sounded like a provincial Italian band; his arias were apt to be repetitive; and the plots he used were hopelessly melodramatic with gore and dead bodies their chief attributes. At that time, most of Verdi's best works were seldom performed. His first great success in Italy, *Nabucco* (1842), had all but disappeared. *Macbeth* (1847), *Luisa Miller* (1849), *Simon Boccanegra* (1857; 1881) and *Don Carlo* (1867; 1884) were mostly historical curiosities. *Un ballo in maschera* (1859) and *La forza del destino* (1862; 1869) were heard occasionally but never attained the popularity of the "big four." *Otello* (1887) and *Falstaff* (1893), completed when Verdi was 74 and 80 respectively, were admired but treated gingerly as "advanced" works.

Verdi lived to be a very old man (88), wrote 26 operas, and was active almost to the end of his life. His creative activity spans the nineteenth century and represents two or three changes in style. When he started to compose, Rossini and Donizetti were still very much alive, although Rossini had ceased writing operas. When Verdi died, Puccini had already written *Manon Lescaut, La Bohème*, and *Tosca*, and Wagner had been dead 18 years.

Verdi came from a peasant background, and it was only through his future father-in-law that he was able to go for a musical education to Milan from the provincial town of Busseto in Parma. His early years were a great struggle. Enough to daunt a lesser man and to stop all musical activity was the death of his young wife and two children within two years (1838–1840). Only his self-discipline and inner fortitude saved him. He gradually made a substantial name in the musical world and later became something of a national hero in Italy. But his career is one long account of battle and argument with impresarios, conductors, singers, and librettists to reach the standard of production we take for granted today. Not all the trouble lay on one side: Verdi could be a difficult, stubborn man; but when it came to musical matters, he was usually right. Although most of his operas were written and commissioned for Italian opera houses (largely Milan, Rome, Naples, Venice), he spent considerable time in Paris. In the mid-nineteenth century it was the artistic center of Europe, and it was natural for Verdi to desire recognition there—he only really attained it at the end of his career. He made several visits to London, but only one of his operas (a lesser effort) was composed specifically for England. There was one trip to St. Petersburg, the only long journey he ever took, for the debut of *La forza del destino*. *Aida* was first performed in Cairo, but Verdi did not go to see it.

Verdi cannot be fully understood if the age in which he lived is disregarded. His mature years were those of the Italian *Risorgimento,* of Cavour (with whom he had a personal friendship), of Garibaldi, and of the growth of modern Italy. The composer was an intense patriot and his early operas were regarded as harbingers of revolution, particularly when they dealt with oppressed peoples overthrowing the yoke of their masters: the Jews against the Babylonians in *Nabucco*; the French against the English in *Giovanna d'Arco* (Joan of Arc); the Sicilians against the French in *I vespri siciliani* (The Sicilian Vespers). The tyrants in Italy's case were the Austrians who controlled much of northern Italy during the first half of the nineteenth century. Verdi's famous chorus, "Va, pensiero, sull'ali dorati" (Fly, thought, on wings of gold) from *Nabucco* (1842) (see p. 79) became a symbol of freedom for 30 years until Italian unification was achieved. Even the cry, "Viva Verdi," which the audience shouted at the composer's successes, became a rallying cry for independence. It was a simple acrostic for *Vittorio Emmanuele, rè d'Italia* (Victor Emmanuel, King of Italy), the ruler of Piedmont and first monarch of a united Italy. At the urging of Cavour, Verdi became a deputy in the first Italian parliament at Turin. But his political career was a brief one, and he soon realized he was destined to be a musician and not a legislator.

Censorship also played a role in Verdi's career. Several operas had to be changed because of their aspersions on authority and royalty. The original version of *Rigoletto*, following Victor Hugo, centered around the French Renaissance monarch, Francis I; the locale was eventually changed to Mantua, and the king became a duke because the censors objected to the portrait of a debauched monarch and considered the play to be immoral. *A Masked Ball* was shifted from Sweden under Gustavus III in the eighteenth century to Boston (!) under an English governor, for somewhat the same reasons. Even though Verdi and his librettists eventually got around most of their censorship difficulties, the process was inordinately time-consuming and frustrating.

What is the key to Verdi as one of the great figures in opera? Essentially, his qualities are those possessed by Mozart: unerring musical strength in melody, harmony, rhythm, and orchestration; ability to create living characters through music; and the sense of what has to be done to fashion an effective musical work for the stage. Yet the two men were in no way alike. They lived in different ages, their musical language was quite dissimilar, and their goals were attained by different means. Verdi's vigor and crudity might have shocked Mozart. Mozart would have recognized the strength and power of Verdi's music but would have preferred his own barbed wit, understatement, and delicate touch. Verdi's vitality is almost overwhelming at times, yet he could be sensitive, delicate, and un-obtrusive when the situation called for it. It was a delicacy, however, that relied strongly on dramatic contrast, on sudden changes in texture and mood[3] that Mozart might have found harsh and abrupt, too lacking in the good taste of his age of manners. Verdi was essentially a romantic and Mozart a classical figure in the history of music, and the two worlds do not meet except at their peripheries.

Verdi's two greatest attributes were his uncompromising honesty and his essential simplicity; in business and musical matters, he was always true to his convictions.[4] He never pretended to be other than what he was—a simple, hard-working Italian musician. By trial and error, he eventually composed some of the finest operas ever written. Verdi was no intellectual, and he often accepted librettos that more sophisticated musicians would have scorned; yet he was consistently shrewd about weak spots in them and had no hesitation about suggesting changes. Collaboration with his librettists in a joint enterprise became a very important factor in the success of his later works. Strong, even violent situations, were necessary to bring out the best in his musical make-up. Without melodrama his music lacks focus. His operas are powerful tragedies, quite different from the opera seria convention of the seventeenth and eighteenth centuries that required an opera to end happily in spite of unfulfilled love, death, or loss of honor. Verdi's operas generally conclude with two or three corpses on the stage. Although the Greek ideal of tragedy as a moral uplift to the spirit is not always attained in the plot, Verdi's music brings it nearer to this goal.

As a musician Verdi was no conscious revolutionary like Wagner. He took the Italian bel canto opera of its greatest period (Rossini, Donizetti, and Bellini) and gradually changed it into a romantic, naturalistic work, a branch of which became the *verismo* of Puccini, Mascagni, and others both before and after his death. Objections at the beginning came from those who loved the human voice: Verdi was accused of drowning it out, of destroying the beauty of its line, of distorting its bel canto tradition. There is some truth in this accusation. But what was lost in subtle vocal control was regained in

[3] "In order to make music, one needs stanzas for *cantabiles*, stanzas for largos, allegros, etc., and all these alternating in such a way that the audience is neither bored nor indifferent." Verdi letter to Cesare de Sanctis (1853) as quoted in Ulrich Weisstein, ed., *The Essence of Opera*, Free Press, (Norton Library paperback), New York, 1964, p. 240.
[4] "I have now been writing operas and wandering from place to place for six years and I have never in the pursuit of success addressed a word to a journalist or asked a favor from a friend or paid court to a rich man. Never, never! I shall always despise this kind of thing. I write my operas as well as I can, then I let matters take their course without any effort to influence public opinion." Letter of 1849 as quoted by Francis Toye, *Verdi: His Life and Works.* Vintage Books paperback, New York, 1959, p. 63.

the dramatic power that made the opera not only music but living theater. Toward the middle of Verdi's life, Wagnerism and its influence threatened to displace every operatic tradition in Europe. But Verdi kept to his own ways: he had clear perception about what he could and could not do and was not to be swayed from his artistic credo. He recognized the lure and magnetism of Wagner's operas but instinctively knew he should not imitate them. Nothing made him angrier than to be told by critics that *Aïda, Otello*, and *Falstaff* were "Wagnerian" in their treatment: by this they presumably meant that the old recitative, aria, and ensemble divisions, particularly in the last two operas, had disappeared, and Wagner's "endless melody" prevailed. *Otello* and *Falstaff* do demonstrate a striking unity in which one section blends into the other, but this came as a result of Verdi's own development (and had little or nothing to do with Wagner). In his effort to attain the most apposite and fitting union of words and music, Verdi was inevitably led to this treatment and achieved it in his own way. If themes or harmonic progression associated with a character or a situation occasionally returned in the opera, they were not "leading motives" as such but living organisms built into the fabric of the music. His creative vigor never allowed him to compose a stereotype. He might be unashamedly vulgar, but the vulgarity is there for a purpose and it keeps the flame of music and drama alive.

RIGOLETTO One of Verdi's works which even a person ignorant of opera has heard of is *Rigoletto*, first presented at the Teatro La Fenice, Venice, in March, 1851. In spite of its reputation as an old standby, it is still one of Verdi's most remarkable creations. He and Francesco Piave, his librettist, were able to fashion a tight-knit, moving, passionate opera from a play so shocking it was originally banned in Paris. *Le Roi s'amuse* (The King Amuses Himself, 1832) by Victor Hugo, deals with the life of Francis I, profligate but able king of France during the early sixteenth century, who had no compunction about satisfying his carnal desires. His court jester, a hunchback named Triboulet, aids and abets him. The king's conquests include the famous Diane de Poitiers (though this has no historical basis: she was the mistress of his son, Henry II) and other ladies at court. When we first see the king, he tells his courtiers he is planning to seduce a pretty girl he has seen at church. The nobles are goaded beyond endurance by Triboulet who mocks and insults them but knows he has the king's protection. They vow vengeance on the jester by planning to abduct his mistress and present her to the king. The father of Diane de Poitiers, M. de Saint Vallier, lays a curse on the head of the king for violating his daughter, and on Triboulet for mocking him. (The play engenders less sympathy for the father by indicating that he had previously arranged a cynical marriage for his daughter with an old hunchback noble.)

In the second act, Triboulet meets a professional cutthroat, Saltabil, who offers to be of service in getting rid of unwelcome enemies. When he is greeted at home by his beloved daughter Blanche, whom he keeps hidden from the eyes of this dissolute world, the jester shows his tender and humane nature. The king disguised as a poor student manages to find his way into the garden when Triboulet is absent, and declares his love (she is the young girl he has seen at church). Shortly afterward, the courtiers, believing Blanche to be Triboulet's mistress, manage to kidnap her with Triboulet's unknowing help—he is blindfolded and his ears stuffed, thinking he is getting the king a woman from the house across the street.

In the third act Blanche is brought before Francis to discover that he is her poor student. He tries to make love to her again; she repels his advances and locks herself in a nearby bedroom. It is the king's room and he has the key. Laughing, he lets himself in. (Presumably he rapes the girl.) This scene caused trouble in Paris and in the opera it had to be modified. Triboulet tries to learn where his daughter is; the courtiers mock him, and he ultimately realizes she is in the king's bedroom. In a magnificent burst of fury, he damns the whole race of courtiers, and attempts to break down the king's door. Blanche finally bursts out of the bedroom and throws herself into her father's arms.

The last two acts, which Piave and Verdi condensed into one, show how the curse works out. Triboulet takes Blanche to Saltabil's hovel outside Paris to show her the king making love to another woman (Saltabil's sister, Maguelonne). But Blanche loves the king in spite of his infidelity and his treatment of her. She substitutes herself in man's clothes for him when Saltabil, paid by Triboulet to assassinate this unknown person, stabs a concealed figure entering the hovel. The body is put in a sack and delivered to Triboulet; as he exults over it, the king is heard singing in the distance. Realizing a mistake, Triboulet tears open the sack to find his mortally wounded daughter. She asks his forgiveness and dies. In the play, at Triboulet's cries, a surgeon and a crowd gather. The surgeon says the girl died because she tried to speak: the blood from her wounds flooded her lungs, and she suffocated. Triboulet gasps, "I have killed my own daughter." The opera is more direct and stronger because there is no surgeon or crowd and Rigoletto's last words are "La maledizione" (the curse), which has enacted its final revenge.

The Austrian censors would not approve the libretto and Verdi refused to alter the plot. The compromise was that the setting was changed from Paris to Mantua, the king became a duke (partial royalty), and names were Italianized—Triboulet became Rigoletto (and his name became the title of the opera, originally called *La maledizione*); Blanche became Gilda; Saltabil, Sparafucile (literally "shotgun" in Italian); Maguelonne, Maddalena. The nobles took Italian names, including Clément Marot, the poet, who was turned into a mere Italian *cavaliere* named Marullo. The explicit scene of the key in Act III was omitted, but Piave and Verdi retained the substance of their opera. Verdi insisted the ruler remain a libertine, the jester be cursed, and the important action of the last act be kept, otherwise, the opera made no sense. The new version was permitted to pass.[5]

Rigoletto has always suffered because certain numbers in the score have become too popular. They have been sung separately out of context—to their detriment. The aria, "Caro nome" (Sweet name) for Gilda is the lovely, meditative, almost rapt utterance of a sweet, young girl, who has fallen in love for the first time and sings of the wonder of it. Often it becomes a mere instrument for coloratura virtuosity. "La donna è mobile" (Woman is fickle) is not an organ-grinder's tune but the sentiment of a libertine duke to whom every woman is like a feather in the wind to be enjoyed momentarily and tossed aside. The quartet in the last act is a miracle of musical and dramatic construction, not just an occasion for four people to sing together. If these selections are firmly fused into the dramatic action, the opera becomes the wholly satisfying entity it is meant to be.

The first thing heard in the prelude is the music which will accompany Monterone's (Saint Vallier's) curse. Whether sung or played in the orchestra, it is a series of repeated notes ending on a dissonant chord. Here it is enunciated by brass and winds (Example 11-6a). The ominous quality of it is immediately recognizable. When Monterone forces his way into the group of courtiers in the first scene of Act I and demands to speak to the Duke, his voice settles on the one note of this motive ("Ch'io gli parli"—Let me speak to him), even before he has laid his curse, and the courtiers cry out his name to almost the same chord as the opening measures of the prelude. This is a premonition of what is to follow. His rather bombastic but

---

[5] Verdi's reply to the management of the Fenice Theater in Venice as to why he could not change some things to suit the censor is revealing: "A hunchback who sings? Why not! Will it be effective? I do not know. But if I do not know, neither does the person who suggested these changes, that is, the hunchback be changed to a man with no deformity. In my opinion, the presentation of this character, so deformed and ridiculous outside, so full of love and passion within, is a fine idea. Indeed, it was precisely on this account that I chose the subject." Quoted by Francis Toye, *Verdi*, p. 71.

Example 11-6   (a)   Verdi, *Rigoletto* (1851)

(You plotted against us, sir;)

(New insult.)

(Ah, may you both be cursed!)

(Ah, you who have boldly disturbed the festivities were guided here by a demon from hell;)

powerful cry for attention: "Si, Monteron . . . la voce mia qual tuono vi scuoterà dovunque" (Yes, Monteron . . . my voice will strike you anywhere like thunder) is imitated mockingly by Rigoletto (not shown). The malevolent side of Rigoletto's character and the wicked thrust of his tongue explain why the nobles desire revenge. The orchestra outlines Rigoletto's gestures before he speaks: a ragged, irregular, chromatic string passage in which he can be pictured jumping obscenely (b). The mocking continues in the orchestra (exaggerated skips) as he further imitates Monterone's manner (c). The winds echo this raillery with a whiplash figure in flutes, oboes, and clarinets at different pitch levels (measure 5, c). Monterone breaks out in a terrible denunciation of Rigoletto (d), supported by full orchestra in forte chromatic ascension (favored by Verdi in other moments of great tension), a literal blast of fury The courtiers say Monterone is crazy and should be arrested, but he turns on the Duke and Rigoletto and defiantly places his curse on both of them (e). Verdi still keeps the formula of repeated notes ending in a striking chord, but this time the voice rises a half step on the third syllable of "maledetti" and the chord is even more sudden in its impact. When Monterone addresses himself directly to the jester a second time and repeats the curse (a strong and fearful threat in a superstitious age), Rigoletto is terror-stricken. The men echo his fright in unison *sotto voce* (a dramatic effect) by singing softly a minor phrase that rises and falls like the surge of their emotions (f). In this powerful scene, Verdi foreshadows the technique he uses with such skill in his later works: recitative, arioso, solo, and chorus forming a dramatic and musical unit.

In the next scene (sometimes labeled Act II), Rigoletto, shaken by Monterone's curse, is coming down the narrow blind alley, bounded by high walls, that leads to his secluded dwelling. It is a dark night and Rigoletto has his coat well pulled up to avoid recognition. Behind him, attempting to approach and talk, is Sparafucile, the professional assassin, with a sword under his cloak. This sinister atmosphere is vividly represented by the orchestra in its opening measures—clarinets and bassoons holding a series of low, dark chords, while underneath, the lower strings mutter in disconnected upward steps. These few measures evoke the picture with amazing brevity and concision (Example 11-7a, measures 1—8). Rigoletto softly sings the familiar phrase (measures 11—12), but this time as description in the past tense. From the orchestra comes a remarkable theme, heard throughout most of the following scene below the voices; it is actually sung only one brief instant, but acts as the dominant motive of the encounter between Rigoletto and Sparafucile. Ernest Newman said the melody "winds its way slowly through the

Example 11-7

orchestra as if, like Sparafucile himself, it was cautiously feeling its way in the uncanny dark."[6] (Measures 14–17, *a*.) It is scored for solo cello and solo double bass muted, with the other strings pizzicato, and winds staccato filling in the harmony. Not the least of this unusual combination is a bass drum at the bottom of the ensemble, making thuds like footsteps along the way (not shown). Further along, the theme is varied by added chromatics below it to give more tension and color (*b*).

Above this ominous background, the two men engage in rapid dialogue:

Sparafucile. *Sir*
Rigoletto. *Go, I have nothing.*
Sparafucile. *Nor did I ask anything   A swordsman—stands before you.*
Rigoletto. *A thief?*
Sparafucile. *A man who can free you for little from a rival. And you have one*
Rigoletto. *What?*
Sparafucile. *Your woman is in there.*

[6]Ernest Newman *Great Operas*, Vintage Books paperback, New York, 1958, vol. 1, p. 83.

Rigoletto. *(What do I hear!) And how much would I have to spend for a gentle-man?*

Sparafucile. *I would want a higher price.*

Rigoletto. *How are you usually paid?*

Sparafucile. *One half is given in advance; the rest is given afterwards*

Rigoletto. *(Demon!) And how are you able to work with such security?*

Sparafucile. *I usually kill in the city, or else under my roof. I wait for the man at evening   A thrust, and he dies.*

Rigoletto. *(Demon!) And how is he brought to your house?*

Sparafucile. *It's easy   My sister helps me   She dances in the streets   and then .*

Rigoletto. *I understand*

Sparafucile (showing his sword). *This is my instrument. Do you need it?*

Rigoletto. *No, not at the moment.*

Sparafucile. *So much the worse for you .*

Rigoletto. *Who knows?*

Sparafucile. *Sparafucile is my name*

Rigoletto. *A foreigner?*

Sparafucile (about to go). *Burgundian.* [The reference comes from Victor Hugo and is not applicable in an Italian location. Piave forgot to remove it.]

Rigoletto. *And where, if the occasion arises? . . .*

Sparafucile. *Always here in the evening.*

Rigoletto. *Go.*

Sparafucile. *Sparafucil. Sparafucil.*

Rigoletto. *Go, go, go, go.*[7]

The dialogue, the orchestra, the music make this one of Verdi's most effective scenes.

In the last act after the quartet, Rigoletto presumes that Gilda is sufficiently convinced of the nature of the Duke's character that she will be willing to flee Mantua for another life. He tells her to go home, get money and a horse, put on man's clothing he has readied for her, and leave for Verona where he will join her the next day After she leaves, the Duke and Maddalena are still seen laughing and drinking together. Rigoletto reappears from behind the house with Sparafucile and counts out money for him. While this happens, Verdi has the orchestra play another brief interlude (heard several times later in the scene) which is not only simplicity but inspired simplicity. Violas, cellos, and basses repeat softly a series of open fifths (no third in the middle) of a D chord. Above this, the oboe sounds a number of high As (Example 11-8a). The effect is remarkably unnerving. In recitative Rigoletto pays out 10

[7]William Weaver, trans., *Verdi Librettos*, Anchor Books, New York, 1963, pp. 21–23. Copyright © 1963 by William Weaver. Reprinted by permission of Doubleday and Company, Inc.

Example 11-8

(a)

(b)

(Humming behind the scenes with mouths closed)

(c)

(Woman is fickle, like a feather in the wind she changes her intent and thought)

(d)

(Gilda: Oh, heaven, take pity; Maddalena: The night is dark, the heaven too angry; Sparafucile: If before the night reaches midnight)

(e)

(Up in heaven, near my mother)

gold crowns to Sparafucile, saying he will give him 10 more when the body is delivered to him at midnight. Sparafucile himself, wants to throw the body into the river but Rigoletto demands it be delivered to him for disposal. Rigoletto leaves. There are sounds of an approaching storm—thunder in the strings, lightning in flute and piccolo. With these naturalistic sounds, Verdi has a chorus of men backstage humming a sliding progression over a held note (b) which is repeated at intervals throughout the scene when the storm rises. The device seems melodramatic, even ludicrous, but it is highly effective in performance; Verdi knew exactly what he was doing. The storm is a good excuse for the Duke to stay the night with Maddalena; he goes to the loft to get some rest. Below, Sparafucile and Maddalena debate what is to be done. Sparafucile tells his sister he gets 20 crowns for killing the man. But Maddalena has taken a fancy to him and pleads for his life, telling her brother to do away with the hunchback himself. Sparafucile indignantly refuses, saying he does not betray a client. Meanwhile, Gilda in man's clothing has returned, drawn by the fatal fascination of her erstwhile lover. She overhears the conversation about the Duke. Sparafucile agrees to kill the first person who might come their way that night and substitute him for the Duke. Gilda determines to sacrifice herself. Verdi compresses the text into a trio, Gilda asking for forgiveness if she should die, Maddalena doubtful that anybody will pass that way on such a terrible night, Sparafucile saying he will do the deed if somebody appears before midnight. It is an anguished moment, and the little burst of melody Gilda sings is doubly poignant (d). She knocks on the door just after 11:30 pretending to be a beggar. Sparafucile does his dirty work. Only the storm is heard, lessening in intensity after the climax of the murder. Rigoletto reappears, Sparafucile delivers the body, and is paid his money. Rigoletto exults over his vengeance and is about to drag the body toward the river when the Duke's voice is heard singing "La donna è mobile" (c), which Rigoletto immediately recognizes. This pause (mentioned on p. 15 as being one of the most intense in opera) brings frenzy to Rigoletto. He tears open the sack to find Gilda still alive but mortally wounded. She tries to calm him, asking his forgiveness in a lovely transfigured phrase (high pianissimo strings and flute in arpeggios) that wrings the heart (e). He begs her not to die. When she breathes her last, Rigoletto, in a tremendous outburst, sings "Ah! la maledizione" (Ah, the curse) to the original motive and falls in despair over her body.

OTELLO   The creative urge in an individual's life generally ceases when old age is reached. Most artists who are painters, sculptors, poets, and composers have done their best work in early life, though there are always exceptions. Maturing rates are obviously different, but energy flags as age increases. Occasionally, a man's greatest artistic accomplishment comes late in life when the accumulation of years has brought wisdom refined by experience, and there is no difficulty with technical problems. If a person is in good health and can summon the necessary energy and concentration, remarkable results may ensue.

Verdi was this kind of creative being. Long after other men would have given up thought of further work, he was still keen enough mentally and physically to be interested in a libretto if it appealed to him. He had no need to compose any more as far as the world was concerned. His fame and renown were more than enough for any man, and he could have occupied his remaining days at Villa Sant'Agata (the country villa he had built near his old home outside of Busseto), puttering in the garden and attending to minor chores.

All his life Verdi had known the Bible and Shakespeare. His Shakespeare, an Italian translation since he knew almost no English, he kept by his bedside and read the plays thoroughly. For some 30 years he had dreamt of setting *King Lear* to music, but attempts to adapt it for opera had been unsuccessful. His *Macbeth* had never entirely satisfied him; the original production at Florence had been in 1847, but the work was revised and new numbers added (ballet particularly) when the opera was given in Paris in 1865.

During the 1870's, Verdi's friends (particularly the Ricordis, the publishing house family in Milan, who were an important influence in the lives of both Verdi and Puccini) tried to get Arrigo Boito and Verdi together to contemplate a Shakespearian opera. At first, Verdi would have none of it: he said he was finished after *Aida* (1871). Moreover, years earlier he had been distinctly cool to the ideas promulgated by Boito and Franco Faccio (another musician, who eventually conducted the first performance of *Otello*). As young rebels in the Italian musical world of the 1860s, they had some biting things to say about the contemporary scene, declaring that Wagner's work was to be the music of the future. Verdi took this to be a slur on himself. But sometime during 1879, Boito wrote a libretto based on *Othello*, which was submitted to Verdi, who liked it, accepted it, but put it away among other possible projects. In the years 1880–1885 Verdi worked with Boito on a revision of *Simon Boccanegra* for Paris and a revised *Don Carlos* for La Scala. When he finally did turn to the "Chocolate Project," as it was called among his friends (Othello was a dark-skinned Moor), the figure of Iago fascinated him the most and *Iago* was to be the title of the opera, to avoid comparison with Rossini's *Otello*, still well-known in Italy of that day. As work progressed, the title was changed to *Otello*.

Verdi began to catch fire with his composition in the mid-1880s when he was 70. After working with Boito on the two revisions, Verdi's attitude toward him changed, and he came to have high respect for the man as librettist and musician. As mentioned earlier (see p. 23) Boito was an ideal collaborator. A musician himself who had completed one opera, *Mefistofele* (1868), and part of another, he was also a man of wide culture and literary interests. He knew English quite well; he had translated several English works into Italian. But in spite of mutual respect on the part of both men, the work proceeded slowly. Verdi was feeling his years—the world was changing and he felt out of touch and out of sympathy. Politically, the Italy which for years had looked to France as an ally was turning toward Germany. In 1882, Italy joined its old enemy, Austria, and Germany in a Triple Alliance. This was a blow to the older generation who felt that everything they had stood for was being negated. Also during these years, many of Verdi's old friends passed away.

But Boito and Verdi kept at their task. There were innumerable changes, cuts, and revisions; except for one major misunderstanding, the two men worked amicably. Finally in February, 1887 (Verdi was 73), almost eight years after the idea had first taken form, the opera was given its premiere at La Scala in Milan. All the musical world was there. An opera from Verdi after a 16-year pause was bound to be a great event. The reception for *Otello* was one of the most tumultuous ever given an opera at La Scala, and it particularly impressed a 19-year-old cellist in the orchestra, Arturo Toscanini, later to become one of the most famous of twentieth century conductors.[8]

Boito's libretto, a masterpiece of language and compression, is commonly recognized as one of the finest ever written for an opera. He omitted Shakespeare's Act I, set in Venice, where the audience

[8]The excitement of that night was described by Blanche Roosevelt, *Verdi: Milan and Otello* (London, 1887) as quoted by Charles Osborne, *The Complete Operas of Verdi*, Knopf, New York, 1970, p. 413. "La Scala has never before held such an audience, and although it was fully an hour before the time to commence, every seat was occupied. The light murmur of expectant voices issuing from three thousand throats, audible, but discreetly indistinct, reminded me of the sounds in an enchanted forest on a summer night   all were frantic to be seated before the curtain rose. Only in Italy could such a scene take place; for here pride of birth, or rank, or position gives way before the homage which a land of song sows in perennial laurel at the feet of her great composers."

"The reception for *Otello* was one of the most tumultuous ever given an opera at La Scala." An historical drawing of the first production of *Otello* at La Scala, Milan, in 1887 (Courtesy of the Victoria and Albert Museum, London)

learns how Otello won Desdemona against the wishes of her father, Brabantio; how Iago already was plotting with Roderigo to overthrow Otello; how Otello before the Doge and the Venetian senate defended his elopement. But Boito managed to include the important motivation of the plot in his first act. Brabantio is lost and so is the pageantry of the Venetian scene, but by concentrating all the action in Cyprus within four acts instead of five (Shakespeare), the drama for music becomes more unified and moves forward to its grim, tragic ending with inexorable thrust.

The dimensions of the characters in the opera are different from those in the play, but they do not change in fundamental quality. Iago, after Otello, is the central figure in the opera—the same in Shakespeare, but his actions there are spread over a wider area and longer period of time. In the opera, his malice and venom explode in the famous Credo of Act II, where he expresses his belief in an evil god. This was Boito's invention: as a device for music, it is splendid, though its dramatic fitness may be open to question. Verdi had definite ideas as to the kind of person who should play Iago. In an often-quoted letter to Domenico Morelli, a Neapolitan friend, Verdi said Iago could not be "a small, malevolent-looking man" because such a person would arouse everybody's suspicion. He must be a tall, thin man with thin lips and small eyes set close to his head like a monkey's and a high, receding forehead with the back of his head well-developed. In the play Desdemona is almost a child-bride who moves in a trance through the events that sweep past her; in the opera, she is a mature woman. Except for the Willow song in Act IV, restrained and delicate, her music is full-blooded. There is less time in the opera for Otello's jealousy to build as it does in the play; it comes on abruptly as if the man by nature was still violent and untamed and not the great hero who had learned patience under suffering. Shakespeare could show "the green-eyed monster" with much more deliberation. Verdi's music puts these problems into perspective. The listener is never conscious of shortcomings because the music adds the overtones of the drama which may be missing in the text. The interludes, for instance, pace the action and continue it consistently The result is one of the masterpieces of the operatic stage.

Otello, even in Italy, has never attained great popularity. There are almost no set arias and few single opportunities for applause. The scenes do not pretend to be glamorous, and, except for the ballet music which Verdi wrote later for Paris, and Desdemona's garden scene in Act II, there is no incidental music. Yet magnificent crowd scenes are highly germane to the drama and always stir the senses: the marvelous storm picture at the beginning when Otello's ship is trying to make the harbor at Cyprus and the crowd describes its progress as seen from the shore; the powerful drinking scene in Act I when Iago and Roderigo deliberately get Cassio drunk in front of the Venetian soldiers in order to stir up a brawl and bring Otello out of his room; the emotional reception of the Venetian ambassadors at the end of Act III when Otello finally hurls his wife to the ground in acting-out his pathological jealousy.

The libretto is written in intensely poetic language—language Verdi was delighted with; it fulfilled his ideal of "la parola scenica," the scenic or stage word he could seize on for direct musical representation. One must either be an Italian to appreciate its fullness and beauty, or else know the opera very well. A good deal of the plot goes on in the ensembles: some of the language gets lost unless great care is taken to enunciate and sing with flawless diction. The music and text are so compact that subtleties of the score demand repeated hearings for complete understanding and enjoyment.

Verdi employs a much more continuous style than he ever used before. It is fashionable to describe it as the Italian version of Wagnerian "endless melody"; but this comparison, plausible on the surface, is hardly adequate for an understanding of Verdi's accomplishment. The opera is completely Italian, and although the orchestra is richer, fuller, and more deliberate, the voice is still supreme and not another instrument, as it is apt to be in Wagner. Verdi sought the most exact realization of tone and word, and if the details are examined closely, one will find they fit precisely in their place. Music does not stop the action; rather there is that unique blend of drama and music which makes an ideal work of art.

The story concerns Venice in the fifteenth century when she was a formidable maritime and economic power. Otello, a Moorish general employed by the Venetian senate and the Doge to protect their interests, falls in love with Desdemona, daughter of a Venetian nobleman, Brabantio, and elopes with her against her father's wishes. Before the opera begins, Otello has defended his elopement to the Venetian senate, been exonerated, and ordered to proceed to the island of Cyprus to defend it against the Turks. The opera opens at Cyprus in the midst of a raging storm. Iago, Otello's ensign, Cassio, his lieutenant, and other soldiers have preceded Otello to Cyprus to await his arrival. Iago, embittered because he was passed over for promotion in favor of Cassio, plots with Roderigo, a disappointed suitor of Desdemona. A sail is sighted, and after great tribulation, Otello's ship manages a safe landing. The crowd hail him as a hero, particularly when he tells them that the Turkish fleet was destroyed in the storm and they no longer need fear an invasion. Otello and Desdemona leave. A celebration is held by the

Cypriots. Iago manages to get Cassio quite drunk; Roderigo deliberately picks a fight with him; Montano, Venetian commander at Cyprus, tries to intervene and is wounded. The uproar awakens Otello who, losing his temper, demotes Cassio. The act ends with a love duet for Otello and Desdemona after the crowd has dispersed.

In Act II, Iago begins to work on Otello's natural suspicion (different race and temperament). Cassio, at Iago's urging, appeals to Desdemona to intercede for his reinstatement with Otello. Otello and Iago see Cassio and Desdemona together in the garden; Iago implies that Cassio is Desdemona's lover and that he, Otello, is being betrayed. The thought grows in Otello's mind when his wife pleads for their old friend Cassio. Iago snatches Desdemona's handkerchief from Emilia, his wife and Desdemona's companion, who picked it up where Desdemona dropped it. Iago tells Otello that Cassio one night talked in his sleep as if he and Desdemona were lovers. Otello is shattered but demands more concrete proof from Iago.

Venetian ambassadors are announced in Act III, but before they arrive Desdemona again pleads Cassio's cause. In a furious scene, Otello openly accuses her of adultery. Iago and Cassio talk about Bianca, Cassio's mistress; Otello, at a distance, cannot hear their words but is convinced Cassio speaks of Desdemona, because he recognizes her handkerchief (which Iago has left in Cassio's room and which Cassio displays). Otello, consumed with jealous fury, strikes his wife in front of the Venetian ambassadors; he succumbs to a fit and faints. Iago exults over the prostrate body.

In Act IV, Desdemona prepares for bed. To Emilia she sings a sad song, "Willow, Willow," about a girl who died through unhappy love, and she prays to the Virgin Mary before retiring. Otello, determined to kill Desdemona for her "crime," enters, awakens her, and declares his intent. She protests her innocence but Otello, beyond reason, strangles her. Her outcry brings Emilia and others. Emilia tells Otello that Roderigo (spurred by Iago) was to kill Cassio, but has been murdered himself and Cassio lives. Desdemona groans and then expires. Iago's villainy of the handkerchief and the plot on Cassio is exposed, and he flees. Otello, realizing his terrible error and what devastation his jealousy has caused, begs forgiveness of those present, stabs himself, and falls over Desdemona's lifeless body.

One of the most glorious musical moments in the opera comes at the end of Act I where, after the tension of the storm and the uproar over Cassio, calm descends on the scene, the heavens clear and stars come out, and Otello and Desdemona sing of their love for one another. Unlike most operatic love scenes, this is not a passionate, tempestuous declaration by two young lovers but a tender, quiet expression of heartfelt emotion by husband and wife. There is a wealth of understanding and compassion in the relation of older man to younger woman and what their love means. Verdi magically recreates this setting by having four cellos (one solo, open-stringed, the others muted) play a seven-measure introduction which for sheer beauty has seldom been equaled (Example 11-9a). The caressing nature of the descending lead cello, the separate entity of each measure with its changing chord patterns, as if the mood was to be savored in several different ways, and the final rest on the dominant D flat of G flat (preceded by a lovely second inversion of the G flat chord in the previous measure) are Verdi's delicate means. When Otello begins to sing, his vocal line on one note imparts tranquillity to his utterance. Underneath, the cellos continue their song but rise up with the voice on the very expressive turn of "s'estingue ogni clamor" (every sound passes away), made even more vivid by the repeated G flats before it. The same is true of the last three measures which give a particular yearning quality to the words in contrast to

Example 11-9

(Already in the thick of night every sound passes away and my furious heart is quieted in this embrace and recovers itself)

(Otello: And you loved me for my misfortunes,
and I loved you for your pity.
Desdemona: And I loved you for your misfortunes,
and you loved me for my pity.)

(Otello: A kiss. Desdemona: Otello. Otello: A kiss. One more kiss.)

the previous phrase, which like the beginning, rests almost entirely
on one note.

The remainder of the scene is a vocal dialogue, recalling how they
met, how Desdemona was enthralled by Otello's telling of his adventures.

Otello. *I described the clang of arms, the fighting,/And the bold rush into the
mortal breech/The attack, hanging like horrible ivy on the rampart by our
nails, and the whistling arrow.*

Desdemona. *Then you led me to the shining deserts,/the burning sands, your native land. /Then you told me of the sufferings undergone/the chains and the slave's sorrow.*[9]

Verdi paints the picture in sharp colors, giving the orchestra full rein. Particularly moving is section (*b*) where Otello and Desdemona repeat lines which Boito extracted from Othello's speech to the Senate in Act I of Shakespeare: "She lov'd me for the dangers I had pass'd. And I lov'd her that she did pity them."

As joy engulfs them, the key suddenly changes and the orchestra sounds the glorious "kiss" motive, which is one of the two themes that Verdi chooses to use more than once in the opera (*c*). It reappears in Act IV when Otello awakens the sleeping Desdemona with kisses but with deadly intent, and at the end of the opera when Otello bids his farewell and falls lifeless over her body. The theme is really a two-measure motive that starts the same way three times but reaches higher on the end of each phrase with the harmonies shifting below. Harmonically the bass acts as an anchor, descending step by step in each measure until the climax is reached in measure 6 and then drops down to a low G before the final cadence. Above in the vocal line, Otello and Desdemona tenderly echo the end of the motive but otherwise are silent. It is a remarkable bit of musical description and one place in the opera where Verdi puts the orchestra above the voice in importance.

The two middle acts contain equally wonderful music: Iago's "Credo" in Act II; the quartet (quite different from *Rigoletto*) with Iago trying to get Desdemona's handkerchief from Emilia, Desdemona pleading her cause, and Otello's jealousy increasing in intensity; and Otello's famous outburst against Iago for destroying his peace and equanimity. Shakespeare's words are paraphrased.

Farewell the tranquil mind! Farewell content!
Farewell the plumed troops and the big wars
That make ambition virtue! O farewell!
Farewell the neighing steed and the shrill trump
The spirit-stirring drum, the ear-splitting fife.
The royal banner and all quality
Pride, pomp, and circumstance of glorious war
Farewell! Othello's occupation's gone.

Iago's description of Cassio's dream is a masterpiece of malignity and planned villainy. The act ends with an oath-swearing duet of vengeance by Otello and Iago.

Act IV has one of Verdi's most striking introductions—one that foreshadows the scene to follow. The setting is Desdemona's

[9] William Weaver, *Verdi Librettos*, p. 345.

Example 11-10

Act IV

(She wept, singing on the lonely heath. The sad girl wept. O Willow! Willow! Willow!)

chamber at night. The events of the previous act have brought her foreboding and dread; her mood is one of deep melancholy. A single English horn plays a haunting phrase, as at the beginning of Act III of Wagner's *Tristan*. It portends tragedy and death (Example 11-10a). The minor tonality, the drooping descent of the melody after an initial rise, the fall from b^1 to g sharp^1 (the b^1 being raised the first time but lowered the second) are characteristic. There are two other musical elements at the end of the phrase: the mournful echo of flutes in low register (measures 4 and 5), and three open fifths in the "chalumeau" (very low) range of the clarinets. These

197 Italian Opera in the Nineteenth Century

three elements speak eloquently together. For most of this introduction, these are the only instruments that play; they are joined
later by solo bassoons and a horn. Emilia asks Desdemona if Otello
was calmer, and in a monotone, she says yes, and that he has requested her to go to bed to await him. She tells Emilia to fetch
her wedding nightgown, and if she should die to bury her in it.
She recalls the song of poor Barbara, a maidservant of her mother's, who died, when abandoned by her lover. It is the Willow
song, taken from Shakespeare, and one of the most touching
moments in the opera. Each of three verses ends with the cry of
"willow" ("salce") unaccompanied, on a falling minor third, but
Verdi treats each verse a little differently. All are preceded by a
little orchestral interlude for winds (b), major in key and the essence of simplicity, but pathetic in feeling. Hopelessness and empti-
ness are emphasized by the extraordinary open F sharps of piccolo
and English horn, three octaves apart, that follow and anticipate
the first note of the vocal line (measures 7 and 8, b). Desdemona's
song is based primarily on the theme heard in the beginning on
the English horn (c). The pathos of the story, the scoring, and the
recurrent "salce's" are memorable in their context and illustrate
the depth of Desdemona's despair. In spite of the static nature of
the song, Boito and Verdi keep the plot moving by interrupted
comments. The first time Desdemona tells Emilia to hurry with her
preparations because she fears Otello is coming soon. The second
time she gives Emilia her wedding ring to put away (a symbolic
act). The third time, in terror, she thinks she hears a knocking on
the door, but it is only the wind. These simple acts relate the song
to what is going on in Desdemona's mind and increase the tension. Most poignant is the farewell to Emilia after saying goodnight. It is a passionate, heartfelt cry, rising to a high a sharp^2, contrasting sharply with the restrained compass of the song. Verdi
concludes by reiterated playing of the flute figure (measures 4 and
5, a) but this time in all the winds over a chromatic falling bass in
the cellos and basses. After her hushed and reverent prayer, she
goes to sleep. Then comes one of the most amazing passages in the
work, accompanying Otello's approach through a secret door. In
the lowest part of the orchestra, solo muted four-stringed double
basses (three-stringed instruments were more usual at the time)
play a sinister theme which advances in short gasps as if Otello
were taking a few steps at a time and halting so as not to disturb
his wife (d). When he comes further on stage, the basses mount
higher. He puts a scimitar on a table and stops in front of a lit
torch, hesitating whether to extinguish it or not. The double basses continue to play, but a scurrying figure in the violas followed

by a low thud in the bass drum (measures 11 and 12, *d*) is added to them. It is a most imaginative bit of scoring. As Otello approaches the bed and stops in front of it, the whole orchestra suddenly swirls up in a tremendous fortissimo. Then as he pulls the curtain aside to look at the sleeping Desdemona, the orchestral winds dwell on the double bass theme, but it is agitated to show the turmoil in Otello's mind. As he bends to kiss her, the "kiss" motive runs through the orchestra and releases the tension for a moment. From here, the action and music work to the climax when Desdemona is strangled, Emilia enters, Iago's plot is exposed, and Otello stabs himself. One of the most moving moments comes when Otello bids farewell to Desdemona in an unaccompanied phrase (see p. 57) that for sheer drama and beauty cannot be matched.

Verdi in this opera and in *Falstaff*, his great comic achievement, written in his late 70s and produced when he was 80, brings a famous Italian tradition to an end. Puccini and other Italian composers travel in a different direction but do not blaze new trails. Verdi sums up in his genius the Italian penchant for melody, forceful, dramatic music, human characterization, and opera as a living, vital force. To travel with Verdi from *Nabucco* to *Otello* and *Falstaff* is to cross a wide terrain. One can be grateful that the leader led the way so directly, so powerfully, and so simply.

SUGGESTED READING

Rossini   Stendhal (Henri Beyle), *Life of Rossini*, rev. ed., Richard N. Coe, trans., Calder & Boyars, London, 1970. Weak on facts, but a lively contemporary account of Rossini, the Italian opera of his time, and the conditions that spawned it.

Toye, Francis, *Rossini: A Study in Tragi-Comedy*, 1934, Norton Library paperback, New York, 1963 Mostly biography, but well-written.

Weinstock, Herbert, *Rossini*, Knopf, New York, 1968. Latest and most complete biography

Donizetti   Ashbrook, William, *Donizetti*, Cassell, London, 1965 Most thorough "life and works" in English.

Weinstock, Herbert, *Donizetti and the World of Opera in Italy, Paris, and Vienna in the First Half of the Nineteenth Century*, Pantheon, New York, 1963 Especially good for background.

Bellini   Orrey, Leslie, *Bellini*, Farrar, Straus & Giroux, New York, 1969

Verdi   Hughes, Patrick C. (Spike), *Famous Verdi Operas*, Hale, London, 1968. Good musical and textual analysis.

Martin, George, *Verdi: His Music, Life and Times*, Dodd, Mead, New York, 1963: Reprint Da Capo, New York, 1979.

Osborne, Charles, *The Complete Operas of Verdi*, Knopf, New York, 1970. Treats all of Verdi's operas.

Toye, Francis, *Verdi. His Life and Works*, 1946, Vintage Books paperback, New York, 1959 Still first-rate.

Verdi Librettos, William Weaver, trans., Doubleday, Anchor Books paperback, New York, 1963 Italian and English for *Rigoletto, Il Trovatore, La Traviata, Aida, Otello*.

Walker, Frank, *The Man Verdi*, Knopf, New York, 1962. Detailed information on certain aspects of Verdi's life.

12 French Opera

French opera outside France has never achieved the wide popularity its Italian and German counterparts have. With one or two exceptions like Gounod's *Faust* and Bizet's *Carmen*, which have consistently held the stage, French opera has had a more rarified appeal to foreign audiences. To the connoisseur, the reasons may be obscure, but not to the general opera-goer. He finds that French opera in general lacks the elemental surge and soaring melody of his favorite Verdi or Puccini, or the overwhelming orchestral excitement of Wagner. It is too reasonable and objective, depending upon the composer and the style of the age when it was written. The visual elements and the ballet assume too much importance. In many cases, blood and thunder are absent, and the whole affair seems anemic compared to Italian vocal melodrama. This attitude has some merit, but it breaks down when faced with the greatest French operas.

Part of the difficulty lies with the French desire that in opera—if there has to be a pecking order—drama comes first and music second. Emphasis upon *raison*, logic, and orderly sequence of events can destroy the grip which music has upon a listener absorbed in the sound of opera and little concerned with the niceties of regulated action. Then there is the French language—a mellifluous sound in the mouth of a skilled interpreter, native or otherwise, but notoriously difficult to sing properly because of its lack of strong accents.

The liquid vowels of Italian, musical in themselves, are absent, and a foreign singer is apt to swallow French words, so that the bite and enunciation of the French tongue is lost. (To the French, poor declamation ruins an opera.) Because words and action are important factors on the stage, French composers have rarely allowed the orchestra to overpower the voice or assume a role out of proportion to the other elements in the opera. The orchestra has tended to subordinate itself to the voice and the formal style often seems rigid to the outsider; whereas Italian opera lets singing be the chief attraction for the audience, French opera will rarely permit singing to overwhelm action.

French opera has had a long and honorable tradition extending from the beginnings of opera itself. This rich heritage is as valuable as it is often neglected. French opera has contributed the dignity of serious drama, the chorus as an integral element within the drama, and the fusion of dance and the visual elements to opera. It has counterbalanced the recurring tendency to overemphasize the voice. At its best, there is a unity of music, drama, and spectacle the art seeks but seldom attains. In all respects, French opera has something important to say.

| Lully and the Seventeenth Century | When most history books speak of opera's beginning about 1600 as an Italian phenomenon, they forget that a kind of opera existed at the same time in France. Since its main emphasis, however, was upon dancing rather than singing, early French opera has often been overlooked. Yet the famous *Circé, ou Le Ballet comique de la Reine* (Circé, or the Comic Ballad of the Queen, 1581), an entertainment staged in Paris for a royal marriage, had songs, choruses, instrumental music for dances, and a primitive kind of plot dealing with Circé's holding cavaliers, gods, and goddesses prisoner in her magic garden until they were released by Jupiter who strikes Circé with a thunderbolt. In 1617, a *Ballet de la Délivrance de Renaud* (Ballet of the Deliverance of Renaud) dealt with a similar story, though this time it was derived from Tasso's *Jerusalem Delivered* (1575); Armida, the enchantress, holds Rinaldo, the hero-mortal, prisoner in her magic garden. Tasso's story has been the source of many opera plots through operatic history. In spite of the rudimentary nature of the plot, all the operatic ingredients were present in these entertainments with the exception of connecting dialogue or recitative to hold them together. There were separate scenes where backgrounds, characters, and dancing could promenade to divert the audience. |

Three factors in addition to the dance, influenced French opera in the seventeenth century. One was the musical pastorale which had its start in Italy, but was quickly taken over in France. The action was simplicity itself: a shepherd loves a shepherdess who either does not love him or is forced to marry another instead of her beloved. The complications were always ironed out in a happy ending. Meanwhile, there were opportunities for dances, discussions about love, and even comic scenes with satyrs. The situations were so stereotyped that everybody knew them and there was no necessity for explanation in recitative.

A second strong influence was Italian opera, brought to Paris by Mazarin (Louis XIII's Italian adviser and cardinal) in the 1640s, partly for political reasons. What impressed the French most in these operas were the scenic effects—that is, "the machines", (of the Italian, Giacomo Torelli, 1608–1687), which for imagination, invention, and resplendence were the marvel of the age. The French audience hardly knew what was going on in the foreign language and the incredibly complicated and bizarre plots, but they could see the marvelous and striking effects. They wanted something similar.

The third influence was classical French drama, which reached its apex in the works of Corneille and Racine from the 1640s through the 1680s. The emphasis in these dramas upon order and reason, backed philosophically by Descartes and politically by the absolutist realm of Louis XIV, breathed the spirit of the age. Each drama adhered to "the three unities" (a single action transpiring in one place and completed in one day). There were no secondary plots and no mingling of tragedy and comedy. The stories were based on mythology, and the characters were mostly royalty. These traits were carried over into musical drama.

When Lully and Quinault, his librettist, began to write French opera, the proportion and clarity of French tragedy was present in their minds as were the rolling alexandrines (12-syllable lines rhyming in couplets). Their first works became known as "tragédies en musique" (eventually "tragédies lyriques"). Passion was created not by the exciting incident but by the expression of speech. The titles of these Lully–Quinault operas (*Cadmus, Thésée, Proserpine, Persée, Psyché*, etc.) indicate the mythological stories on which they were based.

Giovanni Battista Lulli (Jean-Baptiste Lully) (1632–1687), an Italian who came to France when he was 10 or 12, rose from the scullery to become a favorite of the king, a dictator at court, and the best known composer in France—a rags-to-riches saga. He had a keen intellect, great administrative and political abilities, and skill as a violinist, dancer, and conductor. As a favorite of Louis XIV, he was given his own small orchestra ("Les Petits Violons"), from which he learned his orchestral technique. Among his earliest compositions were a series of ballets, in which he and the king both danced. He became associated with Molière and the theater and wrote incidental music for *Le Mariage forcé* (The Forced Marriage, 1664), *Le Bourgeois Gentilhomme* (The Bourgeois Gentleman, 1670), and other comedies. When he, a born courtier and a none-too-scrupulous entrepreneur, sensed the rise of a new kind of musical entertainment, which was to become French opera, be obtained the sole patent of an "Académie de Musique" (the official title of the Paris Opera today is "Académie Nationale de Musique") to produce these entertainments (1672). For the next 14 years he and his librettist, Philippe Quinault (1635–1688), wrote some 15 operas. Quinault is linked to Lully as Calzabigi is to Gluck, da Ponte to Mozart, and Boito to Verdi.

What were these operas like? Almost always they began with a prologue glorifying Louis XIV. In these prologues, attributes like "glory," "honor," and "love" were personified, or gods and heroes of mythology like Apollo and Mars sang the praises of the Sun King. Occasionally, pastoral scenes were introduced. Five acts followed, interspersed with much dance and incidental music (*divertissements* and descriptive symphonies meant to please the eye and ear rather than further the action). Quinault modified the unities and dwelt excessively on the mysteries of love with an inevitable struggle between *L'Amour* (Love) and *La Gloire* (Glory). But his librettos were treated as serious dramatic works and were read widely, even in the eighteenth century. There were no comic scenes and all action was deliberate. Kingly figures predominated in the stories, as befitted the person they were meant to please; the operas were obviously designed to appeal to a monarch and his court, not to a Venetian public. As a consequence, everything was quite formal and stately; and, since time did not matter, the spectacle lasted hours.

Lully made sure that the words could always be understood and his music did not interfere. He aimed at simplicity and clarity in his style (that is, no sudden modulations or jagged intervals). Decoration of the vocal line by the performer was banned except those ornaments written in. Choruses sang simple block harmony. On paper, much of this music looks dull; in spite of arid patches, in a proper stylistic performance, it comes alive (true of early music in general). Lully's great contribution to French opera was a fluid and flexible recitative, beautifully adapted to the French language with changing time signatures to fit different phrase lengths. Little melodic phrases would often appear and reappear in the recitative to be repeated in a rondo fashion and to vary the texture. For the

Example 12-1 Lully, *Armide* (1686)

(Finally he is in my power. This fatal enemy. This proud conqueror. The charms of sleep will ensnare him for my vengeance. I am going to pierce his invincible heart. Through him all my captives will escape from slavery. Now let him feel all my rage! But what trouble seizes me? Who makes me hesitate? What does pity want to say to me in his favor? Let us strike! Heavens, who can stop me? Let us finish! But I tremble! Let us revenge ourselves! I sigh!)

(Come, support my wishes. Demons, transform youselves into lovely zephyrs.)

most part, the composer adhered to a one-note-a-syllable pattern. Lully listened carefully at the Comédie-Française to the famous actress La Champmeslé to hear her accent, the rise and fall of the voice, the speed of the diction. Then he tried to imitate her in his musical line. He also had the knack of writing catchy little airs, quite different from the more developed Italian variety. Many could be danced or sung according to the context. He perfected the overture (see pp. 16, 95), which, in its slow-fast pattern, was a hallmark of his style.

One of the most popular Quinault—Lully works was *Armide* (1686) based on the same cantos (XIV—XVI) of Tasso as the Renaud ballet of 1617 (Gluck used the same libretto almost 100 years later). *Armide* was one of the last works on which Lully and Quinault worked, and in it Lully was freer in his treatment of the conventional musical forms, more romantic, and more emotional than he had been in earlier works. The story centers around the conflict and love of Armide and Renaud. She, a beautiful enchantress, and niece of Hidraot, a magician, is determined to overthrow the redoubtable knight Renaud, the warrior arm of Godfrey and his followers who have come to deliver Jerusalem from the infidels. Armide and her spirits have tried to foil the deliverance by casting magic spells over the Christian knights. In Act II, Renaud falls out of favor with Godfrey and wanders into temporary exile. He falls asleep (scene 3) upon the grass beside a river (really in Armide's enchanted garden). Armide discovers him there, exults, and prepares to slay him with a dart. But as she gazes upon the handsome sleeping knight, she stays her hand; overcome by her feelings, she bids her demons bear Renaud and herself away.

In this famous scene, which opens with a powerful instrumental introduction, Quinault and Lully demonstrate the effectiveness of their collaboration. The text is observation and gloating over triumph (Example 12-1a). When Armide thinks of her vengeance and how Renaud's death will release all her captured followers, she works herself into a fury, ready to strike; but at the moment of execution (measure 12), she weakens. Lully breaks up the line by rests as the series of rhetorical questions repeat themselves. Armide tries to act again (measure 16) on "Frappons" (let us strike), but again something stops her. As the line becomes more agitated, she sings at quicker intervals with short-breathed exclamations. Finally, she can only "tremble" (*frémis*) and "sigh" (*soupire*); she is defeated. After a brief orchestral elision, she breaks into a little air telling her demons to change themselves into gentle zephyrs and waft her and Renaud to the ends of the earth, so they can taste the fruits of love (*b*). The dance by which this is accomplished is the same played previously when nymphs, shepherds, and shepherdesses wrapped the sleeping Renaud with garlands of flowers and hoped he would fall victim to the enchantments of love (c).

Lully creates a scene so touching that it is a tribute to his abilities as dramatist and musician. The recitative deliberately and gradually leads to the climax. Armide's air is by no means a quick change of heart (it shows her inward struggle), but with the dance, she has put herself in stronger hands than hers, and fate takes its course.

Rameau Lully, by virtue of his strong position at court, his dominating personality, and the genuine appeal of his opera to French audiences, put his stamp on French theatrical music for several generations. Though he died in 1687, his king and master, Louis XIV, who lived until 1715, often revived Lully's operas. Composers of succeeding generations found Lully's style amenable to their own creative efforts. Few stood out or pioneered in new directions. Not until well into the eighteenth century did a composer appear who assumed Lully's mantle.

Jean-Philippe Rameau (1683–1764) was the next important figure in French operatic history. A native Frenchman, he did not turn to writing opera until he was 50 years old. The earlier part of his life was devoted to teaching, writing instrumental music (mostly keyboard works), and a famous treatise on harmony (*Traité de l'harmonie*, 1722). He was also an organist. There was little to show he had a bent for the theater. His reputation was a narrow one, gained mainly through his *Pièces à clavecin* (Pieces for the harpsichord) and the controversy that surrounded his harmony treatise. He was not very sociable, and his appearance was likened to that of "a long organ pipe" curved in the middle. Yet during these years he harbored a secret passion for the stage and took every chance to study actors, movement, dance, and voice in Paris. He eventually settled in Paris after living in Dijon (his native city), Avignon, and Clermont-Ferrand. Before he turned to opera, he wrote cantatas and church motets in which he learned to cultivate the voice.

Opportunity for recognition came through a wealthy financier, La Riche de la Pouplinière, at whose home Rameau was in charge of the music. In this grand estate, there was a little theater for musical and theatrical entertainment. Rameau set out to find a librettist. He first applied to Houdar de la Motte, the leading librettist of the day, but was ignored. He then tried Voltaire, whom he met through La Pouplinière and who, in the early 1730s, was by no means the famous man of letters he was to become. The two men collaborated on a *Samson*, but the authorities refused to allow a biblical subject on the stage. Voltaire later published his libretto, and Rameau used his music elsewhere. Finally, Rameau settled on the Abbé Pellegrin, an elderly man with a number of plays and librettos to his credit.

The opera produced by Rameau and Pellegrin was *Hippolyte et Aricie*. It was presented at La Pouplinière's theater in 1733 and later performed at the Académie (opera). Critics gave it a lukewarm reception, calling it "learned" and "filled with too much music." Rameau nearly gave up, but two years later he wrote *Les Indes galantes* (The Gallant Indies, 1735), an opera-ballet, which was an immediate success. *Castor et Pollux* followed in 1737, *Dardanus* in 1739, and a number of other tragedies and ballets through the 1750s. Toward the end of his life, Rameau's work was considered old-fashioned and was violently attacked by Rousseau, the Encyclopedists, and other advocates of simple Italian opera.

As an opera composer, Rameau held fast to the Lully tradition of a flexible recitative and much ballet and spectacle. But Rameau had more ability as a pure musician then Lully, and many of his works can stand beside those of Handel and Bach (Rameau was almost their exact contemporary). A musician's musician, he was a very skilled composer who knew precisely what effects he wanted. He did not cultivate popularity but gave his utmost to create a work of art. Some of his dance and descriptive music is superb. While he was not by nature an experimentalist, he could follow his own wishes and not be bound by those of a monarch. Like all who lived in the baroque age, he believed implicity in the power of music to describe, to illuminate, to depict feelings and emotions. There was surprising passion beneath all his longing for reason and order.

Pellegrin was bold, indeed rash, to select a subject for his libretto that was so near Racine's *Phèdre* (1677) as *Hippolyte et Aricie*. His main source was Euripides' *Hippolytus*, however. He borrowed only the figures of Aricie (the captive princess with whom Hippolytus falls in love) and Phèdre's nurse from Racine. The original story concerns Hippolytus, a proud youth and follower of Diana, who loves no woman. He is the son of Theseus, who is away at wars. His stepmother, Phaedra, falls in love with him, but Hippolytus will not have her. In despair, she hangs herself, accusing, in a letter to Theseus, Hippolytus of being her seducer. Returning, Theseus banishes Hippolytus and invokes the vengeance of Neptune on him. Hippolytus, driving on the beach, is dragged to death when his horses are frightened by a sea monster. Too late, Theseus learns of Phaedra's deceit and Hippolytus' sacrifice.

The opera libretto borrows from Euripides, Seneca, and Racine. Racine explored the motive of jealousy; he has Hippolyte fall in love with the maiden Aricie. She is the last of the Pallantides, and Thésée's (Theseus') rival for the throne of Athens, since her father and all her brothers are dead. Thésée has forced her to enter the service of Diana so she cannot bear children. Phèdre, consumed with jealousy of Aricie, confesses her love of Hippolyte to him; he is appalled. As she threatens to kill herself with his sword, Thésée breaks in. Phèdre and Hippolyte offer no explanation for their conduct. When they leave, Oenone, the nurse, implies to Thésée that Hippolyte was about to force himself on his stepmother. Hippolyte's banishment and death follow, as in Euripides. But in the opera as in Ovid, Diana takes pity on the lovers and reunites them in the last act.

Pellegrin was no Quinault, but he knew how to manage these episodes. Much of Racine's subtlety and interplay of character is lost in the change from play to libretto, but Rameau took the dialogue and powerfully pointed up its dramatic climaxes. Rameau's musical treatment of his own tongue is fitting, particularly rhythm, inflection, and accent in the recitative.

Of the five acts in *Hippolyte et Aricie* the second is perhaps the best. It is largely Pellegrin's invention for strengthening the character of Thésée, in previous plays of minor importance. Thésée seeks to enter Hades to find his friend, Pirithous, who has gone there to abduct Perséphone, Pluto's wife. (In Greek mythology, Theseus went with his friend and suffered imprisonment until released by Hercules.) He is taunted by the Fury, Tisiphone, at the gates, which only Neptune, Thésée's father, can open. Neptune has granted his son three wishes, and Thésée makes this the first of them. Accordingly, the gates open, and Thésée is confronted by Pluto and the three Fates or Destinies. Thésée pleads for his friend, but is denied him by Pluto. He then asks for death for himself, but the Fates say they are the ones who control his destiny. He is eventually returned to earth (his second wish) with the help of Mercury.

The three Fates (*Parques* in French) sing two remarkable trios. The first comes in scene 4 when Thésée begs Tisiphone to drag him to his faithful friend or let him suffer death. The Fates solemnly intervene. The close male voice part-writing in a strict chordal pattern is almost a religious chant; it is very effective after a long recitative. The voices are accompanied only by the continuo which stays discreetly in the background. The sentiments of the text, the harmonic texture, the slow, ritual nature of the music recall the second act of Mozart's *Magic Flute* and Sarastro's priests intoning the Masonic virtues of their realm (Example 12-2a). Thésée's final appeal to Neptune is

Example 12-2

Rameau, *Hippolyte et Aricie* (1733)
Act II, scene 4 (Trio of Fates)

(The supreme will of destiny has placed in our hands the thread of your days.)

(Your fate fills us with sudden horror.)

(c) *Thésée seul (Recit.)* Act III, scene 9 (Thésée alone)

(Such blessings! I shudder when I think of it. If one of them is vengeance, what it does cost in heartache. Why is it that I hesitate to punish such an ingrate?)

answered by Mercury, who asks Pluto to release Thésée. His request is phrased in a quaint diplomatic sally which says that although Jupiter holds sway in the heavens, Neptune rules the oceans, and Pluto is supreme in Hades, they all can agree only if there is common understanding. Pluto agrees to let Thésée go, but asks the Fates to read his destiny. They foretell a terrible doom for him which makes them tremble with fright. This second trio, antithesis of the first, is accompanied by full orchestra of winds (flutes, oboes, bassoons) and strings which, in a series of introductory measures, give the full flavor of Thésée's destiny. The upward rushing scales of the violins continue against a strong dotted figure on a G minor chord in the other strings (*b*). The harmonic drive is built in the bass, starting from G and ascending to A and B flat as each voice enters. This pattern continues through the trio—a vivid tonal depiction of the tragedy that awaits Thésée.

Act III is also splendid. Phèdre appeals to Venus to solve her dilemma. Oenone announces Hippolyte. He, thinking Phèdre desires the throne for her own son by Thésée, offers to support this claim. (In Act I, Thésée has been declared lost because he was last seen entering Hades from which there is no return. His loss enabled Phèdre to declare openly her love for Hippolyte.) Phèdre tells Hippolyte he can have everything; Hippolyte misunderstands, says he has no desire to rule, and only loves Aricie. The crisis ensues: Phèdre confesses her love for Hippolyte, takes his sword, Thésée enters, etc.; the end of the act finds Thésée requesting of Neptune his third wish—revenge on Hippolyte.

To resolve the tension before this, there is a welcome (chorus and dances) for Thésée by his people. The sailors' dances, called airs also, are particularly attractive for their subtle rhythmic quality. Generally in two parts with both halves repeated, their charm lies in tunefulness and rhythmic irregularity. Thésée thanks his people politely, but his heart is not in it. As soon as they depart, he speaks deeply, bitterly, and tragically about the terrible "blessings" that await him. The irony of the opening "Quel biens!" is self-evident with its high E for baritone, held a whole measure (c). Then follows a shudder at the thought of vengeance on his own son (still alluded to as a bitter blessing). Even more striking is the "Vivement" instrumental interlude that echoes these words; Rameau, knowing the power of pure music to express feelings beyond words, shows Thésée's torment by a rapid syncopated rush of strings over a pedal point of F sharp. How can he inflict this on his own son? The question invokes filial pity and tenderness in a melting string passage of four measures (d). The rest of the recitative text is equally passionate with appropriate instrumental reaction: "The blood he betrays speaks to me in his favor. No, no, in a son so guilty I see only a frightful monster. Let him find in me nothing but an avenger." (The passage is a powerful mixture of straight recitative and instrumental reply, anticipating by some years the techniques of the later eighteenth century.) Rameau may not appeal to every taste, but his works deserve a high place in the history of French opera.

Opéra Comique and Grand Opera

For French opera the late eighteenth and the early nineteenth centuries was a time of many cross-currents and little unified direction. After Rameau, the dominant figure in Paris was Gluck in the 1770s. Largely through the influence of Marie Antoinette (daughter of Maria Theresa, Empress of Austria, and now wife of Louis XVI), formerly Gluck's pupil in Vienna, and the French influence at the Viennese court (a diplomat named Roullet), Gluck was launched in Paris. His first original opera of a serious nature was *Iphigénie en Aulide* (1772), followed (1774 and 1776) by the French versions of his previous Italian *Orfeo* and *Alceste*, first heard in Vienna. In spite of the supporters of Italian opera in Paris who launched an all-out attack on this "new" venture, Gluck persevered. His next attempt was a setting of Quinault's *Armide* in 1777 (see p. 206), only partially successful because of the "longueurs" of the five-act libretto. Gluck's French masterpiece was *Iphigénie en Tauride* (1779), derived mostly from Euripides, probably the nearest to a revived Greek tragedy in outstanding musical form. The characterization, the chorus, the use of the orchestra, the reconciliation of musical and dramatic principles in this work made it a model work for years to come and strongly influenced composers like Weber, Berlioz, and Wagner in the nineteenth century.

One aspect of Gluck's creative life in Vienna which has been given little attention was his writing of French opéra comique during the years 1756–1762. Count Durazzo, intendant at the court, wanted to take advantage of a French vogue, and he imported Paris librettos to which Gluck could add airs or write new music (many of these little operas had been put together previously by French composers).

The nature of opéra comique is difficult for the American or English listener to comprehend because so few of these works have ever been performed outside France, yet they have a long and honorable history from the seventeenth century through the nineteenth. The music ranged all the way from popular tunes of a balled nature (called "vaudevilles" in French) to quite sophisticated airs and ensembles. The mark of the genre was spoken dialogue (instead of recitative), and a happy ending. The operas were not necessarily "comic," even though labeled as such, but they were generally light in mood and frequently satirized serious opera. Often they pointed a moral, which to the new bourgeois society of Paris in the nineteenth century was an important attribute.

Historically, one of the most famous ones was Jean-Jacques Rousseau's *Devin du village* (The Village Soothsayer, 1752), which he wrote to prove that French opera could be as simple and delightful as the Italian variety of the day. He actually included recitatives, but in feeling the little work was quite French.

Gluck's best opéra comique was *La Rencontre imprévue* (The Unexpected Meeting, Vienna, 1764), a work almost entirely his own, with many fine airs and ensembles. It was translated into German as *Die Pilger von Mekka* (The Pilgrims from Mecca) and was undoubtedly heard by Mozart sometime in the 1770s, for the story is very similar to *The Abduction*: a pair of lovers are caught in an eastern harem, and the lady has to be rescued from the sultan by her faithful young man. Gluck's music, although French, was a bridge between the world of opéra comique and Singspiel.

Opéra comique flourished in Paris in the eighteenth century alongside serious opera. These works were mostly little comedies with a mingling of dialogue and songs—older "vaudeville" airs or newly composed ones. Some French composers took the music more seriously and began to expand the genre as Gluck had done in Vienna. Instead of little ballads, they wrote more fully developed airs and ensembles with linking instrumental interludes. One of the best of this kind was *Richard Coeur-de-Lion* (Richard the Lion-

Hearted, 1784) by André Grétry (1741–1813), a Belgian who wrote over 40 opéras comiques for Paris. King Richard of England's rescue from secret imprisonment after a Crusade was familiar and endearing. (Richard recognized Blondel, his faithful follower, by the song he sang beneath the window, although he could not see him.) Grétry anticipated the romantic period with his sentimental but affecting melodies which were tuneful and musically gracious. Equally effective were the ensembles, dances, and choruses which gave weight and seriousness to the work.

During and after the French Revolution (1780s and 1790s), two kinds of opera dominated Paris: opéra comique was one; the other was "grand opera" ("grand" in the French sense of large and extensive, rather than necessarily magnificent and sumptuous in the English sense). Gradually it assumed definite form and by the 1830s it dominated French operatic life. Its genesis was in the large public spectacles and fetes introduced to keep the people happy during the post-Revolution and Napoleonic years. These works called for large crowd scenes and processions that were imposing on the stage. The leading opera composer at the turn of the century was an Italian, Luigi Cherubini (1760–1842), whose works (serious opéras comiques) were highly admired by Beethoven. Cherubini's French operas, with those of his contemporary Etienne Méhul (1763–1817), were serious and classical in subject matter, greatly influenced by Gluck. Napoleon's favorite composer was Gasparo Spontini (1774–1851), also an Italian, who ruled operatic Paris for the first two decades of the nineteenth century and Berlin thereafter—no mean feat for a foreigner. His best known work was *La Vestale* (The Vestal, 1807)—a "grand" opera—which combined a love story, a rescue theme, and many crowd scenes in a colorful depiction of ancient Rome. The heroine's innocence is proved by a lightning bolt that rekindles the fire on the Vestal altar. Wagner was so impressed by this work that he openly used it as his model for *Rienzi* (1842), his early grand opera.

Three men were primarily responsible for the popularity and success of grand opera in Paris before the middle of the century: Louis Véron, entrepreneur and director in the early 1830s; Eugène Scribe (1791–1861), a prolific and able librettist; and Giacomo Meyerbeer (1791–1864), musician and composer. Véron took charge of the opera house at a critical time just after the July Revolution of 1830 which established Louis-Philippe as elected king of France. It was a bourgeois regime that prided itself on small virtues, laissez-faire business practice, and the rise of a new class. Formerly the opera belonged to the aristocracy; now it was opened to the new moneyed classes whose tastes were less esoteric. Véron was a born publicist and he promoted opera by a shrewd combination of display and public entertainment—for example, balls were held at the opera house when there was no performance. Spectacle in the opera meant lavish costumes and scenes of great splendor. The auditorium was partially darkened during a performance and the curtains lowered between acts while scenery was changed. New and improved lighting (gas instead of candles) added to the overall effect.

Scribe, a facile playwright of the 1820s and 1830s (over 100 of his plays were performed in these years), knew what the public wanted. The old classical and mythological stories were scrapped in favor of more recent history. Tales of the Middle Ages and Renaissance became common, particularly if they embodied a hero or heroine from a lower class who managed to outwit the aristocracy. Scribe, although fundamentally a playwright, had some experience with opéra comique and he took great pains with his librettos to see that everything worked. He was not finicky about historical accuracy as long as an exciting situation was able to develop. With the exception of Rossini's *William Tell* (1829), (the last opera Rossini wrote before he retired from the stage at 37, and one of the first grand operas), Scribe was responsible for the other famous works of the time: Auber's *La Muette de Portici* (The Dumb Girl of Portici, 1828); Halévy's *La Juive* (The Jewess, 1835); Meyerbeer's *Robert le Diable* (Robert the Devil, 1831) and *Les Huguenots* (The Huguenots, 1836). Most of these works involved spectacular scenes. Fenella, mute sister of Masaniello, Neapolitan fisherman, who leads his people against the Spanish usurper in *La Muette*, jumps into a seething Vesuvius after her brother is killed. Rachel, persecuted Jewess in fifteenth century Constance (*La Juive*), is thrown into a cauldron of boiling oil by a fanatical cardinal who learns too late that Rachel is his own daughter. *Robert* is the story of a struggle between good and evil within the soul of the hero; the most famous scene is a resurrection of nuns who died in carnal sin and shed their grey shrouds in a bacchanalian ballet. *Les Huguenots* has a great marriage scene, a confrontation of Catholic and Protestant soldiers, a bathing ballet, a conspiracy chorus, and a bit of *Ein' feste Burg* ("A mighty fortress") Luther's great hymn. Scribe made his characters prototypes of social classes rather than individuals. His strongest figures are women—persons of passion and conviction; the men tend to be unstable and fickle.

Meyerbeer was a German, whose upbringing in Berlin was that of a cultivated Jewish family. After only mild success with some comic operas and an oratorio, he turned to Italy (Venice) where he became captivated by Italian style, particularly Rossini. He wrote a number of Italian operas which were received enthusiastically by the Italian public. Paris, however, was the mecca for the enterprising opera composer, and the eclectic Meyerbeer went there just as Rossini was pulling the Parisian music theater out of the doldrums with his Italian works revised for the French stage and two original French pieces, *Le Comte Ory* and *William Tell*. Meyerbeer's other two grand operas in Paris, aside from *Robert le Diable* and *Les Huguenots* were *Le Prophète* (The Prophet, 1849) and *L'Africaine* (The African Maid, 1865, performed posthumously). In neither of these did he reach the popularity he had attained earlier, although *L'Africaine* probably contains his finest music.

The Hugenots is Meyerbeer's most effective work. It is grand opera *par excellence*. The number of performances it received in Paris and all over Europe in the nineteenth century was enormous. The story takes place in Paris and Touraine in 1572 during the height of Catholic–Protestant religious controversy in France. It concerns a fictitious episode which takes place on St. Bartholomew's Eve. Raoul de Nangis, a Huguenot nobleman, is in love with Valentine (daughter of the Catholic leader, Comte de Sainte Bris), but she is forced to marry Comte de Nevers, a Catholic lord. Valentine overhears the plot of the Catholic leaders to assassinate all the Protestants that night. Raoul has come to beg Valentine's forgiveness for his refusal to marry her (their proposed union was backed by Queen Marguerite de Valois to bring peace between the two religious groups, but Raoul felt it was a marriage forced for political reasons and that Valentine loved de Nevers). When the tocsin sounds, Raoul rushes to join his people. The slaughter is frightful, but Raoul, wounded, manages to seek refuge in a churchyard with a few of his friends and Valentine who has joined them. The Catholics break in to shoot the unarmed group. Too late, the Comte de Sainte Bris recognizes his own daughter among them. The opera calls for a large cast of characters——five sopranos, five tenors, and six deeper male voices, from baritone to basso profundo. Seven of these are almost equal in importance: Raoul, Valentine, the Queen, de Nevers, Sainte Bris, Urbain (page to Marguerite), and Marcel (servant to Raoul). The settings include a banquet hall in a chateau, a garden with bathing pools, a field on the banks of the Seine, a salon in a Parisian mansion, a barricaded street during the massacre, and a churchyard.

Scribe and Meyerbeer built their acts into a series of great tableaux. Most of the action takes place in the ensembles. There are some splendid bits of recitative and aria, but they are mostly for the lesser characters. Valentine and Raoul perform largely with others, but in Act IV they have one of Meyerbeer's finest love duts. Also in this act, the best in the opera, is the oath-taking and blessing of the swords by the Catholics before they embark on their vengeful mission—a famous chorus in opera.

Meyerbeer pioneered in new orchestral effects, particularly with the brass, and was very influential on younger composers. But his works have now almost entirely disappeared from the repertoire— his bombast and rhodomontade were not attractive to later generations. In his music there is a good deal of repetition, of unmotivated coloratura, of side-shows that have no relevance to the plot; yet for sheer theatrical excitement, Meyerbeer has seldom been surpassed. Some day his operas may return. If they do, they will need solo and choral singing of a high order, and a willingness to spare no expense with the stage settings. Performed again with something like their original intent, they might delight the operatic public.

Berlioz   Hector Berlioz (1803–1869), whom Meyerbeer's popularity over-shadowed but whom Meyerbeer greatly admired, is one of the most interesting figures in the history of music. Unquestionably he was an original genius whose contributions to orchestral technique, the outward forms of music (that is, dramatic works in unclassifiable categories such as concert-opera, dramatic symphony), and writings on music will always be profound. Although he has been called one of the great romantics in art (he for music, Victor Hugo for the novel, and Delacroix for painting are generally cited as the most representative artists of their time), at heart he was a classicist in a romantic age. His later works show tight discipline and self-restraint, very unlike the qualities generally assigned him. Nothing is more deceiving than to characterize Berlioz solely by his first symphony (the *Symphonie fantastique*, 1830–1831), a work subtitled "Episode in the life of an artist," written in his twenty-seventh year, and accompanied by a florid, descriptive program, which Berlioz later retracted, saying he wanted only the titles to the five movements of the symphony given in the program and not the verbiage. This symphony, Berlioz' most famous composition, has forever labeled the composer as a wild-eyed radical, hopelessly in love with an actress he had never met, and ready to overturn the whole Parisian musical establishment.

The real story is more complicated and less dashing. Berlioz came from a cultivated, moderately well-to-do family in Dauphiné (southeast part of France near Grenoble) and was educated by his father, a liberal physician, who taught him the classics (particularly Virgil) and the rudiments of music. When Berlioz first left home and an overly devout mother, he was destined for medicine. His early struggles in Paris, medicine and music vying with each other, are outlined in his *Memoirs*—an incomplete, slightly fictional, but valuable account of his young manhood. His emancipation from his family and the conservative Parisian musical world took many years. On a fourth attempt he finally won the Rome prize from the Conservatoire by sacrificing his principles and writing the kind of piece he knew his judges wanted.

Berlioz' life was a struggle to achieve for music the serious recognition as an art he felt it deserved. As a result of his efforts (concerts conducted throughout Europe; his penetrating pen—most of his life he had to subsist on musical journalism; his own works) he had a lasting influence on European musical life of the nineteenth century, raising standards and lifting sights higher than they had been before.

Since Berlioz was essentially a dramatic composer, it was natural he should be captivated and absorbed by opera. (Gluck, whose mature works he heard at the Opera, and Beethoven, whose symphonies were just being performed in Paris, were Berlioz' musical gods throughout his creative life.) Though his operatic attempts were different from the run of the repertoire and he knew it would be difficult to get them performed, he never gave up trying. However, it limited the number of operas he wrote. There are only three operas but, in the opinion of many astute critics, one of them deserves a very high place among the operas of the century: it is *Les Troyens* (The Trojans, 1859), which some rank alongside Wagner's *Ring*. Berlioz' other two operas were *Benvenuto Cellini* (1838) and *Béatrice et Bénédict* (1862), an opéra comique based on Shakespeare's *Much Ado About Nothing*, composed at the end of his life.

The Trojans is a most demanding grand opera in five acts with complicated stage settings, a large cast, and of considerable length. One of Berlioz' obstacles is his specifications for numbers— so many in the orchestra, so many in the chorus; some are realistic, some not. Yet the general resources asked for are no greater than those of *The Ring* and there has been exaggeration about the opera's length. *The Trojans* runs about as long as Wagner's *Tristan und Isolde* and is shorter than an uncut *Meistersinger*. Wagner was fortunate to have a king finance him in a special theater built to his own specifications; Berlioz had to compete in the commercial theater of his day, and was never successful.

The history of *The Trojans* as an opera is a melancholy one. After many delays and interruptions, Berlioz managed to finish it in the spring of 1858. The Théâtre-Lyrique (not the Opéra or the Opéra-

Comique) showed some interest in producing it but only if the composer consented to give it in two parts. The opera dealt with the familiar story in Greek mythology of the Trojan War and the aftermath of Aeneas' wanderings—his visit to Carthage, Queen Dido's love for him, and his departure for Italy to found a new kingdom. The first part was to become *La Prise de Troie* (The Taking of Troy, originally in two acts but made into three acts and five scenes). It told of the strange departure of the Greeks, leaving behind the wooden horse, and Cassandra's prophecy that doom was inevitable if the horse was taken inside the city walls. The Trojans pay no attention and move the horse. The city is sacked; Priam the king, and Corebus, Cassandra's lover, are killed; the Trojan women, Cassandra at their head, kill themselves; and Aeneas and his followers escape to endure years of wandering. This portion was never performed in Berlioz' lifetime; it was heard 21 years after his death. The second part, *Les Troyens à Carthage* (The Trojans at Carthage) is laid wholly in Carthage. Aeneas and his followers come; Dido, the queen, falls in love with him, but the gods inexorably push him on toward Italy; Dido pleads in vain and then takes her own life as the Trojan ships sail away. This part was finally given with inadequate preparation and many cuts in November, 1863. Only in the twentieth century has the work been heard in its original form and then infrequently. But a complete recording and a corrected score have finally been made, and the work may well find the public it deserves.

Berlioz wrote his own libretto and based it on the Virgil (Books I, II, and IV of the *Aeneid*) he had known and loved in his youth, even quoting key verses of the Latin at the bottom of his score. Founded on an epic in which the will of the gods prevail over human passion, the situations are stronger and more vivid than the characters themselves. Aeneas is the link between the two parts, but because his destiny is always to flee, he takes a lesser role than the two women who dominate the action—Cassandra in the first two acts, Dido in the last three.

In order to understand why this work has had less acceptance than it might, one must know something of Berlioz' characteristics as a composer. His music, on first acquaintance, is not easily grasped. His melodies are long, winding, complicated affairs that lack Italianate lyricism or Wagnerian brevity but have their own particular charm. In a singular way, he is a great melodist. He is fond of complicated cross rhythms, asymmetrical phrases, and other rhythmic irregularities that have to be heard several times to be appreciated. His harmonic construction is often simple but unorthodox, and it can change with bewildering rapidity. He makes hardly any use of coloration, appoggiaturas and other Italian devices that make inner and outer melodic lines immediately attractive. His operatic accompaniment is carefully designed for the orchestra, and it loses everything when reduced for piano in a vocal score (Berlioz never thought in terms of a keyboard instrument; he played flute and guitar). His special tone-colors of the orchestra are sketched with great care; unless the instruments and combinations he designates are used in the proportions he wishes, his music may sound empty or inconclusive.

On closer acquaintance with *The Trojans*, one finds a dramatic power, a skill, and a tautness that are the mark of a great composer. Berlioz seldom falters in his delineation of events, although he dispenses with much interconnecting tissue another composer would think necessary. His recitative is very pliable. He called it "chant récitatif" (song recitative) and tried to get away from the usual marked difference between it and the lyrical portions of the opera. It is both narration and song, and the abrupt changes of earlier opera are dispensed with. Berlioz kept to the traditional patterns of aria, ensemble, and chorus but blended one into the other by transitions. He calls for a large orchestra but not a monster one. His felicity with winds and brass gives delicate, haunting color to the music. The choruses of Trojans and Carthaginians take a direct part in the drama; they comment and act. Some of the most stirring march music ever written accompanies them as they enter Troy or greet Dido in Carthage. Berlioz does not neglect that favorite French ingredient, the ballet; Parts I and II contain some splendid music for it.

Acts I and II show the Trojan people rejoicing at the end to the 10 years' war. They dance and sing, noticing Achilles' tomb and speculating about the huge wooden horse left on the shore. Cassandra foretells doom, but the people will not listen; Corebus, her lover, tries to alleviate her fears without success. Aeneas tells the assembled company how Laocoon, the priest, and his sons were devoured by two terrible monsters who came out of the sea when Laocoon urged the people to burn the wooden horse and hurled his spear against the side of it. The Trojans interpret this as a sign the gods are angry. The horse may be a sacred symbol and must be preserved within the city walls. It is taken in amid rejoicing and in spite of Cassandra's warning. Act II, first scene, shows Aeneas asleep in his room, visited by the shade of Hector, Priam's son, and the former leader of the Trojan forces. The ghost tells Aeneas that Troy has fallen, the enemy is within the gates, he must gather what forces are left and flee to seek Italy where the Trojans will be reborn. The second scene shows Priam's palace with the Trojan women before Vesta's altar. Cassandra tells them that Aeneas has escaped after saving part of Priam's treasure and gathering many of the soldiers, but that Corebus is dead and that she will not surrender. As the Greeks burst into the palace, she and the other women stab themselves. A good deal of this is Berlioz' invention from hints in Virgil but put together masterfully for the purpose of the opera.

Acts III, IV, and V take place in Carthage. Dido, widowed queen, celebrates with her people the seventh year of their settling in Carthage after fleeing from Tyre. The gods have blessed them with fruitful crops and a prosperous land. Dido, alone with her sister Anna, professes unease in spite of good fortune. Anna says Dido needs a husband, but Dido says she will remain true to Sychaeus' memory. The arrival of the wandering Trojans is announced, and Dido receives them hospitably, particularly because the Carthaginians are threatened by their enemies, the Numidians. Aeneas, making himself known, takes up arms in defense of Carthage. Act IV, first scene, is the famous Royal Hunt and Storm, depicted by Berlioz in music of great beauty. Dido and Aeneas, caught by a storm during a hunt, take refuge in a cave and make love. The huntsmen, naiads, nymphs, and the storm are acted in pantomime. The second scene in Dido's gardens tells us that the enemy attack has been successfully repelled, and Dido, acknowledging her passion for Aeneas, still hesitates. Dido's adviser, Narbal, is worried about neglect of matters of state and what will happen when Aeneas leaves, as it is common knowledge by decree of the gods he must. Anna tries to dispel Narbal's fears, saying love is stronger than war or destiny. Dido and Aeneas openly declare their love when Aeneas relates how Hector's widow, Andromache, after years of hesitancy, finally remarried. Dido hesitates no longer. Act V, first scene, shows the harbor and the Trojan ships. Aeneas struggles with his conscience; the ghosts of Priam, Corebus, Hector, and Cassandra appear and tell him he cannot wait any longer. He gives orders to his men to make ready for departure. Dido learns of these preparations and in an agonizing scene accuses Aeneas of treachery and desertion. The second scene in her palace finds Dido spent, her anger departed; she begs her sister to try to detain Aeneas for a few days. But messengers announce the ships have set sail and it is too late. Dido in a passionate monologue shows her grief, rage, and tumult. The final scene is the ritual for the dead. An enormous funeral pyre has been erected with Aeneas' gifts to Dido beside it. Dido bids farewell to her people and hopes the flames will reach to Aeneas at sea. She has a vision of Hannibal crossing to Italy and of ultimate Roman victory. She then kills herself in an enthralling immolation scene. In the background the Roman capitol is shown with the Emperor surrounded by his legions. The Carthaginians sing undying hatred for the race of Aeneas.

Berlioz' music is particularly difficult to describe, but there are some magnificent touches that anticipate the Wagnerian idiom of a few years later. One is Berlioz' ability to take a theme or motive and transform it in subsequent appearances by variation according to the context. A striking instance is the music that accompanies Cassandra almost every time she appears. Berlioz had no set theory about leading motives or musical characterization, but his intention made his musical ideas clear, and instinctively he created his own system whether it is labeled so or not.

In the initial scene of Act I where the chorus has sung along in C and G major, Cassandra suddenly appears among one of the groups. There is an abrupt breaking off on a diminished chord, and the whole atmosphere changes, as the strings play a wrenching ascending and descending octave passage in E flat which immediately conveys her "wild and troubled look" (Example 12-3a). She suspects the sudden disappearance of the Greeks and foretells ill fate, her race doomed, her love for Corebus unfulfilled. When she reproaches Priam and her people for not heeding her warning, the distinctive, off-beat, ascending runs of the strings, marked out in the beginning, once more rumble in the bass beneath the words "Tu ne m'écoutes pas, tu ne veux rien comprendre" (You do not listen to me; you do not wish to understand anything) (b). Even during the later cavatina when Corebus tries to speak of hope and happiness, the same rising pattern appears in the bass as Cassandra interrupts him with "Tout est menace au ciel" (The sky is full of menace), but it is in E major here and not quite so abrupt, as if Corebus' plaint had temporarily halted some of her fears (c). Corebus lyrically sings "Reviens à toi, vierge adorée" (Come back to yourself, adored maiden), but Cassandra persists in her frightful vision of death, rapine, and slaughter for her people, and the sinister motive rises out of the bass again in a tremolo outlining a dissonant chord (d). Then Cassandra feverishly urges her lover to leave the city that very night. The little pattern is shorter to emphasize breathlessness (e), and is heard almost continuously throughout their duet. Later in the act a triumphal chorus and march herald the procession of the Trojans who will push the horse into the city. Cassandra, horrified, hears the crowd approaching ("L'éclat des chants augmente"— the noise of their singing grows louder). The singing persists while underneath the motive runs through the orchestra (f). At the beginning of Act II while Aeneas is sleeping, the directions read: "Noise of distant fighting." The orchestral introduction reminds us of what this fate is to be by the presence of another slightly different rhythmic version of the ascending theme in the bass (g). At the end of the act when disheveled Cassandra tells the other Trojan women of Aeneas'

Example 12-3   Berlioz, *Les Troyens* (1858)

Example 12-5

(Énée: Dido sighs, but her remorse has fled. Didon/Anna: But my/her heart is absolved.
Iopas/Narbal: Everything conspires to overcome her remorse and her heart.)

escape, the violins reiterate the motive before she speaks (*h*). Some
of these recurrences may be buried for the listener under the weight
of the action and the orchestra, but if the ear is sufficiently attuned,
there is keen musical and dramatic satisfaction to be gained by
recognizing and feeling their impact.

On a less sophisticated and more straightforward scale is Berlioz'
use of the famous Trojan March theme through the opera. It is first
heard in the cornets as the procession gathers to enter Troy (Example
12-4*a*). The rapid temporary turn toward another key (A flat) in
measures 5–7, the distinctive triplets, the shifting accents toward
the end are vintage Berlioz; they remain in the memory. In Act III
when the Trojans are about to be received by Dido, the orchestra
plays a minor version of the march (*b*). Although in substance it is
the same as the original, the swinging triplets are gone, and the
minor mode echoes the uncertain fate of Aeneas and his people. In
the last act after the ghosts have urged Aeneas on to Italy, it appears
as a syncopated undercurrent (*c*) when Aeneas tells his men to make
ready to sail. Lastly, it appears in its original form and full orchestral
panoply when Dido is about to die and the vision of future Rome is
seen in the background.

One of the most lovely lyrical moments in the opera (over too
quickly) is the quintet of Dido, Anna, Aeneas, Iopas (Dido's poet),
and Narbal in Act IV after Aeneas has described what has happened

to Andromache and Dido utters her fateful phrase "Tout conspire à vaincre mes remords et mon coeur est absous" (Everything conspires to overcome my remorse and my heart is absolved)—notice that she has finally overcome all thought of her former husband and gives herself entirely to Aeneas. As in a dream, the ensemble rapturously repeats these words (Example 12-5). The love duo that concludes the act is one of the great moments in Berlioz' score. He fashioned the words in imitation of Shakespeare's dialogue of Lorenzo and Jessica in *The Merchant of Venice* (Act V, 1).

In such a night as this/When the sweet wind did gently kiss the trees/ And they did make no noise .. In such a night stood Dido with a willow in her hand/Upon the wild sea banks, and waft her love to come again to Carthage.

Berlioz' words are:

Nuit d'ivresse et d'extase infinie/Blonde Phoebe, grands astres de sa coeur, /Versez sur nous votre luer bénie; Fleur des cieux, souriez a l'immortel amour! (Night of rapture and boundless ecstasy/ Blond Phoebe and you, great stars of her court/ Pour on us your blessed light/ Flowers of heaven, smile on our immortal love).

The remaining verses refer to Troilus and Cressida, Anchises and Venus, Endymion and Diana, and end as Shakespeare does with the two present lovers. The accompaniment of winds and strings imparts a gentle rocking motion to voices that rise and fall in ecstatic happiness (Example 12-6).

The last act is filled with gems of many descriptions. It opens with a little song by a homesick sailor, Hylas, who dreams of his Phrygian homeland. This simple touching melody brings the drama to a humble human level, needed to counteract the searing tragedy to follow. A little later, in the manner of a Shakespeare comic scene to relieve tension, Berlioz has two sentinels ask why there is talk of departure when the land is fruitful, there are wine and women, and life at sea is a dog's life. A humorous counterpoint bounces back and forth in the winds (clarinets and bassoons) to give the background to this digression. A final example is Dido's confrontation with Aeneas when she learns he is leaving. In the middle of their tense dialogue, the strains of the Trojan march are heard, Dido senses Aeneas' trembling at the sound (Example 12-7), turns on him sarcastically, and asks directly if he will leave—this question accompanied by low tremolo strings, whose throbbing echoes the anguish in her heart. The question (measures 5 and 7) is punctuated by piercing woodwind cries. He says he leaves to die but will always love her. Dido's rage overflows, and in a regal outburst (the orchestra in broken chords) she tells him to go, cursing him as

Example 12-6

(Night of rapture and infinite ecstasy)

Example 12-7

(Didon: I see you quiver when the song of triumph proclaims your glory. You are leaving? Énée: I must go. Didon: You are going? Énée: Yes, but to die. Obedient to the gods. I go and I love you!.)

(Didon: Do not let my cries stop you any longer! Monster of piety!
Go then, go! I curse your gods and you yourself!)

a faithless monster to be cast aside. Berlioz is careful to let every
syllable ring out in this memorable passage.

Although the opera's two parts seem to be separable units, they
belong together and should be performed together to show how
one tragedy begets another, and the force of men's will is nothing
in the hands of destiny. Berlioz has captured this epic story with
great skill. Through his music, the human element and the role of the
gods become believable and come vividly alive.

BIZET AND CARMEN The transition from Berlioz and his work to Bizet and *Carmen* is
not a long one in time (*Carmen* was first heard in March, 1875).
Whereas many have heard of Berlioz, his romanticism, his *Fantastic
Symphony*, and his treatise on orchestration, they know little about

his operas. With Bizet the situation is almost the opposite: every operagoer knows *Carmen*, if not by personal acquaintance at least by reputation, but knows little about the man who wrote the music.

Carmen is one of the three of four most popular operas in the repertory today. Its appeal has always been widespread, and there are few people—even those with a very modest knowledge of music—who have not heard of the toreador's song, the habanera, the seguidilla, the fact that Carmen is a gypsy, and the affair has something to do with Spain. *Carmen* is one of the few works in the operatic literature that is not only intensely popular with the public but is also highly esteemed by professional musicians—a happy, though somewhat unusual unanimity. The work is a masterpiece of the dramatic stage, not only because of its sparkling melodies and gay rhythms, but its libretto is one of the best ever written. It is an extremely natural, instinctive work that needs no theory or rationalization to reveal its "blaze of sunlight." Of the host of commentators, two might be selected. Friedrich Nietzsche, the philosopher, and Wagner's erstwhile disciple, turned from the complexities of *The Ring* to *Carmen* in the following way:

Yesterday I heard—would you believe it?—Bizet's masterpiece, for the twentieth time.   How such a work makes one perfect! One becomes a "masterpiece" oneself. This music seems perfect to me. It approaches lightly, supplely, politely. . . . its subtlety belongs to a race, not to an individual. It is rich. It is precise. It builds, organizes, finishes.   . Have more painful tragic accents ever been heard on the stage? How are they achieved? Without grimaces. Without counterfeit. Without the *lie* of the great style.   With this work one takes leave of the damp north.   . it has what goes with the torrid zone: the dryness of the air, the *limpidezza*. . . .[1]

And Ernest Newman writes:

It is the most Mozartian opera since Mozart, the one in which enchanting musical invention goes in hand in hand, almost without a break, with dramatic veracity and psychological characterization. . . This is indeed music muscled in the Mozartian way, the fascinating way of the cat-tribe, the maximum of speed and grace and the minimum of visible effort.[2]

Georges Bizet (1838–1875), like Mozart, was precocious musically. He had a musician father but not one with the driving ambition and hoarding of resources of a Leopold Mozart. If it were not for Bizet's *Symphony in C major*, composed when he was 17, there

[1] Walter Kaufmann, trans. *The Case of Wagner*, Vintage Books paperback, New York, 1967, pp. 157–158.
[2] Ernest Newman, *Great Operas*, Vintage Books paperback, New York, 1958, vol. 1, pp. 247–248.

would be difficulty attesting to Bizet's phenomenal ability. Yet this little work rivals the compositions of Mozart and Mendelssohn at the same age. The effortless movement, the fluid melodies, the rightness of the music are those of a natural genius who only needs maturity to bring his talent to fruition. That Bizet did not wholly do so is a tragedy for music. His death at 36 (he was a victim of ill-health most of his life) cut short a career that had just begun to blossom. He seemed to lack the self-confidence needed to generate his true creative urge. His mature years were filled with abandoned projects. He had to contend with the same Parisian musical philistinism Berlioz did, but he lacked Berlioz' will to overcome adversity.

After his conservatory training, he easily won on a second try the Rome prize for which Berlioz had struggled so tenaciously. The *Prix de Rome* gave the winner a pension from the state for five years; part of the residency was to be in Rome, part elsewhere if desired. A work ("l'envoi") had to be submitted every year to the Académie des Beaux-Arts in Paris. Bizet's Italian years were very happy ones, but they demonstrated the uncertainty of his compositional struggles. Returning to Paris, the only outlet for him was the stage, but it was still monopolized by the Opéra and the Opéra Comique at the Salle Favart. Neither was very promising: the Opéra clung to the grand opera tradition (Cherubini, Spontini, Meyerbeer, Gluck) and refused to recognize native composers; the Opéra-Comique was the comfortable bourgeois home of carefully selected light opera (spoken dialogue, separate numbers, few complications, and a happy ending). From the 1850s onward, there were, in addition, the operettas of Offenbach, which swept Paris of the Second Empire. But Bizet temperamentally was not attracted to operetta, and in any case, Offenbach with works like *Orphée aux enfers* (Orpheus in the Underworld, 1858) and *La Belle Hélène* (The Beautiful Helen, 1864) was uncrowned king of this music.

Although Bizet spent a good deal of his early manhood doing musical hackwork, he did manage to get two complete operas on the stage—*Les Pêcheurs de perles* (The Pearl Fishers, 1863), and *La Jolie Fille de Perth* (The Pretty Girl from Perth, 1867). Both were given at the Théâtre-Lyrique under Carvalho, not in the two main theaters. Unfortunately, neither of these works was successful with the public, although they possess some fine music, particularly *The Pearl Fishers*. The one-act *Djamileh* (1872) is his only other surviving complete opera previous to *Carmen*.

In spite of discouragement, Bizet felt he was on the right track. He suggested to Henri Meilhac and Ludovic Halévy by 1872 the possibility of a libretto from a short novel by Prosper Mérimée,

Carmen, which had appeared 30 years earlier. The adaptation by these two skilled theater craftsmen was not an easy task. To reduce a sprawling story to manageable form for the stage took considerable experience and insight; a great deal of incident had to be omitted, yet the highlights of the plot maintained in logical and dramatic sequence. Mérimée told his story in the first person. touring Spain for archaeological purposes, he fell in by accident with a notorious outlaw; Mérimée befriended the man and gradually learned his story, which is that of the opera. This tale of Don José and his gradual degradation from a simple country boy to a brigand and murderer could obviously be developed more fully and leisurely by Mérimée than it could in the opera, yet it is remarkable how much of its substance the librettists were able to incorporate. They softened the characters of both Carmen and Don José. In the novel, Carmen has a villainous husband, "One-eyed Garcia," whom Don José manages to slay. Don José also kills his company captain, Zuniga, in the course of a fight. In the opera, the one killing (Don José's stabbing of his beloved Carmen) is reserved for the last act where it comes as the denouement of the tragedy. Carmen in the novel is a gypsy prostitute, a pickpocket, a robbers' decoy, and the accomplice of murderers; in the opera, she is a fascinating, willful woman, but not a criminal. The librettists added to the plot the character of Micaela, who as the "pure girl" is the dramatic foil for Carmen. Micaela gives an added poignancy to the tragedy, and her music sets off the wildness of the other woman.

Don José, a simple country boy, has enlisted in a regiment stationed in Seville (in the novel, he had to flee his native Basque country for severely injuring a man in a quarrel). His widowed mother has living with her an orphan girl (Micaela) she has helped to bring up. Part of the soldier's duty is to keep order in the city, particularly in the area of a cigarette factory, whose workers are mostly women. A disturbance takes place in the factory, and one of the girls is slashed with a knife by Carmen, a gypsy, very pretty but wild and independent. Don José is ordered by his captain, Zuniga, to take her to the guard house. Carmen's fascination (she threw a cassia flower in his direction) has cast a spell on Don José, who previously thought himself in love with Micaela. On the way to confinement, Carmen declares her love for Don José and pleads with him to let her escape; she pushes him and runs off. The maneuver is a clumsy, obvious one, and corporal Don José is stripped of his rank and put in prison for a month.

When he is released, he and Carmen meet again at a tavern on the outskirts of the city. Carmen is part of a smugglers' gang which intends to carry on operations outside of Seville. Escamillo, a toreador, has become fascinated with Carmen and means to become her lover. In the tavern, Don José not only disobeys the orders of Zuniga, but threatens to strike him. As a result, he has no choice but to join the smugglers.

The life of an outlaw makes Don José a moody man. Carmen remains with a man only a few months and is tiring of José. But he is so desperately in love he cannot bear to give her up, even after pleas from Micaela who appears at the smugglers' camp to tell José his mother is dying.

The climax occurs when Carmen, no longer in love with José, stands outside the bullring in Seville and tells him she is leaving with Escamillo, the toreador. José, now a desperate, enraged man, makes a last plea to Carmen. Although she knows she is in fatal danger, she refuses to compromise. José draws his dagger and stabs her to death, telling the crowd coming out of the bullring to take him, the murderer.

The opera, a popular masterpiece, is also historically of great importance, for it dispelled the difference in France between opera at the Opéra and opéra comique at the other theaters. A tragic ending had never been tolerated at the "Comique". The character of Carmen went against all previous notions of a heroine: here was a woman who openly seduced a man on the stage and proudly proclaimed a series of other lovers, with allegiance to none. The picture of a man's slow degradation was not the pleasant, facile entertainment the audience expected. And yet in order to understand *Carmen* fully, the opéra comique from which it stemmed must be kept in mind. Originally, like other works in the genre, it had spoken dialogue. Then for a performance in Vienna several months after the Paris premiere (Bizet had died in the interim), recitatives were written by the composer's lifelong friend, Ernest Guiraud. This version of the opera has become the standard one today, although the original version is being heard more often. While Guiraud did a tasteful, skillful job of filling in the gaps, he inevitably had to simplify, and a good deal of Meilhac and Halévy's explanatory text was omitted. The audience gets the main ideas and is carried along by the music, but some of the convincing power of the opera is lost; the libretto is such a fine support for the music, the opera suffers without the full text. The argument comes down to whether spoken dialogue upsets dramatic continuity in opera. Although *The Magic Flute* and *Fidelio* may be special cases, they have managed to survive under this handicap and to maintain their high position in the operatic world.

In *Carmen* Bizet borrowed a number of melodies from other composers, from folk-song collections, and from himself. The habanera

("L'amour est un oiseau rebelle"—Love is a rebel bird) has Bizet's words but the tune (Cuban in rhythm and altered by Bizet) is by Sebastian Yradier, a Spanish-American composer (Example 12-8a). Carmen's defiance of Zuniga when arrested is an old Spanish song modified (b). The lovely entr'acte (Acts II—III) is part of the *L'Arlésienne* music written by Bizet in 1872 (c). José's passionate appeal to Carmen in Act III ("Dut-il m'en couter la vie"—Though it should cost me my life) comes from an earlier Bizet work (d). The entr'acte music (Acts III–IV) is based on an Andalusian song by Manuel Garcia (e). There is nothing wrong with these adaptations. Bizet improved most of them and they are fine additions to the score.

Bizet, however, was not stingy with magnificent tunes of his own written specifically for *Carmen*. Among them are the seguidilla, the chanson bohème, the toreador's song, Don José's canzonetta and flower song, and Micaela's Act III aria. Each one is vital

Example 12-8   Bizet, *Carmen* (1875)

to the character and situation represented, though several have become too familiar through repeated playing. The seguidilla (Example 12-9a) is an important means for Carmen to win Don José and make him release her on the way to prison. Don José has not felt the full force of Carmen's passion and fatal charm; the lilting seguidilla with its promise of future love, dancing, and wine at Lillas Pastia's outside the walls of Seville is seduction incarnate. The so-called "chanson bohème" at the beginning of Act II is more local color than action; it demonstrates the gypsy temperament of Carmen and her friends, Frasquita and Mercedes, and paints an atmosphere(b). The bumptious, cocky personality of Escamillo is summed up in his toreador's song (c)—it echoes the bullring and the men who inhabit it. Carmen will eventually be so influenced by it she will leave José and take up with Escamillo. Newman calls it "a splendid piece of swagger against which the voices and the eyebrows of purists have long been raised in vain."[3] Don José's canzonetta after he has been released from the guardhouse shows the subtle change which has taken place in his personality. No longer the simple country boy newly enlisted, he is now an adventurous dragoon, ready to make his rival bite the dust if necessary (d). His flower song tells the audience and Carmen of the extent of his love: she derides him for wanting to return to quarters at the sound of "retreat"; and he having gone to confinement for her contemplates an even more serious step—desertion. The melody is an inspired piece of writing with none of the repetition of fixed song. José speaks from his heart (e). Finally, there is Micaela's famous aria in Act III (f), a melody that borders on sentimentality but is very appropriate in its place. Bizet comes near to Gounod here, but the portrait of the pure woman next to the violence, jealousy, and passion of the Carmen–Don José relationship is a fine dramatic contrast.

Bizet also creates purely musical devices to speed the drama. One is his use of counterpoint. A particularly fine example is Carmen's dance against the cornet call for "retreat" in Act II. Carmen tries to please her returning lover by concentrating all her energies on fiery castanets and intricate dance-steps. As she continues, sexual and intense, the call for retreat sounds against her "la-la" melody, and the effect is electrifying because of the inevitable conflict of opposites (Example 12-10). Then there is his use of musical reminiscence. A "fate motive" runs through the opera. This theme, characterized by an augmented second interval, is associated with Carmen in two ways: its first form (Example 12-11a) is Carmen

---

[3]*Great Operas*, vol. 1, p. 274.

Example 12-9

Près des rem - parts de Sé - vil - - le.   Chez mon a - mi Lil - las Pas - tia

(Near the ramparts of Seville, at my friend, Lillas Pastia's)

Les trin-gles de sis - tres tin - taient ___ a - vec un é - clat mé - tal - li - que,   Et

sur cet - te é - tran - ge mu - si - que,   Les ___ Zin - ga - rel - las se le - vaient.

Tra   la   la   la ___   Tra   la   la   la ___

(The rods of the sistrums jingle with a metallic clatter, and with this strange music,
the Zingarellas leap to their feet.)

Vo - tre toast je peux ___ vous le ren - dre, Se - ñors, se - ñors car a - vec les sol - dats ___

Tor - é - a - dor,   en   gar - de ___   To - ré - a - dor ___   To - ré - a - dor ___

(I can return your toast, gentleman, for with soldiers... Toreador, on guard! Toreador)

Hal - te - là!   Qui va là?   Dra - gon d'Al - ca - la! ___

Où   t'en vas - tu   par là,   Dra - gon d'Al - ca - là? ___   Moi   je m'en vais

fai - re ___   mor - dre la pous - siè - re   à mon ad - ver - sai - re.

(Halt! Who goes there? Dragoon of Alcala. Me, I'm going to make my rival bite the dust.)

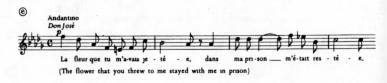

La fleur que tu m'a-vais je - té - e,   dans   ma pri - son ___ m'é - tait res - té - e.

(The flower that you threw to me stayed with me in prison)

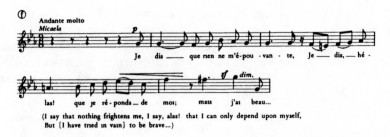

(I say that nothing frightens me, I say, alas! that I can only depend upon myself,
But [I have tried in vain] to be brave...)

Example 12-10

Example 12-11

herself—"fickle, laughing, elusive";[4] the second and more recognizable one, Carmen's fateful hold over José (b). Bizet brings these two ideas in at crucial moments in the opera to point up what is happening and to show the steady heightening of the tragedy. One of the great moments is the full orchestra playing the second form of the fate theme at the very end when Don José stands over Carmen's body and says to the crowd, "Vous pouvez m'arrêter. C'est moi qui l'ai tuée" (You may arrest me. It is I who have killed her). It is a mark of genius to have saved the motive in fortissimo for this climax. The effect is guaranteed to send chills up the spine.

Many more things could be said about this remarkable opera—its superb orchestration (Bizet was a master of the art); its French quality in spite of all the Spanish background; its splendid choruses

[4]Winton Dean, *Georges Bizet, His Life and Work*, Dent, London, 1965, p. 232.

(men, women, and children); its gaiety but at the same time inexorable sense of fate and tragedy; its delineation of live, flesh-and-blood people. These combine to produce a work of art attuned to its subject and one that never falters in its representation on the musical stage. It can be seen and heard again and again with renewed joy and pleasure.

French Opera Through Debussy

To trace the history of French opera from the middle of the nineteenth century through that extraordinary masterwork *Pelléas et Mélisande* by Claude Debussy at the beginning of the twentieth century would be too long a task. Yet some names should be mentioned. The struggle to achieve recognition in the Paris of the middle and late nineteenth century continued unabated with only a few composers of first rank coming to the fore. One who did was Charles Gounod (1818–1893). He managed to break the barrier in both lyric opera and genuine comic opera within the confines of the ruling fashion. Like Bizet, he attained fantastic popularity with one work, *Faust* (1859), which began, like *Carmen*, with spoken dialogue and had recitatives added to it later. In this form, it spread everywhere and has become one of the most popular French operas ever written. Although Gounod was a fine musician with an exceptional gift for lyric melody and music of clarity and balance so favored by the French, his operas lack the substance and power of a Berlioz or Bizet. *Faust*, based on Part I of Goethe's drama and telling of Faust's transformation by Mephistopheles from an elderly scholar into a young man and his tragic love affair with Marguerite, is a remarkably well-knit, attractive work with enough memorable tunes (see pp. 42–44) to keep audiences coming to it for years. The work lacks the dramatic pulse and depth of great opera. Gounod's talent was for lyric utterance and elegance, not the epic or the passions of grand opera. Two of his best works are light comic operas, *Le Médicin malgré lui* (The Doctor in Spite of Himself, 1858), based on Molière, and *Philémon et Baucis* (1860).

The other figure who dominated the French operatic scene later in the century was Jules Massenet (1842–1912), who lived a long life and wrote over 20 operas, the most famous of which are *Manon* (1884), *Werther* (1892), *Thaïs* (1894), and *Sapho* (1897). Massenet is a difficult figure to assess in the twentieth century because, with the exception of *Manon*, his works have disappeared from the opera house. He was a skillful musician whose melody and music appealed greatly to the public of his time. His pupil, Vincent D'Indy, gave the label of "erotisme discret et quasi-religieux" (secret and semi-religious eroticism) to his music, while others more sarcastically called him "la fille de Gounod" (the daughter of Gounod). There is, nevertheless, a good deal of charm to *Manon*, which utilized the same story by Abbé Prévost as Puccini did later for *Manon Lescaut*. Manon, a young girl, becomes enveloped in a life of luxury and dissipation in Paris, even though loved by the Chevalier des Grieux. An episode of supposed cheating at the gambling tables sentences them to deportation to the American colonies. But Manon, broken by the charge of prostitution, dies in des Grieux's arms. (In *Manon Lescaut* they go to Louisiana and Manon dies there. This was in Prévost's story). The pretty songs, from Manon's first air in Act I ("Je suis encore tout étourdie"—I am still all giddy) when she arrives at the inn in Amiens and is captivated by the fine clothes and dresses of the actresses, to "Adieu, notre petite table" (Farewell, our dear little table) in Act II and also "La Rêve de Manon," sung by des Grieux, were the music the public wanted to hear. The songs have worn a little thin today but can be enticing when heard for the first time. Massenet had a gift for sweet, entrancing melody which rang in the ear after leaving the theater.

The culmination of French opera in the late nineteenth and early twentieth centuries was *Pelléas et Mélisande* by Claude Debussy (1862–1918). By the 1890s, the musician in France was much less obsessed by the opera than his predecessors had been. Symphonic music, chamber music, and songs found wide and growing outlet, and the composer could channel his creative energies in these directions rather than try to write an opera. Debussy let his interests take their natural bent; they did not necessarily lead to the stage, though he knew and liked the theater. He bided his time.

Debussy, born outside of Paris to a simple bourgeois family, was fortunate enough to travel extensively in his formative years. At the age of 18, he was taken into the household of Madame von Meck, a wealthy Russian widow, who had a passionate fondness for music. He was the tutor for her children, and travels took them to Switzerland and Italy the first year and Russia the second. Before that, his life had been rather uneventful. His early education came almost entirely from a doting mother who never let him attend a school, but his musical talent was recognized, and at the age of 11 he entered the Paris Conservatory where he received thorough training. He won the Prix de Rome like some of his famous predecessors, but his two years in Italy were not altogether happy ones. Nevertheless he pursued his career assiduously and tried to hear the best music of the day. He was one of the first to recognize the quality of Russian music, although his comments at first are few. The overpowering influence of the time was Wagner, and Debussy like the rest of the musical world came under his spell. In 1888–1889, he went to Bayreuth and heard *Die Meistersinger, Tristan,* and *Parsifal.* In the beginning he was entranced but later paid less attention.

From his early years, Debussy showed an original musical mind. He was determined not to follow the path of others. His friend, Maurice Emmanuel, recounted the time at the Conservatory (1883) when, waiting for their tardy teacher, Debussy went to the piano and played a group of "consecutive fifths and octaves; sevenths which were not resolved at all; shameful false relations; chords of the ninth on all degrees of the scale; chords of the eleventh and thirteenth . . . and all this Claude called a feast for the ear." His life in Paris brought him into contact with artists of the day in other fields: Mallarmé, Verlaine (poetry); Whistler (painting); Valéry (literature). He became well acquainted with the prevailing currents of impressionism and symbolism and tried to apply these theories to his music. Another influence was the exotic in any form, whether Russian music or the Javanese gamelan at the 1889 Paris Exposition. The latter with its pentatonic scale, its new sonorities, and irregular percussive rhythms had a strong influence on Debussy.

During these years he was constantly searching for a possible opera libretto but could not find the right vehicle for his ideas. He is quoted as saying: "I am not tempted to imitate what I admire in Wagner. I conceive dramatic form differently; music begins where words are powerless to express." Music for him was sensibility and improvisation, not rhetoric and the bold statement. Fortunately in 1892 the libretto he had been searching appeared: the Belgian Maurice Maeterlinck's drama, *Pelléas et Mélisande,* published in Brussels. Debussy obtained a copy and absorbed. It. The play was given in Paris in May, 1893. After seeing it, Debussy decided to try a musical setting. But the task was a long and arduous one. He visited Maeterlinck to get his permission (there were further difficulties with the author) and then wrote, revised, and changed for many years. For Debussy there was no need to alter the play fundamentally; he took the language as it stood, with some rearrangements and cuts (scenes were omitted) but no rewriting. Maeterlinck, who was no musician, objected to even mild changes. Eventually the way was cleared and the opera completed and performed in 1902. Some knowledgeable people were deeply affected; others were not so sure.

Maeterlinck's play, under the influence of French symbolism, stresses the uncertainty and mysterious quality of life. Everything is filtered in a dim light. As in painting, there are few definite lines and surfaces, but mood and background are important. Action and meaning take place through suggestion rather than statement. The characters are in the grip of a fate against which there is no struggle. Direct questions are seldom answered. There is a plot—a firm and rational one—but it develops by indirection: events are told through symbols. The language is very simple and plain, ambiguity and ornamentation are avoided.

The story takes place in a legendary kingdom (Allemonde) at a legendary time. Golaud, grandson of the king, Arkel, loses his way hunting and finds a beautiful, young maiden in the forest beside a pool. He eventually marries her and brings her home to his family castle, where live Arkel; Golaud's mother, Geneviève; Pelléas, his half-brother; and Yniold, his little son by a previous marriage. (Golaud is presumably quite a bit older than Pelléas; he has grey hair.) Pelléas falls in love with Mélisande. They confess their love and are overheard by Golaud, who, in a fit of fury, kills his brother (an action not shown on the stage). Suffering agonies of remorse, Golaud tries to get Mélisande to forgive him. But she dies after giving birth to a daughter and never revealing to Golaud what her true relationship to Pelléas was.

The play is in five acts with several scenes in each act except the last one. Everything is shadowy. Nobody ever knows where Mélisande comes from, why she is found by a pool in the forest, why there is a crown at the bottom of this pool, why she is crying. Golaud suspects Pelléas' feeling for Mélisande. He takes him to a deep vault below the castle where there is an evil-smelling pool. Golaud talks darkly about the air of death in the place but does nothing except lead Pelléas out again. The growing love of Mélisande and Pelléas is shown in a magical scene where Mélisande is combing her very long hair. Pelléas is below the tower, trying playfully to hold Mélisande's hand as she leans over the casement; her hair falls all around his head, and he is overwhelmed by its scent, texture, and warmth.

When heard for the first time, the music sounds like continuous recitative and a return to early Florentine music drama in the oldest days of opera. It is subdued (there are only three or four "fortes" in the whole score), and every syllable of the text is heard (Example 12-12). The vocal lines are beautifully adapted to the French language; one must know French or be very well acquainted with the story to grasp the subtlety, beauty, and quiet interpenetration of music and text. Debussy's orchestration is a marvel of color and substance. To feel its full effect, it must be savored and allowed to sink in. Composers have withdrawn the orchestra at moments of tension and climax but very seldom when there is a declaration of love; Debussy removed it entirely in Act IV when Pelléas and Méli-

Example 12-12

Debussy, *Pelléas et Mélisande* (1902)
Act II, scene 1

(Pelléas: You do not know where I am leading you? I come here often about noon to sit down when
it is too hot in the gardens. I am stifling today even in the shade of the trees. Mélisande: Oh! the
water is clear. Pelléas: It is as cold as winter. It is an old abandoned fountain)

Example 12-13

Act IV, scene 3

(Pelléas: You do not know what it is because... I love you. Mélisande: I love you also)

sande say very simply that they love each other. The silence is rapt
(Example 12-13). In spite of the composer's reaction to Wagnerian
music and theory, he does use a kind of leading-motive system in the
orchestra to signify persons and things. But these musical ideas are
never obtrusive. Most of the time they are so transformed and hidden
in the texture they are hardly recognizable. They do not bear labels
and are more associative than representative.

A most important part of the music is the orchestral interludes
which fill the change of scenes. They generally fulfill a dramatic
function by pointing up what has just taken place or what is to
follow. The same is true for the preludes to the acts. Sometimes
Debussy will deliberately introduce a new form of the thematic
material to show the gradual change in the relationship of the
characters: Golaud's growing suspicion; Pelléas' and Mélisande's
budding love; the foreshadowing of tragedy. Debussy's harmonic
means in these interludes and elsewhere have now become
familiar fare in music of the twentieth century, but they were

Example 12-14

Example 12-15

novel: parallel fifth, seventh, and ninth chords with no resolution, whole tone and pentatonic melodic progressions, obscured tonal relationships, and a restrained rhythmic flow. It is important to remember, however, that the tonal devices were employed not to "épater le bourgeois," as Debussy might have done in his conservatory days, but as the embodiment of the poetry and the story. The association of Maeterlinck and Debussy was made easier because they were contemporaries, subject to current fashion and taste. The confluence took place, and it was a happy accident that it did so.

A typical but remarkable scene in the opera is Act II, scene 1. It is labeled merely "Une fontaine dans le parc" (A fountain in the park), and it is the place Pelléas will be killed later. Pelléas and Mélisande, newly acquainted, have come to escape the heat of the day. (See opening recitative, Example 12-12.) Mélisande is fascinated by the fountain (really a deep pool and abandoned well) and lies down on the marble beside it. She plays with the reflection of her arms and her face in the water. In order to get more glint, she takes off her wedding ring and tosses it up and down. Pelléas warns her about falling in the water or losing the ring. She persists. The ring slips out of her hands and sinks out of sight. She asks Pelléas what to say to Golaud. He advises her to tell the truth. The symbolism of this little act in what follows is obvious. Debussy

treats it with the utmost simplicity, making it the more effective.

He begins with a prelude that is in the greatest contrast to the opening of the first act with its overtone of menace and unease. Here all is serene with some reference at the beginning to a motive associated with Pelléas when he enters in Act I (Examples 12-14*a* and *b*). The harps and winds, firmly settled in E major, delicately wrap around each other. When the strings enter, their figure is the rippling of the water in which Mélisande is gazing (Example 12-15). She is entranced by the silence ("Comme on est seul ici . . . on n'entend rien"—How alone one is here; nothing is heard). Pelléas replies: "Il y a toujours un silence extraordinaire" (There is always a remarkable quiet) to be followed by a remote change to a held B flat chord in the lower strings—a startling effect, better than silence itself. As Mélisande continues to play with her ring, bits of a Golaud motive intrude in the background. Pelléas' agitation ("Prenez garde"—Take care) is felt in the broken string chords. When the ring falls, there is merely a harp arpeggio. Mélisande exclaims "Oh" on a high g sharp[2]*. The orchestra tells us the inner feeling by a lone held e and a harp reiteration on two notes. At the end of the scene, Debussy emphasizes Pelléas' reply about the ring to Mélisande by having the word, "la verité" repeated twice with the orchestra silent—a touch all the more dramatic because of its brevity and its understatement.

The opera, in spite of its outer daring, is really a logical continuation of the ideals held for centuries in French opera. The emphasis on declamation and the drama was no different than what Lully and Rameau had espoused. Debussy was severely criticized for his lack of melody, but that was not what he was trying to achieve. He wrote afterwards:

I have tried to submit to a law of beauty that seems particularly to be forgotten when it is a question of dramatic music: characters in a drama try to sing like ordinary people and not in a language of superannuated traditions. This is the reproach which is made about my so-called monotonous declamation where nothing melodic ever appears . a character's sentiments cannot be expressed continually in a melodic fashion since dramatic melody should be different than melody in general.

Debussy disregards the bar line whenever possible to make the flow of language in musical diction more natural. He hesitates to

*See Glossary· Abbreviations.

make wide jumps except at climactic moments where they are all the more striking. Narrow intervals are the norm. Like speech, there is frequent singing on one tone, similar to chanting. Below the vocal lines he is particularly concerned with sonorities—spacing of chords, doubling for special effect, flute or clarinet in low or high register, muted and divisi violins, stopped horns.

While Debussy had enormous influence on twentieth century music in general, few composers have attempted to follow the path of *Pelléas et Mélisande*. The work is too special, too unusual to be imitated. It will always have a restricted appeal because it possesses few of those characteristics in opera that generate applause and attention—the tuneful aria, the high note, the big chorus, the colorful scene. But from those who feel the tug of its unique quality, it will continue to draw sustenance and support and will serve to represent an entrancing union of word and sound.

SUGGESTED READING

General   Cooper, Martin, *French Music: From the Death of Berlioz to the Death of Fauré*, Oxford University Press paperback, London, 1961. Includes chapters on Massenet, Debussy, and others.

Cooper, Martin, *Opéra Comique*, Chanticleer Press, New York, 1949

Crosten, William L., *French Grand Opera: An Art and a Business*, King's Crown Press, New York, 1948. Mostly on the Meyerbeer period in Paris.

Rameau   Girdlestone, Cuthbert, *Jean-Philippe Rameau, His Life and Work*, Cassell, London, 1957, Dover Publications paperback, New York, 1969 Some fine chapters on Rameau's operas.

Berlioz   Barzun, Jacques, *Berlioz and the Romantic Century*, 3rd ed., 2 vols., Columbia University Press, New York, 1969. Particularly good for nineteenth century cultural background. Chapters on Berlioz' operas.

The Memoirs of Hector Berlioz, David Cairns, ed., Gollancz, London, 1969.

Bizet   Curtiss, Mina, *Bizet and His World*, Knopf, New York, 1958. Good for background and biography.

Dean, Winton, *Georges Bizet, His Life and Work*, Dent, London, 1965 Excellent, general study.

Debussy   Lockspeiser, Edward, *Debussy· His Life and Mind*, 2 vols. Cassell, London, 1962—1965. Best biography in English.

Vallas, Léon, *The Theories of Claude Debussy*, Maire O'Brien, trans., Oxford University Press, 1929, Dover Publications paperback, New York, 1967 Interesting chapters on Debussy's attitude toward the French musical theater and Wagner.

13 Nationalism in Opera

As indicated in Chapter 4, operatic traditions in England, Spain, Portugal, Scandinavia, central and eastern Europe were much slower to develop. In many instances they never flowered at all. One of the puzzling historical curiosities is the lack of native opera in English. The language, in spite of claims to the contrary, is no more difficult to set to music than German. It does not possess the liquid vowels of Italian which are musical in themselves, but neither do many other languages. In mid-seventeenth century England, there was a genuine attempt to write English opera on the lines of opera heard in Italy and France. But before 1660, Puritans frowned on music in general and after the Restoration, Charles II, who had spent most of his exile years in France, regarded English music as raw and unformed, preferring French models. In the 1680s there was the bright light of Henry Purcell, but his life was cut too short to follow up what might have been a renaissance of English music after *Dido and Aeneas* in 1689. In the eighteenth century, Handel and his associates dominated the London operatic scene for 30 years (1710–1740) with Italian opera. Later, foreign opera was too strongly entrenched to be displaced. For almost all of the nineteenth century, England was a way station for foreign touring companies, composers, and conductors who prevented native groups from coming to the fore.

The most interesting operatic music of the nineteenth century outside of Italy, France, and Germany came from the Slav countries —central Europe and Russia. Although native arts generally surface when political entities form and a country becomes more conscious of its language and customs, certain races in central Europe had exhibited a cultural heritage for generations without the stimulus of political unity. Poles, Hungarians, Czechs, Slovaks, and Serbs were the most notable examples. Musically, one of the most active areas in Europe was Bohemia, that middle section of the land mass, with Prague as its center. Although fought over for centuries, Bohemia and the Czechs, its dominant race, were intensely aware of their musical tradition, which was firmly grounded in the school system and small villages and towns. Folk song and dance found there a lively outlet. However, composers born Czech found themselves quickly weaned away from local music (considered crude and vulgar) to the reigning international style. (Gluck, earlier, is a case in point.) But the various political upheavals in the first half of the century (1830 in France, 1848 in Germany) stirred much national sentiment in central Europe and were inevitably to have effect in these lands.

| Bohemia and Smetana | Bedřich Smetana (1824–1884) has been called the father of Bohemian operatic music, but he came to it almost accidentally. Smetana's musical training was in the Prague conservatory, which was almost entirely German-oriented. Musically precocious, he was naturally exposed to native Czech music; but when he started to compose, his models were Liszt, Schuman, Beethoven, and Mendelssohn. Smetana had a difficult time trying to earn a living as a musician, and his later life was marred by the same tragedy that engulfed Beethoven—deafness. He accepted an appointment as conductor in Göteborg, Sweden, from 1856 to 1861 but returned to Bohemia when Austria's iron grip over the country was relaxed about 1860. One of the foremost musical aims in Prague at that time was to establish a Czech Philharmonic society and a national theater for drama and opera in the Czech language. Before this the stage had been almost entirely German. Smetana had a prominent role in these native efforts and in 1866 brought out in Prague the first of his Czech operas, *Branibori v Čechách* (The Brandenburgers in Bohemia). This work was written and completed in 1863 but not produced until 1866. While waiting for this historical and patriotic production, Smetana became interested in the idea of a comic opera. At first the venture was taken light-heartedly as a side issue to his more serious |

works. (Smetana always considered *Dalibor* (1868) and *Libuše* (1881)—both serious operas—to be more worthy of his best efforts.) His previous librettist, Sabina, sent him a rather thin tale spun around the story of a young man who leaves his native village but eventually returns to win the girl of his choice. Years later when Smetana's reputation had been established, but almost entirely on the basis of this comic piece, *Prodaná Nevěsta* (The Bartered Bride), performed in Prague, May, 1866, Smetana tried to belittle his early effort. It was a natural reaction. His more serious stage work (four operas) had been shunted aside in favor of this merry opera (almost an operetta), then achieving its hundredth performance (1882). He said then in a speech:

The Bartered Bride.. is actually only a toy. I composed it, not out of vanity but out of spite because after "The Brandenburgers" I was accused of being a Wagnerian and not capable of doing anything in a lighter, national style. So I immediately hastened to Sabina for a libretto and I wrote "The Bartered Bride." It was my opinion at the time that even Offenbach could not compete with it.[1]

While this may be exaggerated, it is nevertheless true that Smetana did not consider the work one of his major efforts, and even his librettist said: "If I had suspected what Smetana would make of my operetta, I should have taken more pains and written him a better and more solid libretto."

In spite of these disclaimers, *The Bartered Bride* after a slow start, swept everything before it and has since become practically the national Czech opera. Although there is no real folk music in it, Smetana made a good deal of it sound as if it were derived from such a source. All good composers, whether Brahms writing an art song that could be mistaken for a folk melody or Stravinsky inserting Russian folk rhythms into a dance, have known that native spirit must be captured although the musical ideas may originate with them. The gaiety, vivacity, and the charm of this score come from Smetana's skill in incorporating Bohemian dance rhythms and melodic fragments that sound like folk music into a unified whole for the operatic stage.

The story concerns the peasant maiden Marenka, who has been contracted by her parents, Krusina and his wife Ludmila, to marry the son of Micha, another peasant. Marenka, however, loves Jenik, whom she knows little about except that he came from the village but has been absent for some time. Kecal, the village marriage broker, is arranging the match but knows he must get around Jenik.

[1]František Bartoš, ed., *Bedřich Smetana. Letters and Reminiscences*, Artiz, Prague, 1955, pp. 254–255.

When Jenik learns that the person Marenka is supposed to marry is Vasek, son of Tobias Micha, he suddenly agrees to let Marenka go for 300 florins, provided the contract of Kecal reads she marries the son of Micha and nobody else. Marenka is desolated by this news and at the urging of her parents half-heartedly gives in to the proposed marriage with Vasek. At the last minute, Jenik reveals himself as the elder son of Micha who had left home because of a disagreeable stepmother, Micha's second wife. The stepmother Hata makes trouble about this newly-proposed union but gives in when Vasek appears in the ridiculous guise of a bear among a group of traveling comedians, and the parents feel he is not mature enough for marriage. Blessings by all are bestowed upon the true lovers.

The Bartered Bride went through several versions before it attained final form. The original consisted of 20 numbers and an overture in two acts, connected by spoken dialogue. It was expanded by the addition of new scenes and dances, which necessitated a three-act structure. Finally, for a performance in Russia, Smetana substituted recitative for the dialogue, and this became the definitive version. Smetana's changes proved helpful, for many of them were dances that added color to the opera; and, in the case of a sentimental, serious aria for Marenka in the third act, provided a nice contrast to the comic business of the other characters.

In the overture, one of the best of its kind, Smetana utilizes thematic material from the opera. The spirit of the work shines in the rustic vivacity of the opening measures with their reiterated syncopations, cross accents, and emphasis on three notes (Example 13-1a). Then comes the memorable stomp of the entire string section in octaves, the rhythmic beat which gets the feet going (b). After a rapid fugato passage built up on B in each string section in turn against a constant eighth-note motion in the other strings, the full orchestral tutti breaks into a gay melodic fragment (c), syncopated and cross-accented, which dominates the rest of the overture. All of this material comes from the finale of Act II where Kecal, Jenik, Krusina, and villagers are gathered together to witness the signing of the marriage contract. At first, Drusina and the crowd seem grateful that Jenik has magnanimously agreed to give up Marenka, but when they learn from Kecal that his reward is 300 florins, they are appalled by his avarice and monetary change of heart. They point scornfully at the man who has bartered his bride (literally, "sold" her)—the theme of the opera. Later in the overture, there is reference to a little phrase (d), also in the Act II finale, which is heard in the orchestra when Kecal tells the crowd what the contract is. It signifies the deception Jenik has undertaken about his paternity and the confidence he has of winning in the end.

Example 13-1   Smetana, *Prodaná Nevěsta* (The Bartered Bride) (1866)

Example 13-2

(Why not sing of joy and gladness)

Example 13-3

The opening chorus of Act I, marked "Con vivacità" (Example 13-2) is typical of exuberant village life on a feast day and sets the scene for the action. There is strong resemblance in it to a Gilbert and Sullivan operetta chorus. Example 13-3 is the introduction to Marenka's aria when she and Jenik, alone, tell of their love. Affective in its simplicity, the music is the essence of lyricism. One of the great attractions of the score are the dances that occur at regular intervals. Act I has a polka in the finale; Act II, a furiant in the first scene (a rapid, fiery Bohemian dance in 3/4 time with frequently shifting accents); and Act III, a galop, performed as a ballet by the strolling players—a quick dance with hopping movements and many changes of steps. Of these, the polka (Example 13-4) was particularly popular. The dance itself was taken into polite society during the century and became a mania. Smetana was one of the first to use it on the stage, and soon his Bartered Bride polka was known all over Europe. Lastly, there is Marenka's third-act aria (Example 13-5). Marenka has learned of Jenik's action and mourns her desertion. The sweetness of this air made it a great favorite in its day and a fine contrast to the more lively parts of the score.

Although the work may be nearer to "spirited musical comedy"[2] than to so-called serious opera, it is a splendid example of spontaneous national spirit and feeling. The tendency to relegate lighter opera to a secondary position because of its style and subject matter is a misreading of operatic ideals. Comedy is a much a part of life as tragedy. In the hands of a gifted composer, it often probes deeper than the overwrought simulation of death and destruction—Mozart and the Verdi of *Falstaff* come quickly to mind. Comedy is the counter and the leaven. It has its rightful place.

Example 13-4

Example 13-5

(Ah love's sweet dream so heavenly fair)

[2] Rosa Newmarch, *The Music of Czechoslovakia*, Oxford University Press, London, 1942, p. 56.

Another important Czech composer, whose work properly belongs to the twentieth century, is Leoš Janáček (1854–1928). In recent years, Janáček's operas have been gaining more and more acclaim outside their native borders because they speak directly to a modern audience. Janáček, a highly personal and individualistic composer, drew on Moravian folk music for much of his inspiration although, like other national composers, he seldom directly utilized folk tunes. He came from a district near Poland and spent most of his professional life in the city of Brno. He first came to attention in 1904 with the production of *Její Pastorkyna*, or *Jenůfa* (Her Foster Daughter), as it is generally called; not until 1916 was it given in Prague, and he became famous overnight. Then followed *Kat'a Kabanová* (Kate Kabanov, 1921); *Příhody Lišky Bystroušky* (The Cunning Little Vixen, 1924), a realistic fairy tale; *Věc Makropulos* (The Makropoulos Affair, 1926), based on a play by Karel Čapek; and *Z mrtvého domu* (From the House of the Dead, 1930), based on a Dostoyevsky novel. These are his best known operas, although he wrote several others.

Janáček's musical language is forceful, colorful, and violent. He was a superb orchestrator and could draw the utmost from his brief themes, which often consist of only a few notes, subject to continual variation. There is much repetition, but the ear is not offended because this repetition has a dramatic purpose and builds up a scene through moments of great tension.

His vocal lines are strongly ruled by the accents and inflections of the Czech language. He was a fanatic believer in carrying the rhythms and inflections of speech into his music; for this reason, his operas are particularly difficult to translate. Yet they come alive because of their overwhelming musical and dramatic effectiveness. The libretto subjects are strong, crude, and naturalistic. *Jenůfa* deals with infanticide and *Kabanová* with suicide; *The Makropoulos Affair* with a woman who lives more than 300 years and has had five different lives; *The House of the Dead* with various downtrodden characters met by Dostoyevsky while in a Siberian prison camp. But Janáček's music is particularly suited to this material and he makes the most of it.

When these passionate operas become more widely known and produced in the world's opera houses, they will find a more permanent place in the repertory; in the meantime, their performances are hailed by opera lovers.

Russia and Mussorgsky Russia was long isolated from the center of European culture by geographical remoteness and political enmity. Not until the eighteenth century was there much contact with the musical life of other nations. Under Catherine the Great (reigned 1762–1796), however, St. Petersburg (Leningrad), then the royal seat, became musically an Italian outpost. Italian composers and instrumentalists flocked to Catherine's court because of royal largesse. Italian opera became the rage as did French and German imports. Nearly 350 operas had their premieres in Russia in the last quarter of the century, 30 appearing in one year (1778) alone.[3]

Not until the nineteenth century did Russian opera become wholly Russian, sung in its native language, with plot and musical material having reference to Russian background. There had been native operas of this sort in the eighteenth century, but most of them lacked quality and substance. By common consent, the first significant Russian works were two operas of Michael Glinka (1804–1857), *Zhizh za Tsarya* (A Life for the Tsar, 1836) and *Ruslan i Lyudmila* (Ruslan and Ludmila, 1842). Although it is questionable how much Glinka was influenced by native idioms (his musical training was taken in Italy and Germany), he did attempt Russian historical and literary themes. *Ruslan* was the first of the Pushkin operas, of which there were many later.

Russian musicians of the next generation divided themselves into two groups depending upon their national or international creative outlook. Of the national group, the best known were five men of differing age and training who banded together to propagate Russian music. The period from 1840 to 1880 saw a great flowering of Russian art and literature (Gogol, Tolstoy, Turgenev, Dostoyevsky were writing) of which musicians were also a part. Not only Russian themes were sought but a realistic presentation of them which would accord with life as it was and not a glossed-over picture. The Moguchaya Kuchka (Mighty Handful, as some critic called them)—Balakirev, Cui, Borodin, Mussorgsky, and Rimsky-Korsakov—were not professional musicians in the early parts of their careers and thus felt freer to experiment along new lines. They came from land-owning or professional families who with the freeing of the serfs in 1861 lost most of their land revenues. As a result, there was pressure to take up occupations at which one could earn a living (a Russian musician then had no other remunerative outlet than to be a performer or have some connection with the church). Balakirev was the closest to a professional musician, even to teaching Mussorgsky, but he started as a mathematician and was a railway clerk for a while. Cui was a military engineer; Mussorgsky, a minor civil servant in the government;

[3]Donald J. Grout, *A Short History of Opera*, Columbia University Press, New York, 1965, p. 455.

Borodin, a teacher of chemistry; and Rimsky-Korsakov, until the age of 30, a naval officer. They were united, however, in a desire to write music expressive of their native land, and were aided greatly by a writer, V. V. Stasov, whose pugnacious articles brought the musicians to the attention of the public. For a time, they pitted themselves against the more eclectic music of Anton Rubinstein and Peter Tschaikovsky, although the Tschaikovsky of some of his operas was far nearer to them than generally supposed.

From the operatic point of view, the two most important figures of the Five were Mussorgsky and Rimsky-Korsakov, although Borodin with his opera, *Prince Igor*, deserves strong mention. The artistic lives of Mussorgsky and Rimsky-Korsakov were deeply intertwined because Rimsky edited much of Mussorgsky's work after his death. (The argument this has aroused in musical circles has been endless, and it will probably continue.)

Modest Mussorgsky (1839–1881), of all the group, was the most original. If it had not been for his somewhat desultory musical education which hampered quick progress, his alcoholism which shortened his life to 42 years, his inability to finish much of what he started, he might have developed into one of the great opera composers. As it is, his reputation is based largely on one work, *Boris Godunov* (1874), which, in spite of mutilations and changes, has remained so moving and powerful a drama it is generally recognized as one of the outstanding operas in the repertoire.

Books on Russian music have put too much emphasis on Mussorgsky's lack of training, as if formal schooling was a *sine qua non* of education. He was brought up in a well-to-do landowning family, and may have had peasant blood from one of his grandfathers. His general education was evidently quite good, and although he never went to a conservatory, his early tutoring in music fundamentals was presumably adequate. His talent and ear for music became manifest quite early. Although his formative years were spent drinking and carousing in a Guards regiment—a favorite dumping ground for young aristocrats—he was seemingly able to get musical instruction. He became facile as a pianist and was an attraction in musical circles with his songs. The West hears too few of these songs because of the language barrier, but many are of very high quality.

Mussorgsky's preparation for opera came through several projects never finished: music for a play, *Oedipus in Athens*, and a setting of Flaubert's *Salammbô*, for which Mussorgsky compiled a libretto. Parts of the music from these works were later incorporated into *Boris*. He also wrote one act of Gogol's prose comedy *The Marriage*

(1868), which he set directly from the text. It was performed private-
ly. These works aimed at musical naturalism. Realism meant sub-
ordinating art to life in the most direct way possible. During
sojourns at his family estate, Mussorgsky also became absorbed in
the folk song idiom of the common people, Emancipation of the serfs
made young Russian intellectuals acutely aware of their peasant
lineage and their folk heritage. Gerald Abraham[4] speaks of several
qualities which can be assigned generally to Russian music of this
period: directness of expression without intellectual complication,
a certain primitiveness, a lack of emotional appeal, a naive delight
in pure sound, and little dramatic development (that is, the operas
were a series of tableaux that progressed like a chronicle or an
epic).

Much of *Boris* is characterized by these features. Yet Mussorgsky
thought of these qualities as strengths rather than weaknesses. In
most of his music, expressive directness comes through a wonderfully close representation of the text. For foreigners who know no
Russian, this union of music and text is particularly difficult to grasp
although its dramatic power can be instinctively felt. Much easier to
hear are the harmonic subtleties which Mussorgsky deliberately
employs since they do not depend upon words. Another feature is
emphasis on modality and the whole tone progression rather than
major and minor scales. The leading tone is omitted; the dominant
loses its strong function of leading to the tonic; cadences are set
differently; the second of the scale is apt to become a dominant. Yet
Mussorgsky does not rely on any set pattern. He often will mix a
modal progression with a major one. His chords may be bare fourths
or fifths (that is, no filling-in of the triad in the style of old Slavonic
church music). Alongside these archaisms are also chords of some
complexity—augmented combinations and added seconds. Unrelated chords are placed next to each other and are repeated over
and over again (the classic place for this is the opening of the Coronation scene in *Boris Godunov* where an A flat seventh chord and a D
seventh alternate for many measures).

But *Boris* is a great deal more than striking harmonic devices. It
is a work that touches the heart, for it shows a man whose remorse
over a murder leads to madness and death, even though he is the
Tsar of all the Russias. Mussorgsky took as his source Pushkin's
play, *Boris Godunov* of 1825. It had 24 scenes, five in prose, the rest
in blank verse. He selected seven of these scenes for his first version of
the opera; several of these scenes were combinations of two or more

[4]"The Essence of Russian Music" in *Studies in Russian Music*, William Reeves,
London, n.d., *passim*.

scenes in Pushkin, and one his own invention taken from hints in the text. Although Mussorgsky took many of Pushkin's lines directly, he also rearranged, cut, or substituted his own words, often to the detriment of Pushkin. Compression was obviously necessary, as it must be for any libretto adapted from a play. He also had to retain the time scale of the original—seven years from Boris' acceptance of the throne (1598) to his death in 1605.

The story is taken from Russian history at the turn of the seventeenth century. Boris Godunov is made Tsar, but he takes the throne reluctantly because he is suspected of having had Dimitri, the young son of Ivan the Terrible (d. 1584), put to death in 1591. (There is considerable historical doubt about Boris' complicity in this affair. Eye witnesses claimed the boy fell upon a knife in a violent epileptic fit but, for political reasons, the death was claimed to be murder by Boris' henchmen. For the purpose of the drama, however, Boris' guilt must be assumed.) In the interregnum between Ivan's death and 1598, the country has been ruled by Feodor, a pious man, Boris' brother-in-law. Grigory, a rebellious young monk, hears the outline of these events from Pimen, an old monk, who saw Ivan's court, fought at the battle of Kazan, and was at Uglick when Dimitri died. Pimen tells Grigory that he is almost exactly the age Dimitri would have been had he lived. Grigory determines to pass himself off as Dimitri come to life (that is, the pretender to the throne). He flees the monastery for Lithuania and Poland—Lithuania then consisting of a sizeable part of present-day Russia. In Poland, he stirs support for his cause with the help of Marina, a Polish princess, and her scheming adviser, Rangoni, a Jesuit priest. Russia, in the meantime, has fallen on evil days ("The Time of Troubles")—famine, pestilence, distrust of Tsar Boris, and open talk of deposing him. Prince Shuisky, treacherous adviser to the Tsar, preys on Boris' half-demented mind about the death of the boy Dimitri. In a meeting of the Duma (Council of the Boyars—nobles), Boris hears a tale about a blind shepherd whose sight was restored while praying at the tomb of the murdered Dimitri. Boris becomes unconscious with this shock. He recovers, and as he feels his death approaching, he pronounces his son, Feodor the new Tsar, and falls dead.

Even today there is great confusion and indecision about how the opera should be performed because there are four versions of it, two by Mussorgsky (1870 and 1874) and two by Rimsky-Korsakov (1896 and 1908). The first, written in 1868–1869 with seven scenes, had no indication of Grigory's involvement in Poland with Marina and Rangoni. The government censors rejected it because it showed the Tsar in such an unflattering light and there was no palliative love scene with a heroine. Mussorgsky then revised his score in 1872 (published 1874 with cuts), adding a Polish Act III of two scenes (one, Marina's dressing room; the other, scene of the garden of the castle at Sandomvi) in which Grigory shows his infatuation for Marina. She, scheming and ambitious, pushes him toward the throne, even after he discloses he is a pretender. A final love duet was also added. Mussorgsky, moreover, eliminated a scene before St. Basil's Cathedral in Moscow where a Simpleton accuses Boris of murdering Dimitri. The Simpleton's music was transferred to a new last scene—the forest at Kromy where Grigory is advancing on Moscow with Polish and Russian support. The authorities also disapproved this version, but after three scenes were given at a benefit, they relented and the work was finally produced in January, 1874. Rimsky-Korsakov made a completely new version of the opera in 1896, after having re-orchestrated portions of it previously. Among other things, he reversed the last two scenes, letting the death of Boris be last as it was in Mussorgsky's original score. This is the version generally heard today. Although many feel that Mussorgsky's original score is far more satisfying dramatically and his "crude" music greatly superior to Rimsky's smoothed-over revision (harmonies changes, etc.), the opera would probably never have found a larger public if it had not been for the work of Rimsky-Korsakov. He was a superb orchestrator and in the Coronation scene and elsewhere made the sound fuller and richer.

It has often been said that "the real hero" of *Boris* is the Russian people. They are depicted as a downtrodden ignorant mass, endlessly patient and suffering, whose real consideration is for amelioration of their own individual lot with little interest in the ways of politics and monarchies. In the first scene, Pushkin shows them gathered in the courtyard of the Novodievitch Monastery where they have been brought to stage a demonstration of support for Boris as the new Tsar. A police officer goads them into raising their voices (really a prayer) to entreat that Russia will find a new monarch, for, inside the building, Boris is hesitating. When the crowd appears apathetic, the police officer treatens to use a whip on them. In a great fortissimo they finally shout out the supplication which they had begun before (Example 13-6). Its changing meters, the mixture of modal and minor scale (for example, the end of the first two phrases dwells on an E natural which would ordinarily be a raised seventh in the minor scale), and the sense of archaic chord progression in measures 9 ff. give evidence of Mussorgsky's ability to invest the chorus with the coloring he desires. In this scene and those that follow the chorus acts both as

Example 13-6

Mussorgsky, *Boris Godunov* (1874)

(Why dost thou forsake us, O Father? Ah! why dost thou leave us, O Father?
Are we not your poor defenseless orphans? Our tears are falling with our prayers)

Example 13-7

(Like unto the bright sun in the sky is the glory of Russia's Tsar Boris)

Example 13-8

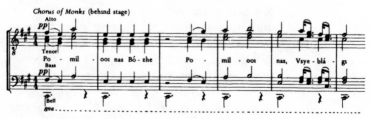

(Have mercy, O Lord; have mercy, almighty Lord!)

an entity and as individuals. When in ensemble, the group express their collective joy or terror; in individual utterance they back up what has been said en masse, or undermine it. In the beginning, several peasants ask each other what is going on; one wants some water; another tells the speakers to keep quiet. Mussorgsky is particularly skillful in giving the crowd a face psychologically and not always treating it as an amorphous mass. Many different situations show the extent of the people's oppression and waywardness. In the Inn scene, for example, where the guards seek the fleeing Grigory and his description is read to Varlaam and Missail, the two rebel monks who have picked up Grigory en route, the guards do not hesitate to add they will hang him if they catch him, even though this is not stated in their warrant. In other words, the rights of the lowly are disregarded by the law. In the revolution scene of the forest at Kromy, the crowd, incited to frenzy, seize two passing Jesuits and threaten to lynch them. The crowd are so inflamed that anybody who is not with them is an enemy and must be dispatched.

In the Coronation scene which is the second half of the prologue, the chorus sings out the familiar "Hymn to the Tsar," a traditional Russian tune which was also used by Beethoven in his second Rasumovsky quartet as a tribute to his patron. It is Mussorgsky's harmonization, however, which gives the melody its pointed thrust. First appearing without any real bass and a held G in the high woodwinds, horn, and strings, the repetition is a full projection by chorus and orchestra of the tune in all its majesty (Example 13-7). The same treatment occurs later after an intervening development where the orchestra and chorus toss the theme back and forth in fragmented movement.

The chorus finds a different outlet in the choirs of monks and pilgrims heard behind scenes. In Act I during Pimen's recitation to Grigory, monks intone a chant in the background, investing the atmosphere with religious solemnity. As Pimen puts out his lamp and prepares to depart, the call for mercy and forgiveness of sins by the choir (Example 13-8), heard above the reverberation of the low bell, is a moving epilogue to Pimen's tale of violence, warfare, and lusts of men. At the very end of the opera when Boris' time has come and he has called for Feodor to tell him to defend the throne, protect his sister, and watch for treacherous boyars, deep bell strokes are heard again, this time in an ominous, dissonant progression below. With them a choir is heard intoning part of the mass for the dead. Boris recognizes the music for his own departure and asks forgiveness for his sins (Example 13-9).

Example 13-9

Chorus of Priests (behind stage)

Boris

Nad-grób-nı vopl!

Sop.
PP

Plách-tye plách tye lyú-di-ye_____ Nyests bo zhiz-nı v noym

Alto

Tenor
PP

Bass

(Chorus of Monks: Weep, weep, people. There is no life left in him. Boris: Funeral tears!)

Example 13-10

ⓐ

Allegretto capriccioso

Hostess

Po-ï-má-la ya_____ sı-za syé-lyez-nyá._____ Okh, tı moı syél yez-yen moï ka-sá-tik syél-yez-yen

(I caught a lovely duck, oh my little duck, my darling little duck)

ⓑ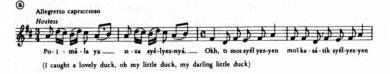

Allegro giusto

Varlaam

Kak vo gó-rod-ye bi-lo vo Ka-zá-nı

(Thus it was at the town of Kazan)

ⓒ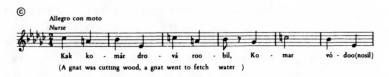

Allegro con moto

Nurse

Kak ko-már dro-vá roo-bil, Ko-mar vó-doo(nosil)

(A gnat was cutting wood, a gnat went to fetch water)

ⓓ

Scherzando

Feodor

Tóo-roo, tóo-roo pye-too-shók Ti dal-yé-kol o-to-shól za mor ye, zá mór-ye

(Turu, turu, little cock. Why have you gone so far? I went away behind the sea)

ⓔ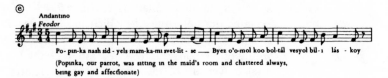

Andantıno

Feodor

Po-pın-ka nash sid-yels mam-ka-mı svet-lit-se_____ Byez o'o-mol koo bol-tál vesyol bil-ı lás-koy

(Popınka, our parrot, was sitting in the maid's room and chattered always,
being gay and affectionate)

ⓕ

Andantıno

Simpleton

Mye-sats syyé-tit, Ko-tyó-nok pla-chet. Yu-ro-di-vı, vsta-vaiı_____ Bó-goo po-mo-lis-ya

(The moon is shining, the kitten is crying. Silly boy, rise now, and pray to God)

259 Nationalism in Opera

Another element which brings out the Russian idiom and gives the opera a distinctive flavor is the numerous ballads injected into the score. Many of these texts were given Mussorgsky by Stasov, his friend and correspondent, who obtained them from collected folk-song sources and suggested that they be inserted in some way. They are not specifically indicated in Pushkin except where he merely writes: "Vaarlam sings." Mussorgsky took these texts and skillfully constructed quasi-folk tunes on them. They serve to relieve the tension and give the composer an added opportunity for character delineation. In each case, Mussorgsky demonstrates an uncanny ability to project an image in a remarkably brief passage. In the Inn scene on the Lithuanian border (Act I, scene 2), the Hostess sits mending an old bodice and sings about a duckling she has found (Example 13-10a); though interrupted by the arrival of the mendicant monks and Grigory, she manages to convey in some 30 measures the bucolic nature of the setting and her simple disposition. The orchestra at the beginning of this same scene has already sounded the opening phrase of Vaarlam's song, in which he, in a roistering mood with a bottle in his hand, relates how Ivan the Terrible routed his enemies at the battle of Kazan. This memorable descending motive (b) with its jarring dissonance at the end depicts the rascally, bibulous, old monk (attached to it for comparison is an example of the Rimsky-Korsakov metric version which makes the accents more regular but robs the original of some of its rhythmic force). In Act II, scene 1, the Nurse of Boris' children Xenia and Feodor tries to distract Xenia from her grief (she has lost her young fiancé) by singing a song about a gnat and a flea (c). But Feodor says the song is hardly cheerful because it ends sadly. He will do better. His song is a little nonsense ditty about a cock, an owl, a sparrow, and a priest whose barn caught fire. The Nurse and he join together on the refrain (d). Later, when Boris comes in to his children, Feodor sings a 40-measure tale of how a parrot in the maid's room could not get his head scratched and getting loose, bit the unfortunate girl who refused to favor him (e). This explains the noise outside which has alarmed Boris, for he fears an uprising. Finally, there is the Simpleton's song, a pathetic telling of a moon shining and a kitten crying (f). In Mussorgsky's original version of the opera, when Boris and his nobles come out of the cathedral, the Simpleton accuses the Tsar Boris of murdering Dimitri; the second version puts the Simpleton in the forest scene but retains his song and his tormenting by urchin boys.

While Mussorgsky had no fixed or theoretical system of motives attached to people and things, he did use a series of themes to be associated with various characters and transformed them ingeniously according to the situation and the setting. These reminiscences, some of an original turn, served to link scenes and episodes which otherwise might seem quite unrelated. It was Mussorgsky's instinctive musical device for giving the opera unity and bringing together episodes separated in time.

In the cell scene of Act I, Pimen writing his long history is introduced by a sixteenth note figure running constantly through the bass—almost a literal scratching of his pen. When he puts the pen down, lost in thought, the reiterated figure ceases and a solemn, hymn-like phrase is heard in the strings (Example 13-11). This theme appears again when Grigory complains of his uneventful life and longs for the excitement Pimen has had. Pimen reminds him that even Russia's rulers turned their backs on the world and took refuge in the monastic life, Ivan the Terrible among them. Pimen's theme appears again when he goes before Boris to describe the shepherd's restored vision after praying at the tomb of the murdered Dimitri. This is the tale that causes Boris' death.

A short motive connected with Grigory–Dimitri (Example 13-12) is heard first when Pimen says that the Tsarevitch, if he had lived, would have been just about Grigory's age. The same theme comes into the Inn scene when Grigory refuses to disclose himself to the guards and escapes by pulling a sword. It sounds softly in the orchestra when Boris mentions the name Dimitri to Prince Shuisky in the next scene. When Dimitri appears in Act III, scene 2 (the Polish act), he is introduced by this phrase. It is heard again when Pimen tells Boris of the shepherd's vision beside Dimitri's tomb—this time an angelic choir in the winds. A less important phrase but lovely in its serenity is attached to Xenia. Boris uses it when speaking of his daughter in Act I, and it makes no further appearance until the end when, just before dying, the Tsar tells Feodor to watch after his sister (Example 13-13).

The themes associated with Boris are less prominent than the others, as if Mussorgsky wanted to concentrate so thoroughly on Boris' text there could be no diversion in the orchestra. Example 13-14a is an introduction to the Tsar in the Coronation scene where he expresses his foreboding about assuming the throne. It does not appear in the monologue but is heard in various places where Boris speaks of the fate which will probably overtake him. Also to be noted is a bass idea (b) that is related to both the Tsar's anger and remorse for his crime. Mussorgsky's famous clock

Example 13-11

Example 13-12

Example 13-13

Example 13-14

scene comes when Boris, choking with fear and guilt, thinks he
sees the ghost of the murdered child. As the clock ticks louder,
he believes he is losing his mind. No motivic material is brought
in, but by virtue of superb declamation and throbbing orchestra
Mussorgsky writes one of the most exciting scenes in opera.

The work makes its impact through a combination of many
factors—Russian background, the people, the folk-song element,
striking delineation of major and minor characters, gripping drama,
and unique music. It demonstrates how one branch of opera, based
on a different tradition, has the flexible capacity to absorb a number
of elements and unify them. Although *Boris Godunov* remains somewhat outside the main stream of operatic history, it retains its
powerful hold on the affections and feelings of those who know it.

SUGGESTED READING

General   Abraham, Gerald, *Slavonic and Romantic Music*, St. Martin's Press, New York, 1968. Some fine chapters on Czech and Russian operatic music.
Abraham, Gerald, *Studies in Russian Music*, Reeves, London, 1935
Newmarch, Rosa, *The Music of Czechoslovakia*, Oxford University Press, London, 1942.

Smetana   Large, Brian, *Smetana*, Praeger, New York, 1971. New biography Considerable attention given to the operas.

Janáček   Chisholm, Erik, *The Operas of Leoš Janáček*, Pergamon Press paperback, Oxford, 1971. The work of a composer whose reputation is growing rapidly in the operatic world.

Mussorgsky   Calvocoressi, Michel D., *Modest Mussorgsky: His Life and Works*, Essential Books, Fair Lawn, N.J., 1956. Good background for *Boris Godunov*.
Leyda, Jay, and S. Bertensson, *The Mussorgsky Reader*, Norton, New York, 1947; Da Capo reprint.

14 German Opera

German opera did not assert itself strongly until the first half of the nineteenth century. Even then it was nearly overwhelmed by Parisian grand opera which dominated the 1830s and 1840s and had as one of its chief exponents the expatriate German, Jacob (Giacomo) Meyerbeer, who was more at home artistically in Italy and France than in his own country.

Any attempt to delineate specifically German traits in opera must take geography and politics into account. Because the twentieth century has seen abundant evidence in two world wars of an aggressive, united nation, the misconception persists that this political entity has deep historical roots. Bismarck and Prussia united Germany only in 1871, and then under forced circumstances. Regionalism has always been a strong factor among Germans and remains so today. Culturally there has been one language and one intellectual background, stemming from the late eighteenth century of Goethe, Lessing, Schiller, Kant, and others. But a city like Paris has never dominated artistic life in Germany the way it has in France. Berlin and Prussia were one distinct region; Munich and Bavaria, another, with gradients in between (for example, Saxony, Württemberg, Hesse, the Rhineland). Austria and Vienna have always stood apart. Austrians speak the same language (with variants) but comprise a separate country with proud roots extending into central Europe. Weber and his followers managed to establish a distinct

German Romantic opera, recognized by all these regions. But Wagner, even with all his ultra-nationalistic talk, began composing under the shadow of French grand opera, and it took him some time to throw off its influence, if he ever did entirely.

The way to a native German opera lay through the Singspiel. In *The Magic Flute*, Mozart proved that a composer of genius could take popular and serious music and combine them into a great work of art. Other hands might have turned out a hodgepodge, but Mozart raised opera to a higher level, although it was hardly recognized as such at the time.

Beethoven and Fidelio Haydn outlived Mozart by some years, though he was much older. But he never ventured so thoroughly into the opera field as Mozart had. During his years in the service of the Esterhazys, Haydn performed a number of his Italian opera buffas as well as some German puppet operas, the music to which has been lost, but he never felt that pull of the stage which was such a strong force with Mozart. Of the great Viennese classical composers, it was Beethoven who attempted to further the cause of German opera. His struggle to do so with one great work was so fraught with difficulty it is a wonder it was ever performed.

The complicated history of *Fidelio* (1805, 1806, 1814), Beethoven's only opera, has often obscured the work's great merits. In spite of weaknesses, it remains Beethoven, and Beethoven at a very high level. The trouble the composer had with his material only partly accounts for the difficulty the public outside Germany has had in accepting this stepchild of one of the world's supreme musicians. First, it is a Singspiel with spoken dialogue, and no recitative has ever been written to it.[1] When the opera has been given abroad, either in German or the native language, the dialogue is generally so severely abbreviated the characters lack motivation and one hardly knows what is going on. Second, the work is a "rescue" opera with a last-minute reprieve by a trumpet call announcing the arrival of the minister, Don Fernando, who saves the imprisoned Florestan and his valiant wife Leonore from possible death. This *deus ex machina* ending has a strong resemblance to the Western sheriff rescuing the hero or heroine in the nick of time from the noose or a bullet. But in the time of the French Revolution, such happenings were possible, and we should not malign them too much. Third, the opera is a

[1] " the first irruption of spoken dialogue into music produces a disagreeable shock if you do not expect it." Donald F Tovey, *Essays in Musical Analysis*, Oxford University Press, London, 1937, vol. V, p. 185.

strange mixture of bourgeois *Gemütlichkeit* and heroic drama, the first act being the chief offender. To have the heroine disguise herself as a man (a difficult problem for mature dramatic sopranos of more than girlish figure) and let the employer's daughter fall in love with "her-him" is a delicate matter in anything but a comic opera.

Florestan, unjustly incarcerated in a dungeon by Don Pizarro, his political rival and governor of the state prisons in Spain, languishes near death. Leonore, his faithful wife, suspects he is in a certain prison near Seville. She disguises herself as a man, "Fidelio" (that is, the faithful one), gets a job as assistant to the head jailor Rocco, and plots to get near the prisoners in solitary confinement. Another complication is that Marzelline, Rocco's daughter, supposed to marry Jaquino, the porter, has fallen in love with her instead. Pizarro learns that Don Fernando, suspecting illegal political imprisonment, is coming on a tour of inspection. Pizarro, fearing he will be found out, goes to the prison to murder Florestan in his cell before the minister arrives. Rocco and his assistant, Fidelio, are taken along on this fateful expedition to dig a grave for the body. Just as Pizarro is about to kill Florestan, Fidelio reveals herself as Florestan's wife, throws herself in front of her husband, dares Pizarro to kill her first, and, as he advances, pulls out a pistol. As the group stand undecided, a trumpet call sounds in the prison courtyard announcing the arrival of the minister. Rocco explains to Fernando what has happened. Pizarro, a thwarted captive, is led away, and Florestan and Leonore are happily reunited.

Beethoven all his life was looking for the right libretto. He rejected comic opera (*Don Giovanni* and *Figaro*, for instance, he regarded as morally repugnant), magic librettos, or stories that did not jibe with his serious purpose. He was particularly influenced, as were many other forward-looking Germans of that day, by the ideals of the French Revolution, in spite of the Reign of Terror. The tyranny of one segment of society over another, the brotherhood of man, the heroism of the individual were vividly alive in the minds and hearts of thinking men. *Leonore, ou l'Amour conjugale* (Leonora, or Wedded Love), as it was called in French by Jean Bouilly, its author, (music by Pierre Gaveaux), was instantly attractive to Beethoven because of its emphasis on unselfish love, loyalty, heroic courage, and triumph over odds. In addition to Gaveaux, the libretto had been set to music in two different versions by two other composers, but a German version was prepared for Beethoven by Joseph Sonnleithner, and the work was given in Vienna, November, 1805. At first, it was a failure, partly due to the occupation of the city by French troops and partly because Beethoven, an inexperienced opera composer, made the work too long, did not arrange the scenes satisfactorily and had difficulty in sustaining the heroic mood. He wanted the characters to develop as themes would in a symphony, but in the opera they remain mostly static. Dramatic conflict on the stage was a different matter from drama conceived in an instrumental work. If the situation lacked noble interest and was involved in the petty detail of opera, Beethoven's inspiration flagged. Nonetheless, he tried the work again in 1806 with cuts and changes (three acts reduced to two, finales rewritten, some musical numbers dropped, a new overture added). But there were only two performances and Beethoven gave up temporarily. Finally in 1814, the libretto was completely revised by Georg Treitschke, a poet of the Vienna theater, as *Fidelio*, and Beethoven's final version had 22 successful performances that year. In this latest form, the opera has survived hardily. The overtures Beethoven wrote for the different versions (Leonore overtures 1, 2, and 3 plus the overture to *Fidelio*—the first overture antedates the first performance) have become more famous than the opera itself. Leonore No. 3, one of Beethoven's greatest achievements, is generally played before the last scene of the second act, although there are those who feel by doing so the form of the whole work is disturbed because the overture is such a powerful piece of drama in itself.

In the 1814 version, the first act opens with a duet—Marzelline trying to fend off Jaquino's attentions. This coy bit of business is straight Singspiel and Beethoven makes heavy going of it; the music for the duet and Marzelline's aria following is appropriately gay and light, but Beethoven seems to be gritting his teeth and gives the impression of not feeling quite at home. Mozart might have passed this off with ease and deftness, but for Beethoven it was a different matter. Jaquino leaves, Rocco meets Marzelline, Fidelio comes in laden with groceries and some heavy chains he has taken to the blacksmith to have repaired. Marzelline and Rocco show concern for his heavy load, and Rocco, who in the next aria is overly impressed with money, congratulates Fidelio on getting such good bargains with the grocer. It is obvious that both Rocco and Marzelline think Fidelio is an appealing and clever young man, whom they already envision as a son-in-law and bridegroom respectively.

This prosaic, down-to-earth dialogue is suddenly succeeded by one of Beethoven's finest ensembles in the score, "Mir ist so wunderbar" (It is so wonderful to me), a moving canonic quartet (Jaquino, tenor, has come back on stage), too lofty and elevated for the situation but a glorious piece of music. The quartet in *Rigoletto* comes to mind in comparison. Beethoven's might be called superior musically, but Verdi never forgets his dramatic situation, and his four

Example 14-1   Beethoven, *Fidelio* (1805; 1806; 1814)

(To me. It is so wonderful. My heart is filled with it. He loves me, it is clear. I will be happy)

(Leonore: How great the danger; how weak the ray of hope. Jaquino: My hair stands up.
Her father favors him . Rocco: She loves him it is clear.)

Example 14-2

(O what joy to breathe easily in the fresh air!)

characters maintain their identities within the ensemble. Beethoven, however, writes almost solely with the music in mind, his four characters being indistinguishable musically, even though there are different themes. The text is:

Marzelline. *My heart is filled with the most wondrous feeling. He loves me, it is clear, and I shall be happy.*
Leonore. *How great is the danger; how weak the ray of hope. She loves me, it is clear Oh what pain!*
Jaquino. *My hair stands up. Her father favors him. It would have been so wonderful. No means occur to me.*
Rocco. *She loves him, it is clear Yes, my girl, he will be yours. A good young couple, they will be happy.*

Beethoven constructs the quartet in splendid symmetrical proportion. The lovely opening phrase (Example 14-1*a*) is first accompanied by two clarinets with violas and cellos pizzicato. It is taken up by each voice in turn at the same or octave pitch. The countersubject is reproduced similarly: Marzelline's phrase (*b*) after being combined with the original theme (*a*) for Leonore, is then sung by Leonore when Rocco enters (bass before tenor). All four themes can be seen together in (*b*) when Jaquino comes in with the main theme. What matters is not Beethoven's technique but his masterly handling of the material.

Another great moment comes toward the end of the act when Rocco, at the urging of Fidelio and Marzelline, allows the prisoners a breath of air, briefly letting them walk in the courtyard. The scene responded to Beethoven's inmost feelings: political prisoners, held without hope of deliverance, suddenly allowed fresh air and a glimpse of the sky. As the men stumble out rubbing their eyes unaccustomed to the sunlight, the strings slowly build on two held chords from the bass upward, sustaining the tension. The second basses then lead off with the phrase, "O welche Lust" (Oh, what joy) and the other male parts come in one by one on top until the whole chorus fortissimo shouts a cry of happiness. (Example 14-2). Their song of joy is brief enough; soon the prisoners are suspicious of this sudden freedom and shrink back to their cells in fear. Rocco appears and the voices die away. This bit of realism has no direct connection with the plot. It is primarily "atmosphere," but Beethoven's music is drama itself.

Act II is the culmination of the opera. Here where Beethoven did not have to deal with the affairs of Marzelline and Jaquino, he concentrated on essentials and reached the height of his dramatic powers. The curtain rises on an almost dark stage depicting the dungeon where Florestan lies; his body, a heap on the floor, is barely perceived. The orchestra pictures the prisoner's surroundings

Example 14-3

Und spür ich nicht lin - de, sanft säu - seln - de Luft?
(Do I not feel a soft, sweet, whispering breeze?)

Le - o - no - ren, der Gat - tin, so gleich,
(Leonora, my wife, even her,)

and plight in a Grave introduction of great dimension and power. Beethoven treats this orchestral interlude like part of a symphony. Four motives dominate. They might be characterized as the poles of Florestan's despair and hope: Example 14-3a being his grief; b, his desperate longing to be free; c, inexorable fate; and d, thought of Leonore. Beethoven intermingles these with other menacing sounds until Florestan raises himself and cries: "Gott! welch' Dunkel hier" (Lord! what darkness here). Then come his equally despairing comments on the gruesome stillness, the desolation, and his terrible trial of existence under these circumstances. These phrases of recitative are separated by orchestral accompaniment drawing on motives heard previously. The thought of God's protection brings him consolation. With it the orchestra plays an anticipation of his aria, "In des Lebens Frühlingstagen ist das Glück von mir gefloh'n" (In the springtime of life all my happiness has vanished) (e). This famous woodwind passage also appeared in the slow beginning of the Leonore overtures, Beethoven linking it with Florestan and his plight. Finally, in fevered imagination Florestan senses a breath of outside air and thinks he sees an angelic light (f). The aria reaches its climax as the key changes, the tempo increases, and Florestan equates the vision with his beloved wife (g). In a frenzy, he believes she will lead him to "freedom in the kingdom of heaven." After this outburst, he sinks down exhausted.

The next part shows Rocco and Leonore approaching the dungeon in the darkness. Beethoven uses "melodrama" here (that is, spoken dialogue interspersed with orchestral comment)—a device to be handled with the greatest care, but very effective at the right moment. This scene and the Wolf's Glen in *Der Freischütz* are two occasions where it has remarkable impact. Leonore is nearly overwhelmed by the darkness, the cold, and the fear of what she will find. The orchestra mirrors her feelings. Seeing no movement from Florestan, Rocco whispers: "Perhaps he is dead," and Leonore replies, agonizingly: "You think so?", the orchestra playing from Florestan's aria referring to Leonore (*e*).

Beethoven builds the tension gradually: a duet for Rocco and Leonore; a trio when Florestan awakens; and a quartet as Pizarro joins them. The trumpet call, mechanical though it may be, is a wonderful dramatic stroke, paralyzing the action of the participants. Jaquino's spoken words after the call break the spell and signify that rescue has come.

If Beethoven could have found librettos that inspired him as much as the second half of *Fidelio* did, the world of opera might have been notably enriched; for in this work German opera has a proud heritage.

Weber Musical Romanticism in Germany found its most ardent exponent in Carl Maria von Weber (1786–1826). Weber came from a large family of musicians, whose forebears were musicians even in the seventeenth century. During his lifetime, several other musical Webers occupied prominent positions in Germany and Bohemia; one of them, Gottfried, was an associate and lifelong friend. Weber was also related to Mozart by marriage; his first cousin, Constanze Weber, was Mozart's wife. If Weber had lived beyond his fortieth year he might have had much greater influence on subsequent opera history. But his death of tuberculosis in 1826 deprived music of a creative operatic spirit just beginning to bloom.

Weber's whole life was involved with the theater. His father, a traveling performer (violinist and double bassplayer), was director of a dramatic company, consisting mostly of his own family, the mother a professional singer and the children playing and singing. Before he was 17, Weber saw as much of Europe and its theaters as others would know in a lifetime. He gained invaluable experience in the operatic and theatrical world, whether it was intrigue, stagecraft, or music. Later he put this to good use. At the tender age of 18, he was appointed *Kapellmeister* at Breslau on the recommendation of his teacher, Abbé Vogler, a man of reputation in the musical world. He went to Stuttgart, Darmstadt, and Mannheim in various positions, some musical, some secretarial. These three cities, like many others in Germany at that time, had their own local ruling establishment headed by a hereditary duke or prince. Generally, they were the seat of government for the surrounding area or region. The rulers furthered artistic interests in music, painting, poetry, and literature as a form of rivalry with the neighboring prince and were proud to have men of culture around them. Weber met able young men of his own age and was saturated with current literature and philosophy. One of his friends was Jacob Beer (Meyerbeer), whose family was to be very generous to him later in Berlin.

For some time, Weber led the life of a virtuoso on concert tours. He was an able pianist and in demand as a conductor. Among his other talents were facility on the guitar and a pleasant singing voice, nearly ruined by an accident in his teens. In 1813, his roving existence came to a temporary end when he was appointed a conductor in the theater at Prague. Here his organizational abilities were brought to bear on administration, stage management, scene painting, and music. In the beginning he had great success. However, politics and the governing structure led to change and after four years at Prague (1813–1817), he went to Dresden where he was eventually appointed conductor of the German opera for life. His struggles to establish a new tradition in the face of Italian operatic influence which had flourished there for 100 years was a difficult one, but he managed to accomplish it and at the same time keep up his own composing.

Weber's three great operas are *Der Freischütz* (1821) written for Berlin, *Euryanthe* (1823) for Vienna, and *Oberon* (1826) for London. All of his operas are Singspiele except *Euryanthe* (see p. 13). Of his early works, two, *Silvana* and *Abu Hassan*, a one-act comic opera, stand out. The three works for which he is known exhibit different faces of romanticism. *Freischütz* is primarily folk music on a large scale, and it laid the foundation for German romantic opera. Its clever libretto drawn from an earlier source by Friedrich Kind gave Weber the opportunity to portray nature as it seldom had been before. The stillness of the moonlight night, the gruesome Wolf's Glen at the witching hour, peasant village bustle, natural human character—all came to life in Weber's music. It was the orchestral sound that fascinated his public: the horns invoking forest and rustic life; his careful woodwind coloring, particularly the clarinets (he cherished them all his life). Then there was music for Agathe, Max, and Ännchen—songs tuneful, memorable and beguiling, easily grasped and remembered.

After the predominance of French ways during the Napoleonic wars, the Berlin public longed for something from their own culture. This opera appeared at just the right moment. Spontini, Italian by birth but French by adoption, had been Berlin's leading operatic figure, backed by the king and his court. But his works, too formal and too cold for the average German, were grand opera without heart. *Freischütz* was to be the opening musical work of a new theater. The excitement was intense. Seldom had a new opera been greeted with such enthusiasm. It was taken up almost immediately by the important opera houses in Germany, and Weber's name was on everybody's lips. As a Singspiel with spoken dialogue, the work has never traveled as well as it might outside of Germany. Like *Fidelio* and *The Magic Flute*, this hindrance has given perhaps slightly more difficulty because the opera is so "echt" German, needing all its dialogue to create the proper effect. The Germans have always taken it to their hearts.

Of perhaps equal significance for the history of opera is *Euryanthe*, Weber's full-blown excursion into medieval romance. *Euryanthe* is the classic example of an opera hailed by critics for its splendid music but damned for its libretto. Part of the fault was Weber's. He was determined to create something different after *Freischütz* and was captivated by medieval tales. (The romantics had a passion for the Middle Ages, which were remote in time, slightly mysterious, and could be clothed with imagination.) When Weber received a commission from the Vienna Kärntnertor Theater, he looked forward to writing a work with continuous music and one that might reflect his recent interest. The librettist he chose was a lady, one Helmina von Chézy, whose song texts he had known. She had no experience with opera and her poetry was stilted and high-flown, but she seemed the best Dresden had to offer at the time. From the dramatic point of view the result was nearly a disaster, even though Weber took great pains in helping work out the libretto and revised it 11 times.

Chézy drew her story from an early French chronicle, *L'Histoire du tres-noble et chevalereux prince Gerard, comte de Nevers* (The History of the very noble and chivalrous Prince Girard, Count of Nevers). The tale, well-known in literary circles—Shakespeare's *Cymbeline* was derived from it, tells of a knight who boasts of his wife's fidelity, and is challenged to a wager by a hated rival who says he can disprove it. The wife, on falsified evidence, is proven false to her husband. The knight, seeking to kill his wife, takes her to a lonely place, where she shields him from an attack by a snake. This magnanimous act stays the husband from his deed, but he abandons her. At the point of death, she is rescued, her innocence proven, the rival shown to have told a lie, and husband and wife united. In variants of the story, the evidence for infidelity ranges from a mole on the breast (only a lover would have seen it) to a ring given by the husband to his wife.

In the opera libretto, Euryanthe and Adolar, the hero, are not married but engaged and very much in love. He pledges Euryanthe to secrecy about the family disgrace involving his sister, Emma, who at the loss of her lover committed suicide with poison from a ring. (Taking one's life was considered a sin by the medieval church.) Her tomb is in Adolar's castle; she was buried with the ring. Lysiart, who also loves Euryanthe, challenges Adolar. After Adolar has told the court of Euryanthe's purity and beauty, Lysiart wagers his property and estates that she is not as saintly as she seems. Adolar, in anger, foolishly accepts the challenge in spite of a warning by the King that tragedy may ensue. Euryanthe unwittingly discloses the story of Emma to Eglantine, who is in love with Adolar and wants to thwart Euryanthe. Eglantine takes the ring from Emma's body and gives it to Lysiart, who by producing the ring proves that Euryanthe has betrayed her trust. (This part of the story is exceedingly weak because an audience finds it impossible to believe that Euryanthe should be killed or deserted by Adolar for violating a family secret. If Lysiart had brutally described some body imperfection which would have proved Euryanthe's infidelity the subsequent action might have been more plausible. But the censor probably would have frowned at this realism.) Adolar with murderous intent takes Euryanthe to a lonely place; the snake episode takes place. Euryanthe is abandoned but finally discovered by the King and his followers, who hear the true story. Eglantine, about to marry Lysiart with Adolar's property, confesses her crime, and is stabbed by Lysiart. The tangle is exposed. Lysiart is captured and led away; Adolar and Euryanthe are happily united.

There have been equally weak librettos in opera but few with the combination of artificial language, confused motivation, and improbable circumstance this one possessed. Weber nevertheless lavished some of his greatest music on it. His dovetailing of recitative, aria, and chorus with an embryonic motivic structure made it one of the most advanced works of its time. Wagner's debt to it is enormous, particularly in *Lohengrin*.

Weber's overture, written last as was customary, makes use of material from the opera, and is a brilliant piece. Beginning with a call to arms (full orchestra, triplets in the strings, accented chords in the winds and brass), the music almost immediately rings out

Adolar's stirring assertion of faith in his God and in Euryanthe. This appears in Act I when he is challenged by Lysiart (Example 14-4). The theme which Weber develops with great skill is the central one in the overture. It reappears at the end of the exposition in the sonata form, triumphantly restated. It is also transformed in the development as the inverted subject of a powerful contrapuntal passage (Example 14-7). The second theme of the exposition in B flat (the main key is E flat) is the second half of Adolar's aria to Euryanthe, which he sings in Act II before the great confrontation with Lysiart to decide the wager. Adolar is in his most resplendent dress, his head a wreath of jewels. The words tell of his great love. The music breathes the Age of Chivalry and presents one of the memorable tunes in the score (Example 14-5). Just before the

Example 14-4

Weber, *Euryanthe* (1823)

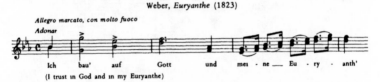

(I trust in God and in my Euryanthe)

Example 14-5

(Oh happiness, I can scarcely comprehend you. Your eye will shine upon me)

Example 14-6

Example 14-7

Example 14-8

Example 14-9

(a) Allegro con fuco

(b) Andante con moto
Lysiart
dolce

Schweigt, glüh'n-den Seh - nens wil -de Trie - be, Ihr Au - ge sucht den Him - mel nur.
(Be quiet, wild impulse of glowing desire. Her eye seeks heaven alone.)

(c)
So weih' ich mich
Strings

(So I devote myself { to the power of revenge }.)

(d) Vivace feroce

Zer - trümm're zer - trümm're schö - nes__ Bild!

(Fall in pieces, lovely image!)

development section of the overture, Weber ceases the orchestral movement. Horns and bassoons with dotted muttering below in the strings are the only sounds heard. The scoring is similar to the start of the *Freischütz* overture where the horns by themselves invoke a picture of the forest at night. Then eight muted violins, joined later by violas, play a Largo, the mysterious chromatic music associated with the ghost of Emma. Euryanthe tells Eglantine in Act I that on one May moonlight night when she and Adolar were about to part, they were visited by Emma's ghost which said she also once loved the way they did, but her hero fell "in bloody strife." Now she, the ghost, cannot rest until "this ring, from which I sucked my death has been wetted by the tears of an innocent one who has grievously suffered and whose fidelity is finally rewarded." The music (Example 14-6) is an ethereal evocation in hushed, sliding, supernatural tones that avoid a tonal center and progress hesitantly from step to step.

In spite of emphasis in the overture on the triumph of good over evil, some of Weber's most interesting music is assigned to Eglantine and Lysiart. At the appearance of Eglantine in Act I, Weber outlines a motive which anticipates the Wagnerian system; it is treated in a less elaborate fashion and its various recurrences lack Wagner's sophistication, yet it is advanced for its time. This idea is first heard after Euryanthe's touching cavatina. Eglantine enters with malicious intent. The motive is largely an outline of a diminished seventh chord (Example 14-8a), but in later variations of it, Weber keeps the arpeggiated sequence and reminds his audience each time of what Eglantine is trying to do. Example *b* is reserved for a recitative when she is alone: "Infatuated woman! that believes in my love." Example *c* is the orchestra interjection in the following aria when she sings: "He scorns me for her: therefore do I complain and in my days of bloom pine away in suffering." In Act II *d* comes when Eglantine steals furtively from the tomb with the ring. The original motive is heard differently each time but plain enough to be recognized. Weber is letting the music take its natural course in character representation.

One of the finest examples of an unfolding scene mixing orchestral introduction, accompanied recitative, aria, and bold tone painting in passionate sequence is Lysiart's opening soliloquy in Act II. Beginning with accented dotted strong figures that stretch over two-and-a-half octaves (Example 14-9a), his rage, jealousy, and determination leap out of the orchestra. "Where shall I hide myself? Where can I find composure? Infatuated heart! you looked upon her as easy prey. Rocks, fall down upon me. You, echo, do not answer the signs of my hopeless heart." But then comes an unexpected human touch, mitigating the portrait of Lysiart as evil. He sings a touching paean to Euryanthe's purity and innocence (*b*). But she loves Adolar and he cannot tolerate this blow to his pride. His mood changes abruptly; rushing, throbbing accompaniment interrupts quick phrases of recitative. Then comes a vivid passage where Weber has the strings in unison and octaves rapidly growl back and forth under Lysiart's whispered cry for vengeance (*c*). Tension builds to a Vivace feroce and the climax (*d*), where his words are: "Fall in pieces, lovely image. From henceforth, sweet pain. Revenge alone can fill this storm-tossed heart." The melodramatic villain is speaking, but the music is so apt and striking, the histrionics assume their place and one is not conscious of exaggeration.

Weber was able to sustain this high level through most of the score. His opposition of the two couples is furthered by open, major keys for Euryanthe and Adolar against a darker, more chromatic world for Eglantine and Lysiart. The music manages, as it often can, to dispel difficulties in the libretto. One forgets the inconsistencies and is carried away by the force of Weber's genius. If the drama had come up to the music in a positive way, the opera might have attained a high place in the lexicon.

Weber's last opera, *Oberon* (1826), was written on a commission from Charles Kemble, the actor-director of Covent Garden Theater (London) in 1824. Kemble wanted an opera as much like *Freischütz* as possible with spoken dialogue and a complete text in English. The taste of the English public at this time was fairly low: standard operas were performed in altered form with extra music added and the work arranged according to the desires of the management. Nevertheless, the offer was attractive to Weber. With his flair for languages, he made progress in English and the subject of *Oberon* was decided on. It was to be a magic opera, and he was sent the libretto act by act from London. The librettist, James Robinson Planché, concocted a hodgepodge of scenes that Weber tried to pull together with his music. There is a little bit of Puck's fairy world (*Midsummer Night's Dream*), an oriental setting, and much romantic coloring, especially for the orchestra. In spite of Weber's best efforts, the work never came off as a whole. There are individual numbers of great beauty but the combined effect is one of disjointedness. Weber knew when he left for London and *Oberon* he might never see his family again; his consumption was rapidly growing worse. Just before he was to return home, he succumbed to the disease. The world lost a distinctive and talented artist.

Wagner   The artistic distance from Weber to Wagner is not a great one. Although Wagner belonged to a much later generation, he often spoke of his debt to Weber. In 1844, 18 years after Weber's death, it was Wagner, the Kapellmeister in Dresden, who arranged the return of Weber's remains to that city and performed music at the graveside.

Richard Wagner (1813–1883) is one of the most significant figures in the history of opera. Although his life and character will always be controversial, his work had far-reaching influence on music. He is one of the few figures in music who wrote prolifically (16 volumes of prose) on what he was attempting to achieve and how he proposed to do it, as well as comments on a multitude of other subjects. His musical aim, simply put, was to create a composite art-work (*Gesamtkunstwerk*) which would unite all the arts through opera and attain a grand synthesis. Since he was both librettist and composer, his ideal was partly fulfilled in his own person. Only the visual elements needed to be equally well-coordinated. Wagner soon realized that the ordinary opera theater could not cope with his ambitions—a special theater would have to be built to perform his works and to show a doubting world they were valid artistically. Wagner, whose whole life was either profound good fortune (he was in the right place at the right time) or a series of calamities, (most of them brought on by his own foolishness), managed to achieve his theater (Bayreuth). He had his works performed there and elsewhere, through the generosity of King Ludwig of Bavaria, although he never fully brought the public with him. It is an extraordinary tale that never lacks for color in the telling.

Wagner the man fascinates and repels. His life has engendered enough books to fill a good-sized library, and even the literature on his music is enormous. It is surprising that psychoanalysis has not probed his childhood more thoroughly to search for the meaning of his subsequent behavior. Wagner and women, Wagner and money, Wagner and the ego, are all topics ripe for speculation. Some episodes in his private life are so unpleasant as to be embarrassing.

A man who at 53 could run away with the wife of one of his star protegés (Hans von Bülow)—the lady 27 and an illegitimate daughter of Franz Liszt—have three children by her out of wedlock; marry her and make the world accept it, was a considerable person, to say the least. Flouting conventional morality might have been tolerated for the exceptional creative artist, but it is more difficult to accept this same artist dictating to Cosima Liszt-Wagner his *Autobiography*, trying to justify his conduct and putting his first wife, Minna Planer, in the worst possible light. Wagner's other aberrations, if they might politely be called that, ranged from the eccentric (while composing he had to wear silk dressing gowns and have attar of roses pumped into his room) to the unpleasant. He had a reputation as one of the most prolific borrowers of all time with little of the money ever repaid; his arrogant and selfish conduct toward friends and foes alike was notorious (". . . Wagner had a constitutional aversion to feeling grateful");[2] his ability to regard human beings merely as they served his own purpose[3]— these are interesting phenomena but only tangentially related to the most important thing about the man: his music.

With all his faults, Wagner was utterly serious in his artistic purpose; by his stubbornness and energy, he single-handedly created an artistic revolution in nineteenth century music. We couple his name with those of Darwin, Marx, and Freud as a seminal thinker and doer. If one of the most original minds of the nineteenth century, Friedrich Nietzsche, could fall under his spell (though he later recanted), there must have been considerable artistic and intellectual attraction to the man.

Wagner came from a bourgeois Saxon background in Leipzig. His father, a clerk in the police department, always passionately fond of the theater, died of typhus a few months after Richard's birth; a few years later the mother married Ludwig Geyer, an actor and a painter, often reputed to be Wagner's real father. While a boy, Wagner's two sisters became opera singers. If the musical theater was in his blood, his early musical training was haphazard and he was largely self-taught. But he persevered and attained competence as a musician. Writing on a large scale was an early occupation; barely in his teens, he undertook long, ambitious tragedies, which came to naught. He matriculated at Leipzig University but left for an opportunity to become chorus-master at Würzburg. During these years, Wagner wrote a number of concert overtures and other instrumental pieces, some of which were performed but almost all are now forgotten.

At 20, he began his first complete opera, *Die Feen* (The Fairies, 1834), produced only after his death in the 1880s. His second opera, *Das Liebesverbot* (Love's Denial), his libretto based on Shakespeare's *Measure for Measure*, was performed in Magdeburg in 1836 when

[2] Eric Blom, *Stepchildren of Music*, Foulis, London, n.d., pp. 126–127
[3] " Wagner is made out to be consciously scheming. It is more probable that he displayed the natural cunning and alteration of love and ferocity which he showed in his relations generally. Wagner's great charm was his impulsive, unpremeditated self-seeking. He was only intermittently a moral being, and his idolators of the nineties who were overawed by his "mind" should have found this out from the wooly inconsistency of his words on almost any subject." Jacques Barzun, *Berlioz and the Romantic Century*, Little, Brown, Boston, 1950, vol. II, pp. 182–183.

Wagner was part of a traveling company. The work was withdrawn after two performances. Following this came appointments to the theaters at Königsberg and Riga in the east, and Wagner's marriage to Minna Planer, an actress in the Bethmann traveling company with him. Neither of the operatic engagements lasted because Wagner was too demanding or incurred debts which made him flee his creditors. In 1839, he went to Paris where for several years he tried to get *Liebesverbot, Rienzi* (his first grand opera), or *The Flying Dutchman* (original version in one act) performed. He and Minna lived in poverty and Wagner supported them as best he could by journalism and hack work. A turn for the better came when *Rienzi* was accepted for performance in Dresden (October, 1842). As a result, Wagner received an appointment to the court opera there as second conductor. In the years 1842–1848, both *The Flying Dutchman* and *Tannhäuser* were given in Dresden. Wagner's position as conductor was precarious—the opera establishment was conservative and bureaucratic. Wagner's desire for change was constantly running up against difficulties: most of his requests were designed to improve the opera (weeding out dead wood in the orchestra, more attention to rehearsal detail, new staging) and were reasonable, but his own life was so tied with debts and troubles he had few allies. When the revolution of 1848 struck Saxony, Wagner joined the provisional forces who wanted to institute a new government. Prussian troops were called in and Wagner had to flee. The sanctuary of Liszt at Weimar saved him temporarily. With a warrant out for his arrest (1849), he escaped to Switzerland.

His first years in Switzerland (1849–1854) were largely occupied with prose writings and the construction of *Siegfried's Death,* which eventually became *Der Ring des Nibelungen. Lohengrin* was given by Liszt in Weimar in 1850 but Wagner never saw it. There were trips to Paris and London but no fixed engagements. In the late 1850s, Wagner fell in love with Mathilde Wesendonck, a married woman. She was partly the inspiration for *Tristan und Isolde,* written in 1857–1859 but not produced in Munich until 1865. During the fifties and sixties Wagner kept working on the four operas of the Ring as well as *Tristan* and *Meistersinger,* which he had conceived earlier but never brought to fruition. For many of these years his only means of support were gifts and loans by friends. But his fame was growing in Germany as a result of performances of *The Flying Dutchman, Tannhäuser,* and *Lohengrin,* and he began to receive royalties. In 1864 came the miraculous promise of financial backing from the young King Ludwig II of Bavaria, who was enthralled by Wagner's music. Plans were undertaken for Wagner to go to Munich to set up under ideal conditions a national opera house. With the production of *Tristan* the following year and other promises, Wagner's future looked hopeful, but his capacity for entanglement soon created trouble— he took up with Cosima quite openly, alienating many of the good burghers, and officials at the court intrigued against him because he had too much influence over the king. The years 1865–1868 were spent partly in Switzerland and partly in Munich because of this unsettled state of affairs. A second triumph was a performance of *Meistersinger* in Munich in 1868 under Hans von Bülow, still greatly devoted to Wagner and his cause in spite of family complications. 1870 saw Cosima finally married to Wagner and plans prepared for the festival theater in Bayreuth. These plans were near collapse in 1874 because of lack of money; but again Ludwig, now near insanity, came to the rescue by supplying the necessary funds, and the *Festspielhaus* (Festival House) was completed. There were further problems, but *The Ring* was performed at Bayreuth during the late 1870s, as well as *Parsifal*, Wagner's final opera. In his last years, Wagner had the world at his feet and saw the fulfillment of his dreams. The foundations were not strong, but the impossible had happened. Wagner, health deteriorating, died in Venice in 1883.

Wagner's artistic principles and theories were elaborated before any of the operas embodying them were completed, but he also wrote on all sorts of musical and political topics. A welter of essays and polemical tracts poured from his pen from young manhood to old age. Like many romantics he wrote too much and a good deal of it is verbose and vague.[4] Yet some of his essays are important for an understanding of his own operas and for aesthetic theories of music in general. On the other hand, many tracts are propaganda for a cause and are interesting only for historical reasons.

His prose can generally be divided into two groups. The first comprises early essays, written before 1842, in which his ideas were stated through a consideration of other men's works. Outstanding among them are "A Pilgrimage to Beethoven," "A Happy Evening," and "On the Overture" (1840–1842). The second group, written mostly in exile in Switzerland, expounded his own views on the problems of opera. Their chief aim was to explain "the composite art-work," which he had been mulling for many years. The most important titles of this group are "Art and Revolution" (1849), "The Art Work of the Future" (1850), and "Opera and

---

[4]To make matters worse, the standard English edition of *Wagner's Prose Works* by Ashton Ellis in eight volumes is often obscure and unreadable. Granted that Wagner's original German is much the same, a new translation is badly needed for the English and American public.

Drama" (1852).[5] Because of Wagner's late musical maturity, he was not entirely consistent between what he wrote in theory and the music he composed in fact. Only *The Ring* follows his theories in some detail. *Tristan* and *Meistersinger* begin to break away, *Meistersinger* particularly being a return to a diatonic tonal world and to rhymed verse which Wagner supposedly eliminated. Wagner was not rigidly doctrinaire; as he applied himself to composition, he realized that his musical instinct had to take precedence over theory. He should not be charged with hypocrisy, but regarded as an artist who had to find the best means wherever it led.

The essay on the overture is a worthwhile bit of criticism. It appeared in the Paris *Gazette Musicale* of January, 1841, a few months after the completion of *Rienzi* and about six months before the beginning of *The Flying Dutchman*. Wagner undertook to summarize the overture prior to his time, dwelling on the purpose of a prologue, the lack of connection between some overtures and the rest of the work, and the desire to sum up the dramatic action of the opera. He speaks of the change which Beethoven instituted with his great *Leonore* Overture No. 3—" . . . far from giving us a musical introduction to the drama, [Beethoven] really sets that drama before us more completely and more affectingly than the ensuing broken action does. This work is no longer an overture, but itself the mightiest of dramas." Mozart achieves another ideal in the *Don Giovanni* overture by contrasting two broad principles: the arrogance of Don Giovanni versus a higher power which destroys him. Beethoven's method is to concentrate everything into one sublime action: the loving self-sacrifice of Leonore. But by reason of its greatness as music *Leonore* ceases to be an overture: "If it is not understood by the hearer, because of his lack of knowledge of the opera, it conveys only a fragment of its real message to him, if it is wholly understood, it weakens his subsequent enjoyment of the drama itself."[6] Wagner declares that Gluck in his *Iphigenia in Aulis* overture and Weber in *Freischütz* and *Euryanthe* were, in a sense, more successful than Beethoven because they summarized the drama without overshadowing it.

When he came to write his own opera overtures Wagner did not always emulate the models he praised. *Tannhäuser* overture does

[5] A condensed version of "The Art Work of the Future" can be found in Oliver Strunk, ed., *Source Readings in Music History*, Norton, New York, 1965, vol. V, The Romantic Era, pp. 134—163. "Opera and Drama" is succinctly summarized in Gerald Abraham, *A Hundred Years of Music*, Duckworth, London, 1949, pp. 97—112. Also see summaries in Ernest Newman, *Wagner as Man and Artist*, Vintage Books paperback, New York, 1960.

[6] *Wagner as Man and Artist*, p. 205.

present the conflict between the world of Venus and the devout pilgrims, but it is more a pageant than a summary of the action ahead. The Prelude to *Lohengrin* poses no conflict—it is Lohengrin coming down to earth and leaving it again (or perhaps the Holy Grail doing the same)—a representation of one event, beautifully drawn, but telling nothing of Elsa's struggle with herself and Lohengrin. In *Das Rheingold* it is the primeval element of the Rhine river; for *Die Walküre*, the storm which precedes the entrance of Siegmund into Hunding's hut. *Meistersinger* is a potpourri of themes (the mastersingers, Walther's love for Eva, the apprentices, and a few others); it is a wonderful piece of music and can stand on its own, though not as summary of the drama. Curiously enough, Wagner never decided on the solution to the overture problem later composers adopted: get rid of it altogether or open the curtain on a few chords.

"Opera and Drama" has three sections, the first two largely analytical, the third a series of proposals. In part one, Wagner acknowledges the criticism of opera as an artform. But he says the fundamental reason for its weakness has not been the degenerate taste of the public or the composers who catered to this taste, but that music has always overshadowed the drama (the old argument). In elliptical language, Wagner says that music, which should be the means of expression, had become the object, while the object of expression (drama) had become the means. In other words, the music of Gluck, Mozart, Rossini, and Weber had determined the shape of their operas, their librettos being completely subordinated. This unequal partnership had to be corrected.

In part two, he tries to show what the essence of dramatic poetry should be to redress the balance. The proper subject of opera was to be *the legend*—intense, elevated, and embracing in a timeless fashion eternal truths. These sagas and myths were to be clothed in a special kind of word language particularly fitted for music. He wanted to emotionalize the intellectual content of the poetry by an intensification of the direct sensory appeal of the verse. The type of verse is spelled out in part three. Three means were to be used—alliteration, condensation, and free rhythm. Consonantal alliteration expresses an intuitive perception of the relationship between different objects (for example, *Lust und Leid*—joy and pain). Condensation permits a higher percentage of root syllables and gets rid of conjunctions and prepositions which have no emotional quality. Free rhythm replaces the regular pulsation of most poetry with normal speech rhythm, making possible an endless degree of subtlety in accentuation for purposes of emotional shading.

Also in part three he goes into more detail about the music. The orchestra was to realize the subtle changes found in this new verse by a series of harmonic modulations which would carry the vocal and melodic lines without any break. The music was to be an immediate expression of feeling and was to represent the inner action of the drama (word and gesture were to make definite the outer action). Since inner action is continuous, the music is continuous (intermissions are Wagner's concessions to human frailty). Transitions between scenes were to be made by orchestral interludes, and within the scene perfect cadences were to be avoided. Voice and orchestra were to be related as two entities, not one subordinate to the other. Since pure instrumental music can express all that is inexpressible in actual speech, it has a new role to play. Motives fashioned by the orchestra would be heard continuously; and through power of association, recall of past emotions, or by anticipation of what is to come, add a new dimension to the musical and dramatic fabric.

The so-called *leitmotiv* (leading motive) system with its labels, development, and structure was never laid out by Wagner himself but by Hans von Wolzogen, an ardent admirer. Wagner merely spoke of "musical reminiscences and presentiments" in the orchestra. He was surprisingly vague and unclear about what these meant. Because many of them are intuitive and not literal, Wagner probably realized anything too specific would tend to destroy the character of the music. He had no wish to turn his *Ring* into a gigantic chess game where all the moves were plotted in advance. The tables of motives should never be taken as an exact science. Musical considerations often made Wagner change his mind, and the listener should be ready to change his also. By various counts, there are some 70 to 100 motives in the *Ring*. The clue to the association of the motive and the idea with which it is associated can be found at its first appearance. In general, the motives are short and of pronounced individual character; they are generally suggested by *pictorial image* (as the fire motives) or by *association* (trumpet figure for the sword motive). Each one aims to convey, in Wagner's language, the essence of the idea and not merely a picture. The motives form a symphonic web which in theory corresponds to the dramatic web of the action. They may be varied, developed, and transformed, according to the changing fortunes of the idea. The orchestra is the basic medium. Motives are rarely sung. The voice makes a kind of free counterpoint to the instrumental melody, but still retains its melodic function.

Although Wagner did not completely revolutionize operatic music, he did bring about considerable change. From the technical point of view, his new harmony started the breakup of the tonal system which had been the foundation of music for three centuries. His most purely experimental opera in this respect was *Tristan und Isolde*; also in this category is the second act of *Parsifal*. In the operas after *Lohengrin* he did away with the old "numbers system" and evolved a continuous chain of "musical periods" which melted one into the other. Whether he achieved a completely satisfying "composite art-work" with them is aesthetically more debatable; but the outward form reached toward this goal. He did make the orchestra (again, only the mature works) a living symbol of the action. If the listener wants to know what is happening, he generally hears it in the orchestra rather than in the voice. Wagner expanded the orchestra, adding more brass and even devising new kinds of horns and tubas to get the sounds he desired. He was a brilliant orchestrator—one of the most effective who ever lived. As a child of his age, he was unconsciously an arch-romantic. His romanticism consisted of "a thorough exploration of the means": for example, harmonic devices to achieve certain ends. In *Tristan*, the feeling of unsatisfied longing comes through discords that do not resolve. In *The Ring* the metamorphoses of motives show continuing development in actions and people; the ring motive undergoes successive transformations from its pure, unsullied state deep in the Rhine to its darkened, troubled condition in the hands of Siegfried and Hagen. Then there is emphasis on orchestral sound per se; and finally, the exploration and unfolding of the myth or legend as the only fit subject for a serious, comprehensive music drama. All of this was a mighty accomplishment.

Wagner's operas can be conveniently divided into three groups. There are four early operas. The first, *Die Hochzeit* (The Wedding, 1832), is an operatic fragment by an 18-year-old boy. *Die Feen* (The Fairies, 1833–1834), a fairy tale based on a supernatural story by Gozzi, is Wagner's first completed opera; it is an overly long essay in German romantic opera under the influence of *Der Freischütz*. *Das Liebesverbot* (Love's Denial, 1835–1836), based on Shakespeare, is an attempted assimilation of the Italian style of Bellini, Rossini, and Donizetti with spoken dialogue and comic scenes. It has some fine music but again is too long. *Rienzi* (1838–1840), based on a novel by Bulwer-Lytton (nineteenth century English historical novelist), is a grand opera in five acts with massive choruses, ensembles, and some catchy tunes. Wagner was attempting to outdo Meyerbeer. This is the opera that started him on his road to fame. He began his career by demonstrating his mastery of a style to which he later became bitterly opposed. These four operas mark the end of his apprenticeship and his mastery of current models. All the librettos except *Rienzi* were written by other people. He was now ready to embark on work more in accord with his own thinking.

The middle period comprises those three operas which launched him into the musical world. They are part of the present-day repertory, particularly in Germany, and each one has individual and distinctive features. *The Flying Dutchman* (1843) is a German romantic opera in the tradition of Weber and Heinrich Marschner (1795–1861), whose *Der Vampyr* (The Vampire, 1828) and *Hans Heiling* (1833) were filled with supernatural and diabolic elements. The Dutchman who roams the seven seas and comes ashore every seven years to redeem a curse on him is a similar subject. Although divided into traditional numbers (arias, accompanied recitative, choruses), the opera has splendid moments with considerable inner dramatic significance. Based on legend, it is the first opera to show Wagner's dawning ability and genius. *Tannhäuser* (1845) unites the grand opera of *Rienzi* with the romanticism of *The Flying Dutchman*. The theme, as in *The Flying Dutchman*, concerns a man's redemption through the unselfish love of a woman. There are large choruses (the song contest) along with spectacular ballet (The Venusberg scene). Set in the Middle Ages, *Tannhäuser* combines historical background with legend—the conflict of sacred and profane love. *Lohengrin* (1850), the last of the group, shows Wagner's further advance toward the new music drama. There is greater emphasis on a simple motivic structure; the orchestra grows in intensity and importance; and a general loosening of the old "number" system is clearly visible. Wagner was ready for the next step.

His mature period comprises the rest of his operas. (Performance dates with most Wagner operas have little relation to the times when they were composed. *The Ring* was not fully performed until years after the first part of it was written.) These operas with their composition dates are:

Der Ring des Nibelungen (1853–1874)
  1. *Das Rheingold* (The Rhinegold, 1853–1854)
  2. *Die Walküre* (The Valkyrie, 1854–1856)
  3. *Siegfried* (1856–1857; 1865–1871)
  4. *Götterdämmerung* (Twilight of the Gods, 1869–1874)

Siegfried was interrupted for *Tristan* (1857–1859) and *Meistersinger* (1862–1867). *Parsifal* (1877–1882), Wagner's last opera, came after the establishment of the Bayreuth *Festspielhaus* in the early 1870s.

◀ "The central scene is the celebration of Holy Communion (Christ's Last Supper)." Wagner's last opera, *Parsifal*, as presented by the New York Metropolitan Opera. (Photo by Louis Mélançon)

The Ring occupied Wagner on and off for 21 years. It is a gigantic achievement even though some of its luster has dimmed with time. Wagner wrote his poems in the inverse order: he started with *Siegfried's Death*, the subject of *Götterdämmerung*, and at the outset all there was to be of a *Ring*; then came the librettos of *Siegfried*, *Walküre*, and *Rheingold*. The music came in regular order beginning in 1853. The drama of *The Ring* deals with mythology. The principle of redemption is again preeminent with the figures of the lost one (Wotan) and the redeemer (Siegfried). Only in *The Ring* does Wagner fully exemplify the theories he expounded in "Opera and Drama." *Tristan* is Wagner's technical and emotional achievement. It is perhaps the greatest representation of love and death in all opera. The work is one-sided in its concentration on Tristan and Isolde alone, but this was Wagner's intention. Very little action takes place—only five things "happen": Tristan and Isolde drink the love potion; the lovers are discovered by King Mark; Tristan is wounded by Melot; Tristan, waiting for Isolde, dies; Isolde dies also. The drama is mostly in the orchestra. Yet the harmonic boldness and musical power of the score make it a unique work in the history of opera. *Meistersinger* is a great work in another sphere. It started out as a light comedy and a short one, but became one of the longest and most appealing of Wagner's operas. The tale of Walther's love for Eva, the goldsmith's daughter; his winning of the Prize Song contest of the Mastersingers; the wisdom and mellow judgment of Hans Sachs; the pettifogging Beckmesser; the atmosphere of renaissance Nuremberg—these come alive in the glorious melody and uniform richness of Wagner's score. In ripe maturity, he forgot some of his theory and let his musical imagination roam. The world will always be grateful. *Parsifal* is regarded by some as a decline in Wagner's powers; others firmly disagree and say it is the climax of his genius. Part of the difficulty lies with the subject—mixing of legend and Christian ethic. The central scene is the celebration of Holy Communion (Christ's Last Supper); many believe it to be a theatrical perversion of a solemn rite. In fairness, Wagner only wanted the work to be performed at Bayreuth under certain conditions. He knew that if it was given in a commercial theater it might be considered a profanation.

To understand fully Wagner's unusual development, further knowledge of one of his earlier works is important. The poem of

Tannhäuser had generated in his mind for many years; in 1843 he completed it. The original title was *Der Venusberg* (The Mountain of Venus). Wagner soon realized (and so did his friends) that the name would provoke laughter and the title was changed to that of the leading character. Even then, the location of the first scene in the mountain of Venus called forth bright remarks from the young bloods of Dresden and Paris when the opera was heard in those places. Wagner combined history and legend in his poem: the Wartburg Contest of Song (thirteenth century history) and Tannhäuser's adventures with Venus (medieval legend via the brothers Grimm). In Act I, Tannhäuser, a young knight, has fallen under the spell of Venus and dallies with her, surrounded by nymphs and sirens. Satiated with pleasure and love, Tannhäuser wants to return to earth but Venus detains him. In desperation he invokes the name of the Blessed Virgin Mary. The Venusberg disappears and he finds himself at the foot of the Wartburg (hill in Thuringia, Germany, near Eisenach, on top of which is the famous castle that was the scene of song contests in the Middle Ages, and also the place where Luther in the sixteenth century wrote the German Bible). Tannhäuser is discovered by the Landgrave and his knights who astonishedly welcome him back to their midst. Reluctant to join them, Tannhäuser finally accedes when Wolfram von Eschenbach, his friend, says that Elisabeth, the Landgrave's niece, has awaited the day when Tannhäuser would return. Act II is the song contest in the hall of the Wartburg, the winner to have Elisabeth's hand in marriage. Elisabeth greets Tannhäuser before the others arrive, and they proclaim their happiness at seeing each other again. The theme of the contest is the Nature and Praise of Love. Other knights sing of courtly and chivalrous love; Tannhäuser, of a more earthly variety. Challenged outright for this boldness, he forgets restraint and describes Venus' charms as being the ultimate in love. He is damned by the entire assemblage who threaten to kill him. Only Elisabeth forgivingly defends him. The Landgrave says the sole hope for his salvation is to go to Rome to beg absolution from the Pope. Act III is the same hillside which appeared at the end of Act I. Elisabeth and Wolfram await the arrival of pilgrims from Rome. Tannhäuser is not among them. In despair, Elisabeth departs to ask the Virgin to receive her soul. Tannhäuser in rags finally enters and tells Wolfram about his bitter pilgrimage; the Pope has not only refused him penance but said that only when leaves grew from his staff would Tannhäuser find salvation. Now Tannhäuser in desperation seeks Venus again. As he is about to depart, in spite of Wolfram's horrified pleas, pilgrims approach bearing Elisabeth's body Tannhäuser, overcome by the sainted character of his beloved, falls prostrate over her bier. The pilgrims show the Pope's staff with green leaves as a miraculous token of Tannhäuser's pardon.

Wagner had trouble with the ending of the opera. In the legend, Tannhäuser returns to the arms of Venus when the Pope denies him absolution and is to stay there until Judgment Day. This would hardly do. Friends and Lüttichau, the intendant of the Dresden court theater, urged Wagner to let Tannhäuser and Elisabeth be reunited at the end when the leaves bloom on the staff. But Wagner's decision to have them both die was in accord with his theory and philosophy: death brings release and redemption with all the old wounds

Example 14-10

Wagner, *Tannhäuser* (1845)

Allegro
Tannhäuser

Dir tö - ne ___ lob! Die ___ Wun- der sein ge - prie - sen,
(All praise resound to you! Your wonder be extolled)

Example 14-11

Allegro
Elisabeth

Dich, teu - re Hal - - le, grüss ich wie - der
(You, treasured halls, I greet you once again)

Example 14-12

Adagio
Elisabeth

Ich fleh' für ihn, ich fle - he für sein Le - ben;
(I pray for him. I pray for his life;)

Example 14-13

Lento
Elisabeth

All - mächt' - ge Jung - frau, Hör' mein Fle - hen
(All powerful Virgin, hear my prayer)

Example 14-14

Moderato
Wolfram

O du mein hol - - der A - - bend - stern,

wohl grüsst' ich im - - mer dich ___ so gern:
(O you, my beautiful evening star. I always so gladly greet you:)

291 German Opera

closed. The two characters were also temperamentally too different to be brought together in a "soap-opera" conclusion. To the medieval mind, any person who sold his soul to the Devil in the form of "lustful love" had to be punished, even though the legend indicated otherwise. Elisabeth's sacrifice enables Tannhäuser's sins to be forgiven.

The plot has three groups of people: 1. the Knights of the Wartburg and Elisabeth; 2. Venus and her sirens; 3. pilgrims and monks. They are drawn together through Tannhäuser. The central problem of the opera is pagan versus Christian, profane versus sacred love. Venus' realm belongs to German folklore—like the Wolf's Glen and *Walpurgis Nacht*, haunts of the devil, but the devil may make them attractive.

The opera has a strong element of the spectacular in it. The Venusberg scene calls for an elaborate ballet, the Knights' Hall of the Wartburg is filled with pageantry, and the procession of the pilgrims in the last act has long been famous (see p. 80). Aside from these great choral and dance scenes, there are a number of set pieces which have attracted audiences: Tannhäuser's Song to Venus (Example 14-10); Elizabeth's Invocation to the sacred halls of the Wartburg before the contest starts (Example 14-11); her prayer for Tannhäuser after he has sung in praise of Venus (Example 14-12); her own prayer to the Virgin (Example 14-13); and Wolfram's well-known Song to the Evening Star (Example 14-14).

In the last act after Elisabeth has despaired of finding Tannhäuser, she leaves Wolfram alone on stage. Night has descended. Suddenly he sees the evening star and it gives him hope. Violins play tremolo as he declaims its beauty. Then a quiet modulation leads to a series of broken chords as Wolfram takes up his harp. The strings play pizzicato, and the woodwinds sustain above. The melody itself was regarded as rather daring in its day because of its frequent chromatic shifts and changes from major to minor and back again. But Wagner would never have written anything like it later. It is an old-fashioned aria with a four-measure introduction, four-measure vocal phrases, a definite beginning and end, and a lovely epilogue of a cello playing the melody. Although some of its magic has worn off with overfamiliarity, it illustrates Wagner's capacity to write the kind of melody his audience would love.

A different sort of attraction—the grander, more resplendent kind—comes in the orchestra at the entrance of the knights in Act II, scene 4. If bands at high-school graduations have not worn down the capacity of the sensitive listener to hear this processional music with fresh ears, its thrill can still be recaptured. The six motives ring

Example 14-15

out in succession and Wagner orchestrates them superbly (Examples 14-15a–f).

If the Song to the Evening Star and the Processional Music point to the past, there are parts which look to the future. One of these is Tannhäuser's description in Act III of his Rome journey. As he tells the story to Wolfram, who has great pity for him, each of his moods is reflected in text and music. The divisions fit naturally one into the other and create a splendid unit. "The Journey" is also one of Wagner's first steps toward a new declamation where voice and orchestra assume equal importance in the music. Much of the musical material has been anticipated in the purely orchestral introduction to Act III which is a tone painting of Tannhäuser's pilgrimage before he actually tells about it.

The narrative text is divided into six sections, each separated by a few measures of orchestra. The first tells of Tannhäuser's *deep yearning for pardon* because of Elisabeth's forgiveness of him ("Inbrunst im Herzen wie kein Büsser noch sie je gefühlt—More fervent in heart than any other pilgrim ever had felt"). The second describes the *Rome journey* and tells how Tannhäuser made his way as difficult as possible, shunning hospices and Italy's fair scenes, taking the route through ice and storms ("Wie neben mir der schwerstbedrückte Pilger die Strasse wallt' erschien mir all zu leicht. . . . — As the heaviest burdened pilgrim near me set on his way, it seemed to me his load was all too light"). The third is *Rome* itself where bells were pealing, heavenly songs were heard, and voices were raised in hope and worship ("Nach Rom gelangt' ich so zur heil'gen Stelle, lag betend auf des Heilig-thumes Schwelle. . . .—I arrived in Rome and found its holy places, where I lay kneeling on their thresholds"). The fourth is a description of the *Pope*: how penitents fell before him and thousands were forgiven their sins ("Da sah ich ihm durch den sich Gott verkündigt—Then I saw them through whom God makes himself known"). The fifth is *Tannhäuser's audience* with the Pope when he fully confesses his sins. But the Pope consigns him to damnation for consorting with Venus; salvation will come only when the Pope's staff turns green. Tannhäuser, in hopeless despair, falls unconscious. When he awakens, the pilgrims' songs are anathema to him, and he flees ("Da naht' auch ich, das Haupt gebeugt zur Erde. . . .—Then I also drew near, my head bowed to the earth"). The last is his desire to *return to Venus* and to taste those joys once again ("Dahin zog's mich, wo ich der Wonn' und Lust so vielgenoss, an ihrer warmen Brust—Then pull me toward that rapture and bliss I once enjoyed on her warm breast"). Wolfram tries to prevent Tannhäuser from moving toward Venus, now appearing in a distant rosy light. Only when Wolfram cries out "Elisabeth" does the vision of Venus disappear and Tannhäuser fall to his knees as Elisabeth's funeral train approaches.

Each section is enhanced by the music. At the beginning before Tannhäuser speaks, a motive of woe (Example 14-16a) with solemn reiterated horns and a sliding upward chromatic progression, both outlining a diminished chord, is heard in the orchestra. This was played when Tannhäuser first appeared after the pilgrims had left. As he is about to begin his narrative, an uneasy chromatic string passage, initiated by violas, serves as introduction (b). This was heard in the orchestral prelude to the act with the pilgrims' chorus to indicate Tannhäuser's wretchedness when starting on his journey. It continues at the beginning of the second section (Rome journey) but is succeeded by more conventional accompaniment, as Wagner goes through D minor, A minor, E minor, and ends in F major. A sudden

Example 14-16

jump to D flat announces Tannhäuser's arrival in Rome (third part), and a few measures later the flutes and high winds enunciate a new motive which personifies the Feast of Grace in Rome (c). It resembles the so-called "Dresden Amen," sung in the Royal Catholic Church in Dresden and later used by Wagner in *Parsifal*. When it is heard, Tannhäuser describes his impression of the Holy City. At the mention of the Pope (fourth section), the orchestra becomes agitated in tremolo string and wind accompaniment. But when the text tells of the Pope granting absolution to thousands, the Grace theme in trombones and tuba becomes implacable and threatening. Tannhäuser's audience (fifth section) brings back *b* as his unease increases. Here Wagner drifts away from any key center and leads to the climax of the Pope's words: ("If you have shared in evil lust, if you have kindled Hell's embers, if you have dwelt in the hill of Venus, now you are forever damned: as this staff in my hand will never put forth fresh green, so can you never find salvation out of Hell's hot fire." The orchestra, except for three repetitions of *a*, drops out so the words can be clearly heard. The Feast of Grace ends in a deceptive cadence, and as Tannhäuser yearns for a return to Venus (last section), the familiar strains of the Venusberg music (played in the first scene and the overture) (*d, e,* and *f*) float through the orchestra. It is a dramatic ending to a forceful narration.

There are two versions of *Tannhäuser*—the Dresden original of October, 1845, and the Paris version of 1860. In the late summer of 1859, Wagner went to Paris after completing the score of *Tristan.* While he was there, Napoleon III ordered a production of *Tannhäuser.* Wagner rewrote a good deal of the overture and the Venusberg scene, making it sound richer and more like *Tristan,* made cuts in Act II, and revised parts of Act III. The work was translated into French, and the Paris opera went to great trouble to prepare the production thoroughly. There were two difficulties: an incompetent conductor directed the work (composers were not allowed to conduct their own operas in Paris); and a riot broke out during the first performance.

Parisian opera was very fashionable, and one of its strongest coteries was a group of young aristocrats who called themselves the "Jockey Club." It was their custom to arrive at the opera after a late dinner about the beginning of the second act. The management customarily staged a ballet then or at the end of the act because the ladies in the ballet were mistresses of the young men and the "Jockey Club" wanted to see them dance. Management warned Wagner of this custom and tried to get him to insert a ballet in Act II. He could not very well do so without ruining the dramatic plan of his opera, so he refused. The "Jockey Club" arrived primed to "get" the German. Their boos and catcalls created one of the famous scandals of the musical stage. After three performances the opera was withdrawn. Today this Paris version of the music is seldom performed except for the overture, which itself has three versions. The last version came in 1870 when Wagner eliminated the pompous ending of the pilgrim chorus return (frenetic strings below the theme) and had the music flow into the Venusberg scene without interruption.

When one approaches Wagner's monumental conception of a drama demanding four operas, not one, and a series of characters and situations continued one opera to the next, judgment and logic give way to the imagination. Many scenes in the sprawling drama, *Der Ring des Nibelungen,* aim at the senses rather than the reason. But the music is able to transcend difficulties and create a work of grandeur.

The impressiveness and beauty of the tragedy are not in question;

it is the mood of the listener which is at stake. What is needed is an uncluttered and childlike state of mind. If we are to take *The Ring* seriously (and sometimes it is difficult to do so), we should regard it not as a fairy tale but a "tragedy, Hellenic in its scope and proportions, dealing with one of the great problems of human existence [the lust for power] and reflecting the operations of the quickened mind and conscience of humanity in its impressionable childhood."[7]

Parts of the story may be found in the folklore of all peoples: Achilles dipped by his heel in the Styx; the sword pulled out of the altar by King Arthur in tales of the Round Table; the wicked suitors of Penelope vainly trying to bend the bow, which only Ulysses, disguised as a beggar, can do. So Siegfried, bathed in the dragon's blood, is invulnerable except for the place behind his shoulder, where he is struck by Hagen; and Siegmund draws the sword Nothung, out of the ash tree where it has been placed by Wotan.

The Ring is celestial because it concerns Wotan, the chief god — its real hero. The contest waged by gods, dwarfs, and giants for power comes about as a consequence of the sin committed by Wotan and his efforts to repair it. The result is destruction of the gods, but destruction followed by a new creation: the self-sacrifice of Brunnhilde, a loving woman (the theme of most Wagnerian operas), removes the curse from the earth. Progress is from a state of sinlessness (the Rhinemaidens play with the gold at the bottom of the Rhine) through sin and its painful consequences to expiation. The Teutonic gods were created in the image of man, yet they were idealized beings. In the Golden Age before sin, nobody wanted the gold, and the Rhinemaidens watched it carelessly. But when Alberich, the dwarf, approaches with lust for power and treasure, the old age is wiped away. He renounces love and steals the gold, but Wotan in turn steals the gold from him, including the ring fashioned from it, and the helmet (Tarnhelm) which provides invisibility for the wearer. Yet the gods must pay gold to the giants for building them Valhalla, Wotan's dearest dream. One sin is piled on another. The curse Alberich puts on the ring begins its work when the brother giants Fasolt and Fafner argue who should possess parts of the treasure, and Fafner strikes Fasolt dead. These events of *Rheingold* are prologue to the main part of the drama, which begins with *Walküre*.

Wotan can clear his guilt only by having his offspring, conceived of a mortal mother, through their own free will solve the dilemma of the gods. This elaborate rationale wears thin when we see Wotan

[7]Henry E. Krehbiel, *Studies in the Wagnerian Drama*, Harper & Row, New York, 1898, p. 113.

intervening and controlling mortal lives, but the theory of the Teutonic myth was that only human beings had the capacity to put the curse to rest. This interesting ethical reversal—gods, being superior beings, are generally the ones to solve petty human problems—is central to the drama. The gods have sinned; only human beings not tainted can expiate their sin.

In Act I of *Walküre*, Siegmund, who knew his father only as Wälse (therefore the son is a Wälsung), is exhausted after fighting and fleeing from his enemies. He takes refuge during a storm in Hunding's hut. Sieglinde, Hunding's wife, pities the stranger and feels a strange fascination for him. On Hunding's return home, the discovery is made that Siegmund is an enemy; the laws of hospitality prevent an immediate duel, but Hunding says that in the morning he and Siegmund must fight. When Hunding has retired, Sieglinde points to a sword buried in the ash tree. A strange man in grey left the sword just before her betrothal to Hunding (she was forced into the marriage), saying a hero would pull it out. Siegmund, desperately in need of defending himself on the morrow and remembering his father promised him a sword in time of trouble, triumphantly withdraws it from the tree. He reveals his name to Sieglinde. They are twins, children of Wotan by a mortal, but do not know their real parentage. They passionately embrace and flee into the night.

Act II finds Wotan telling Brunnhilde, his favorite Valkyrie daughter, (the Valkyrie maidens are nine warrior daughters of Wotan and the earth goddess Erda) to protect Siegmund in the coming struggle with Hunding. Fricka, Wotan's wife and the guardian of marriage vows, commands Wotan to kill Siegmund because he has violated the laws she upholds. Wotan ruefully assents and withdraws his order to Brunnhilde, saying Siegmund must die. In the fight, Brunnhilde, disobeying Wotan, intervenes to help Siegmund, but Wotan at the last minute steps between the two warriors and Siegmund is pierced by Hunding. Brunnhilde flees with the frightened Sieglinde and the shattered pieces of Siegmund's sword, trying to avoid her father's wrath. In a contemptuous gesture by Wotan, Hunding falls dead.

Act III is the top of a rocky mountain. Brunnhilde gives Sieglinde courage to live since she will bear a son who will be the greatest hero of all. The pieces of Siegmund's sword must be kept for him to be forged anew. Brunnhilde stays to face Wotan's anger. Wotan sternly decrees that Brunnhilde will fall into a magic sleep, become a mortal, and be possessed by the first man who finds her—her punishment for disobeying him. Brunnhilde accepts her fate but pleads that her discoverer be a great hero, not just any man; she begs for the protection of a wall of fire through which only a hero can pass. Wotan agrees, kisses away her godhead, and surrounds her rock with flames.

In *Walküre*, the characters are people with human passions and failings. Siegmund goes through great trials to show the heroic fiber of his character, yet he breaks two sacred laws: he carries off another man's wife; and the woman is his own sister. He is a pawn in the gods' struggle. Sieglinde is tender and passionate, reckless and wise. She has resolution but also impulsiveness. She knows pathetic fear when Hunding approaches; she also knows she has sinned and must be punished. Brunnhilde is the most heroic of Wagner's women. It will be the sacrifice of her life in *Götterdämmerung* that will solve the gods' dilemma. By her transformation from a Valkyrie maiden to mortal woman she symbolizes the change from the rule of the gods to the carrying out of fate through men. She is the symbol of love and affection. She will not permit a wrong to be committed to a human being, even if the wrong is ordered by the supreme god. Wotan in his harangue with Fricka is portrayed all too clearly as the hapless husband of a determined woman. His hope for salvation through Siegmund, his mortal son, is rudely dashed. He is caught in his own mesh—he knows that Fricka is right and Siegmund cannot be allowed to defy the laws of mankind. But worse is Brunnhilde's fate. She is his own second sight, the image of godhead in woman, and she must now be used as the instrument of his purpose wherever that may lead. It will lead to Siegfried, the offspring of Siegmund and Sieglinde, who will pass through the flames and make Brunnhilde his bride. But after Siegfried's death, Brunnhilde will return the ring to the Rhine and immolate herself, as the world is engulfed in flames and water. The cycle has come full circle.

The first scene of *Walküre* shows Wagner bringing to the drama all his craft as librettist and composer. The stage setting is the interior of Hunding's dwelling built around a mighty ash tree. Before the curtain rises, the orchestra plays wild and turbulent music representing the storm from which Siegmund seeks shelter. It is built largely on one motive (Example 14-17a). For the first part, the violins and violas reiterate a D, whose constant rumble creates tension while the lower strings below play a scale-like ostinato figure that moves continually up and down portraying the storm. When the curtain rises, the storm gradually dies down, Siegmund lifts the latch on the door, staggers to the fireplace, and throws himself on some bearskins before it. As he does so, the orchestra sounds his motive, a descending, stepwise figure (bass of *b*) that tells his despair and woe. Sieglinde enters, thinking her husband has

Example 14-17

Wagner, *Die Walküre* (1875)
Act I, scene 1

Example 14-18

Sieglinde

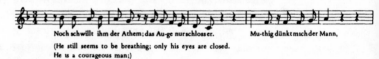

Noch schwillt ihm der Athem; das Au-ge nur schloss er.   Mu-thig dünkt mich der Mann,

(He still seems to be breathing; only his eyes are closed.
He is a courageous man;)

Example 14-19

returned, and is astonished to find a stranger on their hearth. As she exclaims about the appearance of the man sleeping, she comes nearer. Siegmund's motive combines with a new lingering upward phrase in the violins (c) signifying Sieglinde's pity and compassion for him. Sieglinde's words show Wagner using the abbreviated and alliterative speech (Stabreim) he described in "Opera and Drama." "Schwanden die Sinne ihm? wäre es siech? Noch schwillt ihm der Athem; das Auge nur schloss er. Muthig dünkt mich der Mann, sank er müd' auch hin." (Example 14-18) (Is he unconscious; perhaps he's sick; yet he's still breathing, only his eyes are closed. The man seems brave to me, but he sank down exhausted.) The vocal shape of "das Auge nur schloss er" outlines the descending Siegmund motive, and Wagner further illustrates the words by a decisive fifth on "Muthig" (courageous) and a rise of a third on "müd" (tired) (not shown). Siegmund wakes and begs for water; she brings him some from a drinking horn. As he quenches his thirst, the two look at each other more closely—there is a remarkable resemblance, though nothing is said of this yet. The orchestra reduces itself to a single line. As their gaze continues, divisi cellos and bass play a lovely new theme (Example 14-19*a*) which Wagner will use as his chief musical source in the love duet concluding the act. The scoring for the lowest strings is magical in its intensity and beauty. Siegmund thanks Sieglinde for his refreshment and asks her whose wife she is; Sieglinde tells him. Siegmund has a premonition of danger and laments his lack of sword and shield; he tells her how he lost them in battle. Sieglinde's interest in his plight grows, and the orchestra weaves the pity motive into a major key along with further treatment of Example 14-19*a*. But at the end of the phrase, Wagner suddenly turns it toward the minor as the directions read: "Siegmund sighs deeply, and gloomily lets his eyes sink to the ground." He tells Sieglinde she has harbored an ill-fated man, and he must leave. A somber chord (*b*), associated through the opera with Siegmund's ill-fate, sounds just before he sings: "Misswende folgt mir wohin ich fliehe—Misfortune follows me wherever I wander." Sieglinde impetuously asks him to stay. As they look at each other, the orchestra combines a different musical idea with the rising and descending thirds (*c*). Commentators have labeled the first two measures "Wälsung's woe"; whatever it may be, the music and Sieglinde's words hold Siegmund back. He decides to stay and declares: "Here Hunding shall find me," as the orchestra moves into a symphonic interlude built on *c* in D major. This change from predominantly minor tonality immediately brightens the music and pictures the growing love between the two.

Although this scene, and many like it in *The Ring*, seems a formless mixture of quasi-recitative and song flowing one into the other with the orchestra providing the links, there is more structure to it than one might imagine. A German scholar, Alfred Lorenz, analyzed Wagner's mature operas in several volumes called *The Secret of Form in Richard Wagner* (Berlin, 1924). In these works, he found musical organization which determined the dramatic form. His conclusion was that Wagner's compositional process was a

Example 14-20

Act III, scene 3

(a) Lebhaft

(b) Tutti — ff

(c) Leb' wohl, du küh - nes, herr - li -ches Kind!
(Farewell, you valiant, splendid child!)

(d) Muss ich dich mei - den, und darf nicht — min - nig mein Gruss dich — mehr grüs - sen,
(Must I leave you, and may not my welcome any longer greet you,)

(e) Strings
Winds

(f) Etwas langsamer
Trbs.,Horns
p ben marcato

(g)

(h) Poco rall.
Zum letz - ten Mal, letz' es mich heut' mit des Le - be - woh - les letz - tem Kuss!
(For the last time let me be comforted with a farewell kiss!)

(i) Trombones
Tuba
Cellos
English Horn
Horns
pp express
Timpani

The Magic of Opera

Wer mei - nes Spee - res Spit - ze fürch tet, durch-schrei - te das Feu - er —— nie!

(He who fears my sharp spear's point shall never cross through the flaming fire!)

simultaneous realization of text and music, in which the music was often the determining factor. Individual phrases and patterns of larger organization had sections like ABA and AA′B or ABACADA where A is musically clearly recognizable on its return. While Lorenz in his desire to make everything fit often pushed his theories to absurd lengths, his basic premises were sound. As long as his patterns maintained flexibility and did not attempt to stretch all of Wagner's music on a mighty Procrustean bed, the analysis was highly revealing and indicated that Wagner's structural power was formidable.

Lorenz divides this first scene of *Walküre* into four periods, exclusive of the prelude. One and two are ABA and AA′B; three is AA′B; and four is five different sections of various lengths. The initial two periods have much validity and demonstrate fairly conclusively the organization Lorenz outlines. Periods three and four, however, make the music try to fit a preconceived pattern, and the result is dubious. At any rate, Wagner's mind functioned in this manner, and it is highly rewarding to watch the components assume rational and distinctive form although on the surface they seem free and rhapsodic.

One of the famous lyrical portions of the opera, the last scene when Wotan bids farewell to Brunnhilde and surrounds her with fire, has a similar logic to the first scene in that it is a continuous unit. But the sections are more lyrical, and the whole part is sung by Wotan. There are three main divisions. In the first, Wotan is distraught as he contemplates the fate he has decreed for his daughter, but he can take some comfort in knowing that only a hero will penetrate the flames. Part two is a tender farewell leading to the kiss which will put Brunnhilde to sleep. In part three, Wotan summons Loge, the god of fire, and commands that he surround Brunnhilde's rock with fire; Loge does not actually appear, but his presence is felt when Wotan strikes the rock three times and at the third stroke flames encircle the mountain. As Wotan departs, the opera ends.

Wotan's farewell is preceded by Brunnhilde's begging her father to protect her from all except a hero. The familiar Valkyrie motive bursts out solemnly and slowly in bass trumpet, trombones, and tuba unlike its original lively appearance (Example 14-20a) in the ride of the Valkyrie maidens. Here it means the union of father and daughter, and befits the majesty of the chief god. Immediately following comes two measures of the motive of Brunnhilde's sleep; the orchestra will bring this motive to symphonic fruition at the end of the opera (b). Wotan's vocal line (c) is a true melody and it pours forth in lyrical splendor. Example d is the first of a series of poignant rhetorical questions Wotan addresses to Brunnhilde. Wagner repeats this musical phrase several times in a reversion to the time-honored practice of aria and song. When Wotan refers to the flames that will surround the rock, the fire music associated with Loge in *Rheingold* sounds through the orchestra (e). Then Wotan sings. "Denn einer nun freie die Braut" (Only one will free the bride) and the listener hears Siegfried's motive majestically enunciated in the brass, telling in advance that he is the hero (f).

As Wotan holds Brunnhilde in a long embrace, the orchestral interlude leading to the second section dwells in rich sequence (g) on a theme played earlier in the scene when Brunnhilde told her father of Siegmund's valiant refusal to abandon Sieglinde, even to dying a hero's death. Siegmund's forceful speech moved Brunnhilde so strongly she determined to protect him and defy Wotan. The theme is a triumphant E major assertion of Brunnhilde's affection for the Wälsung.

The second part of Wotan's address is more intimate. He refers to Brunnhilde's sparkling eyes when she came to him bringing heroes to Valhalla. But he must bid her farewell with a kiss (h), a motive actually sung here but also winding contrapuntally through the orchestra in the peroration of the opera. Wotan decries the fate that deprives him of his beloved daughter, and the musical equivalents of "death" (unexpected resolution of minor chord) and "renunciation of love" rise to the surface (i). As he bestows upon her the fateful kiss, the magic sleep motive appears in the orchestra (j). It is a chromatic half-step descent of some striking and unrelated chords finally settling into E major. At this point the orchestra

interlude to the last section begins with an instrumental development of *b*. It is a beautiful representation of Wotan lowering Brunnhilde on to a grassy mound, closing off her face with her helmet,
and covering her body with the great steel shield of the Valkyrie.

Suddenly the music changes into a massive descending bass line
(Compact or Treaty with the other gods, *k*), as Wotan summons
Loge to surround the rock with fire. The magic fire music increases
in brilliance as the flames shoot higher (*e* and other themes). Wotan's
final words are sung to an abbreviation of Siegfried's motive (*l*), he
who will pass through the fire. Siegfried's theme combines with
Brunnhilde's slumber theme (*b*) to show their eventual union. A
magnificent orchestral finale blazes forth these two motives and
the kiss motive in contrapuntal and symphonic splendor as Wotan
gazes sorrowfully on Brunnhilde and slowly turns to depart. It is
a dramatic and musical spectacle of the highest order and never
fails to thrill those who see and hear it.

Although Wagner's reputation has fluctuated with the years
(idolatry in the 1890s and early 1900s, denigration between the
two world wars) there will never be any question about his ability
to create a magic that captures the senses, and even drugs them.
People may complain about the narcotic, hypnotic element in his
music; they attempt to throw it off, but eventually succumb. His
superb ability as an orchestrator always makes the music sound,
even if the quality may be thin. Yet his contribution to opera is
more than merely sensory; his grandiose dreams had vision and
certainty and they came true. He attempted a new kind of music
drama that broke with the past. His influence on music of the
twentieth century has been very great. For years composers tried to
come out from under his influence and did so only when they found
a new direction. Wagner and Verdi, the two great operatic pioneers
of their age, achieved different solutions to the same problem. Their
names will remain prominent in the history of the art.

SUGGESTED READING

Beethoven   Bekker, Paul, *Beethoven*, Dent, London, 1939 Chapter on "Beethoven's
Dramatic Works" includes good discussion of *Fidelio*.

Weber   Warrack, John, *Carl Maria von Weber*, 2nd ed., Cambridge University Press,
London, 1976.

Wagner   Donington, Robert, *Wagner's Ring and Its Symbols*, Faber & Faber, London,
1963. Jungian psychological interpretation of *The Ring* and its motives.

Newman, Ernest, *The Life of Richard Wagner*, 4 vols., Knopf, New York, 1933–1946; Reprint Cambridge University Press. New York, 1976. The monumental biography in English. Particularly valuable for social and historical background.

Newman, Ernest, *The Wagner Operas*, Knopf, New York, 1949. The best and most complete discussion of the operas for both librettos and music.

The Ring of the Nibelung, Stewart Robb, trans., Dutton paperback, New York, 1960. Fine introduction and English translation. Lacks German original.

Tristan and Isolde, Stewart Robb, trans., Dutton paperback, New York, 1965 Both German and English on opposite pages.

Westernhagen, Curt von, *Wagner, A Biography*, 2 vols., Cambridge University Press, London/New York, 1978.

White, Chappell, *An Introduction to the Life and Works of Richard Wagner*, Prentice-Hall, Englewood Cliffs, N.J., 1967 Splendid introduction to the composer and his works.

15 Late Romantic Opera

Opera at the close of the nineteenth century and the beginning of the twentieth follows no regular pattern, least of all with respect to continuing tradition. Italian and German composers after Verdi and Wagner were all too aware of the power of these two and could hardly escape their influence, even if they wished to. Yet to imitate would have been fatal. It was not so much a question of striking out in a new direction as of remaining within the main stream and still keeping one's individuality.

This was easier for an Italian than for a German. While Verdi was the acknowledged hero of his day, there was considerable demand for other Italian operas. The repertory had to be filled because the public wanted to hear something new. Verdi's *Otello* and *Falstaff* (1893) were jewels in an old man's crown, but they were an end, not a beginning. Others had to take up where he left off.

The predominant literary current in France and Italy during the 1880s and 1890s was naturalism. Zola's and Flaubert's novels of unadorned bourgeois life, covers stripped off, startled and influenced their contemporaries. The musical counterpart in France was *Carmen*. In Italy, the movement turned to "verismo" (realism; the truthful), which was no different from naturalism but merely more blunt and open. Life was to be pictured realistically even to seeking out the sordid and brutal and making the impact upon the emotions as pointed as possible. While melodrama in Verdi (for example, *Rigoletto*) had dealt directly and powerfully with emotional issues, there was some palliative or romantic element to counteract the sensational and not allow it to monopolize the drama. Later, the sensational became an end in itself, though not enough to lose its human touch; otherwise it would have become "grand Guignol."

In Italian opera the most striking examples of "verismo" were Pietro Mascagni's *Cavalleria rusticana* (Rustic Chivalry, 1890) and Ruggiero Leoncavallo's *Pagliacci* (Clowns, 1892), contemporaneous with late Verdi. These two classic works (now generally performed together in one evening), were sensational successes in their day but have not weathered the years as well as they might. They brought instant fame to both composers. The remaining operas of these two men sank into obscurity, and Mascagni and Leoncavallo have become one-opera composers. Both *Cavalleria* and *Pagliacci* have admirably taut librettos—everything fits, there is no waste motion. But the music, even with its wonderful improvisational quality which seizes upon the essence of hate, jealousy, and love in a Sicilian village and in a traveling theater company, lacks staying power. The melodies in *Cavalleria* and the motives in *Pagliacci* are catchy and emotionally tingling but they fade out. Seen a second time, the shock value of the drama is gone, and something is needed to take its place. *Pagliacci* is better than *Cavalleria*, but the two are always linked together and put on the same level. Both will probably hold their own for some time; the general audience is not satiated that easily. It is difficult to foretell the future; another generation must pass before a fair assessment of these works can be made.

PUCCINI   Of greater permanence is the composer who is in the same veristic camp but shows more durability; Giacomo Puccini (1858–1924) is one of the most famous names in opera. Although his general musical reputation does not equal that of Giuseppe Verdi, his works rate very high in the eyes of the public, and they will probably hold the stage for years. The big three by Puccini (comparable to *Rigoletto*, *Trovatore*, and *Traviata* for Verdi) are *La Bohème* (1896), *Tosca* (1900), and *Madama Butterfly* (1904). Less frequently heard are *Manon Lescaut* (1893); *La fanciulla del West* (The Girl of the Golden West, 1910); and *Turandot* (1926), left unfinished and completed by his friend, Franco Alfano. There is also a series of one-act operas: *Il Trittico* (The Tryptich, 1918), comprising *Il tabarro* (The Cloak), *Suor Angelica* (Sister Angelica) and *Gianni Schicchi*. The third is one of Puccini's best works—a genuine comic opera. He wrote three other operas but they are seldom performed.

As indicated previously (p. 39), Puccini is a difficult composer to assess properly His popular works are so well-known we are apt to be patronizing about them, which is a mistake. They have musical and dramatic faults, but there is a power and a thrill about them as operas that always moves an audience. Puccini's ability to stir the emotions through musical means is unquestionable. Sometimes these means—piling one effect upon the other; tricks in orchestration; insistent repetition of certain motives—border on the meretricious. But if an art is to be judged by its ability to reach the hearts and emotions of an audience, then Puccini's art succeeds admirably. He is the Tschaikowsky of opera—an exceedingly skilled craftsman, a composer of fluent melodies, and a musician with an uncanny ability to dramatize elements at the right moment. He once said: "My laws are those of the theater: to interest, to surprise, to move."

Puccini came from a long line of musicians and exhibited talent at an early age. He was born in Lucca and educated at the Conservatorio in Milan. He is one of the few composers to attain fame and fortune almost from the beginning of his career, although, like everyone else, he had his ups and downs. His first opera, written in his student days, was a success, but the second one, *Edgar*, was a failure. It was not until *Manon Lescaut* that he really came before the public eye. A great aid to his career was his close association with the Milan music-publishing house of Ricordi. Giulio Ricordi was almost a father to the composer, and it was Ricordi who commissioned and brought to fruition many of the Puccini operas. Ricordi was more than a publisher: he helped to find librettists, steered them through the shoals of collaboration with Puccini; and encouraged the composer to do his best work. Puccini was an exacting taskmaster in the construction of a libretto. Many versions were tried and torn up; revisions were countless. At times Puccini would write the music he wished and the librettists had to put words to it. Since Puccini had an instinctive lyric gift and dramatic eye, this close supervision generally had good results. Its great drawback, however, was that many of his operas lack the necessary motivation to provide a satisfying work of art, some of his works become a series of colorful scenes with a dramatic thread running through them rather than coherent drama.

A common criticism of Puccini is that his characterizations tend to be very much the same. Most of his heroines are Mimis (the seamstress in *La Bohème*) or his heros Rodolfos, the poet in the same opera. Everything comes to the surface quickly and tragedy results. Although the outer circumstances may be similar (the women are generally the suffering ones), the scenes and people are different.

Mimi, Tosca, and Butterfly are closely related but they dwell in contrasting environments.

On one matter there can be no doubt: Puccini's ability to write a melody—short phrases, motivic bits, even a simple cadence that has a memorable melodic contour. These melodies sweep over the listener. Puccini devised them so they return again and again in slightly different forms but do not sound stale or over-repetitive. Many of them are motives rather than long melodies, but they all possess a strong lyric quality. They are not greatly transformed when they return, the way Wagner's are apt to be, to suit different circumstances and situations. Mostly there is merely a change of tempo or transposition to another key. This is done so skillfully it sounds like a change without being one. In the arias, his longer melodies show a typical Italian "sensuous warmth"[1] that comes from a line with stepwise movement. There are few large skips and none of the jagged, instrumental writing for voices found in composers who think through instruments rather than through the voice. An effective Puccinian device is to have the voice begin in a monotone on one note while the melody is delineated in the orchestra (for example, the famous "Che gelida manina" of La Bohème, Act I). As the aria gathers passion and excitement, the voice takes over the melody and moves on to a thrilling climax.

Puccini uses exotic harmony for color. He draws on everything—Wagnerian chromatic alterations, parallel unresolved discords played in succession, all kinds of augmented triads, and intervals involving the whole tone scale. A favorite harmonic and rhythmic device is a succession of ostinato chords—two or three chords repeated and repeated to distraction. Although his orchestra is a large one, he is careful not to overload it at points of tension and climax. His texture is always clear and his handling of instruments is superb.

Another effect—it can hardly be classified—is Puccini's use of silence; at moments of electric anticipation, the music will halt for several measures. Conductors are less than enthusiastic about these silences because it is difficult to contain either the audience or the orchestra.

Tosca (1900) has always been a favorite opera with those who like to explore the human psyche. It is a thriller. Joseph Kerman calls it a "shabby little shocker"[2]—a bon mot that only partly hits the mark. There is attempted rape, torture, two suicides, an execution, and a

[1] Mosco Carner, Puccini, A Critical Biography, Duckworth, London, 1958.
[2] Opera as Drama, Knopf, New York, 1956, p. 254.

murder in it. None of the principals survives. The second act where Cavaradossi is tortured and Tosca stabs Scarpia with his own knife as he attempts to rape her is one of the most macabre in all opera. Its musical tension is overwhelming, and there are few who can be unaffected by it.

The plot was taken from a French play by Victorien Sardou (1831–1909), one of the most popular playwrights of his day (he wrote over 70 plays for the French stage). Sardou was a very clever master of stagecraft, whose reputation declined markedly after his death. He excelled in the realistic and was often accused of borrowing other people's ideas, but his plays kept their appeal. *La Tosca* (1887) became particularly famous because it featured the well-known actress, Sarah Bernhardt, who made it one of her leading roles. Puccini saw it in Milan and although he understood very little French, the ideas were conveyed to him instantly and he saw its possibilities as an opera libretto. After many tribulations, the play was boiled down, even with the help of Sardou himself, although the two who did most of the work were the Italians Illica and Giocosa, Puccini's collaborators on previous operas. A good deal of the political background and explanation was lost but the main features of the play survived. The first act in particular is difficult to unravel because of events that have taken place before the opera begins. The setting is Rome about 1800 when Napoleon's fortunes were varying throughout Europe, but his followers were still the young and idealistic who saw in him the great Republican and liberator bringing new life to the political scene.

Cavaradossi, a young painter, who has lived in Paris and has republican sympathies, is in love with a famous singer, Floria Tosca. She is both exceedingly jealous and religiously devout and possesses a fiery, artistic temperament. Cavaradossi, painting in the church of Sant' Andrea della Valle in Rome, helps an old friend, Angelotti, who has taken refuge there, to escape. Angelotti had been imprisoned in Sant' Angelo castle because he offended the royalists in Naples. The police chief, Baron Scarpia, tool of the monarchy, is a diabolical lecher and sadist, who under the guise of a smooth exterior, has managed to satisfy his desires in his line of work. He learns of Angelotti's escape and vows to capture him; his own professional reputation is at stake—the Queen at Naples threatens to have his head if Angelotti is not found and put away. Scarpia traces Angelotti to the church and suspects Cavaradossi of hiding him.

He determines to get information from Tosca by leading her to think that Cavaradossi loves some other woman. In Act II, his minions capture Cavaradossi, bring him to the Palazzo Farnese (Scarpia's headquarters), and in Tosca's presence begin torturing him to find out where Angelotti is. In spite of Cavaradossi's pleas to Tosca not to say anything, his screams of anguish are too much for her and she reveals the hiding place. In the meantime, Scarpia promises Tosca to spare Cavaradossi's life if she will give herself to him. Tosca, in agony, assents. Scarpia says he cannot let Cavaradossi go freely but must pretend to have him shot in order to satisfy his superiors. As Scarpia moves to take Tosca, she seizes a knife from his desk and stabs him to death.

In Act III, Cavaradossi's execution is to take place at 4:00 A.M. He bids farewell to the world. At the last minute, Tosca comes to him in prison and reveals the plan: he will pretend to be dead; the firing squad's bullets will be blanks; the jailors are bribed; the lovers will escape from Rome together. The firing squad enters, Cavaradossi stands erect. Of course, Scarpia had no intention of letting the painter escape—the bullets are real, and Tosca discovers the horrible truth. Just then, Scarpia's henchmen burst in to capture Tosca—they have discovered their chief's murder. Tosca, having no desire to live, throws herself from the parapet of the castle.

One of Puccini's finest acts from a dramatic and musical viewpoint is Act II: Cavaradossi's torture in the Farnese palace; Tosca's revelation of Angelotti's hiding place to spare her lover; and Tosca's stabbing of Scarpia as he tries to force himself upon her. The action goes so swiftly and tellingly a few musical gaucheries are forgotten and the spectator is enthralled.

The last two scenes are particularly powerful. Cavaradossi is led away and Scarpia thinks he has won Tosca. He pushes her into the room and proposes to resume his interrupted supper, hoping to deal with her more diplomatically. The orchestra runs the first measure of Tosca's and Cavaradossi's love duet from Act I (Example 15-1a) with a Scarpia motive heard at the beginning of the act. The Scarpia motive indicates his deadly purpose (a, measures 2 and 3—a descending triplet figure over a held bass chord. See b for the beginning of the original Act I duet). Musically, the two characters confront each other in this elision of themes.

Scarpia's diplomacy takes the form of a stepwise, insinuating phrase which rises and falls seductively (c) and is echoed in the orchestra by another slurred downward motive (d). Ingratiatingly he offers Tosca a sip of wine. Tosca suddenly looks him straight in the face and leaning her elbows on the table in a quasi-speaking tone asks contemptuously "Quanto?" (How much?). Actresses who say this in a guttural voice make it a chilling moment as the orchestra drops out except for a tremolo on two notes. Scarpia laughs and says he does not take money from ladies but chooses other forms of payment. He launches into a passionate aria, saying this is the hour he

Example 15-1   Puccini, *Tosca* (1900)

(Do you wish we find together some way to save him?)

Property of G. Ricordi & C., S. p. A., Milan.

Example 15-2

(I have lived for art)

(I gave flowers to the altar)

Property of G. Ricordi & C., S. p. A., Milan.

has been waiting for. Tosca's beauty and her hatred of him have made him especially desirous. The savage climax comes when he advances toward her with open arms and sings: "Ah! in that moment (Tosca had cursed and reviled him) I swore you would be mine." The orchestra doubles his vocal line in four peremptory chords which Puccini accents and marks "Sostenuto" (e). Tosca backs toward the window and then toward the door, hoping to escape. As Scarpia pursues, she screams. Suddenly the roll of distant drums is heard, stopping Scarpia momentarily. He tells her it is his men preparing a gallows for those about to hang; Cavaradossi will go in an hour unless she acts sensibly. At this moment she breaks down in grief. Two clarinets a third apart hold their notes for seven measures as tense preparation for Tosca's famous "Vissi d'arte" aria. This piece, sung by some ladies from a prone position on floor or sofa where they have flung themselves, is really an invocation. Tosca says she has always lived for art and love, never harmed a soul, given liberally to the church and the Madonna. Why has the Lord repaid her in this manner? The opening phrases (Example 15-2a), an introduction, are accompanied in parallel string chords with no bass, the third in root position—a sound suggesting a church chant to emphasize Tosca's religiosity. The main part of the aria is Tosca's theme heard at her entrance in Act I (b). The voice is counterpoint to the melody in the orchestra and only at the cadence (c) do the two themes join. This "Tosca" cadence is used over and over as her trademark. At the end (the aria formally has a free ABA' structure), the cadence gives Tosca an opportunity for extension and elaboration as she goes to a high B flat (b²)*.

There is a knock on the door: it is Spoletta, Scarpia's chief lieutenant, who says that when they surrounded Angelotti in his hiding place, he killed himself; now they await Scarpia's word on what to do with Cavaradossi. Scarpia looks significantly at Tosca and there are two dreadful silences. She finally nods her head, weeping with shame, but insists that Cavaradossi be released immediately. Scarpia says he cannot do this but must have everybody think Cavaradossi died; there will be a pretended execution—Spoletta will manage it. After Spoletta goes, Scarpia turns to Tosca saying he has fulfilled his promise, now she must fulfill hers. She insists on a safe-conduct pass to enable her and Cavaradossi to leave the country. As Scarpia goes to his desk to write one, the orchestra plays an ominous 10-measure theme (Example 15-3a— violins on G string muted), which reappears in altered form during Act III when Tosca describes to Cavaradossi what she has done.

*See Glossary· Abbreviations.

Example 15-3

(What eye in the world can be compared to your black, ardent one?)

Property of G. Ricordi & C., S. p. A., Milan.

Example 15-4

Property of G. Ricordi & C., S. p. A., Milan.

When Tosca goes to the table where the glass of wine was left, she suddenly sees a knife which she hides behind her with infinite precaution. This mime is carried out to the accompaniment of a striking phrase in the orchestra (b). Scarpia finishes writing the pass, folds it, puts his seal to it, and advances toward Tosca with open arms. As he says, "Finally you are mine," she stabs him full in the breast. He staggers, choking, trying to get at her. She backs away, reviling him, telling him to die. He does so with a final shudder. Tosca goes to the table, dips a napkin in the waterjug, washes her fingers, arranges her hair, and looks for the safe-conduct pass on the desk. She sees it in Scarpia's clenched fingers,

"She backs away, reviling him, telling him to die. He does so with a final shudder." The emotion of Puccini's *Tosca* is reflected in Tosca's face as well as in her music. (Photo by Louis Mélançon)

pries it loose, hides it in her bosom, and lets Scarpia's arm fall lifeless to his side, the orchestra playing Examples 15-3a and b. Her final words are: "And before him all Rome trembled."

About to leave, she puts two lighted candles on the floor on each side of Scarpia's head, takes a crucifix from the wall and places it on his breast. Before Tosca leaves the room, the orchestra plays a bit of Cavaradossi's Act I aria (c, derived from d), presumably to remind the audience for whom Tosca has committed this deed. Just before the curtain falls, the orchestra whispers Scarpia's main theme (Example 15-4a) very softly and ends it in an E minor chord (death). This treatment of it is the greatest contrast to the same progression at the end of Act I when, above the Te Deum of the choir in the church, Scarpia plots to send Cavaradossi to the gallows and to take Tosca. There the final chord is a triumphant E major (b), heard in the same way at the beginning of the opera. Scarpia then is sure of his triumph and the music reacts accordingly.

This Act II stage realism and the music accompanying it has thrilled generations of opera-goers. It is fairly easy to pick holes in it—melodrama, discontinuity in the music, parading of themes without reason—but Puccini had an instinctive flair for the musical stage and knew when to press forward and when to hold back. His themes are memorable; they are inexorably bound to the characters they personify and serve to make vivid their actions and emotions. Puccini may some day suffer eclipse, but so far in the twentieth century, he is still a staple in the repertory. No opera house can do without him.

Germany Wagner's influence even after his death was so strong that few German composers could resist it; long, pretentious cycles of operas were undertaken but most of them came to naught. In reaction to Wagnerism, there was a resurgence of folk and magic opera, but few held the stage. Perhaps the one worth mentioning is Engelbert Humperdinck's *Hänsel und Gretel* (1893), a fairy-tale opera, which in spite of its Wagnerian flavor, manages to make a direct, simple, and heartfelt appeal. There are songs and dances for children, semi-folk melodies, a touch of the supernatural, and a prayer tune that dominates the overture and three scenes of the opera. It is the theme by which the work is recognized.

STRAUSS After Wagner, one German figure, whose long life spanned several artistic generations, brought a powerful voice to opera of the twentieth century. Richard Strauss (1864–1949) started his operatic career as a convinced Wagnerian, engendered strong controversy by the "modernism" of his middle works, and turned back to neo-classicism for his remaining years.

Strauss came from a musical family in Munich. His father was the principal horn player in the Munich Opera orchestra (he was a virtuoso who supposedly advised Wagner how to make Siegfried's horn-call playable), and his mother was a member of a well-to-do brewing family. Strauss' early musical training was conservative and classical; his teachers even regarded Brahms as too advanced. He attended the University of Munich but soon decided on a musical career. Not until the 1880s when he came under the tutelage of Hans von Bülow, who had him appointed assistant conductor at Meiningen, did Strauss begin to branch out on his own. Liszt, Wagner, and Berlioz were his gods. His first important creative efforts were symphonic poems: *Aus Italien* (From Italy, 1887); *Don Juan* (1889); *Tod und Verklärung* (Death and Transfiguration, 1890). During the 1880s and 1890s Strauss was primarily known as a first-rate conductor who from assistantships at Munich and Weimar went to Berlin as director of the Philharmonic and, later, conductor at the Royal Opera House. He attempted to put aside time for composition as well as he could while traveling extensively all over Europe. The later 1890s saw the writing of *Till Eulenspiegel* (1895), *Don Quixote* (1898), and *Ein Heldenleben* (A Hero's Life, 1898). His first opera, *Guntram* (1892), was based on a Wagnerian "redeeming female"; the second, *Feuersnot*, was partly Wagnerian, but showed Strauss as a much more independent workman with rich orchestration, brilliant choruses, and pointed musical characterization.

The first evidence of Strauss as an operatic iconoclast and pioneer came with *Salome* in 1905. The play by Oscar Wilde was adapted directly by Strauss himself with cuts and considerable compression. The story of Salome's desire for the head of John the Baptist, the sultry decadence of Herod's court, the dance of the "seven veils," the crushing of Salome to death after she kisses the dead lips of John, is still a shocker. The one-act opera, both because of its subject and the dissonant, violent music that Strauss put to it, was a "cause célèbre" and Strauss was pushed to the forefront of the avant-garde. The music is one of his most original scores. In spite of later developments and a tendency to belittle Strauss' achievement, *Salome* remains a work striking in symphonic structure, treatment of *leit motiv*, orchestral sound, and realization of a dramatic nightmare.

Elektra (1909) is the first of Strauss' operas written in collaboration with Hugo von Hofmannsthal. This partnership, the correspondence of which has been preserved, was one of the most fruitful in operatic history. Hofmannsthal was a poet and dramatist of great ability. Although the two men were temperamentally very unlike, they recognized each other's qualities and were able to achieve a fine working relationship. Hofmannsthal had made a new one-act version of Sophocles' *Electra*; Strauss saw it in Berlin and marked it down for future operatic treatment. Eventually when the two men decided to collaborate the work was written. *Elektra* marks an intensification of the Strauss of *Salome*, although some view it as a decline. The subject is equally shocking but has the virtue of being a distasteful action for a purpose: the dwelling on vengeance rather than sexual pathology gives the shock a loftier setting. There is the same masterly and complex harmonic vocabulary, rich scoring, and intense musical characterization found in *Salome*. The recognition scene between Orestes and Electra is particularly vivid. Brother and sister are united in their vengeful obsession: they will kill their mother and her paramour, Aegisthus, who killed their father.

Der Rosenkavalier (1911), the next of Strauss' operas, is now one of the classics of modern opera. Its success in the international repertory is rather unusual because the text and the music are so localized: it is an Austrian comedy, and one is hardly able to appreciate its full humor and beauty without some knowledge of Vienna, its dialect, its jokes, its easy-going ways, and its love of music, particularly waltzes. Yet the librettist and the composer raised the work above the level of a regional comedy and give it lasting significance. With this work, their collaboration came to full flower. There was compromise and struggle on both sides. Their correspondence gives valuable insight into the perils and difficulties of building an operatic edifice. By keeping the end in view, however, difficulties were resolved, and the result was a triumph.

The opera began with Hofmannsthal as a simple little comedy to last at most two hours; it eventually became almost as long as *Meistersinger* with much of that opera's pageantry, humor, and expansiveness. The story is simple enough in its general outline but there is complexity beneath the surface. It takes place in Vienna of the eighteenth century, the reign of Maria Theresa (1740–1780), and relates the tale of another Marie Theres', Princess of Werdenberg, wife of Field Marshall Werdenberg. She is called *Marschallin* or *Feldmarschallin* (that is, the wife of the Field Marshall); her husband never appears—he is away hunting, an occupation that seems to fill his days. As Ernest Newman[3] puts it, his wife, a vibrant woman of 32, pursues another kind of venery during his absence—dalliance with lovers, the present one of whom is a 17-year-old boy of the aristocracy, Octavian. His full name is Count Octavian Maria Ehrenreich Bonaventura Fernand Hyacinth Rofrano. To make matters more complicated, the collaborators determined that Octavian should be sung by a woman (the part is written for mezzo-soprano), and since Octavian spends a good part of the opera dressed as the servant girl Mariandel, the confusion about sex comes full circle. Unlike Cherubino, whom Mozart and da Ponte picture as a lovelorn adolescent, Octavian makes love to two women onstage, kissing and fondling them, and the opera opens with Octavian and the Marschallin getting out of bed. During the opera's early performances this opening scene had to be modified to soothe the sensibilities of the north Germans (not the Viennese). A representation of love-making between a 17-year-old boy and a mature woman could have degenerated into crudity and bad taste, but the music and light nature of the affair place it in perspective.

The story concerns Baron Ochs, a lubberly country cousin of the Marschallin, who comes to Vienna to marry Sophie Faninal, the

[3]Ernest Newman, *Great Operas*, Vintage Books paperback, New York, 1958, vol. 1, p. 408.

"Ochs ıs very taken with him-her and is eager to pursue the chase further." Walter Berry and Chrısta Ludwig play Ochs and Octavian ın Strauss' *Der Rosenkavalier*. Octavian, a young man played by a woman, is dressed as a maıd through much of the opera. (Photo by Beth Bergman)

young daughter of a rich Viennese bourgeois. Her dowry will recoup the Baron's declining fortunes and the marriage will elevate the Faninals into the aristocracy. Ochs is everything the ruling class should not be—lecherous, boorish, stingy with his money, fat, cowardly when it comes to physical danger, and quite insensitive to anybody's feelings but his own. It is easy to play him as a caricature—his recital of his amorous adventures in the country sounds like a rooster let loose in the henyard—but he is made such a figure of ridicule and scorn, and he takes his beating with such good grace, we end by feeling sorry for him.

When a marriage is to take place in the Lerchenau family (the Baron's pedigree), the custom is for a silver rose to be presented by a friend or relation to the bride. Octavian is chosen for this mission, but when he sees Sophie, he falls deeply in love with her and she with him. Meanwhile, the Baron behaves with such grossness towards his intended bride she will have none of him; Octavian, enraged by the Baron's behavior to Sophie, draws his sword and pinks Ochs in the arm. Faninal and his household feel themselves disgraced.

In the last act, Octavian, seeking further revenge on Ochs and trying to disgrace him completely with his intended in-laws, enlists the aid of two shady Italians, Valzacchi and Annina, to entice Ochs to a disreputable rendezvous where he will be caught by Faninal and Sophie in a compromising position with the servant girl, Mariandel (Octavian in disguise). In the first act, when Ochs, fresh from the country, bursts in on the Marschallin and Octavian, Octavian has had to don female costume and pretend to be a servant to avoid disclosure of his and the Marschallin's love affair. Ochs is very taken with him-her and is eager to pursue the chase further. The scene in Act III where Ochs is exposed is German comedy at its broadest—heads pop in and out of secret cupboards; four little bastards come in wailing "Papa"; a discarded mistress (Annina) makes an appearance; and a Commissary of the Police investigates the noise and uproar. Finally, the Marschallin is brought to the scene and dominates the situation. Ochs, in spite of his attempted bravado, is told firmly that Sophie is not for him. The Marschallin, recognizing the love of the two young people for each other, renounces Octavian in a moving scene which is one of the most beautiful in the opera. In the first act she had foreseen the time when they must part—the difference in their ages made it inevitable—but the break has to be endured with dignity.

In the end, the central figure of the opera is the Marschallin, whose beauty and noble bearing shine through the charade and give a bitter taste of partial tragedy to the world of comedy. Without her, the opera is apt to become farce. Her observations on life, on the passage of time and what it does to all human beings, her acceptance of the world as it is, and her renunciation of her beloved Octavian, make her one of the great characters in opera. As played and sung by great actress-singers, she has become beloved of the Viennese and all others who relish the true marriage of music and drama.

Hofmannsthal's libretto with its clever situations, its peculiarly fit use of language (Mariandel the servant is made to speak low Viennese dialect; Ochs in a polite mood tries to intersperse his conversation with French and Italian expressions to show his upbringing; the Princess addresses Octavian as "'Du" (familiar), "Sie" (formal), or "Er" (ultra-formal) depending on her mood and the situation), and its interweaving with the music is greatly responsible for the subtle flavor of the work. But it is Strauss' music which puts the capstone on the collaboration and turns the comedy into sterling opera.

Strauss was a master of the orchestra; in size, color, and density he took it farther than it had gone. His quicksilver passage from one mood to another is magical in its effect, although it wears thin with repetition. After Wagner, the use of leading motives to express a character or a situation became *de rigueur*. Strauss is not as specific as Wagner, but he does utilize a set of themes to personify people and situations, and they are moderately changed when the position demands it. In *Rosenkavalier*, the musical foundation of these themes is the waltz, although Strauss knew full well that the waltz belonged to the nineteenth century and not to the Austria of Maria Theresa. Yet through the other Strauss (Johann) the waltz had become so readily associated with Vienna, Richard Strauss felt he could use it with impunity. The devoted opera-goer, once he has heard these waltzes, seldom forgets them. They are constructed in such a way that Strauss can break them up, extract part of a phrase, or change their scoring to get the effect he wishes. He changes key with startling rapidity to give color and variety to his score. A recognizable defect is his perilous skirting of the obvious—the chord sequences become banal and overripe, or he repeats a phrase that cannot stand repetition. In his later operas, these Strauss trademarks become more obtrusive, but in *Rosenkavalier* they are only in the background.

The beginning of the opera has always posed a problem for the actors and the stage director. Strauss chose to write "'eine Einleitung" (an Introduction) that is really a musical depiction of the ending of a night of love. (Hofmannsthal's stage directions indicate the Marschallin is in bed with only her arm visible, Octavian is kneeling on a footstool beside her.) The musical introduction (rare for Strauss; in his other works the curtain came up immediately) presents the two characters by developing their themes.

Strauss was able to accomplish both of his objectives. The very first notes of the introduction, played by the horns, show the impetuous, youthful ardor of Octavian, followed by a more chromatic, languorous answer to the bold assertion of the opening measures (Examples 15-5*a* and *b*). (The pastime of motive-labeling, a game that began with Wagner, continued with later composers: some commentators find in these first two motives a representation of Octavian first and the Princess second.) Whatever it may be, this opening music and the coy repetition of the strings in *c* are generally associated with Octavian alone—his eagerness and rapture.

Halfway through the introduction the orchestra calms down and at "Molto più tranquillo" plays a lovely, syncopated oboe and string line, characterized by a descending leap of a seventh (Example 15-6*a*). Strauss develops this motivic bit more fully in the duet between the Marschallin and Octavian at the end of the act. Then come two unmistakable ideas—both associated with the Marschallin and her love for Octavian (*b* and *c*). The second, with

Example 15-5   Strauss, *Der Rosenkavalier* (1911)

Example 15-6

its octave leaps and sudden change to a distantly related altered chord in the second measure, are characteristic of the late Strauss and give a distinctive touch to his musical construction.

The many waltzes through the opera are integral parts of the score. They are not ballet or interpolated music but are woven into

Example 15-7

the musical fabric. They are seldom sung but have definitie associations with a situation or a character. Their lilt, their varied pacing, their tunefulness add immeasurably to the charm of the work, and put a lovely varnish over some of the rough edges and boisterous antics of Baron Ochs and the other comic characters.

In Act I after the little black boy has brought the Marschallin's chocolate and Octavian has come out from hiding behind the screen, the two lovers resume breakfast. Octavian sits near her and the Marschallin strokes his hair. In the background the orchestra plays a delicate waltz tune (Example 15-7a), more nearly a minuet, as they look at each other tenderly. The music is the counterpart of the action—a pensive, charming little tune. Later, after Ochs has burst into the room and has eyes only for the pretty chambermaid, Mariandel, b is heard as Ochs makes a proposition to her ("Have you ever had supper tête-à-tête with a gentleman?"). The insinuating nature of this tune with its downward chromatic motion followed by a leap upward is the ideal background to the "gentleman's" advances and puts a light cover over their grossness. Previous to this when the Marschallin discovers the noisy voice outside is not her husband's but her country cousin's, and Octavian steps out in maid's clothes before Ochs enters, Strauss makes Octavian's theme (Example 15-5a) into a full-fledged waltz melody (Example 15-7c), of which the beginning is the first notes of the opera. It is a delightful transformation, which Strauss uses several times in the second and third acts.

In Act II, one of the best-known waltzes in the opera is heard when the Baron calls on Faninal, Sophie, and the household. In front of Octavian, who has just presented Sophie with the silver rose, he behaves so outrageously to Sophie (pawing her, praising her physical good points as if she were a filly in a stable), the assembled company is outraged. Ochs, to back up his clumsy overtures, says Sophie will discover overnight what a fine fellow he is (d): "With me no room is too small for you; without me, every day is anxiety; with me, no night is too long for you." The waltz lifts the words and situation above the commonplace and transforms the Baron's crude attentions into light-hearted courtship. Strauss indicates that the repeated upbeats of this captivating tune be played glissando by the violins to get the proper sentimental and alluring effect. At the end of the act, the Baron, wounded slightly by Octavian's sword, has recovered with the help of some wine. A note from Mariandel saying she would like to join him the following evening, brings thoughts of pleasure and he softly sings to himself the same words and tune of d, adding he has "the luck of the Lerchenaus" (e). This gay conclusion with the fat Ochs dancing around the room always brings applause. Music and action fit together like hand in glove.

In Act III, after the pantomime when the stage is being set for the tête-à-tête of Ochs and Mariandel, the lights are lit on the supper table and the "enraptured" couple enter. Music in the background onstage consists of another lively waltz (*f*), suggesting the forced gaiety of this cosy occasion. A series of waltzes enliven the scene, the last of which is a delightful tune (*g*), to be played when: "Octavian leans back coquettishly in his chair with half-closed eyes. The Baron rises: the moment for the first kiss seems to have come. When his face is quite close to his companion's, he is suddenly struck by the likeness to Octavian. He starts back and instinctively grasps his wounded arm."

Some of the finest scenes in the opera involve the Marschallin. Their bittersweet taste is sentimental, yet serious. At the conclusion of Act I the Marschallin realizes that time will eventually take Octavian from her. At the end of the opera when the farce is exposed, Ochs finds that Mariandel is Octavian, and Sophie and Octavian are in love. In a trio of surpassing beauty—one of the finest of its kind ever written—the Marschallin firmly, sadly, but without cynicism or bitterness renounces what hold she may have had on Octavian and quietly leaves the two young people alone to declare their mutual love.

The Marschallin's famous soliloquy in Act I comes after Ochs has departed and she is left alone with her thoughts. Ochs takes his leave, his heavy and clumsy tread mirrored in the orchestra (Example 15-8*a*—a series of reiterated tonic and dominant notes in the bass with an ungraceful scurrying in the violins). The Marschallin with unexpected vehemence says to herself: "There he goes, the bloated worthless fellow, who catches the pretty young thing and a bit of money with her, as if it had to be." She is under no illusions about the nature of a marriage with the Baron, and has only profound pity for the young girl, fresh out of a convent, who is forced into a marriage not of her own choosing. But it is the way of the world. She takes a hand-mirror and gazes into her own face. For moments there is only music (*b*), a nostalgic, oddly old-fashioned tune, bright but fragile. She well remembers a similar girl (herself) not too long ago. But where is she now? The music also asks the question, the first desk violins swooping down softly onto a diminished chord (*c*). How can it be that the little "Resi" (Marie Theres') is now a grown woman and the Field Marshall's wife? Soon it will be the old Princess Resi (*d* derived from *b*, but darkened). Why does the Lord let it happen? Why does he not hide it? "It is all mysterious, deeply mysterious; yet one

Example 15-8

has to bear it. But it is in the 'how' that the whole difference lies." Hofmannsthal's delicate lines on the passage of time and the onset of middle age are accompanied by a most touching allusion to Example 15-6a, one of the earlier Marschallin love themes when time with Octavian seemed to stand still. The orchestra drops to nothing so the words can be heard.

Lotte Lehmann, whose acting and singing of the Marschallin, is a wonderful memory to those who saw her, speaks of this scene in the following manner:

What the Marschallin should be doing here is standing quietly, half-smiling, pensive. She has learned to smile the wise smile of a woman tried and tested by life, the smile that carved out of youth's passionate rebellion, is one of life's greatest and most gratifying victories... She very definitely must avoid conveying the impression of sadness; the music here is joyfully moving ... the dim, distant past .. is remembered only as one remembers a sentimental song of yesteryear, a trifle sad, perhaps, in a sweet, warmly pleasant way.[4]

Strauss' remaining operas never attained the popularity of *Der Rosenkavalier* although the next two, both on Hofmannsthal librettos, *Ariadne auf Naxos* (1912; 1916), a chamber opera drawn partly from Molière, and *Die Frau ohne Schatten* (The Woman Without a

[4]*Five Operas and Richard Strauss*, Ernst Pawel, trans., Macmillan, New York, 1964, p. 158. Reprint DaCapo, New York, 1982.

Shadow, 1919), a magic fairy tale, have splendid music. Strauss wrote eight more operas in the 1920s and 1930s, but few of them have held the stage except in Germany. He outlived his time. Music in the early decades of the twentieth century was changing too rapidly for a man schooled in an older tradition. The Strauss technical equipment and luscious sound are in these later works but the heart seems to be lacking. Opera pointed in new directions. One had to turn a corner or be swept aside by the new ideas that overran the artistic world between the two world wars. There was no time to look backward and the future was highly uncertain.

SUGGESTED READING

Puccini   Ashbrook, William, *The Operas of Puccini*, Oxford University Press, New York, 1968. Discussion of the individual works.

Carner, Mosco, *Puccini, A Critical Biography*, Duckworth, London, 1958. The best combination of biography and opera analysis in English.

Hughes, Patrick C. (Spike), *Famous Puccini Operas*, Citadel, New York, 1962.

Puccini Librettos, William Weaver, trans., Anchor Books paperback, New York, 1966. Italian and English for *La Bohème, Tosca, Madama Butterfly, Gianni Schicchi,* and *Turandot.*

Strauss   Del Mar, Norman, *Richard Strauss, A Critical Commentary on his Life and Works*, vol. I, 1962, vol. II, 1969, Barrie and Rockcliff, London. Best biography in English.

Mann, William, *Richard Strauss, A Critical Study of the Operas*, Oxford University Press, New York, 1966. Thorough study of background and music to all the operas.

16 Opera in the Twentieth Century

Although we are already some 70 years into the twentieth century, it is very difficult to single out specific composers or styles that tower over others. Detachment and perspective on one's own age is sought but seldom attained—events are too near at hand. The cliché that every generation experiences rapid change in social, economic, and political conditions can be applied with particular force to our own century. Two world wars, economic disruption, and the rise of competing political systems (capitalism and state socialism) both antithetical to art, are events not easily shrugged off. And there has been a veritable revolution in music itself— the abandoning of tonality, foundation of music since the seventeenth century. If the early and middle twentieth century can be characterized at all in opera, it is by the multiplicity of styles. No age can cut itself off entirely from its past, and so conservative efforts have lingered and been cherished. On the other hand, experiments in electronic media and other radical offspring have been common, though few have appealed to the public. The more radical, far-reaching attempts for a "new opera" occurred in the earlier decades of the century; the later decades concentrated on other fields of music. In the midst of this diversity, however, several works can be mentioned that seem to have lasting quality as musical drama. For the most part, they represent trends of the times.

Berg   Alban Berg's *Wozzeck* refutes the notion that opera is wholly a
museum piece. This extraordinary work, first heard in its entirety on
the stage in December, 1925, in Berlin, is written in a complicated
and dissonant idiom. The word "atonal," which describes a work
without tonality, is frowned upon by modern theorists but it describes the musical nature of this opera. Aside from its harmonic
idiom, the work has a complex musical structure and it deals with
a sordid subject; nevertheless, *Wozzeck* is now generally accepted
as one of the finest of modern operas. Its dramatic power and
musical quality are so compelling that audiences, even those not
enamored of Schönberg and his school—of which Berg was a
member, are gripped by its totality and come to hear it again and
again. It is one of the few genuine "modern" operas not in a tonal
idiom which has held the stage.

Alban Berg (1885–1935) was a Viennese of comfortable circumstances and good education who early demonstrated his
musical ability. The decisive musical influence in his life was his
years of study with Arnold Schönberg, 1904 through 1910. He
became an ardent disciple of Schönberg's theories, but always kept
his own individuality and integrity as a creative artist. He did not
compose a large quantity of music because with his keen interest in
delving into the secrets of musical composition, everything had
to be thoroughly thought out and formed. He could not let a composition alone until it had reached a state of near perfection. He
was appalled by the usual criticism of Schönberg and his followers
as being "chaotic, atonal, and formless"; atonal might apply to
Schönberg's music, but the first and third adjectives were wide of
the mark and Berg was determined to prove this. His music and
that of Arnold Schönberg are among the most tightly organized
pieces ever written. An analysis of *Wozzeck* already fills a good
size book, and the same is true for various works of Schönberg.
The appeal and justification for Berg's music, comes not from a
lengthy technical analysis; it is interesting primarily because it
shows that music departing from the old norms of tonality must
have some other guiding principle to give it coherence and unity.
It has power as sheer music and, in the case of *Wozzeck*, remarkable aptitude for the operatic medium.

Berg himself was quite specific about this when he wrote about
Wozzeck:

However much may be known about the musical forms in this opera, the
strict and logical "working-out" of this or that, the craftsmanship of the
various details   from the moment when the curtain goes up until it falls
for the last time, there should be nobody in the audience who is aware of

any of these various fugues and inventions, suites and sonata movements, variations and passacaglias: nobody filled with anything but the idea of this opera, which transcends the individual fate of Wozzeck. And I believe that in this I have been successful.[1]

The play *Woyzeck*, upon which the opera is based, dates from the 1830s. Georg Büchner (1813–1837), a playwright almost unknown until recently, died tragically early from typhus. *Woyzeck* and *Danton's Death*, also by Büchner, seem to belong to the post-Freudian era, not 100 years before it; they shatter one's comfortable generalizations about the Victorian era and the early nineteenth century. Büchner, born in the same year as Verdi and Wagner, was a sensitive young man greatly influenced by the revolutionary events of his time, particularly political uprising in Germany. In *Woyzeck* he wished to portray the unfortunate lot of downtrodden lower classes who were cannon fodder for the armies and so much cheap manpower for the growing industrialization of Europe. Berg saw the play in Berlin in 1914 and was so taken with it that he determined to set it to music. World War I intervened and Berg had to do military service. Because of his health, he was relegated to guard duty in Vienna. Experiences common to all who have served as enlisted men in an army helped Berg point up the sorry situation of Wozzeck, who was an ordinary soldier of no education or background. After the war, Berg returned to his music and completed the opera by April, 1921. He tried peddling it to various German and Austrian opera houses but nobody would touch it. Extracts of it were given in concert form in Frankfurt in 1924, but not until 1925, in Berlin, was the opera produced in its entirety.

Berg's chief problem in setting *Woyzeck* to music was compressing it. Büchner had a plot but chose to provide a number of psychological situations which threw light on the chief characters but did not directly advance the story. Berg wanted to keep the original language of the play and not construct a libretto as such. Even though some of the scenes were very short, he reduced the total from 26 to 15, five in each act. He also made some minor omissions and charges in the text. The musical interlude or transition between each scene is important to allow time for the necessary scene change but also because the music points up something that has just happened or is about to happen.

The story concerns Johann Franz Wozzeck, a pitiable soldier in a German regiment.

Uneducated, uncomprehending, he is the slave and the butt of everyone,

[1] *Pro Domo*, 1928.

not only of the Captain of his regiment, whose regimental servant he is, but of the Doctor, who laughs at him to his face, regards him merely as an interesting subject for scientific experiment, and uses him for demonstration purposes to the students. His one thin ray of sunshine in a dark world is the trull by whom he has had a child; and she is stolen from him by the boastful Drum Major, who makes use of his physical superiority over the wretched Wozzeck to humiliate him in the eyes of the other soldiers. Over almost everyone and everything of first-line significance in the drama there broods the shadow of something like incipient madness: no one is wholly normal.[2]

Wozzeck, who has a fixation that the world is closing in on him and that he will be annihilated in some great natural catastrophe, is finally unhinged by Marie's unfaithfulness. His common-law wife is as downtrodden as he. Aside from the child by Wozzeck, her main solace in life has been the various men with whom she has cohabited. Wozzeck takes Marie to a lonely pond in the woods and plunges a knife in her throat. Unbalanced by this act, he goes to a tavern where his fellow soldiers are and tries desperately to drown his sorrows. His comrades see blood on his arm and accuse him of violence. He rushes back to the place of the murder. When he finds the mutilated body of Marie, the moon, the clouds, and the pond seem to swallow him in a sea of blood. To wash it off he wades out into the pond and is drowned. In the last scene, outside Marie's hut, children playing tell Marie's child that his mother is dead. The child rides his hobby horse faster, saying "hop, hop." Finding himself alone, he runs off after the others.

Berg's musical language is a flexible idiom founded on Schönberg's. Of two devices used, the new one is *Sprechstimme* (see p. 52), to heighten the declamation. Much depends upon the interpreter to make the proper effect; some singers have the knack; others merely sound uncomfortable. The old device is the construction of each scene in one of the standard musical forms—rondo, sonata, theme and variations, fugue, suite, ABA, and passacaglia—to give the unity and cohesion which tonality, repetition, and sequence once supplied. Berg was not dogmatic about his use of these forms; they were a means to an end. The five scenes of the third act are freer: they are called *inventions*—on a theme, note, rhythm, hexachord, and eighth note movement. In reality, they are free developments of these ideas and do not follow set patterns. Interestingly, these instrumental forms adapt well to Berg's vocal medium. They help to unify the voice and orchestra and make the resulting music a satisfying whole.

It is difficult to investigate any one scene of *Wozzeck* because

[2]Ernest Newman, *Great Operas*, Vintage Books paperback, New York, 1958, vol. 2, p. 416.

"The Doctor uses the soldier as the subject in an experiment to see what effect certain foods will have on him." The doctor's study is the scene for much of the irony and tragedy of Berg's *Wozzeck*. (Photo by Louis Mélançon)

all of them bear on the drama. One of the most interesting is Act I, scene 4, where the Doctor, who gives Wozzeck three pence every time he sees him, uses the soldier as the subject in an experiment to see what effect certain foods will have on him. The picture is bitterly ironic because the food the Doctor prescribes is usually far too expensive for Wozzeck; he is lucky to get gruel and a common soldier's fare. The scene is cast in the form of a passa-caglia with 21 variations—the ground theme appears in some form in each variation. Berg anticipates modern twelve-tone organization in that the passacaglia theme has twelve tones and each variation uses the original progression, but there is no attempt to organize the musical material in a strictly serial manner. Berg lets the music develop naturally; when it is per-formed, there is hardly any sense of its being divided into a number of variation segments.

The setting is the Doctor's study on a sunny afternoon. The Doctor rushes to meet Wozzeck as he comes into the room.

Doctor. *What do I see, Wozzeck? Are you a man of your word? Eh, eh, eh!*
Wozzeck. *What then, Doctor?*
Doctor. *I saw you just now, Wozzeck. You were coughing and barking in the street like a dog. Do I give you three groschen every day for that? Wozzeck! That's bad. The world is bad, very bad. Oh!*

Example 16-1

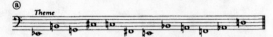

ⓐ Theme

ⓑ Clar.

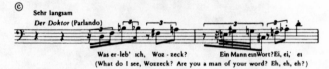

ⓒ Sehr langsam
Der Doktor (Parlando)

Was er-leb' ich, Woz - zeck?   Ein Mann ein Wort? Ei, ei, ei
(What do I see, Wozzeck? Are you a man of your word? Eh, eh, eh?)

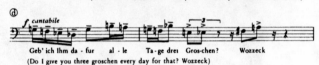

ⓓ f cantabile

Geb' ich Ihm da - fur   al - le   Ta - ge drei Gros-chen?   Wozzeck
(Do I give you three groschen every day for that? Wozzeck)

ⓔ Var. I

Die Na - tur kommt! Die Na - tur   kommt! A - berglaube, ab-scheu-li-cher A-ber - glaube!

Hab'ich nicht nachgewiesen,dass das Zwerchfell dem Willen un-ter-worfen ist,   die Na - tur,   Wozzeck!
(If Nature calls! If Nature calls! Superstition, wretched superstition.
Have I not proved that the diaphragm is subject to the will? Nature, Wozzeck!)

ⓕ Var. 16

Example 16-2

Langsame (♩.=56-60)
Marie
p

Mä - del, was fangst du jetzt   an? _____   Hast ein klein Kind und kein   Mann!

Ei.   was frag' ich dar - nach, _____   Sing' _____ ich die gan - ze Nacht:
(Maiden, what will you sing now? You have a small child but no husband.
Why should I ask about that? I'll sing the whole night through!)

Wozzeck. *But Doctor, if Nature calls one!*

Doctor (flaring up). *If Nature calls! If Nature calls! Superstition! Wretched superstition! Have I not proved that the diaphragm is subject to the will?* (Flaring up again.) *Nature, Wozzeck! Man is free. In man, individuality is changed into freedom.* (Shaking his head, more to himself.) *Have to cough!* (Again to Wozzeck.) *Have you eaten your beans, Wozzeck? Nothing but beans, nothing but beans as vegetables. Mark my words. You do it. Next week we begin with some mutton. There will be a revolution in science* (counting on his fingers): *protein, fats, carbohydrates, and next, oxyaldehydanhydrates* (sudden anger). *You are coughing again* (goes up to Wozzeck; suddenly stops). *No. I cannot get angry. Anger is bad for the health, it is unscientific. I am quite calm, my pulse is its usual 60. Be careful of the person who gets angry over a man. If it were a salamander that was unwell.* (More vigorously.) *But really, Wozzeck, you do not need to cough so!*

(The music for this text includes the theme and the first five variations.)

This farrago of nonsense shows the Doctor to be as pathological as his subject. To him, Wozzeck is just another object, with no comprehension of his life, his fate, or his reason. As in other scenes of this first act, showing Wozzeck in relation to different people in his environment—the Captain, Andres, Marie, and the Drum Major, this one portrays the poor man as uncomprehending and dazed in the midst of sinister forces. When he says to the Doctor: "... nature has vanished, and the world's so dark, so dark that you have to grope around it with your hands. I mean, it passes away like a spider's web," one glimpses the depth of his despair and the gradual unhinging of his mind.

A passacaglia in eighteenth-century terms is a continuous variation based on a repeated theme which normally appears in the bass but can be transferred to an upper voice in each variation. Generally the theme appears in the form it takes at the beginning. The succession of tones which Berg uses is Example 16-1a: it has no tonal base; it is merely a series of notes. The clarinet first enunciates the musical idea by itself (b). Then the theme appears in the bass in greatly augmented form while above it the Doctor sings his first phrase (c) and the rest of the text to Wozzeck's "If Nature calls!" This first vocal phrase contains most of the notes of the original but in a different rhythmic and melodic order. Two brief smaller motives are prominent within it: the rising third when the Doctor pronounces Wozzeck's name, and the three notes of "ei, ei, ei," taken from the end of the theme and heard several times in the course of the scene. Example d is another phrase which Berg emphasizes later. Variation 1 has the theme spread out and carried by a horn in a middle register. The vocal line also touches on these notes in various places and adds another dimension to the variation (see circled notes of *e*, which correspond to the opening part of *a*). Variation 16 shows another treatment of the theme unadorned in the bass, while string chords above present combinations of the tones found in the series (*f*). The miracle of this complicated structure is that the listener is not consciously aware of its close formal logic but is carried along by its unfaltering musical and dramatic force.

Berg does not avoid traditional means when he finds them useful. In Act I, scene 3, after Marie has slammed the window on her neighbor, Margret, who has been stridently accusing her of promiscuity, she turns to her child and sings him a little cradle song (Example 16-2). The tonal shape of the phrases and the repetition of the first measures at a different pitch cling to an older idiom but are consistent with the particular situation. The same is true of the poignant last scene of the opera where Marie's and Wozzeck's child is playing with other children before they interrupt to say his mother is dead. The nursery rhyme (Example 16-3) is repetitive musically; the

Example 16-3

Rin - gel, Rin - gel, Ro - sen-kranz, Rin - - - gel-reih'n,   Rin - gel, Rin-gel, Ro - sen-kranz, Rin -

(Ring around the roses. Ring in a row.)

Example 16-4

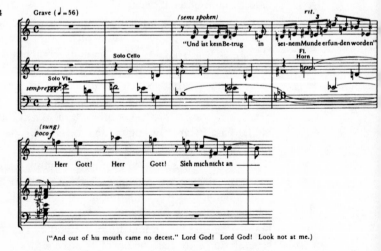

("And out of his mouth came no deceit." Lord God! Lord God! Look not at me.)

tragic nature of what has happened is made all the more penetrating by the simple song of the child.

Berg makes an important distinction in his score between *Sprechstimme* and regular singing. In the first scene of Act III, Marie is reading by candlelight the biblical story of Mary Magdalene and bewailing her own frailty. At the end she asks the Lord to take pity on her. The reading occurs in Sprechstimme, but her reactions to the words are sung (Example 16-4). The orchestra begins the theme softly underneath her semi-sung narration. At her sung words, there is a great outburst (not shown here) uncovering her inner distress.

Wozzeck proves that opera in a nontonal medium and a musical language unfamiliar to the audience can be dramatically and musically viable. Berg continued to develop his highly organized musical language with great originality and force. He wrote another opera, *Lulu* (1937), in the strict twelve-tone idiom, but its last act was only one-third completed (now heard in its entirety from new sources).

Britten One of the most heartening signs for English-speaking opera lovers has been the recent resurgence of opera in English. Opera in England and America was long regarded as an import which people went to see more for social than for dramatic reasons. This attitude has changed with the advent of radio, television, and the phonograph. Opera can be heard in ways never known before, and the English-speaking public can accept the idiom on its own terms.

The composer who has probably done most to put English-speaking opera back on the stage is Benjamin Britten (1913–1976). Although he has his adversaries, there is no question that he speaks authoritatively as a composer immensely skilled in stagecraft, the voice, and the orchestra. His style is basically conservative, but his touch is so deft and convincing that his works are recognized as contemporary creation, not imitation of the past. Because Britten's training and background have been eminently practical (he has earned a living by writing documentary film music, music for radio playscripts, and songs for special occasions), he has been regarded by some as a journeyman whose style is essentially eclectic (a pejorative term today). Whatever criticism is aimed at him, however, his operas have been popular, and they are among the few English works accepted into the international repertory.

Britten's first opera to gain recognition was *Peter Grimes* (1945), the one by which he is still best known. He composed two chamber operas, *The Rape of Lucretia* (1946) and *Albert Herring* (1947), a comic work, then he returned to the sea (*Peter Grimes* is the tale of a fisherman and a fishing village) in a full-scale setting of Melville's story, *Billy Budd* (1951). *Gloriana* came in 1953 for Queen Elizabeth's coronation, *The Turn of the Screw* (a chamber opera modeled on the Henry James story) in 1954, and *A Midsummer Night's Dream* in 1960. He has also written several mystery plays with music for church performance. These works are quasi-operatic and make considerable use of boys' voices. Much of Britten's music was first presented at the Aldeburgh, Suffolk, festival, started by Britten, his friend Peter Pears, the singer, and others. Aldeburgh, Britten's home, is a small village on the sea. Thus it is no accident that two of Britten's finest works deal with seafaring life.

Peter Grimes' libretto by Montagu Slater is based on George Crabbe's poem, "The Borough"—a series of 24 "letters" in heroic couplets describing an eighteenth century village much like Aldeburgh. Crabbe (1754–1832), a realist before his time, did not hesitate to paint Peter Grimes in a harsh light; the man had few redeeming features. He obtained orphan boys from London, beat them, and worked them to death on his fishing trips. The Borough (the town), finally became aroused, forbade him to take any more apprentices, and ostracized him. He eventually went mad and died.

Slater had to ameliorate this forbidding figure. In the libretto, Peter is too proud to come to terms with society, yet the audience sympathizes with him as the outcast hounded by his own people. There is some truth in the accusations of his town people; but their prejudices and blindness never give Grimes a chance; he is defeated by his own shortcomings and the village's baleful threats. Other names in the opera were taken from Crabbe but Slater also fashioned living characters of his own invention.

The opera has a prologue and three acts of two scenes each. In the prologue, Grimes is brought before Swallow, the coroner and mayor, and a crowd of villagers for an inquest into the death of his apprentice. The verdict is death by accidental circumstance, and Grimes is acquitted. But the villagers show clearly they still believe him guilty of death by negligence. Ellen Orford, widowed school-mistress, tries to comfort Peter.

In Act I, in spite of village disapproval, Ellen Orford, agrees to fetch Grimes' new apprentice. A storm comes up. Captain Balstrode, a retired merchant skipper, tries to get Grimes to seek a new beginning elsewhere, but Peter is obsessed with proving his innocence, making money, and marrying Ellen. At "The Boar" that night, the situation is tense. Mrs. Sedley, the town gossip, awaits her supply of laudanum; "Auntie," the proprietress, tries to keep her two "nieces" away from Bob Boles, a drunken Methodist preacher; and the crowd fears the raging storm, which already has flooded the coast road and swept away part of the cliff by Peter Grimes' hut. When the cart arrives with Ellen and the new apprentice boy, John, Peter insists, to everybody's dismay, on taking the boy directly to his hut.

In the first scene of Act II, Ellen discovers that Grimes has been abusing his new boy—she finds him with body bruises and torn clothes. When Grimes and Ellen quarrel, Mrs. Sedley overhears and spreads the word that "Grimes is at his exercise" again (maltreating his apprentice). In scene 2, a party of men march on the hut to investigate for themselves. Grimes, who has been berating the boy, decides on a quick flight: he orders the boy to take the fishing nets and go down the cliff (dangerous because of the storm), to the boat below. The boy slips and falls to his death. When the crowd enters, they find an empty hut.

Act III opens with a dance at "The Boar." Peter and his apprentice have not been seen for days. Mrs. Sedley tells that an embroidered jersey which Ellen gave to the boy has been washed up on the beach. Swallow summons a posse to find Peter. A fog comes up. Ellen and Balstrode go to Peter's boat and find him half-insane. Ellen wants to lead him home, but Balstrode says Grimes must take his boat out to sea and scuttle it. This he does as dawn breaks. The Borough wakens; it is another day. In spite of the grim nature of the story, it has humor and compassion supported by Britten's music.

The plots of *Wozzeck* and *Peter Grimes* have much in common though their musical language is vastly different. Both works concern misfits of society who gain the audience's compassion. The protagonists have fixations which lead to their downfall, and both men have women who shelter and befriend them but whom they eventually renounce. In *Peter Grimes*, Britten has six interludes: at the beginning of each act and between the scenes of each act. They serve the same function Berg employed in *Wozzeck* —to link the action. Unlike *Wozzeck*, *Peter Grimes* emphasizes the chorus. The villagers, men and women, are participants in the story: they act and their actions affect Grimes; they persecute him; he wishes to defy and subdue them; they indirectly cause the fatal accident in Act II. The other powerful element in the drama, the sea—at rest, in a violent storm, in a fog, on a sunny day— ebbs and swells in the music. At the beginning of Act I the music is based on three motives which represent the sea in various moods.

While the composer rarely reverts to the separate number formula of earlier opera, he does write arias, recitative, choruses, and interludes that are distinguishable from each other but flow together without break. His music is superbly adapted to English. For once, the English-speaking listener feels he is hearing his own tongue in an unforced, natural, and skillful way set to dramatic music. Some of the dialogue goes so rapidly that the singers must be experts at enunciation to project the words clearly.

Various examples show Britten's ability to portray mood and situation. At the end of the prologue, Ellen and Peter sing unaccompanied a moving duet.

Peter. *The truth, the pity, and the truth.*
Ellen. *Peter, come away.*
Peter. *Where the walls themselves gossip of inquest!*
Ellen. *But we'll gossip too and talk and rest.*
Peter. *While Peeping Toms nod as you go. You'll share the name of outlaw too!*

Example 16-5a follows. Ellen sings in E major, Peter in A flat to show their separateness. But there is a link with the enharmonic G sharp and A flat on "find" and "until" which are the same notes.

Ellen. *There'll be new shoals to catch, life will be kind. Unclouded the hot sun will spread his rays around.*
Peter. *Ah! only of drowning ghosts! Time will not forget—the dead are witness, and fate is blind.*

They join and sing together, in their different keys; the tempo slows and their voices come together in octaves (*b*). They yearn for peace and harmony, and Britten shows musically their common purpose. All through the opera (Examples 16-8a and *b* are instances as well as here), Britten uses the interval of a major ninth as a symbol of both Peter's hope and his maladjustment to society. The passage marked "Recitativo without measure" with dotted lines to indicate natural breaks in the voice is a splendid illustration of Britten's way with the voice and his feeling for diction translated into sound.

In Act I, when Jim Hobson refuses to bring Peter's new apprentice from the workhouse, Ellen volunteers and puts the Borough to shame. The chorus says: "Ellen, you're leading us a dance fetching boys for Peter Grimes because the Borough is

Example 16-5   Britten, *Peter Grimes* (1945)

Example 16-6

Example 16-7

Example 16-8

What har - - bour shel - ters peace

Peter mezzo voce

We strained ____ in - to the wind hea - vi - ly la - den

Example 16-9

Pub con - ver - sa - tion ____ should de - pend on this ____ e - ter - nal mo - ral

So ____ long as sa - tire ____ don't des - cend to fis - ti - cuff or quar - rel

Allegro molto (Refrain)

We live ____ and let live, and look ____ we keep our hands to our - selves

Example 16-10

Old Joe has gone fish - ing and Young Joe has gone fish - ing and

Bring them in sweet - ly Gut them com - plete - ly Pack them up

Pull them in in han' - fuls and in

O haul ____ a - way

you know has gone fish - ing and found them a shoal ____

neat - ly sell them dis - creet - ly

care - ful and in pan - fuls

____ O haul ____ a - way

343 Opera in the Twentieth Century

afraid. You who help will share the blame." Her reply is a chant-like aria (Example 16-6) of utmost simplicity and beauty (a measured descending scale with final upward turn) to fit her Christian words. The text continues with biblical allusion: "And let the Pharisees and Saducees give way to none. But whosoever feels his pride is deep, there is no corner he can hide even in sleep."

Peter's utterances are mostly short soliloquies. When Balstrode in the first act tries to get Peter to leave the Borough and seek a new life elsewhere, Peter replies: "I am native, rooted here .../ By familiar fields,/Marsh and sand/Ordinary streets/Prevailing wind." His vocal line has a haunting jagged beauty (Example 16-7), and below it Britten emphasizes this fatal tie with a two-measure ostinato theme which winds through the texture. One of the loveliest moments in the score comes after Peter enters "The Boar" and an uneasy silence settles over the group; he muses aloud about the stars and nature ("When the Great Bear and Pleiades") in measures of intense beauty.

Folk song plays an important part in Britten's music. He has arranged many folksongs and weaves the feeling of them into his music. Balstrode, trying to calm the crowd in "The Boar" during the storm, sings a regular ballad with refrain that is roistering and catching. Everybody joins the chorus (Example 16-9). At the end of the act when the drunken preacher Boles threatens to break a bottle over Peter's head and there is the making of a riot, Ned Keene, the apothecary, starts a round in 7/4 meter and averts a crisis. The piece is Britten at his cleverest and most appealing. Nothing could be more English than the words and the four tunes (Example 16-10); the odd rhythms and accents make the music pure frolic.

Other Contemporary Operas
Many other contemporary operas and composers could be mentioned. If the discussion is restricted to opera in English, two other names immediately come to mind. Gian Carlo Menotti (1911–   ) was born in Italy, but he is really an American composer who has spent most of his life here. Menotti is one of the few modern composers who has managed to bring his works

successfully before the public. He really belongs more to musical theater than to opera although his dramas are cast in operatic form. *Amelia Goes to the Ball* (1937), *The Old Maid and the Thief* (1939), *The Medium* (1946), *The Telephone* (1947), *The Consul* (1950) —his first full-length opera, *Amahl and the Night Visitors* (1951), *The Saint of Bleecker Street* (1954), and *Help! Help! The Globolinks* (1969) are all viable, strong musical plays. Several of them were written specifically for radio and television. In some instances, the drama is more powerful than the music. Menotti writes his own librettos, and there is no doubt that they are strong, well-constructed, and plausible. Of all his operas, *The Consul* is probably best known. It has been performed many times in Europe. Menotti's popularity and his proximity in feeling and execution to Broadway should not be considered a drawback. Americans badly need the realization that opera is a living art, not something drawn from a musty museum of old favorites. But Menotti, as a twentieth century successor to Puccini, has dated too quickly; the music to his melodramas often does not match the librettos. Nevertheless, he has contributed significantly to American musical drama. Millions of listeners who never knew what an opera was have been captivated by the **sight and** sound of his television productions. This is a considerably achievement.

Igor Stravinsky (1882–1971), one of the musical giants of the twentieth century, is not generally associated with opera because his works in the operatic medium are not readily classifiable. *Le Rossignol* (The Nightingale, 1914) is a chamber opera written in Russian; *Oedipus Rex* (1927), called an opera-oratorio, draws on Sophocles but is written in Latin—a narrator tells the story in whatever the language of the audience may be; only *The Rake's Progress* (1951) is a standard opera in the common frame of reference. The libretto, written in English by W. H. Auden and Chester Kallman, was inspired by Hogarth's eighteenth century paintings of "The Rake's Progress," which tell a story in themselves. Stravinsky composed his opera in a neoclassical idiom, there are divided recitatives, arias, and ensembles in the music (Stravinsky said he thought of Mozart when he was writing). In spite of this deliberate reversion to the past, however, Stravinsky does not let his audience forget that the work belongs to the 1950s—not 200 years earlier. His characteristic touches stamp the work as contemporary.

The Rake's Progress has aroused great controversy because it looks backward. Probably only a composer of Stravinsky's ability could have brought it off at all. When dealing with Tom Rakewell and Anne Truelove, the two lovers, the opera has moments of considerable lyric beauty. The grotesque figures of Baba the Turk and Sellem the auctioneer, however, are caricatures difficult to believe. But Stravinsky manages to pull the affair together in an opera that may well find a place in the modern repertory.

What might be called "folk opera" has also been quite popular in twentieth-century America. Fictional and historical subjects dealing with plain people in the colorful American past have appealed to the imaginations of various composers. One of the best known works is George Gershwin's *Porgy and Bess* (1935), which has achieved international status through its clever mixture of jazz, popular tunes, and some operatic music. Gershwin's picture of the hopes and heartaches of Catfish Row in Negro Charleston carries great conviction. It may outlast more weighty operas, though its musical language is closer to the popular theater than to traditional opera. Other composers who have occupied themselves with American themes are Douglas Moore (*The Devil and Daniel Webster*, 1938; *The Ballad of Baby Doe*, 1956); Aaron Copland (*The Tender Land*, 1954); Carlisle Floyd (*Susannah*, 1958; *The Passion of Jonathan Wade*, 1962); Virgil Thomson (*The Mother of Us All*, 1947); and Jack Beeson (*Lizzie Borden*, 1965).

In New York of the 1960s, several operas in a more dissonant and serial vein by American composers (North and South America) have at least proved that contemporary works are not entirely neglected: *Nine Rivers to Jordan* (1969) by Hugo Weisgall; *The Visitation* (1966) by Gunther Schuller; and two works by the Argentinian, Alberto Ginastera, *Don Rodrigo* (1964) and *Bomarzo* (1967), might be mentioned.

In France, Francis Poulenc wrote *Les Mamelles de Tirésias* (The Breasts of Tirésias, 1947), a surrealist, comic work, and *Dialogues des Carmélites* (Dialogues of the Carmelites, 1957), a moving opera. Luigi Dallapiccola's *Il prigioniero* (The Prisoner, 1950) in Italy deserves strong mention. Names which come to mind in Germany are Werner Egk, Carl Orff, Boris Blacher, Gottfried von Einem, and Hans Werner Henze. Serge Prokofiev and Dimitri Shostakovitch have written a number of operas conforming to "Soviet realism," but Prokofiev's charming work, *The Love for Three Oranges*, (1921), has been the most popular Russian work in the West.

Finally, mention should be made of Arnold Schönberg's, *Moses und Aron* (Moses and Aaron) (first stage performance, 1957), an extraordinary cross between oratorio and opera. Although he completed two acts by 1931 and lived another 20 years, Schönberg never finished the work. The opera has been compared to a biblical mystery play. It is drawn directly from the third chapter of Exodus. Those who have seen it have hailed its great dramatic effectiveness.

Enormous demands are made on choral and orchestral forces which portray a Voice from the Burning Bush, a dance around the Golden Calf, and other familiar biblical episodes.

Contemporary opera is being written and performed, but it has a difficult time holding the stage. Emphasis in these works largely has been given to the text and the plot, the music taking a secondary role. Themes of guilt, despair, and uncertainty generate considerable dramatic power, but the musical thrust has been mostly through the orchestra rather than the voice. The voice has tended to become just another instrument, and melodic expression as known in the past has taken a new form. Audiences need time and repeated hearings to become used to this new language. Singers are reluctant to learn these trying, difficult roles for one or two performances; and an impresario trying an unfamiliar modern work always has the specter of low box-office receipts hanging over his head. Hope remains; every so often the cynical observer is confounded by the willingness of the public to hear something new and to be excited by it.

The Present and the Future

One of the favorite pastimes of contemporary critics and composers is to declare that opera is dead. If recent activity in the United States alone is any criterion, this statement can hardly be supported. A survey for the season 1969—1970 shows that 40 major opera companies in this country were responsible for 1104 performances, or 26 percent of the total given. (The complete number of opera companies was 648; 301 are public groups and 347 belong to colleges and universities.) The leading 40 companies with an estimated cost of $40 million had an attendance of about 2.5 million people. Of the works performed, 178 were in the standard repertory and 163 in the contemporary repertory (contemporary means composed during the last 40 to 50 years). Seventeen American operas were given world premieres.[3] The extent of college and university activity alone is noteworthy. A recent college survey[4] listed 450 "directors of opera." Opera, then, is being given in one form or another, and it is hardly "dead" from the numerical standpoint. The charge is directed primarily at the large international opera houses which get the most public-

---

[3] Maria F Rich, "Plus ça change . U.S. Opera Survey," *Opera News* (November 21, 1970), 14—16.
[4] *Directory of Music Faculties in American Colleges and Universities*, College Music Society, Binghamton, N.Y., 1970.

ity; community and college opera is forgotten because much of it is not professional. The critics base their estimates on the Metropolitan, San Francisco, and Chicago Opera Companies and tend to ignore what is happening elsewhere.

The voices of doom are really speaking of the aesthetics of grand opera rather than numbers in attendance. Their lament pertains mostly to the choice of works given; they are in effect speaking of the dilemma that inflicts all contemporary music—the gap between audience and composer. Ours is the first age in musical history to reject in large measure what the contemporary composer is writing unless it is couched in a conservative, tonal idiom. This fact is crucial because it determines most musical life today. Before the nineteenth century, almost everything performed was contemporary. If a work was 20 years old, it was old-fashioned and out-of-date. Later audiences may have found a Verdi or Wagner work unappealing for one reason or another, but they went to see it. Most contemporary music, opera and otherwise, is box-office poison unless there is some special attraction or the composer is already a well-known figure.[5]

Opera's reputation as the most conservative branch of present-day music has turned away lively musical minds. A distinction must be made between large, commercial opera and the enterprising college workshop: the increasing activity among smaller groups bodes well for the future of opera. But many composers are disenchanted; a few say, only half-jokingly, that the only salvation is to blow up the large opera house and start anew.[6] They despair of penetrating the veneer of social snobbery, worship of the big voice, and safe repertory which to them characterizes opera. They hope rising costs and lack of government support will spell the end of this kind of enterprise. Because they fundamentally believe in opera as an art form, however, they point to the possibilities inherent in new media and trust that salvation may lie in that direction.

The difficulty as already said, is not opera itself but the kind of opera which reflects contemporary musical trends and ideas. There is no reason to despair so long as the old-fashioned historical spectacle does not completely usurp the operatic stage. A new work may not be able to have as prominent position as it once had, but if it be heard, and more than once or twice, there is guarded cause for optimism.

---

[5] Opera, moreover, needs repeated exercise to prove its worth. Most great opera composers have come to their finest works only after three or four previous attempts.
[6] Pierre Boulez, "Opera Houses?—Blow them Up," *Opera* (June, 1968), 440–450.

"For television's generally cramped studio space and small receiving screen, the spectacle and voluptuous sound of grand opera are out of place." Britten's opera, *Owen Wingrave*, was written specifically for television with these problems in mind, and was presented on the National Educational Opera Theater on May 16, 1971 *Owen Wingrave* in the Maltings at Snape with cameras and other television equipment (Courtesy of National Educational Television and the British Broadcasting Company)

Opera on Film and Television   Films and television have become the most popular entertainment media in the Western world today, and numerous attempts have been made to bring opera to them. A television show reaches more people in one sitting than decades of opera-going would. The first televised Metropolitan Opera production reached a larger audience than have all the operas performed in the theater since its founding in 1883. Films of opera have been made in Europe in some quantity but with variable results. They have ranged from direct filming of stage production, to studio performances with live artists, to sound tracks of a well-known singer with an actress on the screen (*Aida* of 1954 had Renata Tebaldi's voice and Sophia Loren's acting). In the United States, filming of opera has generally been popularization of a famous opera by bringing the setting and characters into modern focus and rearranging the original libretto and music (*Carmen Jones*, 1955; *The Naked Carmen*, 1969). Menotti is one of the few composers to direct his own opera in a film version. For *Th·· Medium* he recorded the sound track and then reworked the staging.

During the late 1940s and 1950s, the National Broadcasting Company Television Network had its own opera company which gave a number of enterprising and enriching operatic performances. Productions eventually became so expensive they were discontinued. Recently, the Ford Foundation in conjunction with National Educational Television has presented television opera that may mark the beginning of a new cycle. There are now 160 educational television stations in the United States, and if they present opera, they may attract an audience which could never afford the price of a ticket to the opera house.

Any music drama transferred to a film or television immediately runs into new problems. The camera close-up of a person singing is a delicate maneuver. Facial contortions, to a certain extent inevitable, have to be minimized in the picture. Popular singers crooning into a microphone do not need as much breath or body support as an opera singer does and consequently there is less distortion. The camera cannot probe too closely; distance may lend some enchantment. Since romantic opera (which includes most of the repertory) is largely illusion, this illusion has to be preserved. Opera stars attain success through their voices, not their svelte figures or handsome faces. They do not depend on their appearance the way a film star must, and so it is not always wise to put them on the screen. And singers with reputations have no great desire to subject their voices to the rigors of film takes and television rehearsals under hot lights. Since the screen is a visual medium, that image is paramount.

Young, attractive singers with good voices (and there are many) should be the mainstays of an opera film or television performance. They can satisfy both eye and ear.

For television's generally cramped studio space and small receiving screen, the spectacle and voluptuous sound of grand opera are out of place. The time limits of television often make a one-act opera more feasible; for a longer opera, cuts and scene rearrangements can impair artistic unity. English is essential—any translation must be free and colloquial rather than literary

Although television and films pose similar problems, films made in Europe have usually followed the operatic stage production closely. If the opera is native, there is no need of translation. Germans and Italians used to the routine opera conventions are not so bothered by close-ups as an English or American audience would be. The advantages of seeing a famous singer and of retaining the fine elements of a production are difficult to reproduce unless filmed. Even these productions appear stilted when they try too hard to capture restricted stage movement and forget to use the camera's flexibility. Consequently, film and television producers abroad have often resorted to pre-recording the music on tape and then playing it back while the singers or actors mouth the words. Synchronization is very difficult; many listeners may not notice the occasional slip, but the knowledgeable person will immediately be disconcerted by the two forms of communication.

Finally, there are the purely technical difficulties of sound as filtered through film equipment or broadcast for home television. High-grade audio equipment is rare in the movie theater and practically nonexistent on the average television set. Since so much of opera is the power and beauty of all-encompassing sound, whether in the glowing resonance of an acoustically splendid auditorium or over a good audio system in one's living room, poor equipment is a great drawback. However, technical improvements through research engineering are being made. Operas on a screen—original opera movies and live television shows would be best—have enormous potential for a large public. Every effort should be made to develop them through these media, which could do much to draw opera into the currents of late twentieth-century culture.

Operatic Experiments By now the reader is aware of the growing belief that opera must change if it is to remain a popular art form. Not only the younger generation, but attentive people of all ages seek in art a living, vital experience. Much that is new and experimental will fade, as it has in the past; but films, television, and electronic equipment are here to stay.

Compared to the stereophonic splendors of movie sound tracks and their own record libraries or to the slick visual polish of TV spectaculars and Broadway musicals, mounted standard operas have the look of so many pressed flowers, or those antique photographs of female relatives that have been lovingly restored and hand-tinted into a simulacrum of present-day vitality.[7]

This is exaggerated, but there is much truth in the images.

Most recent experiments have involved multimedia—combinations of electronic music, dance, film, pantomime, the visual arts, and some form of singing. This new musical theater has studiously avoided the word "opera," with all its connotations. Much of its inspiration has come from modern ballet companies who in the last 20 years have created a veritable revolution in the dance. If the electronic element is removed, a good deal of what remains was pioneered earlier in the century. Stravinsky in *L'Histoire du soldat* (The Soldier's Tale, 1918) wrote a chamber work that is read, acted, danced, and sung with orchestral background. In his *Oedipus Rex* a narrator and a male chorus comment in Greek style upon action carried forward by soloists on the stage. Arnold Schönberg's *Die glückliche Hand* (The Lucky Hand, 1924) has one real singing voice with occasional interjections from two others, a chorus that sings and murmurs tonelessly, and various mute characters who act in pantomime. Kurt Weill (1900–1950) wrote one of the first socially conscious operas in *Die Dreigroschenoper* (The Threepenny Opera, 1928) on a Bertolt Brecht text (modeled after John Gay's *Beggar's Opera*). It is a series of popular ballads in dance rhythms (mostly jazz) strung together with spoken dialogue. Darius Milhaud's (1892–1974) *Christophe Colombe* (Christopher Columbus, 1930) was perhaps the first opera to include film sequences in its plot. Happenings on different levels of consciousness are portrayed simultaneously in different parts of the stage with pantomime, ballet, and film to help distinguish the various groups; sometimes there are tableaux, sometimes only movement and singing.

Recent "stagings" have concentrated on electronic tape, with light projections to pick out or create visual images in a kaleidoscopic pattern; the tape is a sound collage to fit the patterns. The sensual and visual have become so important to the theater that narrative and logic are often missing; there may even be no plot at

[7] Gian Carlo Menotti, "A Point of Contact," *Opera News* (December 27, 1969), 9

all. The flow of ideas is purposely nondirectional, and operations of chance, silence, symbolism, and psychological penetration dominate the stage. The music is stylistically a mixture of many elements— pure electronic sound, "rock," jazz, a nineteenth-century waltz.

The most telling criticism leveled against this experimental theater is that it has distorted the human voice. When the voice is asked to act like a mechanical instrument or to reproduce sounds that take away its natural lyricism, opera becomes a different form of art. The melody to be sung—jagged, irregular, with great intervallic leaps—robs the voice of its inherent lyric capacity. However, melodies by Beethoven, Verdi, and Wagner were all criticized as being unsingable in their time, but they gradually won acceptance. Likewise, vocal lines of advanced twentieth-century composers will undoubtedly become understandable if they are heard often enough. But if the voice becomes mere sound manipulation on tape its lyrical and dramatic function disappears and a new use evolves.

Because the past has such a heavy hold on the opera house and most contemporary music provides such a marked break with the past, it is difficult to prophesy the future of opera. Undoubtedly the stable 50 operas in the standard repertory, with minor additions and subtractions, will continue to fascinate and draw opera-goers here and abroad. There is too much beauty, emotion, and drama in these works for them to be discarded. Economics may change their presentation, but they will live on with a certain vigor. The audience however, may shrink unless the works are brought closer to the communities' needs and desires. Aside from "relevance," these needs generally include an understanding of the text, a good ensemble, a live production, and voices of quality (not necessarily super-quality). When these needs are met, opera is not only a highly pleasurable and exciting venture but a union of the arts that can blend to attain grandeur. Given these conditions, opera's future may be assured.

SUGGESTED READING

Berg   Redlich, Hans F., *Alban Berg, The Man and his Music,* Calder, London, 1967
Reich, Willi, *Alban Berg,* Cornelius Carden, trans., Thames and Hudson, London, 1965.

Britten   White, Eric Walter, *Benjamin Britten, His Life and Operas,* University of California Press, Berkeley, 1970.

Stravinsky Ledermann, Minna, ed., *Stravinsky in the Theatre*, Farrar, Straus & Giroux, New York, 1949; Reprint Da Capo, New York, 1975. Chapters by individuals who worked with Stravinsky on various productions.

White, Eric Walter, *The Composer and His Works*, University of California Press, Berkeley, 1966. Mostly a register and discussion of individual works.

Schönberg *Arnold Schönberg: Letters*, Erwin Stein, ed., Eithne Wilkins and Ernst Keiser, trans., St. Martin's Press, New York, 1965. Account by Schönberg of his activities and ideas.

The various issues of *Opera News* and *Opera* magazine provide both historical and up-to-date information on opera productions (professional) in the United States and England. *Opera News* is the official publication of the Metropolitan Opera Guild and is geared mostly to the Saturday afternoon broadcasts of the Metropolitan Opera during the fall, winter, and spring months. It includes a plot summary of the work to be broadcast and some commentary on it with pictures, plus general articles of a historical and topical nature and reviews of other productions here and abroad. *Opera* magazine is published in England and aimed primarily, but not wholly, at an English audience. It gives more comprehensive coverage (particularly of Europe) than *Opera News* and provides similar kinds of articles, often in more depth.

For those primarily interested in opera in the United States, the best source for new productions, brief biographies, music publishers, appointments, etc., is the *Central Opera Service Bulletin*, ed. Maria F. Rich, Metropolitan Opera, Lincoln Center, New York, N.Y. It treats operatic organizations throughout the country and also many in Canada.

ADDED READING LIST
(Mostly books published since 1972)

Alexander, Alfred, *Operanatomy*, 2nd ed., Crescendo Publishing Co., Boston, 1974. Some unfamiliar operatic territory, e.g. the conductor, score-reading, voice technique, etc., examined in a fresh, easy manner.

Donington, Robert, *The Opera*, Harcourt, Brace, Jovanovich, New York, 1978. Somewhat too detailed but interesting coverage, particularly of earlier period.

Gishford, Anthony, *Grand Opera*, Viking Press, New York, 1972. Mostly pictures, but very good ones.

Kolodin, Irving, *The Opera Omnibus*, Dutton, New York, c.1976. Anecdotal and amusing. Demands knowledge of opera and its ways.

Lang, Paul Henry, *Critic at the Opera*, W. W. Norton, New York, 1971; re-titled *Experience of Opera* in 1973 paperback edition. Compilation of reviews on most famous operatic composers. Literate and absorbing.

Marek, George, *The World Treasury of Grand Opera*, Harper, New York, 1957. A series of essays on opera by famous composers, singers, writers, etc. Among the best selections of its kind.

May, Robin, *Opera*, Hodder and Stoughton, London, 1977. Quite good as a general history.

Orrey, Leslie, *A Concise History of Opera*, Thames and Hudson, London, 1977. Excellent pictures with a brief running account of the history of opera.

Schmidgall, Gary, *Literature as Opera*, Oxford University Press, New York, 1977. A mature and very readable emphasis on the literary backgrounds of operas by some leading composers. The music is also discussed.

Swanston, Hamish F.G., *In Defence of Opera*, Penguin Books, London, 1978. A rather idiosyncratic but lively defense of opera's various traditions. Needs knowledge of the repertory.

Glossary

Abbreviations   Fr.—French; Ger.—German; Ital.—Italian

Most musical notes in the text are named according to the following system:

C D E F G A B   c d e f g a b   c¹ d¹ e¹ f¹ g¹ a¹ b¹   c² d² e² f² g² a² b² etc.

Definitions   The brief definitions given below are for the purpose of clarifying technical terms used in the text. They are cursory; for fuller information the reader should consult *Grove's Dictionary of Music and Musicians, Harvard Dictionary of Music,* 2nd ed., *The Oxford Companion to Music,* or any other good modern music dictionary.

Accidentals   a sharp, flat, double sharp, etc., sign occurring temporarily in the course of a piece, not part of the key signature.

Acoustics   the science and physical basis of sound.

Alexandrine   applicable to verse: a line of six poetic feet.

Appoggiatura   (Ital., a leaning)—Either (1) an unharmonized auxiliary note falling or rising to an adjacent harmonized note as an ornament; or (2) an accented nonharmonized note adjacent to a less accented harmonized one.

Apron   the stage area in front of the curtain.

Aria   an organized air or song of some complexity.

Arietta   a light, less hightly developed air.

Arioso   a song-like section of recitative, something in between pure recitative and aria.

Arpeggio   a broken chord in which the notes are heard in succession, not simultaneously

Augmented interval   an interval increased in size by raising the upper note a semi-tone.

Augmented triad   a chord consisting of two major thirds.

Ballet   dramatic entertainment given by dancers in costume with musical accompaniment.

Basso buffo   a bass voice taking a comic part.

Basso cantante   a smooth bass voice especially suited for lyric parts and utilizing the upper register of the voice.

Basso continuo   musical shorthand of a figured or unfigured bass line to indicate harmonies played over this line on a keyboard instrument.

Basso profundo   the lowest bass voice.

Bel canto   (Ital., beautiful singing)—a style of singing that emphasizes beautiful tone, a legato line, good phrasing, and clean articulation of words.

Brass   collective term for instruments made of brass or other metals and blown directly through a cup-shaped or funnel-shaped mouthpiece.

Cabaletta   originally a simple Italian aria. Later, the concluding brilliant portion in quick tempo of a two-part aria, or the whole piece.

Cadence   a progression of chords that ends a section or phrase of music.

Cantata   (Ital., sung piece)—a short sacred or secular vocal work for voices with instrumental accompaniment.

Castrato   a male castrated in youth to maintain a soprano or contralto voice.

Cavatina   an aria consisting of one lyric section.

Chorale   a German metrical hymn tune.

Chord   any simultaneous combination of three or more notes.

Choreography   the invention and design of dancing in a ballet.

Chorus   (1) a body of singers with several people on each vocal part; (2) refrain of a song.

Chromatic   notes produced by accidentals that lie outside the major or minor scales.

Coloratura   (made-up Italian, not a real word)—elaborate ornamentation of vocal line. A coloratura voice is one that specializes in singing this line, generally in a high register.

Comprimario   (Ital., with the principal)—singer who specializes in secondary operatic roles.

Consecutive intervals   any interval between two parts which is immediately followed by the same interval in a different position.

Contredanse   (Ital., contradanza)—a country dance, either French or Italian.

Counterpoint   the simultaneous combination of two or more melodies.

Countertenor a high-pitched male voice which generally sings falsetto or some combination of head and chest tones.

Da capo (Ital., to the head)—Literally, go back to the beginning. An aria in three sections of which the third is musically the same as the first. The sign D.C. occurs at the end of the second section.

Diminished interval an interval lessened from its original value by a semi-tone.

Diminished triad a chord consisting of two minor thirds.

Dissonance or discord intervals or chords that sound jarring and seem to need resolution. Concept of what is jarring has changed radically throughout the history of music.

Divisi an orchestral direction given to an instrumental group (for example, the first violins), indicating they are to subdivide and play different parts.

Dominant the fifth note of the scale in relation to the keynote. Chord upon this note.

Dotted (rhythm)—dots placed after a note indicate time value of note is extended by a half. A series of these notes will generate a jagged rhythm.

Dynamics gradations of loudness and softness in music.

Enharmonic two notes or chords that are notated differently but have the same pitch (for example, G sharp and A flat).

False relations relation set up when two notes of adjacent pitch (for example, F and F sharp) occur simultaneously or in succession in different lines or parts of music.

Falsetto sound produced by adult males above normal pitch, in which only the edges of the vocal chords vibrate. Can put male voice into contralto or soprano register.

Fine (Ital., end)—word shows where da capo aria comes to an end after direction to repeat the first part.

Fioritura (Ital., flowering, flourish)—ornamental figures elaborating a plainer melodic passage.

Forte (Ital.)—loud.

Fugato a brief passage using fugal technique.

Fugue a contrapuntal composition for a given number of parts or voices· built on one or more thematic subjects. Voices enter in imitation of each other.

Furiant a Czech dance in quick triple time with syncopation.

Galop a quick dance in 2/4 time.

Gavotte French dance in duple or quadruple time generally beginning in second half of measure.

Heldentenor (Ger., heroic tenor)—a powerful tenor voice demanded in Wagnerian and other dramatic roles.

Hexachord a system of dividing the scale into six-note units.

Impresario (Ital., one who undertakes an enterprise)—manager of an opera company. In Germany, he is called the *Intendant* (superintendant).

Interval the distance in pitch between two notes whether struck together or separately.

Intonation perception by listener or performer whether music is in tune.

Inversion a device whereby a theme is turned upside down: the descending intervals go up; the ascending go down. In a chord, the root of the chord goes into the upper part.

Key the precise tonality of a piece of music which uses the major and minor scales as its base and accepts certain relationships between the notes and the chords built on them.

Leading motive (Ger., *leit motiv*)—a theme used to represent a character, an object, a mood.

Leading tone the seventh degree of the scale; so-called because it pulls toward the tonic or key-note.

Legato a direction for performance that says a line or melody should be played smoothly without break.

Madrigal a secular chamber composition for voices. Flourished in the late Middle Ages and the Renaissance. Assumed many different forms. Literary merit of the text was a strong factor.

Major scale the eight-note scale in which there is a half-step between the third and fourth steps and the seventh and eighth. It can begin on any note. A major chord is constructed of notes taken from the major scale.

Measure the metrical distance of music included between two vertical bar lines.

Melisma a group of notes sung to a single syllable.

Meter the basic unvarying pulse or regular recurring accents of a piece of music. The time signature of this pulse appears as a fraction at the beginning, the numerator being the number of beats in a measure and the denominator their length. 4/4 means four quarter notes in a measure.

Minor scale takes different forms according to whether it is ascending or descending. Most common ascending pattern gives a half-step between two and three and between seven and eight, the rest being whole steps.

Minuet dance in triple time that became popular social dance of the eighteenth century.

Modes scales prevalent in the Middle Ages and earlier. They can be determined by starting on any white key on the piano except B and going up eight notes.

Modulation a temporary or permanent change from one key center to another.

Motet a sacred composition for several voices with or without instruments. Assumed many different forms from the thirteenth to the seventeenth centuries.

Mute a contrivance to reduce the volume of an instrument or to modify its tone: for bowed instruments, a damper at the bridge; for brass, an object of metal, wood, or fiber placed in the bell.

Obbligato (Ital., obligatory)—a direction indicating that an instrument has a special or obligatory part to play.

Octave the interval that has eight steps, counting both one and eight which are the same note at different pitches.

Ostinato a persistently repeated musical rhythm or figure.

Overture **(Prelude)**—the introductory orchestral movement of the opera. May or may not have any connection with the music that follows. Used in earliest opera to quiet the audience.

Passacaglia music in which a theme is continually repeated. Most often it appears in the bass.

Pedal point a note sustained below changing harmonies above.

Pentatonic five notes. Pentatonic scale—a five-note scale.

Percussion instruments that are played by being beaten: timpani, cymbals, triangles, etc.

Piano (Ital.)—soft.

Pitch exact height or depth of a musical sound according to the number of vibrations necessary to produce it. Standard A = 440 vibrations to the second with all the other notes standing in relation to it.

Pizzicato (Ital., pinched)—direction indicating that bowed instruments (the strings) are to be plucked by finger and not bowed.

Polka Bohemian dance in 2/4 time.

Polyphony really the same as counterpoint except it is a more embracing term. Literally· several voices.

Proscenium the space between the curtain and the orchestra in a theater.

Recitative speech-like singing in which a certain amount of freedom in performance is allowed.

Relative a common key signature is shared by one major and one minor key throughout the series. They are relative to one another.

Resolution in a very general sense, the progression from discord to concord.

Ritornello (Ital., a little return)—a recurring passage in a seventeenth and eighteenth century work which may form a thematic and harmonic basis for the whole piece. Not necessarily exactly the same on each recurrence.

Rondo a type of composition in which a section of music keeps coming back after other musical episodes in between. Formal pattern is ABACA, or something similar.

Root the bottom note of a chord when the chord is in basic or fundamental position.

Scale a progression of single notes upwards or downwards in steps.

Score the complete copy of the music showing all the different parts for performers with the notes appearing vertically over each other so the progression may be easily seen.

Sinfonia (Ital.)—seventeenth and eighteenth century instrumental piece out of which the later symphony grew.

Singspiel German light opera with spoken dialogue.

Soubrette (Fr., cunning, shrewd)—light soprano comedienne.

Spinto (Ital., pushed)—a voice which combines both lyric and dramatic elements.

Sprechstimme (Ger., speech-song)—a kind of speech-singing where all musical elements apply except pitch. Notes appear as crosses on the staff to show approximate pitch.

Staccato   performance indication of dot over a note. Means note is played short and detached.

Stagione   (Ital., season)—operatic system that concentrates on one or two works over a period of weeks rather than a different opera every night (repertory).

Strophe   similar to a stanza in poetry

Suite   instrumental work in several movements. In the seventeenth and eighteenth centuries the movements were generally dance forms.

Tempo   (Ital., time)—the pace at which a piece of music proceeds. Generally given in Italian at the beginning of the music (allegro, andante, etc.).

Timbre   (Fr., tone color)—the tone quality that distinguishes music played on one instrument from another.

Tremolo   (Ital., shaking, trembling)—rapid reiteration of a single note by back and forth strokes of the bow on a stringed instrument.

Triad   the basic three notes of a chord. The fourth note of a chord generally doubles one of the other three.

Triplet   a group of three notes of equal time value occupying a beat or other fraction of a measure normally filled by a time unit of one beat or its subdivision into even numbers.

Tutti   (Ital., all)—used in music for solo performer or performers and orchestra to indicate places where orchestra plays without soloists.

Unison   united sounding of the same note.

Whole tone scale   scale progressing entirely in whole tones.

Woodwinds   type of instruments (wood or metal) which are blown directly or by means of a reed. Holes shorten or lengthen the wind column.

Index